TRANSPORTATION
BY
MONTGOMERYSHIRE
COURTS
1788-1868

BRIAN OWEN

Published by
The Powysland Club

Published in 2003 by
The Powysland Club
Llygad y Dyffryn, Llanidloes
Powys, SY18 6JD

ISBN 0-9541139-0-X

Printed and bound in Wales by
St Idloes Press
Unit 8, Maesllan Enterprise Park, Llanidloes
Powys, SY18 6DF

Dedicated to the Memory of
Joan
A dear Wife, Mother and Grandmother

Contents

Acknowledgements

Research of this magnitude cannot be undertaken without the dedicated support of others who, when approached, were readily prepared to assist me. Grateful appreciation must be acknowledged to the Librarian and Staff of the National Library of Wales; the National Library of New South Wales; the Archives Office of New South Wales; the Archives Office of Tasmania; the Archives Office of Western Australia; the Archives Office of Powys and the Public Record Office, Kew, London. The reproduction of text and document from the Quarter Sessions, Court of Great Sessions and Assizes are by permission of the Controller of Her Majesty's Stationery Office and Public Record Office.

I am deeply indebted to Tom and David McVey, Dorchester, who spent a considerable amount of time in examining records in the Public Record Office. As research progressed in England and Wales, it became evident that to follow the outcome of individual convict lives, relevant records held in Australia needed to be researched. How fortunate I was to find the expertise of the late Norma Ruck, whose untimely death in Sydney, came suddenly towards the end of her research of the New South Wales archives. Prior to her death, she was able to put me in touch with Loreley Morling in Perth and Dianne Snowden in Hobart, who both diligently undertook the analysis of the Western Australia and Tasmania archives respectively. At the same time, Joan Reece, a friend of Norma Tuck, came to my assistance and ensured that the remaining New South Wales records were researched. Without the valued and experienced assistance of these ladies, the content of this publication would have been inadequate. Through this relationship, I achieved valued friendships which culminated in Dianne Snowden visiting Llanidloes one morning when we were able to spend a few hours together. I must return to Montgomeryshire and pay my sincere appreciation to the support afforded to me by E. Ronald Morris, a valued friend. I was able to take full advantage of the tremendous historical knowledge that he possesses and his willingness to persevere and encourage me played a significant part in any achievement that this book may realize.

I must also pay tribute to Robert Edwards, St Idloes Press, Llanidloes, for his valued contribution in the production of this book which has greatly enhanced its content.

Through the generosity of the Powysland Club in accepting my research as a suitable historical project relating to criminal activities in Montgomeryshire in the eighteenth and nineteenth centuries, publication has been achieved. On behalf of the Powysland Club both E. Ronald Morris and Murray Ll. Chapman spent many an hour editing my initial attempts to provide a draft which warranted publication. I am indebted to both who ensured that the outcome finally reached the high standard which they always achieve. A group of members of the Publications Committee of The Powysland Club has been responsible for subsequent copy-editing, and for the provision of an index to the text.

I must finally thank Mark; Simon and Margaret; Alison and Steven; Jason; Lee; Sarah; Jemma and Ashley, who, as members of my family, have patiently waited for the completion of this book.

BRIAN OWEN
January 2001

Foreword

Few readers of British colonial history will be unaware of the part played by the transportation policy of banishing criminal offenders to Australia and, prior to that, to North America. Transportation to Australia began in 1787 and ended in 1868. While there were many British who were economic and voluntary emigrants to Australia, the majority of the rest were convicted criminals sentenced to varying periods of a punishment little better that slavery.

Some of the convicts had turned to crime, largely theft, owing to the abject poverty in which they lived while others appear to have been wandering organized thieves. The difference between them is not always clear. Times were bad for the majority of working people living in the early period of industralization and the long war with France. The penal code was extremely harsh, with capital punishment meted out for a great number of offences.

This new book examines the impact of transportation on a small, largely rural county such as Montgomeryshire and complements more general histories of the system, such as one may read in Robert Hughes's *The Fatal Shore*. In Brian Owen's book one reads of the working of this system and the consequences for some unfortunates who fell foul of the law. One reads of their trial before the local courts, of their voyage to a far off land, their treatment in Australia and the subsequent lives of those convicts who managed to survive their long sentences.

Brian Owen has researched deeply into the events which led many to the 'hulks' or to transportation. He has put together their interesting and tragic story gleaned from contemporary newspaper, legal and prison records, comments and letters of officials who accompanied the condemned on the outward voyage and the large amount of material relating to the latters' subsequent lives, in the Australian archives. To familiarize himself with the latter, the author was in close correspondence with professional researchers in Australia.

Some of the convicts, a few, were fortunate and managed to lead a fairly tolerable life after serving their sentences. Others failed to reform their ways and suffered further punishment in penal settlements such as Norfolk Island and Port Arthur, etc. Others again, male and female, were overpowered by the penal system and did not survive their sentence. Some of their lives make fascinating but often sad reading, like that of the female petty thief Ann Glossop arrested in Newtown, who met a tragic end in New Zealand.

Now, we have a local picture of transportation as it affected our county and the narrative brings home to the reader the real nature of its impact on the lives of Montgomeryshire inhabitants.

The author is to be congratulated on his venture and commitment to elucidating the details of this absorbing but sad period in the history of Montgomeryshire. Readers, especially those who inhabit our county, owe him a considerable debt for such devotion to this study.

E. RONALD MORRIS
January 2001

Abbreviations

ADM	Admiralty
AONSW	Archives Office of New South Wales
AOT	Archives Office of Tasmania
ASSI	Clerk of Assize
BER	Bermuda
BT	Board of Trade
CF	Certificate of Freedom
COD	Copy of Document
CON	Convict
CP	Conditional Pardon
CPMI	Convict Permission to Marry Index
D	Dixson Library
EJ	*Eddowes Journal*
ENG	England
FS	Free by Servitude
GIB	Gibraltar
GS	Great Sessions and Government Servant
HO	Home Office
HRA	Historical Records of Australia
HTG	*Hobart Town Gazette*
HT and SR	*Hobart Town and Southern Reporter*
HRONSW	Historical Records of New South Wales
ML	Mitchell Library
MONT COLL	Montgomeryshire Collections
M and P	Musters and Papers
MT	Ministry of Transport
NCSI	New Colonial Secretary's Index
NI	Norfolk Island
NLW	National Library of Wales
NSW	New South Wales
PCOM	Prison Commissioners
PP	Parliamentary Papers and Port Phillip
PRO	Public Record Office
QS	Quarter Sessions
R	Reel (Microfilm)
SC	*Shrewsbury Chronicle*
SG and NSWA	*Sydney Gazette* and *New South Wales Advertiser*
SJ	*Salopian Journal* and *Surgeon's Journal*
SRO	Shropshire Record Office
T	Treasury
TAMIOT	Tombstone and Monumental Inscriptions of Tasmania
TAS	Tasmania
TL	Ticket of Leave
VDL	Van Diemen's Land
WA	Western Australia

Tables

That a greater curse cannot be inflicted on any community, but especially a younger one – a colony in a kind of immature and uninformed condition – than by pouring in a large proportion of the most worthless of mankind. It is infecting the very heart's blood of Society.

(Letter from Nassau Senior to Lord John Russell,
12 September 1846.
NLW Nassau Senior Papers, c.1866).

'A new way to make a Man'.

On Tuesday at the Town Hall, a young lad named W. Burton, was charged by his father with stealing two pairs of stockings; a handkerchief; a waistcoat, etc. The Magistrates did not wish to send him to prison, but the father said he was determined to have him sent to trial because he wished him to be transported, for that would make a man of hime.

(Derby Reporter. Poor Man's Guardian, No. 114.
10 August 1833).

Montgomery County Gaol
(By permission of Ms Eva Bredsdorff, Curator, Powysland Museum)

The 'Pitt' convict ship (which transported Ann Glossop to New South Wales in 1791
(By permission of the National Maritime Museum, Greenwich, London)

Female Penitentiary or Factory, Parramata, New South Wales
(Augustus Earle, 1793-1838. Watercolour. Rex Nan Kivell Collection, NK 12/47.
By permission of the National Library of Australia)

Millbank Penitentiary, circa 1829
(By permission of Jones & Co., London. Drawn by Tho H. Shepherd and engraved by J. Tingle)

Convicts exercising in Pentonville Prison
(By permission of Frank Cass & Company Limited, London.
The Criminal Prisons of London and Scenes of Prison Life, by Henry Mayhew and John Binny.
First Edition 1862. New Impression 1968)

The 'Warrior' hulk with the sulphur washing ship in the distance
(By permission of Frank Cass & Company Limited, London.
The Criminal Prisons of London and Scenes of Prison Life, by Henry Mayhew and John Binny.
First Edition 1862. New Impression 1968)

*Tombstone of Morgan Miles, located in
Buckland Cemetery, Tasmania*
(By permission of
Dianne Snowden, Hobart, Tasmania)

*Tombstone of John Bumford, located in the
General Cemetery, Ross, Tasmania*
(By permission of
Dianne Snowden, Hobart, Tasmania)

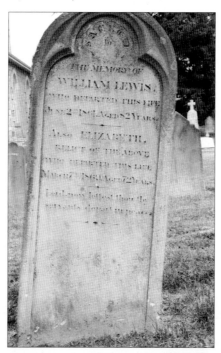

*Tombstone of Elizabeth Lewis (Williams), located
in St Luke's Churchyard, Bothwell, Tasmania*
(By permission of Dianne Snowden, Hobart, Tasmania)

CHAPTER ONE

The Plight of the Transportees

Transportation as a punishment can be traced to 1597 when the term "exile" was introduced in an Act of Parliament.[1] This was followed in 1666 by an Act[2] which provided for transportation of "notorious thieves spoil-takers" convicted within the counties of Cumberland and Northumberland to the American colonies. Both these counties border Scotland which had a separate legal jurisdiction and the purpose of the 1666 Act was to avoid cross-border crimes being committed. Later Transportation Acts[3] required the exiles to undertake compulsory labour at the places to which they were transported. By 1717 an Act was passed which enabled the contractor, who transported the criminals, to put to auction and sell the unfortunate offenders.[4] The American War of Independence (1775-1783) brought to an end that destination and in 1783-84 an Act[5] was passed which included a provision "to appoint to what place beyond the seas, either within or without His Majesty's dominion, offenders shall be transported." Two Orders in Council[6] made on 6 December 1786, determined that the two Australian colonies of New South Wales and Van Diemen's Land, the small volcanic island called Norfolk Island and Bermuda be chosen as penal settlements. In May 1787, the First Fleet departed from England with its convict complement heading for Botany Bay in New South Wales. There were no Montgomeryshire offenders amongst these men and women who were the first of approximately 160,000 convicts who followed during the succeeding 80 years.

The loss of the American colonies as a suitable place of penal settlement was quickly noticed at home. County gaols throughout Britain gradually became overcrowded and by 23 May 1776 (16 Geo III c43), the decision was taken to place offenders on board hulk ships located on the River Thames and elsewhere Assize courts[7] and quarter Sessions in England and Wales were given an alternative location which could accommodate offenders, thus relieving county gaols of an acute situation. A number of Statutes[8] passed between 1775 and 1779, deemed that all male offenders sentenced and found guilty of committing grand larceny or any other transportable offence, with the exception of petty larceny, should be sentenced to a term of imprisonment on a hulk ship.[9]

Transportable offences including grand larceny is the theft of goods the value of above one shilling, receiving or buying stolen goods, petty larceny, i.e. the theft of goods with a value under one shilling, assault with intent to rob and manslaughter.[10]

Crimes warranting the death sentence, during the early years of transportation were numerous and included murder, arson, burglary or housebreaking at night, highway robbery, housebreaking during the day, picking pockets above one shilling, shop-lifting above five shillings, stealing above forty shillings from a house, stealing linen, maiming or killing cattle, stealing horses, cattle or sheep, stealing woollen cloth from a tenter field and servants stealing their master's goods to the value of forty shillings were in many cases commuted to that of transportation. By 1844, capital felonies had been reduced to high treason, murder, wounding with intent to commit murder, robbery including wounding, burglary with assault and intent to murder or wound and malicious arson to an inhabited house.[11]

Following confirmation of a transportation sentence, arrangements were made for convicts to be removed from county gaols to the hulks or London penitentiaries, where they were confined pending a sufficient number being available for removal to a convict ship.[12] During the early years hulks were placed under the supervision of overseers appointed by the Crown amongst whom were Duncan Campbell and his brother Neil. In addition, Duncan Campbell secured for himself the post of contractor, and thereby was able to assume complete control of the hulk system. John Howard, when visiting the hulks in 1776, reported his dismay as to the manner in which prisoners were being kept.[13] This system was soon proven open to abuse. By 1812, hulks had been located at Woolwich, Sheerness, Portsmouth and Langston harbour at Portland. The appointment of an Inspector of hulks with responsibility to:

> Visit the hulks each quarter in order to examine diligently the state of such houses of confinement, the behaviour and conduct of the several officers; the treatment and condition of the prisoners – and to report same to both Houses of Parliament.[14]

This brought about immediate improvement in the system, although concern was still expressed as to the moral requirements of offenders, particularly about the younger age groups. As demands upon the hulks became problematic following the end of the Napoleonic War, the Government appointed John Henry Capper, in 1814, to supervise the hulks. He occupied the post until 1847, during which time conditions on board the hulks became more humane. From the time that convicts were locked down for the evening until the hatches were re-opened the following morning, it was stated that:

> They are left entirely to themselves . . . Under these circumstances there can be no doubt of the prevalence amongst the convicts of gambling, swearing and every kind of vicious conversation.[15]

It is to their credit that following this form of incarceration some convicts attempted to perform a task on their own account such as making shoes, clothes, toys and trinkets produced from bone. Some even took the opportunity to read their Bible or Prayer Book and although no schoolmaster was provided to help them, some of the more literate attempted to teach those less fortunate to read and write. Selection of convicts from the hulks, to be placed on convict ships, was from male convicts under 50 years of age, who had received a life sentence or 14 year transportation. If there was insufficient available from this category then the remainder were chosen from the most unruly of those who had received a seven year sentence. Female convicts were categorized as being suitable if under 45 years of age and in good health.

Batches of chained convicts were then taken to the quayside and sent out to the waiting ship, where it was not uncommon for them to wait for a period of weeks or even months before a sufficient number were on board to enable the long sea voyage to commence. It is evident that many of these unfortunate men and women suffered from ill-health, in some cases illness brought with them from their county gaol, whilst others had contracted their illness from conditions prevailing in the hulks, resulting, in some cases, in premature death.

Many journals of ship surgeons identify the final fate of these prisoners and some of their observations on Montgomeryshire convicts are presented in Chapter 5. The well tried and tested system developed by the Admiralty for the American colonies was perpetuated following the loss of those colonies. They chartered contractors to carry out this task but since these contractors sought to secure as big a profit as possible from each voyage, scant attention was given to the welfare of the convicts. In consequence the Home Office amended their contractual arrangements for the Second Fleet and insisted that party-payment be deferred until safe arrival in Australia. Over the following years conditions on board the ships became more hygienic and the care of prisoners was greatly improved by the ship surgeons being given responsibility for their well being. Thomas Galloway, a surgeon with experience of five voyages between 1830-1836, advised a Parliamentary Select Committee:

> *That he was responsible for all convicts whilst on board and for dispensing disciplinary action such as flogging or solitary confinement.*[16]

Sea voyages from England to Australia, some 12,000 nautical miles, proved lengthy and, although the direct route became usual, variations along the way took place. In 1792, the 'Pitt' arrived at Port Jackson following 212 days at sea, having called at Cape Verde Islands, Rio de Janeiro and the Cape of Good Hope.[17] On board were Ann Glossop, Charles Evans and William Owen who had been convicted in Montgomeryshire Courts. In 1818, the 'Lady Castlereagh' arrived in Van Diemen's Land after a sea voyage of 171 days following a call at Sydney.[18] On board were William Cook, Edward Edwards and John Jones, Montgomeryshire convicts. By 1833, the 'Camden' arrived at Sydney having followed the direct route in 149 days.[19] Included in her complement were Benjamin Davies, John Humphreys and Joseph Parry, Montgomeryshire convicts. The three Llanidloes Chartists, Lewis Humphreys, James Morris and Abraham Owen, and James Corbett of Newtown were transported on the 'Woodbridge' and, following the route via the Cape, arrived at Sydney in 1840 after 133 days at sea.[20] By 1822 a muster of male and female convicts took place, arrival followed by disembarkation to Sydney gaol for the men and the female factory at Parramatta for the women. They were allowed to take their belongings with them. At Hobart, settlers were notified in advance of the pending arrival of a convict ship so that they could be present and be given the opportunity of selecting servants from amongst them.[21]

In the early years female convicts were abused; it being reported that half of children born each year in the colony were illegitimate.[22] By 1810, convicts employed by the Government were divided into gangs working from six in the morning until three in the afternoon, following which they were allowed free time to do as they pleased. Any misbehaviour warranted an appearance before a local magistrate or for a more serious offence before a Bench of three magistrates. Up to 300 lashes could be metered out as punishment but for more serious crimes approval by the Governor was required. Some offenders found themselves allocated to a gaol gang for a specified period, working twelve hours each day with no relief for any personal labour.[23]

Those females who arrived at Parramatta factory were allowed to bring their own bedding and personal belongings and were accommodated in a room built for the reception of pregnant women; others were lodged in the town and many cohabited with male convicts. Their work in the factory consisted of picking, spinning and carding of wool. A weekly food ration of four pound ten ounces of flour and the same quantity of meat or two pound of pork was issued. The children who accompanied their mothers were maintained by the Government at half the ration of the women. Women accompanied by children, received scant attention by settlers and as a consequence remained at Parramatta for an undetermined length of time. The factory building provided only minimum necessities with dirty wool used for beds amongst the spinning wheels. Cleanliness, in these conditions, left much to be desired. Females arriving at Hobart were placed in a depot and on occasions they were allowed to visit the town and mix freely with their contemporaries. Illegitimate children were placed in a nursery with their mothers until such time that they were of an age to be removed to an orphan school. It was a common practice for convict women to obtain work as servants to enable them to obtain money by theft or prostitution and return to the depot to spend their ill-gotten gains.[24] During their detention in the factory, women were placed in one of three classes, viz. (i) those newly arrived in the colony and those returned from assignment, (ii) those who had received punishment and were not ready for the first class, (iii) those who were serving a period of punishment.[25] Immediately a convict ship was ready to disembark, the Colonial Secretary or his representative went on board, carried out a muster and listened to complaints. Male convicts were then taken ashore to the barracks whilst female convicts went to the penitentiaries. As time went by female convicts were allowed to by-pass this arrangement and proceed directly into the employment of settlers. An official (the Principal Superintendent of Convicts) had the task of classifying all recently arrived convicts, the majority of whom were allocated or assigned as servants to settlers with the remainder staying in the employ of the Government. Arrival in Australia introduced a form of segregation for male convicts. Government work necessitated men being required to perform labouring tasks and they were supplemented by convicts returned by settlers who found them to be unfit for service. Part of this workforce included those who had committed minor offences in the colony, whilst those who had committed more serious offences were required to work in irons. Many of these men were classed as being of a "very depraved character" and endured conditions far worse than their more fortunate compatriots who had been selected for assignment, a system described later in this chapter.[26] By 1820, it had been decided that various tasks of labour, such as clearing un-cultivated land and preparing it for ploughing, burning of timber, digging clay and making bricks and agricultural work could be carried out by gangs comprising twelve men.[27] Evidence presented to a Committee of the House of Commons on Gaols in 1819 stated that:

> *Punishment for those committing and found guilty of misdemeanour when working for the Government, included a period in a gaol gang, corporal punishment or transfer to the coal river (Newcastle). More serious crimes required committal followed by trial. Transfer to a gaol gang required a convict to work all day without benefit of time off in which to carry out any personal labour. This punishment took the form of repairing and building roads and any other aspect of the most laborious work required. Transfer to the coal river necessitated the convict to be fully employed in the breaking and other relevant aspects of coal mining. The use of chains was made necessary if a convict displayed un-manageable habits.[28]*

Road parties were made up of criminals of the worst character and were required to work in irons or alternatively be sent to a penal settlement. Chain gangs were reported as being:

A form of punishment as severe a one as could be inflicted on man and the condition of the convict in the chain gangs was one of great privation and unhappiness. From sunset to sunrise they are locked away in caravans or boxes in which they were unable to stand upright or sit down at the same time. They worked under a military guard whilst working and were flogged for the least offence.[29]

In Van Diemen's Land, probation gangs were made up of convicts who had previously been sent to Norfolk Island and also of those sentenced to transportation for a lesser period than a life sentence. Their hard labour duties were undertaken for a period up to two years.[30] On 25 January 1833, by Command of Lieutenant Governor George Arthur, regulations were issued for the introduction of a penal settlement on Tasman's Peninsula. Convicts to be sent there were to include those under colonial sentence of transportation or imprisonment and hard labour; those transportees on arrival whose crimes committed in Great Britain were of an atrocious nature and those known as gentlemen convicts. Male convicts were classified into one of four categories:[31]

(1) *First class which included all transportees on arrival except educated convicts. They were employed in hewing and cutting timber, drawing it to the water edge or in being employed in any other hard labour as required They were not allowed to work lazily and were dressed in yellow.*

(2) *Chain gangs which consisted of convicts who had been sentenced to the gang by a police magistrate or had been sent to work in chains. They were required to wear chains and yellow clothing with the word 'felon' stamped on it. They slept in separate cells, were not allowed to talk amongst themselves and were given the heaviest and most degrading work.*

(3) *Relief gangs comprised of convicts who had received the Commandant's blessing for good conduct. They wore grey or blue clothing and worked in agriculture or horticulture. The more able were appointed as constables or messengers.*

(4) *Educated convicts formed a distinct class, wearing grey clothing and were employed in gardening, fencing or farming.*

Clothing issued to men involved in Government work included a coarse woollen jacket, a waistcoat of yellow or grey cloth, a pair of duck trousers, a pair of worsted stockings, two cotton or linen shirts, a neck handkerchief and a woollen cap or hat. Hard labour warranted that a pair of shoes were issued on a quarterly basis. The general appearance at a muster before church doors at Sydney and Parramatta was that of cleanliness and decency.

Hammocks and bedding in the barracks and sleeping quarters were kept in a hygienic state and although there was no regular supply of soap, enough was issued for most purposes. Long water troughs and towels were available each morning before work. Barbers were attached to the barracks and shaved the convicts twice each week. At Hobart Town at each Sunday muster, convicts were allowed to dress as they pleased.[32]

Between 1800 and 1810, convicts were assigned to settlers who were then required to clothe, feed and accommodate them. Their work was allocated by the settler and at the end of their shift of duty, they were allowed to work on their own accord for the rest of the day. Punishment could not be inflicted by the settler who was required to report any incident to a local magistrate. Reform of convict character was noticeable in such surroundings when they were separated from their previous companions.[33] Although this system remained after 1810 it was noticeable that by 1830, there was an over demand for convicts and it became a matter of favour to obtain their services which was open to abuse and complaint. All applications, for convict labour, had to be processed by a government official. Upon receiving his allocation, the settler was obliged to send for the convict within a certain period of time and to pay £1 per head for the clothing and bedding of each assigned convict. During the period of assignment, each convict was entitled to 12 lbs wheat or 4½ lbs salt pork, 2 oz salt, 2 oz soap each week, 2 frocks or jackets, 3 shirts, 2 pairs trousers, 3 pairs shoes and a hat or cap each year. In addition, each man received one good blanket and a palliasse or wool mattress which remained the property of his master. A more liberal allowance was evident in Van Diemen's Land. Male assigned convicts were divided into one of the following classes, i.e. field labourers, domestic servants or mechanics. The last class included those who were superior to the other classes. Their previous criminal record and sentencing, age or the nature of their offence were not taken into consideration. However, any previous occupation played a significant part in determining assignment; domestic servants arriving in Australia were placed into similar occupations where they could expect to be fed, clothed, well treated and receive wages. Those chosen to be mechanics had an occupational background such as blacksmith, carpenter, mason, cooper, wheelwright or gardener. They were fortunate in being eagerly sought after by settlers, and recognition of their qualifications enabled convicts to exact a degree of indulgence from their masters, to ensure receipt of wages and to be granted permission to work on their own account after completing their allotted tasks. Minor misdemeanours such as drunkenness would be overlooked by the settlers. Sir George Arthur[34] was able to confirm:

> That the assigned convict was deprived of liberty, exposed to all the caprice of the family to whose service he may happen to be assigned and subject to the most summary laws. His condition in no respect differs from that of the slave, except that his master cannot apply corporal punishment by his own hands, or those of his overseer, and has a property in him for a limited period, idleness and insolence of expression or of look, anything betraying the insurgent spirit, subject him to the chain gang or the triangle, or hard labour on the roads.

In New South Wales magistrates were authorized to inflict 50 lashes as a sentence for drunkenness, disobedience of orders, neglect of work, absconding or abusive language to the master or overseer. Additionally, the convict could be punished with a period of imprisonment, solitary confinement or labour in irons with a road gang. Female assigned convicts, who were fortunate to be placed with respectable families, received adequate food, clothing and other indulgences. It is noticeable, in words of Sir Edward Parry, one time Commissioner of the Australian Agricultural Company,[35] that some were considered to be:

> As bad as anything could well be . . . hardly conceive anything worse. At times they are excessively ferocious and the tendency of assignment is to render them still more profligate; they are all of them, with scarcely an exception, drunken and abandoned prostitutes, and were any of them inclined to be well conducted, the disproportion of sexes in the penal colonies is so great, they are exposed to irresistible temptations . . .

As a result many respectable settlers were not inclined to receive convict women into their employ, preferring instead to choose male convicts to carry out domestic tasks.[36] Due to the inequality between male and female convicts permission was granted allowing female convicts to marry free men, although they were supervised by the police. Any minor crime warranted a return to the Parramatta factory but some females were sent to penitentiaries when their crime deserved punishment by solitary confinement and being placed on bread and water, employed on picking wool or the breaking of stones. Due to a shortage of work available at the factory, many women preferred to be sent there instead of being assigned. Expectant mothers were sent to the factory and it is evident that the factory took on the role of a lying-in hospital. Following the births, mothers and their babies remained for a period and even illegitimate children under 3 years of age were to be found within the factory confines. At Hobart and Launceston, female convicts undertook spinning, picking of wool and needlework, such duties being classified as severe. More serious crimes, committed by male convicts, warranted a sentence of re-transportation from New South Wales to penal settlements located at Norfolk Island or Moreton Bay, whilst those from Van Diemen's Land found themselves at Macquaries Harbour or Port Arthur.

Norfolk Island was described as:

> *A small and most beautiful volcanic island situated in the midst of the ocean, 1000 miles from the eastern coast of Australia and inaccessible, except in one place, to boats.*[37]

Major Thomas Wright, Commandant at Norfolk Island between 1846 and 1853, advised that convicts sent to Norfolk Island should include both those condemned in England as capital felons, convicted and pardoned and sentenced to transportation for life and also those convicted of a capital offence in New South Wales for a second time.[38]

Sir Francis Forbes, Chief Justice of Australia, in evidence confirmed that:

> *The experience furnished by these penal settlements had proved that transportation is capable of being carried to an extent of suffering such as to render death desirable and to induce many prisoners to seek it under its most appalling aspects . . . that he has known many cases in which it appeared that convicts at Norfolk Island had committed crimes which subjected them to execution . . . because there was no chance of escape and that they stated they were weary of life and would rather go to Sydney and be hanged. One Norfolk Island convict, placed before Judge Burton for sentencing, pleaded "Let a man be what he will when he comes here, he is soon as bad as the rest, a man's heart is taken from him and then is given to him the heart of a beast".*[39]

As a result of similar appalling stories regarding Norfolk Island, Dr William Bernard Ullathorne, a Catholic priest and vicar-general of New South Wales, visited Norfolk Island in 1834 and presented a damning account of what faced him:

> *On my arrival at Norfolk Island . . . I immediately proceeded . . . to the gaol . . .*
> *The commandant furnished me with a list of the thirteen men who were to die . . . I said a few words to induce them to resignation and then I stated the names of those who were to die, and it is a remarkable fact that as I mentioned the names they, one after the other, as their names were pronounced, dropped on their knees and thanked God that they were to be delivered from the horrible place . . . It was the most horrible scene that I ever witnessed. Those who were condemned to death appeared to be rejoiced.*[40]

Captain Alexander Maconochie, RN (1787-1860), confirmed this view of the conditions at Norfolk Island and reported that conditions in these places were beyond comprehension. Flogging, being place in irons or confinement in gaol on bread and water, was the normal daily life faced by the offender. The arrival of Maconochie to Norfolk Island in 1837 introduced some degree of improvement in the plight of the convicts. In a "Report on the State of Prison Discipline in Van Diemen's Land" in 1838, Maconochie noted:

> The mind of a person disposed to commit a crime is precisely that of a gamble . . . He hopes that if he commits a crime he will escape detection; that if detected, he will escape conviction; that if convicted, he will be pardoned or get off with a few years in the hulks or penitentiary; that if transported he will be sent to New South Wales; that if sent to New South Wales, he will be as well off as are some of this acquaintances and make a fortune.[41]

The Chief Superintendent of convicts in Van Diemen's Land, confirmed:

> That the work allocated to convicts is of the most incessant and galling description the settlement can produce, and any disobedience of orders turbulence or other misconduct is instantaneously punished by death.[42]

John Barnes, surgeon,[43] at Macquarie harbour, was able to draw a vivid and harrowing picture in his description of a:

> large bay situated on the western coast of Van Diemen's Land, probably about 10 miles in length and about 7 miles in breadth. There are several small islands scattered about the bay, two of which were occupied as penal settlements. The other islands were generally used, one as a place of burial another as a garden ground or something in kind for the employment of the convicts. In the early years convicts were sent there for minor offences and were divided into two classes, i.e. the newly arrived and those who had been the for a period of time and placed in the chain gangs. The major form of punishment took place on a small rock up to a mile out in the bay and the more refractory offenders spent their time at this place in heavy irons. Other punishments included stopping their rations of meat; placement in a chain gang to work in irons and the most dreaded form of punishment being worked in water building piers about the island, or flagellation with the cat-o-nine tails. it is relevant to record that the cat used at Macquarie harbour is what is called a thief's cat or a double cat-o-nine tails. It did not comprise more than the usual number of tails but each of those was a double twist of whipcord and each tail contained nine knots. It was a very formidable instrument indeed. Many attempted escape and were never heard of again. Others committed crimes so that they could be returned to Hobart to attend a criminal court and thereby gain some respite from Macquarie harbour. It may not be known that even free settlers in Van Diemen's Land, having committed crimes, found themselves sentence to transportation and being sent to Macquarie harbour.[44]

John West, taking a passage from *Paradise Lost*, by John Milton, considered Macquarie harbour as being:

> Rocks, caves, lakes, fens, bogs and shades of death, where all life dies, death lives and nature breaks. Perverse all monstrous, all prodigious things, abominable, unutterable.[45]

Port Arthur, was seen as:

> *A small and sterile peninsula of about 1000 acres, connected to Van Diemen's Land by a narrow neck of land, which is guarded day and night by soldiers and by a line of fierce dogs.*[46]

John Russell, assistant surgeon with the 63rd Regiment, was able to confirm:

> *He had formed the panel settlement at Port Arthur in 1830 . . . Convicts sent there had been twice convicted or sentenced to another term of transportation since arrival in the colony. They included the worst characters sent out from England, such as men who were desperate house breakers, having bad police characters against them and murderers. Offenders were occupied in felling timber and sawing it up for use in public works. Some men were employed in trades such as shoe-makers, blacksmiths and nailers. A limited classification takes place and the worst offenders are worked in irons. Punishment takes the form of flogging, working in irons and solitary confinement. A chain of dogs "very fierce and always kept fed with raw meat" supplemented the military post and as a result attempts to abscond became rare.*[47]

Fear of flagellation was greater than assignment to hard work in road parties or chain gangs amongst male convicts, and a witness of the aftermath of such punishment and its effect on unfortunate offenders, is testified by the following observation:

> *I have seen men, for a various offences, scoured until the blood had dripped into their shoes and I have seen the flesh tainted and swelling on a living body from the effects of severe flagellation . . . upon a charge of an overseer that the prisoner neglected his allotted task. After being flogged he must again instantly to the fields . . ., for him there is no compassion.*[48]

Whilst the majority of convicts sentenced to transportation found themselves in Australia, some found their destination to be Bermuda. Here their daily routine consisted of an eight hour day with an iron round their legs, performing rock excavation, building work, and if fortunate, the opportunity of carrying on with their own trade. They were given one hour for lunch preceded by breakfast before going to work. Their diet consisted of salt meat on alternate days and pulse or pudding on one day. Clothing was made of linen with the name of the ship or hulk to which they belonged, printed on their flannel waistcoat and coarse linen frocks and trousers. Punishment was either corporal punishment or imprisonment and the stopping of their spirit ration.[49]

In 1790, an Act,[50] allowed such severe sentences to be remitted. The governor of New South Wales was empowered to grant pardons thereby allowing convicts their freedom at the expiration of their original sentence so that he or she was able either to remain in the colony or return to their original homeland. Given a decision to remain in New South Wales, the Government granted, to single men, 30 acres of land, and to married men, 50 acres.

Tools, stock and food were also provided in order that they could establish a sound independence.[51] In his despatch to Viscount Goderick dated 21 November 1832, Major General Richard Bourke noted:

An absolute pardon, when issued under the Great Seal of England, but not before, restored the individual to all the rights of a free subject in every part of His Majesty's dominions from the date of the instrument. A conditional pardon, when approved by His Majesty, through the Secretary of State, but not before, restores the right of freedom from the date of the instrument, within the colony, but it bestows no power of leaving the colony and no right whatever beyond its limits. A ticket of leave, is a permission to the individual to employ himself for his own benefit and to acquire property on condition of residing within the district there in specified, on producing his ticket before the magistrate, at the periods prescribed by the regulations and of attending divine worship weekly, if performed within a reasonable distance, but he is not allowed to remove into any other district without the express sanction of Government and in that case, the individual reverts to the situation and prisoner of the Crown in every respect.[52]

The issue of a ticket of leave enabled a convict to work for himself and, as a consequence, be removed from the list of convicts who were provided with food by the Crown.[53] By 1827, convicts were considered to be eligible to obtain a ticket of leave if the following criteria applied:

1. *A 7 year transportation sentence of which 4 years had been served with one or five years with two masters.*
2. *A 14 year transportation sentence of which 6 years had been served with one, 8 years with two 10 years with three masters.*
3. *A life sentence of transportation of which 8 years had been served with two or 12 years with three masters.[54]*

With his ticket of leave a man found no difficulty in obtaining work as he was preferred to those convicts recently arrived in the colony. He was able to fill vacant positions as police constables, overseers of road parties and chain gangs, while the better educated found themselves able to obtain a position such as superintendent of estates, clerks, bankers, lawyers or shop keepers. Prospects of marriage to a free woman was an added attraction. Female convicts, by 1829, were able to obtain their ticket of leave after 2 years served of a 7 year sentence; after 3 years for a 14 year sentence and after 4 years for a life sentence. Regulations, issued in 1849, for ticket of leave holders in Van Diemen's Land, specified that holders had to register their residence, or any change of residence upon arrival, at a police station. Movement between districts was not allowed without a police magistrate's pass. Absence between 10pm and daybreak was prohibited. Each December and June, holders had to report to a police station, was required to obtain and keep personal property and good conduct warranted the holder being allowed to keep his ticket.[55] As the years went by, convicts who had obtained a pardon, became known as emancipists or expirees. Some had accumulated great wealth but the majority remained labourers or small shop keepers, while a minority became cattle stealers, receivers of stolen goods, keepers of illicit spirits and squatters.[56]

By 1837, a House of Commons Select Committee, under the chairmanship of Sir William Molesworth, presented a detailed account of evidence taken from individuals engaged in the transportation system. Some of its findings were able to confirm that:

1. *The marriage of female convicts brought about a reformed character.*
2. *The habits of the colony confirmed drunkenness.*

3. *Juvenile prostitution was more common than in any other country.*
4. *Corporal punishment of 50-75 and even 100 lashes; solitary confinement and months or even years of hard labour in chains, for crimes such as petty theft, drunkenness, insolence, disobedience or even quarrelling.*
5. *Most convicts have a dread of flogging than a sentence of hard labour.*
6. *Settlers apparently prefer flogging as a punishment for their convict servants.*
7. *Substitution for transportation for a lesser sentence should be carried out in penitentiaries at home or abroad and only those sentences for longer periods should be sent to Van Diemen's Land and Norfolk Island.*[57]

By 1839, the probation system was introduced as an alternative to assignment. Probation was granted to gangs of convicts composed of offenders who had arrived in Van Diemen's Land following detention at Norfolk Island and also to convicts sentenced to a term of less than a life sentence. They were to be employed on government work in those areas not yet settled and the period of hard labour was not to exceed two years. For this purpose a number of probation stations were set up in various locations in Van Diemen's Land. Following a specified period in the probation gangs, the convicts were placed into one of three probation classes. Those in the first class were required to obtain the consent of the Governor to obtain any work for themselves. The second and third classes (distinguished from each other by such mitigation of toil or any other petty indulgences), were allowed to work with prior approval, on the understanding that the Governor was informed. Wages for the first class were to be 50% of entitlement, 75% for the second class with the third class being allowed their full entitlement. Employers of both the first and second classes were required to place, in the Savings Bank, wages held on behalf of the convicts. The period of probation passes was followed by a ticket of leave system which was only valid in the colony, as noted earlier. Within their original sentence period, convicts were eligible to receive either a conditional or absolute pardon, the first preventing the individual from living in certain countries such as Great Britain, whereas the latter did not carry such conditions.[58]

In 1837-38, a Select Committee recommended that the existing system of transportation should be abolished and, as a consequence, the British Government determined that, as from 22 May 1840, transportation to New South Wales should be terminated.[59] It was not until 24 December 1849 that the last convict ship 'Adelaide' arrived in New South Wales and not until 26 May 1853 that the 'St Vincent' convict ship disembarked the last convicts at Hobart. The Penal Servitude Act of 1853,[60] stated that a sentence of transportation could not be passed upon any man who had been sentenced for less than 14 years. For the rest, penal servitude was enforced whereby two years imprisonment was spent in England of which the first nine months was to be spent in solitary confinement.

As an alternative location to send offenders, a Select Committee of the House of Lords in 1856, decided that Western Australia should continue to be used,[61] having received its first complement of convicts in 1850. In his evidence, Captain Edmund Yeamans Walcott Henderson, one time comptroller-general of convicts in Western Australia, confirmed that he had arrived with the first party of convicts in 1850. No preparation had been made for their reception and it was necessary to rent and furnish accommodation. The convicts were well behaved but no form of incarceration was available. Colonists were apprehensive about employing the men and as a result it was decided that they be employed in building a permanent prison whilst some were used as road parties, clearing and making roads; all had been sentenced to 14 or 15 years transportation and were selected because of their good conduct in prison while in England. They had embarked from Portland prison but, as time went by, a much worse type of convict arrived, many having been sentenced to death. Formerly they would have gone to Norfolk Island. Each convict, upon arrival, had to serve out his time on public work in prison at Fremantle or elsewhere, and, if given a good conduct record, would be entitled to receive a ticket of leave, the issue of which was similar to the system operating in New South Wales. Prisoners, in Western Australia, selected for employment with the settlers, received a minimum of £1 per month as it was calculated that a man could clothe himself and get all his necessities for £7 a year. The balance of £5 was an annual deduction put towards the cost of the voyage out to Australia.

A probationer pass confirmed that the individual had behaved himself and so was given permission to work outside the prison environment in any private services for wages. The issue of a ticket of leave, although it granted certain liberties, could be restrictive. As the years passed by, many convicts took the opportunity to leave Western Australia to find their fortune in the gold fields of the western states. Capture warranted severe punishment by hard labour but it was evident that as further contingents arrived from England, a comparable number successfully made their escape.[62]

By 1867, transportation had ceased altogether and, with the arrival in Western Australia of the 'Hougoumont' convict ship on 9 January 1868, Australia finally received its last transportees.

CHAPTER TWO

A Welsh Rural Scene

Montgomeryshire, during the transportation era (1788-1868), was a county where the main employment was based on the agricultural and weaving industries. The majority of the population resided at the main towns of Llanidloes, Newtown and Welshpool, where manufacturing industries were based. Other population centres were the smaller towns of Montgomery, Llanfyllin and Machynlleth, and the villages of Llanfair Caereinion and Llangurig.

The Severn valley provided a convenient communication link between Llanidloes, Newtown, Montgomery and Welshpool, but access to the other centres of population necessitated crossing the mountainous terrain. Bands of vagabonds and pickpockets moved freely from fair to fair. There is no evidence in the earlier Great Sessions records that the terrain was an impediment, in fact it harboured outlaws. The area of the county was approximately 485,351 acres with a fluctuating population of around 50,000, i.e. one person per ten acres.

Evidence given to a Royal Commission on the Handloom Weavers in 1838, by the Rev. E. Pugh, Vicar of Llanidloes, confirmed that:

The best weavers, under the best masters, average about nine or ten shillings per week. The average wages of all taken together are bout seven shillings. Spinners earn, on an average, about twelve shillings. Children are taken into the factories at about from nine to twelve years. The inference, therefore, to be deducted from the foregoing statement, is that the weavers (who constitute the bulk of the population), are generally poor and unable to pay for the education of their children, even though the trade, as regards this place, is some what brisker than it used to be. The weavers are given to drink, they are improvident, their houses are dirty and their families are trained in ignorance, which is attributed to the occupation of females in factories. Between poverty one on the hand and want of education on the other, the condition of Llanidloes presentes a picture darker by many shades than any town of its size in the principality, except Merthyr Tidvil. Insubordination, defiance of all authority, dishonesty, nightly depredation, fighting, drunkenness and profligacy are the predominant habits of people . . . the mass of the population may be said to have been cradled in ignorance and inured by habit and example to vice . . . the immoral and insubordinate habits of the town must first be corrected by means of the civil power.[1]

The local population, through no fault of their own, were poor, and harvests proved to be insufficient to meet its own needs. An increase in population had exacerbated the situation. Rents were high and the return of soldiers from the Napoleonic war had maintained a high level of unemployment. The setting up of a House of Industry at Forden in 1796 had alleviated the situation in the parishes which it served with in excess of 500 inmates in residence during 1817. The Poor Law Amendment Act of 1834 brought additional facilities to house the non able bodied poor, when Poor Law workhouses were built at Caersws, Llanfyllin and Machynlleth, but these hated 'Bastilles' did nothing but incite the poor against Authority.

13

Whilst there was a significant number of criminals moving in and out of the county, as evident in criminal records throughout England and Wales, the number was increased by the resident population who flouted law and order. The following table indicates the respective parishes from where the transportees were committed and it is clearly evident that the county parishes nearest to the English border had the greatest incidence of law breaking.

Parish	New South Wales	Tasmania	West Australia	Port Philip	Norfolk Island	Bermuda	Gibraltar	England	Total
Alberbury	1							1	2
Aberhafesp		2							2
Berriew	2	2	2					3	9
Bettws								1	1
Buttington		2			1	1			4
Carno	2								2
Cemmaes		1					1	3	5
Churchstoke	2	1							3
Dolfor			1						1
Forden	1	2						4	7
Guilsfield	2	4	1			1	2	1	11
Hyssington		1							1
Kerry	1	3				1		1	6
Leighton		2							2
Llanbrynmair		2						1	3
Llandinam	1		1					2	4
Llandrinio	1	1	1						3
Llandyssil				1					1
Llanerfyl	1	1							2
Llanfair Caer		1	2					1	4
Llanfechain		1						1	2
Llanfihangel	2							1	3
Llanfyllin	1	1						2	4
Llangadfan	1								1
Llangurig	2	1	1					2	6
Llangyniew		1				1			2
Llanidloes	7	4	1					3	15
Llanllugan	1								1
Llanllwchaiarn	1	1	1					3	6
Llanmerewig	1	1				1			3
Llanrhaeadr YM	4							1	5
Llansantffraid	1	1				1			3
Llanwddyn		1		1					2
Llanwnnog				1				2	3
Llanwrin		3							3
Llanymynech	1								1
Machynlleth	1	4	1		1			2	9
Manafon	2								2
Meifod	1	3		1		2		2	9
Mochdre								1	1
Montgomery	1	4	3						8
Newtown	3	10	2	2				2	19
Penstrowed		1							1
Pool Quay			2						2
Trefeglwys	1							4	5
Tregynon		2							2
Trewern		1							1
Welshpool	2	14	8			2		10	36
Not Known	27	13	7			1	3	60	111
Total	**74**	**89**	**37**	**6**	**2**	**11**	**6**	**114**	**339**

By 1839, a report on the establishment of Constabulary Forces highlighted the problem that confronted the magistrates at the time:

> . . . it appears that the lodging houses are now operated for the reception of vagrants, thieves or other description of persons who are now found in the most remote county towns. The following is the description of the characters by which they are now infested, given to us by an informant Mr Thomas Yates, solicitor of Welshpool, who made some enquiries for us in Wales. After describing the increase of thefts and robberies in the town and neighbourhood of Llanfyllin, he states:
>
> This town, though small, is much infested with prostitutes. Formerly the bold unblushing prostitute was unknown here; but now there are at least seven or eight who prowl the streets. One of them has been following her trade in Liverpool, and has recently introduced at Llanfyllin the system of inveigling and then robbing the men which (as is supposed) is now generally adopted. There are three lodging-houses for tramps, one of which is the most notorious house in the parish. The constables are frequently obliged to enter it, especially about fair times, in order to quell the disturbances and excesses created by trampers. This disorderly house is kept by a woman known by the name of "Old Peggy". She never lets a tramp go to bed without money or money's worth, and the broken victuals that a tramp beings home is sold by her to poor persons who keep dogs, such as rat-catchers etc. One man told Mr D . . ., a druggist in the town, that for tuppence, "Old Peggy", would give him scraps enough to keep his dog for a week or more. This druggist stated that "Old Peggy", has often come to him saying, "God bless you Doctor, sell me a hap'orth of tar." When first applied to, he asked, "What do you want with the tar?" The reply was "Why, to make a land sailor. I want a hap'orth just to daub a chap's canvas trousers with and that's how I makes a land sailor, doctor." The tramps have increased beyoned all calculations. About a fortnight ago, two fellow, half-naked, went to a farm house about a mile and a half from the town (the wife of the farmer only was at home), and pleaded starvation. The good woman offered food, when they threatened her, and said "D–n your grub, we want money and must have it." The woman had none, or she would, in her alarm, have given it to them, being terrified with their threatening language. The fellows at last consented to take food of which they put a large quantity into their bags and departed, no doubt to sell it to their friend "Old Peggy". The constables of this town never interfere with the tramps, nor even enter their lodging-houses, unless the neighbours call upon them to enter in order to quell a riot, and as there is no place where these tramps are less annoyed, it is no wonder that they swarm in this district, in proportion as others are more severe. The trick of going half-naked is new in this part of the mountains, although not so in other parts of the Principality. As in other places, they travel with their women, who carry their warm clothing in a bundle. There are seven beer-shops in the town, besides nine public-houses. The sergeant-at mace informed me that these beer-shops, as well as the public-houses, keep open all night, or as long as they have any customer whom choose to serve with drink, and that neither he or any of the other constables ever interfere with them, unless specially called upon as they do not like to inform against a neighbour. In reference to the drunken habits of this place, a gentleman, whom business required to stop there some days, observed there was not a night, from dusk to daylight, but he heard constant rows and fighting in the streets. When he was there a desperate assault took place at the inn-door, when one man had his eye nearly kicked out, and the other had his collar-bone much injured . . .[2]

However, in the nearby village of Llansantffraid it was recorded that:

> . . . the roads of the parish were so neglected, so deeply rutted, and so soft, that all traffic had to be carried on horseback . . . the general moral of the parish is also good, although drunkenness prevails to an extent not at all to our credit, yet the attendance on religious worship, and the almost total absence of crime, speaks highly in our favour the wages of workmen are comparatively low, seven shillings per week victuals, is about average . . .[3]

Between these places is the village of Llanfechain, for which the following contemporary description of farm houses and labourers cottages indicates the standard of housing within the county:

> . . . the farm houses are very inferior and the buildings not adequate to the wants of the farm. Many are very old, ill constructed, and ill arranged. There are yet to be found in them house floors of very rough pebble pavement . . . the living rooms are exceedingly low and the sleeping rooms confined and not sufficiently separated from each other. The offices likewise are too small and insufficiently ventilated and too close to the kitchen . . . the cottages, for the most part, are lamentably deficient in accommodation, and in some cases are unfit for the dwellings of human beings . . . Many consist of two rooms only, and these often on the ground floor. The windows are so small as to admit but little light, and are not made to open. No ventilation can therefore be obtained but through the door; and the bad construction of the building is at the same time calculated to give admission to the chilling blasts of winter. The side walls are often constructed of plastered wattles affixed to a framework of beams of more or less scantling. The floors are laid with pebble pavement, and sometimes with mud only, incapable of being thoroughly cleansed. The sleeping apartment . . . is not subdivided so as to admit any separation of sexes. No drains externally to carry off the house slops or the rain which drips from the eaves . . .[4]

Llanrhaeadr-ym-Mochnant, a village lying on the border with the county of Denbigh, was noted for its attraction for a criminal element:

> . . . this neighbourhood was infested by a gang of thieves and housebreakers. Their rendezvous was at a house on the Montgomeryshire side of Llanrhaeadr village and the house retains the name of "uffern" (hell) to this day (1790). This gang was dispersed by . . . Mr Jones of Squennant, whose house they attempted to break into. Traditions are still current relating to these desperadoes and that they were in the habit of supplying human bodies to distant surgeons for anatomical dis-section. Some subjects it is said they obtained from graveyards, but they did not scruple to commit murder to enable them to carry on their horrible trade. One night they went to Squennant with burglarious intent, but were defeated by the vigilance of the house-keeper. The owner, Mr Jones, upon his return home, sent a messenger in the disguise of a surgeon's assistant in search of a subject for anatomical study, to the wife of one of the gang, and she being alone at home . . . replied "that the men had had ill-luck the previous nights but she was expecting them home that night early". The remark was the cause of them being apprehended and brought to justice. The sequel, the gaol files, of the County can best tell.[5]

It is evident that the county attracted both itinerant criminals and that the less fortunate residential element also turned to lawbreaking. The apparent increase in crime which occurred, not only in Montgomeryshire, but throughout England and Wales, necessitated reform.

CHAPTER THREE

Crime, Detection and Punishment

To keep the level of crime under control the general public were financially encouraged to make every effort to apprehend perpetrators of as many known crimes as possible. To this end, the well-to-do tradesmen and inhabitants of Welshpool, and elsewhere in the county, formed an Association for the Prosecution of Felons. Prior to 1826, witnesses were not paid expenses in attending court to prosecute suspects but received payment thereafter. The Association was formed in Welshpool in 1807 and the following extracts from the Rules and Regulations set out its main purposes:

> *Whereas several horses, sheep and other cattle have been stolen, and frequent burglaries, felonies and larcenies of various kinds committed in the parish of Pool and its neighbourhood, and the offenders have often escaped justice for the want of immediate pursuit and effectual prosecution . . . we . . . form ourselves into a society and to raise funds for the prosecution of all such offences committed against the property of either of us. That if any person or persons commit or perpetrate any murder, manslaughter, burglary, felony or larceny; that when any bullock, horse, sheep, pig . . . shall be feloniously stolen . . . shall be prosecuted . . . at the expense of this Society. The Association also offered rewards for the apprehension of suspects and their prosecution which varied from 5 guineas for arson, burglary and theft or injury of a horse; 3 guineas for the theft or injury of cattle and 1 guinea for lesser offences.[1]*

Examples of offences which resulted in a sentence of transportation of Montgomeryshire convicts are as follows:

In 1784, Hugh Jones, of unknown origin, was sentenced to death at the Summer Great Sessions having committed an unknown felony, but this was commuted to 7 years transportation.[2] At the Great Sessions held at Pool, 28 July 1785, John Evans of Llanfechain parish, a labourer, was sentenced to death but commuted to 7 years transportation for having stolen on 14 May 1785, a black gelding worth £5.[3]

In 1787 Lewis Proctor (Matthews), of Pool, was caught attempting to steal flannel to the value of £10 from William Tibbott of Berriew at the Poole market. When charged for his offence he "went two or three times on his knees and begged they would let him go, repeatedly promising, if he should go, he never would do so again". He was sentenced to 7 years transportation.[4]

The first female convict to be sentenced to transportation from Montgomeryshire was Ann Glossop. Evidence was given at her trial in 1791 by Charles Pugh of Weston, Churchstoke, a farmer, who had witnessed Ann Glossop stealing nine yards of printed velvet valued at twenty shillings from the shop of James Moore in Newtown. Ann Glossop was sentenced to 7 years transportation.[5]

Salisbury Davies at Llanfyllin Fair on 24 June 1792, was arrested and committed to Montgomery Gaol for picking the pocket of Mr Richard Davies of Llanfyllin, and stealing a purse containing twelve guineas, two half guineas, four half crowns and one shilling. It was recorded that:

> Some of the members of the Llanfyllin Association for the Prosecution of Felons, being informed that Salisbury Davies was a very suspicious character, properly took the precaution of directing a person to watch him the whole day, which fortunately proved the means of his being detected about noon, and preventing his committing any further depredation on the public. Mr Davies, it seems, had imprudently taken out his purse in a public house, in the presence of the prisoner, and put it in his waistcoat pocket. Salisbury Davies twigged it, and in the space of a few minutes boned it too, with as much dexterity as tho he had served a regular apprenticeship to the noted Mr Barrington. It is hoped that this will be a caution to farmers and others, who frequent fairs and large markets, not to shew their money, thus publicly, or to carry it in so unguarded a place as a waistcoat pocket.[6]

He was sentenced to 7 years transportation, but, for some unknown reason, never left Montgomery Gaol. It is possible that his general state of health did not allow the Authorities to remove him and so he remained in the county gaol. Salisbury Davies had completed his 7 year sentence by the summer of 1799 but was still within the precinct of the gaol awaiting discharge. A cruel twist of fate meant that he was destined never to set foot outside the gaol; for on 10 August 1799 he was murdered by fellow prisoner Aaron Bywater, who had been committed as a lunatic a few weeks previously, for the murder of Jacob Stanley at the Bears Head Inn Newtown. The Coroner's inquisition, held on the same day as the murder, recorded that Davies was stabbed by Bywater inflicting a single mortal wound. At the Great Sessions held in early 1800, Bywater was indicted for the murder of Salisbury Davies. Furthermore, the evidence entered by the Coroner Charles Thomas Jones, Treasurer of the county, recorded that, in addition to using a knife, Aaron Bywater had access to a hatchet, valued at sixpence, and with it struck Salisbury Davies on the head causing a mortal wound of two inches in length and half an inch in depth. Witnesses named included Mary and Richard Davies, David Stephens and Francis Allen of Maesfron, Trewern, solicitor and a deputy steward for certain manors for Lord Powis.[7] Salisbury Davies was buried in the churchyard of Montgomery Parish Church, 11 August 1799.[8]

On 8 August 1795, Edward Barrett of Tregynon was indicted for burglary, but the trial jury found him guilty of the lesser charge of grand larceny. On 27 May 1795, at about midnight, Barrett had entered the dwelling house of David Davies of Tregynon, and stolen eight cotton handerkerchiefs, valued at seven shillings; five pieces of tape, valued at three shillings; six papers of pins, valued at two shillings; four pound of sugar, valued at two shillings and sixpence and three quarters of a pound of brimstone, valued at one shilling. During the course of the trial in the Town Hall, Welshpool, some of the timbers supporting the wall gave way with the floor sinking several inches. The court was cleared of all persons with the exception of those concerned with the case of Edward Barrett, which ended in a seven-year sentence to transportation.[9]

Mary Griffiths was charged with having committed three offences within a week during June 1801. The first two charges related to breaking and entering an inn in Montgomery from where she stole a piece of bacon belonging to the owner and some clothing belonging to a servant girl. She had visited the inn at night while the servants slept before a fire. The third offence, took place a few days later when she had taken lodgings with the Evans family at Llanwyddelan.

She shared a room and bed with Catherine Evans, and both went to bed on the Sunday evening at 10 o'clock. At half past three in the morning when Catherine Evans awoke she found Mary Griffiths missing from her bed. Catherine also found that her personal clothing had disappeared. Following Griffiths's apprehension, the bacon was found to be an exact fit to the bacon flitch remaining at the inn. Mary Griffiths was sentenced to 7 years transportation.[10]

An accessory to a crime was also liable to a sentence of transportation. Margaret Richards (Senior) received a sentence of 14 years transportation in August 1801 for receiving a stolen length of flannel from her daughter Margaret Richards (Junior). The daughter only received a sentence of one month's imprisonment during which time she was privately whipped.[11]

In some instances newspapers or printed notices and posters were used as a means of distributing information to apprehend and indict suspects. The following example was placed in the *Salopian Journal*, 18 September 1805:

> *Two men are detained in Montgomery gaol on a charge of felony and from their appearance and other circumstances are supposed to have committed offences in Brecknockshire and between that county and Montgomeryshire, where they were lately travelling and begging in the character of sailors, with a young woman in their company. The one is called Thomas Webster and says he is a native of LIanfair (Caereinion) in Montgomeryshire. He is about 30 years of age; stout made; 5'6" high; long dark brown hair; grey eyes; long visage; pale complexion and had lost a front tooth from the upper jaw. Has on a blue sailor's jacket; light coloured swansdown waistcoat; white trousers and round hat with a black ribbon tied in a bow. He is supposed to have been convicted of a felony in Meironethshire in or about 1793, sentenced to transportation but escaped.*

With Thomas Webster was his accomplice John Green and, following capture, they appeared before the Spring Great Sessions 1806 when they were convicted and sentenced to 7 years transportation. Only part of their sentence was carried out in a Portsmouth hulk, as both were granted pardons on the understanding that they served abroad in the army.[12]

The need to enlist men in the army or navy during the Napoleonic War gave magistrates judicial power to commute a sentence to active service. Besides Webster and Green two other convicts, Daniel Lowe and Richard Wainwright, had their 7 year sentences to transportation rescinded (on 16 July 1807), to serve in the Plymouth Division of Marines instead.[13]

There was variability in the severity of the sentences given to convicts, even at the same court session, as in the cases against Edward Thomas and Hugh Dawson. At the Spring Great Sessions 1819, Edward Thomas, aged 40 years, was convicted of manslaughter and sentenced to be confined in the County Gaol for one year and be fined the sum of one shilling. Hugh Dawson, aged 19 years, was convicted of picking the pocket of Jeremiah Evans of Llanrhaeadr-ym-Mochnant, and stealing the sum of nine pounds. For this offence he was sentenced to 7 years trans-portation.[14] At the Great Sessions held at Poole 25 March 1824, David Jones of Newtown, labourer, was convicted, that at Newtown on 27 August 1823, he stole five gold sovereigns, two Newtown Bank notes for payment of one pound each and two other promissory notes for payment of one pound each belonging to Evan Roberts. Examination of Andrew Breeze of Newtown, constable, before George Arthur Evors JP confirmed that David Jones received a 7 years sentence of trans-portation. Following a period in the 'Justitia' and 'Gannymede' hulks at Woolwich he obtained a Free Pardon on 16 January 1828.[15] At the Spring Great Sessions held on 29 March 1827, Richard Jones, a 63-year-old man from Leighton, was indicted for the manslaughter of Edward Gardner of Trelystan. The coroner recorded that Richard Jones had struck Gardner with a scythe causing a mortal wound upon his temple, one inch long, and three inches deep. The trial jury found Richard Jones not guilty of murder, but guilty of manslaughter and he was given a 14 year sentence of transportation.[16] Two further cases were dealt with at the Summer Great Sessions 1827. John Tude(o)r was indicted for the theft of a pig valued £3, on 1 May 1827, belonging to Richard Morris of Gaer, Forden and the theft of three pigs valued £5, on 23 June 1827, also belonging to Richard Morris. John Tudor was acquitted on the first offence but convicted on the second offence, for which he received a 7 year sentence of transportation.[17]

At the same Sessions, John Evans, labourer, was indicted for stealing on 11 July 1827, eleven shillings in money belonging to Arthur Watkin the Elder, a silver tea spoon (value two shillings), two other spoons (value one shilling) and a mug belonging to Arthur Watkin the Younger. Evidence given by Arthur Watkin the Elder of Buttington taken on 13 July 1827 indicated that the offence was committed at the time of the Buttington Wake when there were a considerable number of persons at Arthur Watkin's house during the night. John Evans, had been employed in keeping the door of one of the rooms of the house in which there were persons dancing. On being apprehended, John Evans begged to be allowed to go as he had a wife and children. Evans was convicted and sentenced to 7 years transportation.[18]

Itinerant gangs of persons who committed criminal acts included the following three men, Henry Beastall, John Farren and Jonathan Roose. They had been identified as a gang of horse thieves and were indicted in July 1831 for stealing from Dolanog House, Welshpool, a bay mare belonging to Mr David Jones and a black gelding belonging to Mr Henry Jones (Surgeon). They were each sentenced to death commuted to life transportation.[19]

An analysis of data indicates that of the known place of residence of each transportee, the most significant number (118), lived outside the county of Montgomery. This clearly suggests that at least 70 per cent of transportees, whose place of residence is known, were itinerant. It is probable that this figure is higher, as those whose place of residence is not given were of no fixed abode.

NATIVE PARISHES OF CONVICTS

Parish/County/Country	Total	Parish/County/Country	Total
Abermule	1	Berriew	2
Bettws	1	Carno	1
Churchstoke	1	Forden	1
Llandrinio	2	Llanidloes	7
Llanwnog	3	Llanllwchaiarn	2
Llanfyllin	4	Llangurig	1
Llansantffraid	1	Llanfair Caereinion	1
Llanwyddelan	1	Llanymynech	1
Machynlleth	1	Montgomery	1
Montgomeryshire	6	Newtown	9
Pool Quay	1	Trefeglwys	1
Welshpool	2		
Abingdon	1	Ayr	1
Barabados	1	Beguildy	1
Bishop's Castle	1	Birmingham	8
Brecknockshire	1	Brandon	1

Bristol	1	Broseley	1
Brymbo	1	Carmarthenshire	1
Cardiff	1	Chirbury	1
Cork	1	County Antrim	1
County Donegal	1	Denbighshire	2
Derby	1	Dover	1
Dublin	1	East Haddington	1
Edgware	1	Elton	1
Exeter	1	Hagley	1
Hamilton	1	Hanwood	1
Kent	1	King's Lynn	1
Kinnerley	1	Liverpool	5
London	1	Londonderry	1
Loughborough	1	Llandrillo	1
Llanerchymedd	1	Llansilin	1
Llanystymdwy	1	Macclesfield	
Manchester	2	Malvern	1
Meliden	1	Merthyr Tydfil	2
Merioneth	2	Much Wenlock	1
Newcastle	1	Newport	1
New York	1	North America	1
Nottingham	1	North Wales	2
Oldham	1	Oswestry	2
Paisley	1	Plymouth	1
Radnorshire	1	Reading	2
Salford	1	Saxony	1
Shrewsbury	1	Shropshire	10
Somerset	2	Southampton	2
South Wales	1	St Albans	1
Stockport	2	Staffordshire	3
Stourport	1	Stroud	1
Tenbury Wells	2	Ulverston	1
Warrington	1	Warwickshire	1
Westbury	1	West Bromwich	2
Whitehaven	1	Woolwich	1
Wolverhampton	2	Worthen	3
Yeovil	1	Not Known	170

Total   **339**

A summary of the above indicates that 51 came from Montgomeryshire; 20 from the rest of Wales; 86 from England; 5 from Ireland; 3 from Scotland; 4 from abroad with 140 from no known abode.

Some offenders pleaded by way of petition to avoid being transported. Edward Dodd, who was convicted at the Quarter Sessions held on 16 October 1834 and sentenced to seven years transportation, was indicted for the theft of a double barrelled percussion gun, a writing desk and a shooting jacket belonging to Mr Gill of Rhiewargoed in the parish of Llanwddyn on 17 June 1834. Whilst he remained in the county gaol awaiting transportation, Edward Dodd wrote the following letter dated 16th October 1834 to The Right Hon. C. W. Wynn:

Sometime ago I lived with Mr Gill in the capacity of a butler and I must say that I was very ill treated by him. One morning he was going from the house to Liverpool and he asked me what cash I had of his that he wanted it. I went to my dresser and found I had £4.14s.6d., which I gave him and he immediately told me that I may go about my business, that he would not employ me no longer and he went off I was thunderstruck at the time not having the least idea of leaving . . . with besides my 4 months wages, which was £10 more and had no settlement with him whatever. On my way after him to Liverpool, I made so free as to call upon your Honor at

Llangedwyn, to ask your advice what to do in my distress, not having a sixpence in the world. Your Honor was going from home that day and you have kindly promised to assist me at a future date I went after him to Liverpool and begged for a settlement with him as much as possible, but he never did from that day to this I went to an Attorney there and my answer from him was that . . . he would have nothing to do with him. I went after him again from thence to Hereford and begged again for a settlement, but all in vain. I applied there to an Attorney, but he, the former, gave me the same denial that he would have nothing to do with such a character, so I am robbed for £16 to £18 by him and no redress except your Honor, and the rest of the Magistrates may be pleased to take compassion upon me, and I humbly beg that the penalty due to my crime may be mitigated in consideration of myself being so . . . by him that I have often been reduced to hunger and starvation on account of him I humbly beg, for God's sake, that your Honor may be pleased to look upon me in mercy in the midst of Judgment, and the Eternity will be long enough to reward you, when time shall be no more, is the earnest prayers of Your Honour's

Humble Servant.

This petition was to no avail and, on 29th August 1835, Edward Dodd left for Van Diemen's Land.[20]

For women who were sentenced to be transported there was the vexing problem of what should become of their children.

In 1834, Ann Roberts, who was a first offender at the age of 21 years, was described as a sober and industrious farm servant. She had been convicted of breaking and entering the house of Richard Harris of Cil in the parish of Berriew, on 30 April 1834 and stealing a cotton gown, a silk handkerchief, some roast veal and what remained of two puddings. Ann Roberts was convicted and sentenced to 7 years transportation. She was returned to Montgomery gaol to await her fate and, by 16 October 1834, the visiting magistrates considered her to be a fit person to be removed to a penitentiary, but with a proviso that her friends be asked to maintain her infant child. They ordered that steps be taken to obtain her transfer from the gaol to an appropriate penitentiary. On 8 January 1835, Ann Roberts stated to the authorities that she was willing to part with her infant, but that her friends were unwilling to maintain it. The magistrates decided that the said child be removed to its parish in Flintshire,[21] and that a proper person be found to accompany the child and all expenses be paid by the County Treasurer. As a result of these arrangements, Ann Roberts was removed from the gaol and the child taken to Flintshire, the cost of the latter being £5.8s.5d. Ann Roberts left for Tasmania on 26 December 1835, leaving her illegitimate child to the care of the Poor Law Authorities in her native place of Meliden Flintshire.[22]

During the years of transportation, there were well known gangs in the area such as 'The Forty Thieves' and 'The Thimble Riggers'. John James and Edward Ingram were indicted for stealing a sovereign from the person of Edward Watkin of the parish of Tregynon at Newtown Fair on 28 March 1837. Both were sentenced to 7 years transportation, which had the desired effect of clearing Newtown of all the known 'Thimble Riggers'[23] Mary Ann Aubrey, known as one of a gang called 'The Forty Thieves' was in the Newtown area during Christmas 1838, when she stole cash from Owen Jenkins of Newtown whilst he was on his way home from chapel. She received a sentence of 10 years transportation.[24]

Transportees came from varied occupations but, as would be expected in a rural county, the greatest proportion were involved in agriculture. They included 36 labourers, 23 farm labourers and 17 ploughmen.

CONVICTS BY OCCUPATION/CALLING PRIOR TO TRANSPORTATION

OCCUPATION	N.S.W. Male	N.S.W. Female	T.A.S. Male	T.A.S. Female	W.A. Male	P.P. Male	N.I. Male	Total Male	Total Female
Boot/shoe maker	2				1			3	
Butcher	2		1		1			4	
Blacksmith			2					2	
Baker			1					1	
Butler			1					1	
Bricklayer			1					1	
Boatman					1			1	
Carpenter	1		3					4	
Cook		1		1					2
Cattle Jobber			1					1	
Cigar Maker					1			1	
Confectioner					1			1	
Dairymaid		1		1					2
Dealer			1					1	
Dressmaker				1					1
Engineer			1		1			2	
Farm Labourer	12		12				1	25	
Flannel Weaver	3		2		2			7	
Farm Servant		1		3					4
Fireman					1			1	
Groom	1		2					3	
Grinder			1					1	
Grass Cutter			1					1	
Gardener					2			2	
Horse Doctor	1		1					2	
Hawker			1					1	
Iron Moulder					1			1	
Joiner						1		1	
Labourer	8		6		18	4		36	
Laundress				3					3
Lathe Render			1					1	
Mason			1					1	
Miller/Fuller	1				1			2	
Manned Navigator	1							1	
Nurse Girl		1							1
Ostler					1			1	
Ploughman	3		14					17	
Public House Servant		1							1
Ropemaker			1		1			2	
Sawyer	2		3					5	
Servant		4		1					5
Shoeing smith	1							1	
Silk Weaver	1							1	
Skinner/Tanner	2							2	
Glass Grinder	1							1	
Shepherd	2							2	
Shoemaker			1					1	
Shopkeeper			1					1	
Sailor			2					2	
Saddler			1					1	
Spinner			1					1	
Silk Dyer			1					1	
Stoker					1			1	
Striker					1			1	
Tinman	1							1	
Tallow Chandler	1							1	
Tailor					1			1	
Tanner/Currier							1	1	
Whitesmith	1							1	
Waggoner			1					1	
Not Known	14	4	12	1	1	1		28	5
Total	**61**	**13**	**78**	**11**	**37**	**6**	**2**	**184**	**24**

NB. This Table only includes those convicts sent to Australia and Norfolk Island.

There was only one occasion in the county (in 1839), when a significant civil commotion occurred, owing to the impact that Chartism had on various parts of Great Britain. The consequences of this outbreak are well documented elsewhere.[25] Convictions for those in the disturbances in Montgomeryshire included four offenders who received sentences of transportation: namely Lewis Humphreys and Abraham Owen of Llanidloes and John Ingram of Newtown, 7 years, and James Morris of Llanidloes, 15 years. In the case of Lewis Humphreys the Authorities published the following notice:

> *By Her Majesty's Command £100 Reward Whereas Lewis Humphreys late of Llanidloes shoemaker and Thomas Jerman of the same place carpenter, were apprehended at Llanidloes on the 30 of April last (1839), on a charge of felony, and rescued by a Mob, and have since absconded. This is to give notice that the above reward of one hundred pounds will be given to any such person who will re-apprehend, or give such information as will lead to the re-apprehension, of the above mentioned persons; and that fifty pounds will be paid to anyone who will re-apprehend or give such information as will lead to the re-apprehension, of either of the said two persons.*
>
> *The said Lewis Humphreys (called Jehu) 8 is a shoemaker, about 30 years of age, 5 feet 10 inches high, of dark forbidding countenance, muscular high cheek bones and shoulders, has dark hair, black whiskers, and probable wears a blue coat, stripped trousers and cap. The said Thomas Jerman is a carpenter, aged about 30, stands 5 feet 8 inches high, stoutly made, has broad round shoulders and short thick neck, a round wide face, small eyes, and wide mouth. When last seen had on a blue or brown coat, light yellow cotton waistcoat with a sprig pattern upon it, white trousers with stripes on it, and light stripped cotton neckerchief. The fingers of his right hand are slightly contracted, and the third and fourth fingers of his left hand are much contracted. Both are natives of Llanidloes. The reward above mentioned, will be paid by the Mayor of Llanidloes, who is authorised by Her Majesty's Secretary of State to offer the same.*

Whilst Lewis Humphreys was re-apprehended and received his transportation sentence, Thomas Jerman made his escape to Liverpool from where he emigrated to America.[26]

Marking of livestock with owner's identification marks was not unusual but the extent to which it extended is illustrated in the case of Maurice Jones. In 1846, he stole a goose from Mrs Martha Williams of the Herbert Arms Inn, Kerry. When the goose was found it had been partly feathered and its feet, severed. John Hamer, servant to Mrs Williams, identified the goose by its feet, which had a punch hole and a slit in the neck that he had made. Maurice Jones, who had been courting crime for upwards of three years, was sentenced to seven years transportation.[27]

Criminal acts carried out by related persons were infrequent. One such instance occurred in 1847, when the brothers John and Edward Hancox broke into the house of Samuel Brown, an ironmonger and blacksmith of Montgomery, on Sunday evening 5 December, when the Brown family was at chapel. One of the brothers had previously been employed by Mr Brown. They stole eleven pounds sixteen shillings and two coats. Both received 10 year sentences to transportation.[28]

Available data has enabled an analysis to be made to determine if those sentenced to transportation had previous convictions. The following table, indicates that 51 males had committed one previous offence and four females had committed two previous offences. One individual, (James Robinson), clearly a habitual offender, had been apprehended on no less than fourteen occasions. The record indicates that the sentence of transportation was given to those who had previous convictions; nevertheless, there were those who were transported after committing just one offence, probably as an example to others.

NUMBER OF PREVIOUS CONVICTIONS

Convictions	NSW M/F	TAS M/F	WA M	NI M	PP M	Total M/F
None	16/-	2/1	1	-	-	19/1
One	8/-	24/2	18	-	1	51/2
Two	-/3	3/1	7	-	-	10/4
Three	-/-	-/-	1	-	-	1/-
More	-/-	-/-	3	-	-	3/-
Not Known	37/10	49/7	7	2	5	100/17
Total	**61/13**	**78/11**	**37**	**2**	**6**	**184/24**

NB. This table only includes those convicts who were sent to Australia and Norfolk Island.

In general, property which had been stolen was returned to its rightful owner when the offender had been apprehended.

In the case of Evan Turner, who had stolen 6 pigs from the Meifod area in 1848, he was found, following his capture by the police, to have £5.17.6 on his person. At his trial it was decided that the chief constable be empowered to distribute the money amongst those persons from whom Evan Turner had stolen the pigs. Evan Turner was sentenced to 7 years transportation.[29]

From an analysis of age groups of the criminals, it is evident that the majority were in the 20-29 year age group, as shown in the following table for both male and females. This is consistent with the pattern found in England and Wales. It is perhaps significant that of all offenders indicted in Montgomeryshire under the age of 19 years, only 31 male and 5 female were transported, being less than 10% of all age groups.[30]

AGE OF CONVICTS

Ages	NSW Male	Female	TAS Male	Female	WA Male	PR Male	NI Male	Ber Male	Gib Male	England Male	Female	Total Male	Female
10-19	4	1	6	3	6	1		1	2	11	1	31	5
20-29	29	6	46	6	21	4	1	6	3	36	1	146	13
30-39	13	3	17	2	8		1	2		17	1	58	6
40-49	7	1	4		2	1			1	11	4	26	5
50-59	2		3					1		3	1	9	1
60-89			1							3		4	
70-79										1		1	
NK	6	2	1					1		24		32	2
TOTAL	**61**	**13**	**78**	**11**	**37**	**6**	**2**	**11**	**6**	**106**	**8**	**307**	**32**

Abbreviations: WA. Western Australia; PP. Port Phillip; NI. Norfolk Island; Gib. Gibraltar.

One of the youngest offenders was Fanny Bennett of Worthen who, according to official records, was only 13 years of age, although on her arrival in Van Diemen's Land she was recorded as being 16 years old. She had already been an inmate at Montgomery gaol, serving a three month hard labour sentence for stealing clothing, when the Rev. J. Lloyd, Chaplain to the gaol and Rector of Llanmerewig, took pity on her and found her employment at the rectory where she took up her duties as a live-in housemaid on 28 July 1848. On the morning of 19 August she went missing, taking with her 1 black whittle (value ten shillings), 2 small shawls and an umbrella belonging to fellow servant, Jane Evans. She did not get far before she was tracked down by the police. On 19 October 1848 she was given a 7 year sentence of transportation to Van Diemen's Land, where she lived to marry twice when she was 20 and 73 years of age respectively.[31] Another young offender was Elizabeth Davies (Grist) who, when aged 17 years, stole a large bundle of clothing from Martha Ridge, the wife of William Ridge, a farmer, of Churchstoke.

At the Quarter Sessions held on 4 January 1849, the Justice told Elizabeth Davies that she had been tried twice before and each time she had received admonitions as to her future conduct and all to no purpose; that he had to remark, at the last Sessions, she and her mother were in trouble. Her previous offences in 1847 and 1848 included stealing one half sovereign, one shilling and one gauze scarf from Eliza Austin, one pair of shoes from William Pryce and one gown from Eleanor Davies for which offences she had spent 14 days imprisonment. Mr Ridge advised that he had taken the prisoner into his service without a character reference. On hearing this admission the Justice replied:

> that if all farmers and others took thieves into their service owing to not taking the trouble to obtain their character, they must not expect that the county would allow them anything to their attendance in prosecuting them.[32]

In Montgomeryshire there was only one case of murder for which the death sentence was commuted to transportation. Ishmael Jones, a 44 year old farm labourer of Llanfair Caereinion was tried in March 1862. He had conceived on some real or fancied ground, a jealousy towards his wife, Ann Jones, on hearing something pass between his wife and an Evan Evans on the highroad. Having allowed a considerable time to elapse between that time and the committing of the crime, he, on 30 December 1861, while in the garden with his wife digging up potatoes for dinner, with a spade used for the purpose, deliberately, by repeated blows, fractured her skull, causing her death.

The prosecution stated that the prisoner had been married to the deceased woman for a number of years but that their marriage had not been a happy one. It appeared in the mind of the prisoner, "that an improper intimacy existed between the deceased woman and a person named Evan Evans, who was a neighbour of the prisoner". The deceased woman frequently visited Evan Evans, in whose company she was last seen alive on the 30 December.

In his summing up to the trial jury the Judge stated:

> This case has lasted for some time . . . not too long because no time can be too long when spent investigating a charge so serious a character as that made out against the prisoner . . . there can be no doubt that the prisoner did wilfully deprive his wife of life . . . it has been urged that the prisoner was hypocondrical but there has been no evidence to show that he was in any state of mind that did not render him responsible for his acts . . . I would advise you to look at the act and consult not your feelings but your judgment . . .

The jury took half-an-hour to consider their verdict of wilful murder but strongly recommended mercy. The Judge then asked the prisoner what he had to say why sentence of death should not be passed upon him, but he remained silent. Putting on the black cap the Judge ended the proceedings by saying:

Ishmael Jones, you have been convicted of the crime of wilful murder, and that, the murder of your own wife. The jury have felt themselves bound to come to the conclusion . . . and I am bound to say that I entirely concur in the verdict . . . they have accompanied their verdict by a strong recommendation to the Crown, who alone can give it effect . . . I warn you not to be sanguine about the outcome. . . let me advise you to turn your thoughts to that which your soul needs . . . it remains for me to pass upon you the sentence that you be taken from the place where you now stand to the place whence you came, and from thence to a place of public execution where you shall hang by the neck until you are dead, that your body shall be buried within the precincts of the gaol wherein you have been con fined, and may God have mercy upon your soul.[33]

Ishmael Jones' death sentence was commuted to penal servitude for life. Following a period at Portland prison he was sent to Western Australia on 11 January 1864.

During the 1860s at least 17 instances of arson were committed mainly in the eastern parishes near the English border. In each case, sentences of penal servitude were followed by transportation to Western Australia. In July 1863 William Brannan and Thomas Brown set fire to a haystack at Montgomery. Their evidence at the Quarter Sessions dwelt on the fact that they were taking a rest from their travel in close proximity to a farm, when the farmer approached and ordered them to leave the vicinity as he suspected them of being guilty of committing arson to his haystacks. Both received 8 year sentences of penal servitude. Later the same year James Foster and Thomas Riley, in their defence, confirmed that they had only stopped at the Francis's farm near Leighton for food when Mary the farmer's wife scolded them. Being upset by her unfriendliness, they decided to fire nearby stacks of oats and barley. Both were found guilty and received sentences of 8 years penal servitude. Just prior to Christmas 1863, James Booth was arrested, having set fire to hay in the Newtown area. At his hearing it was reported that he had a previous felony conviction and, prior to passing sentence, Mr Justice Crompton told James Booth that:

to all appearances you had committed the crime for the purpose of being sent out of the country. In that you will be greatly disappointed. You will be kept like slaves, working for others for the long term to which I think it is my duty to sentence you.

He was sentenced to 8 years penal servitude.

In March 1864 John Mcintyre was accused and found guilty of setting fire to corn at a farm in Pool Quay. This was a second conviction as he had previously stolen a cape in January 1864 and been sentenced to 2 months hard labour. The chairman of the magistrates confirmed that:

it appeared the prisoner had recently been discharged from gaol, and this was almost his first act, and that animated by an insane dislike to the farmers, as a class of men.[34]

The only female to be indicted for arson was Elizabeth Williams. In 1827 she had been caught setting fire to a stack of hay in Trewern belonging to Thomas Davies who had bought the farm from her husband. The crime was committed following the death of her husband 6 months after the sale, and, as a result, she was sentenced to death. Following a Royal Pardon her sentence was commuted to life transportation.[35]

Throughout the transportation period the main industries that were available to the local population were agriculture and weaving. Offences relating to the flannel trade were generally punished by severe transportation sentences as indicated by the following table:

Year	Name	Offence	Sentence
1787	Lewis Proctor	stealing flannel	7 years
1800	Richard Cadman	stealing flannel	Life
1801	Margaret Richards	accepting stolen flannel	14 years
1805	Evan Morris	stealing flannel	7 years
1818	Mary Hughes	stealing flannel	7 years
1818	Richard Pugh	stealing flannel	7 years
1823	Francis Webb	stealing flannel	7 years
1828	David Powell	stealing flannel	Life
1828	Richard Morris	stealing flannel	7 years
1828	Edward Williams	stealing flannel	7 years
1828	David Rees	stealing flannel	7 years
1829	Edward Williams	stealing flannel	7 years
1832	David Jones	stealing flannel	7 years
1844	Evan Astley	stealing wool	10 years
1844	Edward Griffiths	stealing wool	7 years
1845	William Evans	stealing flannel	7 years

Whilst the majority of trials would have reflected the solemnity of the occasion, instances occur when some degree of humour entered into the proceedings. One such example occurred in 1843, when John Walden, John Hartell and John Bradbury, were convicted of an audacious burglary at the home of Miss Ann Davies of Pool. They had stolen a gold watch, a gold key; a watch guard, a scarf and a silk handkerchief. Whilst at the same house, they had also stolen a top coat, a black coat, a waistcoat, a dressing gown and a silk handkerchief belonging to the Revd. Joseph McIntosh who was staying there as a guest. Each received a 15 year sentence to transportation and it is recorded that at the end of the trial one of the convicts beckoned Mr McIntosh towards him and with the most perfect nonchalance said:

> Will your honor comfort me with a sixpence or give me the old coat end waistcoat, as a remembrance of your honor.

Needless to say the Mr McIntosh declined.[36]

Sentencing of all offenders was governed by Government Regulations of the day and the lack of adequate custodial facilities at both local and national level accentuated the situation. Local Magistrates and Assize Judges would have been acutely aware that any decision on their part, following a guilty verdict by the jury, would have to be tempered by the character of the individual, the degree of the committed offence and whether or not any previous criminal acts should be taken into consideration. The least transportable sentence of seven 7 years was given to 46% (142 men), while 65% (21 women) received a similar sentence. Commutation of the death sentence to transportation occurred in the cases of 17% (54 men) and 15% (5) women.

TYPE OF SENTENCE

Term of	NSW Male	NSW Female	TAS Male	TAS Female	WA Male	PR Male	NI Male	Ber Male	Gib Male	England Male	England Female	Total Male	Total Female
7 Years	27	10	30	8		2		8	1	62	3	130	21
10 Years	2		24	2		3		2	4	13	1	48	3
14 Years	3	2	3					1		7	1	14	3
15 Years	1		6				2			2		11	
20 Years									1			1	
Life	2		7							2		11	
Life (14 Yrs.)			1									1	
Death (2 Yrs.)										2		2	

Death (7 Yrs.)	4									12	1	16	1
Death (Life)	12	1	6	1						3	1	21	3
Death (14 Yrs.)	10		1			1				2	1	14	1
Penal Servitude													
4 Years										1		1	
6 Years					1							1	
7 Years					10							10	
8 Years					15							15	
10 Years					6							6	
14 Years					3							3	
15 Years					1							1	
Death (Life)					1							1	
Total	**61**	**13**	**78**	**11**	**37**	**6**	**2**	**11**	**6**	**106**	**8**	**307**	**32**

The plight of a family following the transportation of the 'Bread Winner' was precarious.[37] The wife and two children of Evan Griffiths who was sentenced in 1844 to seven years transportation, found it necessary to apply for admission to the Newtown and Llanidloes Union workhouse at Caersws, because of destitution. Ishmael Jones, who was transported for having murdered his wife in 1862, left behind five children, some of whom were admitted to Llanfyllin workhouse.

The following tables indicate that for male offenders, burglary and house-breaking, were the most common offence,[38] followed by stealing of sheep (26) and horses (26). There is no clear pattern of offences committed by female offenders, although burglary and housebreaking offences (4), theft of clothing(s) and shop items (4) were the most common.

TYPE OF CRIME COMMITTED BY MALE OFFENDERS

CRIME	NSW	TAS	WA	PP	NI	BER	GIB	ENG	TOTAL
Burglary/Housebreaking	10	35	13	2		2	3	24	89
Murder			1						1
Manslaughter								1	1
Stabbing	1				2				3
Larceny unspecified						1		5	6
Larceny – food	1	1						2	4
Larceny – clothes	6	2	1			1		3	13
Larceny – household items	4	3	1	2		1		9	20
larceny – work items	4	5					1	8	18
Larceny – shop items		1				1		1	3
Larceny – mail								1	1
Receiving stolen goods								3	3
Assault on person			1						1
Theft from person		4	1	1				5	11
Robbery with violence		2					1	2	5
Robbery on highway	2	2						1	5
Stealing – pigs	1	1				1		1	4
Stealing – sheep	9	2	2					13	26
Stealing – cattle	1		1	1				2	5
Stealing – horses	11	11						4	26
Stealing – fowls	2	3				1		4	10
Wounding cattle	1	3							4
Felony unspecified	3	2						16	21
Training/Drilling	3								3
Forgery	1								1
Arson			16						16
Bigamy								1	1
Perjury								1	1
Uttering forged banknotes	1	1					1	2	5
TOTAL	**61**	**74**	**37**	**6**	**2**	**8**	**6**	**109**	**307**

TYPE OF CRIME COMMITTED BY FEMALE OFFENDERS

CRIME	NSW	TAS	ENG	TOTAL
Burglary/Housebreaking	2	2		4
Larceny – clothes	1	3	1	5
Larceny – household items		1		1
Larceny – work items	1			1
Larceny – shop items	2	1	1	4
Receiving stolen goods	3		1	4
Assault on person	1			1
Theft from person		3	1	4
Robbery/on highway	1			1
Felony unspecified	2		4	6
Arson		1		1
Total	**13**	**11**	**8**	**32**

It is not clear whether or not local Associations for the Prosecution of Felons were effective; it was still incumbent on the victim of an offence to take the initiative in apprehending and prosecuting felons. In view of the expenses incurred in undertaking this duty, many offenders were allowed to escape.

Since medieval times, constables were appointed for each township at the manorial courts and were drawn from the residents of the particular township. It was an office which the appointee served unwillingly. The state of affairs resulting from this is well illustrated in a report prepared in December 1833 by Mr T. J. Hogg, Assistant Commissioner, empowered to hold an Inquiry into the Municipal Corporations of England and Wales. For the Borough of Llanfyllin he indicated that:

> . . . the sergeants at mace act as constables and the Yeoman assists them when he is required. There are four constables in the town which is divided into four wards policed by one constable. The ordinary force is not sufficient at the fairs; the assistance of special constables is then required;the constabulary force is inefficient; the constables being mechanics and tradesmen to which duties they are more attentative besides keeping the peace. At these fairs there is usually great turbulence, disorder, savage, rude and riotous behaviour. The people come from the hills where they live on buttermilk and when they taste the strong ale to which they are much addicted, they are apt suddenly to fall a fighting in a very barbarous manner.[38]

Hugh Jones, Mayor of Llanidloes in 1837, was a stalwart man and occasionally acted as his own constable. On 10 April 1834 he apprehended Lewis Humphreys for assault on Pryce Owen at Llanidloes and removed him safely to the crib (lockup) at the local Market Hall.[39]

The Rev. E. Pugh Vicar of Llanidloes, in his submission to the Royal Commission on the Hand-Loom Weavers in 1838, told W. A. Miles Esq, Assistant Commissioner that:

> there is no police fit to be so called . . . unless the town is supplied with a stipendiary magistrate and an efficient police, it may become necessary to have recourse to extreme measures . . . and that if there was any chance of success, . . . he should immediately petition Government on the subject.[40]

The somewhat lax approach taken by the constables is taken from the following newspaper article:

A considerable time ago, a person named Goodwin, was strongly suspected of having stolen two sheep from Vaynor Park Berriew, which he was supposed to have sold at Newtown fair. The constables received instructions to be on the alert and Goodwin was arrested in South Wales and forwarded in company with the constable of Berriew to Shrewsbury, on his way to Montgomery (gaol). Being late in the evening when they arrived at Shrewsbury, the constable and prisoner went to bed in Frankwell, the latter being handcuffed, but so sound did the constable sleep, that he was unconscious to his charge escaping handcuffs and all. Weeks have since passed by without tidings of the prisoner, but in the early part of last week, a person from Montgomeryshire happening accidently to step into a hedgeside alehouse on the road from Wrexham to Chester, discovered Goodwin composedly enjoying his pipe and pot and took him at once into custody. He was transferred immediately to the jurisdiction of the Magistrates of Montgomery, who have committed him to Shrewsbury gaol for trial. It is useless to observe that in no part of the second journey of the captive, was the constable found napping.[41]

There was a need to improve this situation by the introduction of a paid constabulary. The Chartist riot in Llanidloes during 1839 brought it own particular need for adequate policing, when three Metropolitan policemen (Banks, Davies and Garrett) were sent for, with additional police support from William Blenkhorn of Newtown, constable Armishaw of Welshpool and bailiff Andrew Breeze of Newtown. With them a band of upwards of 300 special constables were recruited from the surrounding parishes as the initial response by Authority to quell the disturbance. With no significant result, it was necessary that their efforts received support from the 14th Light Infantry from Brecon and the Montgomeryshire Yeomanry Cavalry before law and order could return to the town.[42] Even after this major local disturbance, and four men being sentenced to transportation,[43] it is noted that by 22 October 1840, Thomas Hayward, Mayor of Llanidloes, had written to the magistrates:

that the council do agree that the Borough be consolidated with the county for the purpose of joining in the county constabulary force, provided the inhabitants of the Borough are not charged in respect of the adoption of the said 1839/40 Acts of Parliament with any expence.[44]

At the same time the town clerk of Welshpool, who had received instruction by his council to answer the same questionnaire, replied in the following vein:

that the council do respectfully decline to agree for the consolidation of the Borough force with the county establishment at present.[45]

Following receipt of two letters from the Secretary of State, Home Department, on 28 February 1839 concerning the establishment of a more efficient Constabulary Force, the matter was placed before the Quarter Sessions held on 9 April 1840. A Committee was formed to look into the provision of a Constabulary Force in Montgomeryshire. As a consequence to this local investigation, a requisition was signed by the Justices of the Peace for the county pursuant to the directions of the Acts of Parliament passed in 1839/40,[46] which declared it expedient to organize a paid Constabulary Force for the whole county of Montgomery, that such a force should consist of a Chief Constable, two Superintendents and twelve Constables, that their salary be £200, £90 and £75 for the two grades of Superintendent per annum respectively, and not less than sixteen shillings and not more than twenty shillings per week for the constables. The county constabulary was established in July 1840.[47]

It was not until 1841 that a policeman was stationed in Llanfair Caereinion. The first task of the newly formed force was clearing the county of highwaymen who robbed farmers and others returning from market, often with considerable force. Ninety-eight such robberies were reported to have taken place in the year 1842 alone. It was reported that this form of crime had been eradicated from the county by the year 1850. Disorderly conduct by mobs was also prevalent in these years. Farm fires were frequent but had greatly decreased by the year 1860.[48] In order that they were able to carry out their duties, constables were equipped with cutlasses, belts and staffs, all marked MCC and numbered.[49] By January 1841 a constable was stationed at Garthbeibio.[50] By 1843 constables were instructed to take down, in writing, all the particulars of a robbery or any felony, as soon as they received information, and, also to take down, in writing, the examination of all persons who were able to give any information on the subject. These would then be reviewed by the chief constable and superintendent. It was noted that, as the rural police had conveyed prisoners to the county gaol in 1842, a saving of £57 had been made, which was in addition to a saving of £20 achieved by policemen attending as witnesses for the trial of offenders.[51] In 1843, Kerry parish made a request that a policeman be stationed there.[52] In April 1845, Major Newcombe, chief constable, resigned his post[53] and by 17 July William Baird had taken it up.[54] On the recommendation of Colonel Cartwright, HM Inspector of Police, the county force was increased in 1857 by the appointment of two sergeants and five constables, the constables being stationed at Cemmaes, Churchstoke, Llangurig, Meifod and Penybontfawr.[55] At a meeting of the Constabulary Committee held on 8 April 1863, after a period of 18 years in the post, Mr Baird, chief constable, reported personal debts amounting to £2,687.14.1. Upon being called upon to resign, he declined to do so, whereupon it was ordered that he be removed from his office and that the deputy chief constable, Superintendent Hodgson, be instructed to carry on the business of the force until a new chief constable could be appointed.[56] In July 1863, Mr John Hodgson, acting chief constable, was appointed to the vacancy, at a salary of £250 per annum plus £30 per annum for expenses.[57]

CHAPTER FOUR

Incarceration

Throughout the transportation period (1788-1868), all offenders within the boundary of Montgomeryshire would have found themselves, following capture, removed either to the county gaol or house of correction, both located in the county town of Montgomery. Local lock up facilities would have been utilized in some instances, but the general state of these places did not provide adequate detention for more than a few days.

Highlighted in a 1833 Royal Commission Inquiry into the Municipal Corporations in England and Wales, a report presented by Mr T. J. Hogg, assistant Commissioner, gave the following account of facilities then available at Llanidloes:

> . . . *there is no gaol within the Borough except a small crib under the Town Hall; it is the property of Lord Mostyn and in the keeping of Thomas Morgan the lessee of the Town hall and of the tolls. It was represented as an unfit place for the confinement of any person and that nobody had been put in it for two or three years. The last prisoner was a shoemaker, a stranger to the Borough, who was committed for a felony in stealing cloth and was convicted of that offence and transported for 7 years.*[1]

The itinerant shoemaker was David Rees, indicted 11 August 1828, having stolen flannel with force and arms, from the tenter field belonging to Richard Brown of Llanidloes. Sentenced to 7 years transportation, he died on the 'Justitia' hulk on 22 February 1829.[2]

During the period 1842-1843, prisoners held in the lock up at Newtown included John Williams and Richard Morris. They had entered the house of Edward Middleton of Newtown and stolen wearing apparel and, as a result, had been sentenced to 10 years transportation, John Williams served out his sentence on the 'Warrior' hulk at Woolwich until he was pardoned 25 April 1848. Richard Morris, however, went to Van Diemen's Land on 21 November 1844.[3]

As was the case in other counties of England and Wales, Montgomeryshire found it necessary to make adequate provision for the incarceration of offenders who committed criminal acts within its boundaries. During the transportation era, two such gaols were built in the county town, the first about 1734 and the latter in 1832. During a visit to the gaol in 1788, John Howard, as part of his extensive inspection of gaols in the country, was able to ascertain that William Davies, gaoler, received ten pounds for escorting tranportees from the gaol to the London hulks.[4]

Doctor James Nield, a government inspector, visited the gaol in 1803 and found confined therein a criminal lunatic, Aaron Bywater, who, having already been committed for the murder of Jacob Stanley of Newtown, and found not guilty due to insanity, immediately upon arrival at the gaol, murdered an inmate, Salisbury Davies, who was waiting to serve a transportation sentence.[5]

Prior to removal from the county gaol, either to a hulk ship or penitentiary, transportees were issued with a supply of new clothing. In 1819, Mary Blakemore, Mary Hughes and Maria Jones were issued with one bedgown, two petticoats and one apron each. Prior to their removal they had been reported as being of a "very disorderly" nature and were admonished that any further such conduct would warrant solitary confinement.[6] Mary Williams, having received a 7 year transportation sentence in 1832, was removed with a new set of clothing, consisting of one woollen gown, one cotton gown, one cotton petticoat, one flannel petticoat, three shifts, two neckchiefs, three pairs stockings, two pairs shoes, one black apron and one black bonnet. When she eventually left the gaol, Mary Williams was the last transportee to leave the old county gaol.[7]

As a result of the Chartist riots of 1839, included amongst the convicted was John Ingram, having been sentence to 7 years transportation. Whilst in gaol, he had been observed by another prisoner, Edward Williams of Llanwnnog, who, on oath, stated that John Ingram was training and parading other prisoners who had paid Ingram three pound ten shillings for their instruction.

No doubt this evidence added to the case against John Ingram.[8] A visit to the gaol in 1853 by Mr Perry, an inspector of Prisons, drew attention to a complaint received from the prisoner, John Williams, who had complained that the Rules and Regulations were not displayed. It was confirmed by the gaoler that Williams himself had taken down the notices and, although only recently committed for vagrancy, Williams had previously been transported from Montgomeryshire to Bermuda and Gibraltar in 1844 for stealing gearing and was a generally bad character. Further, in his report, Mr Perry questioned the role of the surgeon, with particular reference to the case of Thomas Lewis. He had been sent to London on 28 April 1848, awaiting transportation. He was eventually returned to the county gaol suffering from venereal disease, a complaint which which should have been noticed before leaving the gaol and had not been recorded in the journal of the surgeon, although he had been treated for catarrh and dyspepsia. Another case concerned Eliza Thomas, who was in the gaol over a period of time waiting transportation, but her complaint of venereal disease was also not noted, she only being treated for spasms. Mr J. P. Wilding, surgeon, in his submission stated:

> Not feeling justified in exposing the persons of prisoners, especially females for the purpose of examining for venereal disease, and that the report being to direct such an examination, I declined following it out and thought no more about it.

The visiting justices were of the opinion that sufficient care was not taken by the surgeon in the examination of prisoners on their admission to gaol and requested that the surgeon exercise a stricter scrutiny in future.[9]

As soon as convenient after receiving sentences of transportation or penal servitude, arrangements were made for the removal of prisoners from the county gaol to London or Portsmouth where they were admitted either to the hulk ships at Woolwich or the penitentiaries at Millbank or Pentonville. On 26 June 1788, Lord Sydney, Secretary of State, wrote the following letter to the High Sheriff of Montgomeryshire:

> His Majesty, having been pleased to give direction that Edward Evans, David Morris and John Griffiths, together with all the other male convicts under sentence of transportation in the gaol of Montgomery, except E. Jenks, should be removed from thence on board the hulks at Portsmouth and committed to the charge of Duncan Campbell Esq overseer of the convicts on board those hulks. I am commanded to signify to you the king's pleasure that you do forth with cause the said convicts, if upon being examined by an experienced surgeon, they shall be found free from any putrid

or infectious distemper, to be removed on board the said hulks where they are to remain until their sentences can be carried into execution or be otherwise disposed of according to law. You will send with the prisoners an account of their ages and respective sentences.[10]

It is possible that Evan Jenks was allowed to stay at the county gaol due to his age being 55 years and, after a three year period, he was granted a Royal Pardon 23 June 1791. As a result of this directive, the three men and another from Montgomeryshire, namely Lewis Proctor, held the distinction of being the first men to be sentenced to transportation in Montgomeryshire and to be sent to Australia. They did not form members of the convict complement who embarked on the 'First Fleet', but faced the degradation, untold misery, illness and death of those who had the misfortune to embark with the infamous 'Second Fleet', when they eventually left England on the 'Surprise' convict ship 19 January 1790. For eighteen months they had languished in a hulk ship and, in an anonymous publication, the following harrowing description creates a vivid description:

. . . a black melancholy looking vessel, lying alongside the dockyard at Woolwich. The ship has three decks, divided into wards, galleries, workshops, storerooms, rooms for the sick and a chapel, and has no less than six hundred men on board. These are separated into classes according to their scale of good or bad behaviour and at the expiration of the day's labour, they are only permitted to associate with convicts belonging to the same class as themselves . . . No convict is allowed to be without an iron upon one or both his legs.[11]

Between 1815 and 1850, at the very least, the following thirteen men from Montgomeryshire suffered illnesses which resulted in death whilst serving out their sentence on board a hulk ship.

Name	Hulk Ship	Date of Death
Thomas Gumm	Justitia	19 February 1815
John Rowlands	Justitia	25 January 1818
David Austin	Justitia	9 October 1818
Hugh L. Dawson	Justitia	14 December 1819
John Pryce	Justitia	27 October 1820
John Humphreys	Gannymede	25 December 1838
John Kinsey	Warrior	25 August 1850

In addition to the hulks located in England, similar arrangements were made in Bermuda and Gibraltar, to which locations some of the Montgomeryshire convicts were sent. John Beavan, as a result of breaking and entering property, arrived in Gibraltar 7 January 1845 and, six years later, obtained his discharge 8 February 1851. John Roberts, following a ten year conviction in 1849 for robbery with violence, went to Gibraltar where he died 10 September 1852. John Evans, having stolen property at Buttington in 1827, found himself in Bermuda where he died 30 March 1834. John Jones, fared better; following committal in 1845, he served out his sentence in Bermuda and, upon being discharged, emigrated to Nova Scotia. Likewise, Maurice Jones, following a seven year sentence in 1846, arrived in Bermuda and eventually also emigrated to Philadelphia 13 March 1850. Following representation to parliament concerning the brutal manner in which convicts were treated on the hulks, an *"Inquiry into the State of the Hulks"*, was carried out in 1847. Amongst the vast amount of evidence placed before the Committee, the following statistical evidence includes details concerning six Montgomeryshire men:

Date arrived in hulks	Name	Age	Offence	Health State
'JUSTITIA' HULK				
23 December 1844	Evan Owen	61	Stealing 3 geese	Asthmatic
26 January 1846	John Hankinson	21	Stealing clothes	Defective sight
'WARRIOR' HULK				
12 May 1842	John Jones	21	Stealing fowls	Good
3 April 1843	John Williams	21	Burglary	Broken Leg
3 April 1843	Edward Williams	22	Housebreaking	Good
22 February 1847	Samuel Wilkinson	18	Stealing fowls	Diseased Heart

Evan Owen of Llanwnnog had been committed 17 October 1844; John Hankinson of Oswestry on 20 October 1842; John Jones of Newtown on 7 April 1842; John Williams of Newtown on 7 March 1843; Edward Williams of Llanystymdwy, Caernarfonshire on 7 March 1843 and Samuel Wilkinson of Welshpool on 2 January 1845. It is evident that John Jones had spent upwards of five years in the hulks and it is probable that they all served out their sentences in these dreadful conditions, as none of them left before completing their sentences.[12] Although the removal of convicts from county gaols was to be carried out as swiftly as possible, there is evidence that this was not always the case. In a letter from Whitehall, dated 27 March 1837, to the High Sheriff concerning the removal of Rowland Evans and Richard Bliss to the 'Justitia' hulk, their arrival at Woolwich did not take place until 18 May 1837, when the hulk overseer signed a receipt confirming their arrival.[13]

The urgency about removal to the hulks was apparent when the Chartists Abraham Owen, Lewis Humphreys, James Morris and John Ingram were moved during the first week of August 1839, from Montgomery to Shrewsbury gaol, where they remained overnight and the following day continued their journey by the stage-coach to Wolverhampton. This was followed by a rail journey to London and their final destination where they arrived 8 August 1839.[14]

Between 1845 and 1848, the gaoler at the county gaol received in excess of £80 for payment in conveying and escorting the following convicts to Millbank and Pentonville penitentiaries, to await transportation:[15]

John Davies	Hugh Humphreys	John Peters
William Storey	Charles Case	Edward Simmons
John Brown	Michael Kelly	John Stokes
Henry Fisher	Samuel Wilkinson	William Evans
Eliza Thomas	William Bradley	John Kinsey
Evan Turner	Thomas Lewis	Richard Owen
John Hancox	Edward Hancox	James Harvey
William Thompson		

As indicated from the above list, convicts were removed from the county gaol to London penitentiaries where they remained until sufficient numbers were available to fill a convict ship complement. At Millbank a "mixed system" was evident but at Pentonville a "separate system" was favoured. Employment consisted of kitchen cleaning and baking duties while the greater proportion found themselves occupied in making clothes for soldiers, biscuit bags, hammocks, shirts, handkerchiefs, cloth coats and trousers. Female convicts were occupied by picking coir, washing, ironing and needlework.[16]

As is the case in present times, when convicts considered that they had sufficient grounds for an appeal and petitions, these were placed before the authorities on their behalf. Royal Pardons were issued and signed at His Majesty's Command by the Secretary of State and addressed to the Justices of Assizes for the Chester Circuit and the High Sheriff of the county of Montgomery. An example of a Royal Pardon would be as follows:

> *Whereas Hugh Jones and John Evans were, at several Great Sessions held for our county of Montgomery; viz Hugh Jones at the Summer Great Sessions in 1784 and John Evans at the Summer Great Sessions in 1785, and severally received sentence of death for the same, and whereas some favourable circumstances have been humbly represented unto us on their behalf inclining us to extend our Grace and Mercy unto them and to grant them our Pardon for their crimes on condition of their being severally transported beyond the seas for and during the term of seven years. Our will and pleasure, therefore, is that you give the necessary directions for the transportation of them, the said Hugh Jones and John Evans beyond the seas for and during the term of seven years respectively, and that they be inserted for their crimes on the said condition in our first and next General Pardon that shall come out for the Chester Circuit and for so doing this shall be your warrant. Given at our court at St James', the thirty-first day of March 1786, in the 26th year of our reign.*[17]

During the Napoleonic War, it was possible for convicts to avoid the fear of transportation. The need of the country for men to join the army, navy or marines was vital in order to ensure victory. Daniel Lowe and Richard Wainwright, both having been sentenced to seven years transportation for committing felonies, were, at their hearing in 1807, granted permission to join the Plymouth Division of Marines. Following examination by a surgeon and found fit and able, they were handed over to the military. What alternative future faced them is unknown.[18]

Following conviction 25 March 1824, for stealing money, David Jones was removed to the 'Gannymede' hulk at Woolwich. Still imprisoned there in 1827, his name appears upon a Return of 15 male convicts who had served more than half their term of sentence, and, who, on account of their orderly and uniformly good conduct, were selected by the overseer with the support of the chaplain, as being the best behaved men on board the hulk. David Jones was recommended as deserving the Royal Mercy and the following application was made on his behalf:

Name:	David Jones	Age: 34
Crime:	Stealing money	Convicted: Montgomery
Date:	25 March 1824	Sentence: 7 years
Time served:	3yrs 9mths 6 days	
Character:	former character good, very useful as leading hand on board 'Gannymede'.	

As a result of this petition, David Jones obtained a Free Pardon 16 January 1828.[19]

On one occasion an interesting Petition was placed by a group of people. This was on behalf of Richard Morris who, in 1828, was sentenced to seven years transportation and by 1832 had spent half his sentence on board the 'Gannymede' hulk at Woolwich. It would seem that he left many friends behind in Newtown, who in 1832 felt justified in placing a petition to Lord Melbourne, Secretary of State. The petition, shown below, clearly indicated that Richard Morris was held in high esteem by his friends and neighbours:

The Humble Petition of us the undersigned being Gentlemen, Tradesmen and others of the Inhabitants of Newtown, Montgomeryshire, North Wales, humbly sheweth that your Petitioners are well acquainted with Richard Morris, the object of this Petition, and in whose behalf we humbly pray that this may obtain a compassionate hearing. The said Richard Morris resided in this town, by trade a staymaker; has a wife and six children, whom he maintained by his honest and industrious industry, was always considered of good repute as an honest and industrious man until the Spring Sessions March 1828, he was tried and convicted at Welshpool for a confederacy in offering on sale a stolen piece of flannel and sentenced to seven years transportation and has been confined ever since on board the 'Gannymede' hulk at Woolwich. That we your Petitioners from our thorough knowledge of the said unfortunate convict for upwards of 20 years, and been acquainted with the occurrence which he was convicted, are convinced that he was innocent of the said crime, and that he had no tendency of a habitual inclination to violate the laws of his country of which opinion, Mr Andrew Jones his prosecutor, finally unites, and joins us in praying that in consideration of his former good character and the contrition and penitence he has manifested near 4½ years confinement, that your Lordship will be pleased to consider in as much as to get him restored to his afflicted wife and family, at His Imperial Majesty's pleasure, and we the undersigned will have the pleasure to employ him to enable him to support his wife and family as heretofore, and as in duty bound your Petitioners will ever pray. Signed:

Andrew Jones prosecutor, John Jones manufacturer, David Owen overseer, William Bevin manufacturer, Rich Gittins churchwarden, Samuel Evans manufacturer, John Jones manufacturer, John Matthews manufacturer, Thomas Syars manufacturer, Edward Jones manufacturer, Richard Williams overseer, Lewis Williams grocer, Thomas Williams manufacturer, C. Gittins manufacturer.

This Appeal must have received favourable consideration. Richard Morris was granted a Pardon 29 November 1832.[20]

In 1831, David Owen of Trefeglwys and Edward Rees of Llangurig, had been tried and found guilty of maiming a mare and gelding, the property of David Edwards of Fronvellan, Montgomeryshire. David Owen received a seven year sentence while Edward Rees was given a life sentence. One Petition stated that David Owen was twenty one years of age, a flannel weaver by trade, had a wife and one young child, who were now destitute of support. He was of an impeccable character, having worked for the same master for 12 years. This was signed by the mark of David Owen and supported by James Morgan, David James, John Pugh, Samuel Breeze, David Pugh, William Tilsley, Jonathan Tilsley, Matthew Davies, David Davies, Edward G. Lloyd, Richard Thomas, John Lloyd, David Jarman, Edward Edwards, Richard Davies, David Hamer, William Savage and Evan Evans. The petition for Edward Rees confirmed that he was thirty-six years of age, had a wife and five small children under 10 years of age, was the principal support of his young family, and that this was his first offence, signed by the mark of Edward Rees, and supported by Lewis Miles, Daniel Davies, John Davies, Richard Brown, Edward Rees and Thomas Richards. Both Petitions proved of no avail. David Owen was transported to New South Wales and Edward Rees found himself in Van Diemen's Land.[21]

A degree of clemency was to be found in the case of a minority of offenders. During their stay in the county gaol at Montgomery, William Jones and Hannah Maria Evans, serving a 14 and 7 year transportation sentence respectively, were considered by Richard Baxter, surgeon to the county gaol in 1837, in view of their respective medical condition, to be unsuitable for transportation, as indicated in the following Report presented to the Justices 14 July 1837:

> *I have had William Jones aged 55 years, a convict in the gaol under sentence of transportation for 14 years, under my care and beg to represent that he is afflicted with rheumatism and is otherwise so debilitated in constitution that he is not in a fit state to be removed, and from his state and age, I am of the opinion that the chance is that he will never be in a fit state of health to be transported.*
>
> *I have also had Hannah Maria Evans aged 17 years, another convict in the gaol under sentence of transportation for 7 years, under my care, and have to represent that she is labouring under a pulmonary complaint which renders her unfit to be removed at this time, and I am of the opinion, and the probability is, that she will never recover and that confinement will of course tend to hasten her dissolution.*

Upon receipt of this Report, the visiting magistrates, Charles Thomas Jones and Devereaux Mytton, stated that:

> *William Jones had been convicted twice, yet his offences were of a minor description and considering his advanced age, and that he had a wife and several young children, and that he is rather respectably connected, and as he is an infirm man, we think him a fit person to receive the Royal Mercy Hannah Maria Evans has also been convicted before, but as her offences were stealing some trifling articles of wearing apparel, and as she has been . . . good services and has some respectable connections, and considering her youth and believing that she is not of depraved habits, and as her health is in a precarious state, we consider also that she is a fit person to receive the Royal Mercy.*

Accompanying this Petition, was the following letter from Lord Robert Clive, dated 20 July 1837, addressed to Lord John Russell, Home Secretary:

> *I have the honour to endorse to your Lordship, a statement placed in my hands yesterday respecting two prisoners now under sentence of transportation in Montgomery gaol. I had an opportunity of conversing with both the visiting magistrates at the Assizes and they are both satisfied that under the circumstances, the prisoners are fit objects for Her Majesty's gracious and humane consideration. I have the honour to request your Lordship will be pleased to take a favourable opportunity of submitting the case of these prisoners to Her Majesty, upon such occasion, as may seem most suitable to your Lordship.*

Both William Jones and Hannah Maria Evans had their sentence reduced to one year's imprisonment which probably was served out in the county gaol.[22] In 1838, two surgeons, namely Richard Baxter and E. T. Johnes, brought influence to bear upon the future of Thomas Owen who had received a 15 year sentence to transportation for sheep stealing. When the time arrived for his removal from the county gaol, both doctors ascertained that Thomas Owen complained that he had consumption and, upon visiting and examining him on 31 December 1837, Dr Johnes stated:

> *I have this day visited the prisoner Thomas Owen and do not find his state of health worse than should naturally expect that of a person to be who had been accustomed*

to an active life in the open air; and which has been changed to the confinement of a prison, and the depression of mind necessarily following such a sentence the prisoner is labouring under. Mr Lloyd the gaoler; informs me that he has repeatedly seen him discharging blood by coughing and vomiting. Complaints of this description usually ends in consumption and I cannot under such circumstances sanction the removal of the prisoner according to this sentence.

Richard Baxter confirmed that he perfectly agreed with the above observations and as a result the case was placed before Lord John Russell, Secretary of State.[23] Thomas Owen did not reach Australia and it can be assumed that he was eventually pardoned and released from gaol.

It is interesting to ascertain the various methods available to the convicts in order that they might be allowed to obtain remission from serving their full sentence. The following table highlights, in a few instances, the reasons why remission was achieved:

CONVICTS WHO RECEIVED REMISSION OF SENTENCE

Location	Type of Remission	Male	Female	Total
HULKS IN ENGLAND				
	By Death	13		13
	Pardon/Discharge	47		47
	Escaped	1		1
GIBRALTAR				
	By Death	1		1
	Pardon/Discharge	5		5
BERMUDA				
	By Death	1		1
	Pardon/Discharge	10		10
PENITENTIARIES IN ENGLAND	By Death	1		1
	Murdered	1		1
	Pardon/Discharge	19	4	23
	Escaped	2		2
JOINED ARMY OR NAVY	Napoleonic War	7		7
CONVICT SHIP	Prior to Embarkation	1		1
NOT KNOWN		14	4	18
TOTAL		**123**	**8**	**131**

Following time spent in either the county gaol, penitentiary or hulk ship, with the probability that a pardon was unobtainable, it is possible that many of these poor wretches welcomed the news that finally they were being removed to a transport ship and be faced with a long and unknown sea voyage that could be both dangerous to life and limb, and, for some even ending in death, followed by burial at sea.

For others, illness caught whilst on board proved to be fatal upon dis-embarkation soon after reaching their final destination, but, for the majority, it was now the beginning of a new venture thousands of miles away from their homeland.

CHAPTER FIVE

Sea Voyage

Two hundred and eight convicts from Montgomeryshire found themselves transported on convict ships destined for Australia between 1788 and 1868. The first four Montgomeryshire convicts (Edward Evans, John Griffiths, David Morris and Lewis Proctor), were sent on the 'Surprise' as part of the Second Fleet in 1790. The last ship to arrive with convicts was the 'Hougoumont', which left England on 12 October 1867. Amongst her convict complement of 280 men was James Robinson who had been sentenced in Montgomeryshire to 10 years penal servitude for stealing a watch and chain. The following table summarizes the destinations and number of voyages on which the convicts from Montgomeryshire were transported.

	Ships	Convicts
New South Wales	43	74
Van Diemen's Land	55	89
Port Phillip	4	6
Norfolk Island	2	2
Western Australia	16	37
Total	**120**	**208**

The 'First Fleet' convicts were maintained in a healthy condition throughout the voyage as they were for the majority of subsequent voyages. However of all the voyages that took place during the transportation era, that of the Second Fleet must be the most infamous. Three ships ('Neptune', 'Scarborough' and 'Surprise') left England on 19 January 1790, and arrived in New South Wales 26/28 June 1790 with a complement of 939 male and 78 female convicts (1,017 embarked of whom 11 died before leaving England); on board were the first four Montgomeryshire convicts. The master of the 'Surprise' was Nicholas Anstis. The naval agent for the voyage was Lieutenant John Shapcote, who, in his letter dated 24 April 1790 to the Commissioners of the Navy, confirmed that the fleet had arrived in False Bay, Cape of Good Hope on 13 April 1790, and that:

> . . . the soldiers and convicts, to a very large number, are exceeding ill with the scurvy, and as our stay here will be short, I have, in consequence of representation from the surgeon's mate of the troops and the different surgeons of the ships, ordered the masters to issue to them fresh meat every day, with a sufficient quantity of vegetables . . . The surgeon's (William Waters), opinion I herewith transmit, likewise the number of convicts that have died (in the 'Neptune', forty-five males, one female since our leaving England.' In the 'Surprise', eight males and in the 'Scarborough' fifteen males) . . .

The voyage continued 29 April 1790 and Lieutenant Shapcote himself died on board the 'Neptune' on the voyage from the Cape to New South Wales.[1]

On 13 July 1790, Governor Phillip wrote to the Rt. Hon. W. W. Grenville, including the following comments:

> . . . I will not Sir; dwell on the scene of misery which the hospitals and sick tents exhibited when those people were landed, but it would be a want of duty not to say that it was occasioned by the contractors having crowded too many on board those ships, and from their being too much confined during the passage. The convicts having the liberty of the deck depended on the agent and on the masters of the ships; the agent died on the passage and the masters say it was granted as far as was consistent with their own safety and that many of the convicts were sick when sent from the hulks . . . while the masters of the transports think their own safety depends on admitting few convicts on deck at a time, and most of them with irons on, which prevent any kind of exercise, numbers must always perish on so long a journey, and many of those now received are in such a situation from old complaints, and so emaciated from what they have suffered on the voyage, that they will never be capable of any labour.[2]

Captain Hill, 2nd Captain of the New South Wales Corps, who was on the 'Surprise' with a detachment, wrote on 26 July 1790 to Samuel Wathen of Woodstock, England, with further evidence concerning this voyage:

> The bark ('Surprise') I was on board of was indeed unfit from her make and size to be sent so great a distance; if it blew but the most trifling gale she was lost in the waters of which she shipped so much; that from the Cape, the unhappy wretches the convicts, were considerably above their waists in water . . . In this situation they were obliged for the safety of the ship, to be penned down; but when the gale's abatted no means were used to purify the air by fumigation, no vinegar was applied to rectify the nauseous streams issuing from their miserable dungeon. Humanity shudders to think that of nine hundred male convicts embarked in this fleet, three hundred and seventy are already dead and four hundred and fifty are landed sick and so emaciated and helpless that very few, if any of them, can be saved by care or medicine . . . The irons used upon these unhappy wretches were barbarous. The contractors had been in the Guinea trade, and had put on board the same shackles used by them in that trade, which were made with a short bolt, instead of chains that drop between the legs and fasten with a bandage about the waist, like those at the different gaols; these bolts were not more than three-quarters of a foot in length, so that they could not extend either leg from the other more than an inch or two at most; thus fettered, it was impossible for them to move but at the risk of both their legs being broken. Inactivity at sea is a sure bane, as it invites the scurvy equal to, if not more than, salt provisions . . . even when attacked by disease their situation was not altered, neither had they any comfort administered.[3]

In an undated letter (about July 1790), the Rev. Richard Johnson wrote to a Mr Thornton, in which he gives a graphic account of the landing of the Second Fleet:

> I was first on board the 'Surprise'. Went down amongst the convicts, where I beheld a sight truly shocking to the feelings of humanity, a great number of them laying, some half and others nearly quite naked, without either bed or bedding, unable to turn or help themselves. Spoke to them as I passed along, but the smell was so offensive that I could scarcely bear it . . . Some of these unhappy people died after the ships came into harbour; before they could be taken ashore – part of these had been thrown into the harbour, and their dead bodies cast upon the shore, and were seen laying upon

the rocks . . . The landing of these people was truly affecting and shocking; great numbers were not able to walk, nor move hand or foot; such were slung over the ship side in the manner as they would sung a cask . . . Upon their being brought up to the open air some fainted, some died upon deck, and other in the boat before they reached the shore. When come on shore many were not able to walk, to stand, or to stir themselves in the least, hence some were led by others. Some creeped upon their hands and knees, and some were carried upon the backs of others . . . Besides the sick that were in the hospital previous to the arrival of the fleet, there was now landed not less than four hundred and eighty-six sick . . . At first they had nothing to lay upon but the damp ground, many scarcely a . . . to cover them. Grass was got for them to lay upon, and a blanket given amongst four of them . . . The misery I saw amongst them is unexpressible; many were not able to turn, or even to stir themselves, and in this situation were covered over almost with their own nastiness, their heads, bodies, cloths, blanket, all full of filth and lice. Scurvy was not the only nor the worst disease that prevailed . . . some were exercised with violent fevers, and others with a no less violent purging and flux . . . Sometimes for days . . . they have been to the middle in water chained together, hand and leg, even the sick not exempted, nay many died with the chains upon them . . . When any of them were near dying, and had something given them as bread . . . the person next to him or others would catch the bread etc, out of his hand, and, with an oath, say that he was going to die, and therefore it would be of no service to him. No sooner would the breath be out of any of their bodies then others would watch them and strip them entirely naked . . . have buried not less than eighty-six since they landed – eighty-four convicts, one child and one soldier.[4]

Despite the trauma of the voyage Edward Evans, John Griffiths and David Morris survived this horrific experience and were landed from the 'Surprise', but they did not live long after their arrival, probably as a result of harsh treatment during the sea voyage. Lewis Proctor does not occur in the official records of those who survived and probably perished at sea.

Illnesses amongst the convicts during the voyage was treated by the surgeon superintendent on board. During the voyage of the 'Lord Wellington' in 1818, Mary Blakemore and Maria Jones, convicts from Montgomeryshire and four others, were treated by the surgeon Ed F. Bromley who stated that these women:

. . . were dreadfully scalded by the coppers upsetting in a sudden squall . . . Ag Calcis was applied to the scalded parts . . . their bowels were kept open with saline purgative, and when much inflammatory action took place, they were bled and kept on low diet. Several of them got well in the course of a month (and discharged in July), but Maria Jones, who was by far the worst, was not cured for three months.[5]

Although disturbances en route were minimal, it was necessary on some voyages for the authorities to take immediate action, due to the lack of adequate supervision. One such instance took place when the convict ship 'John' sailed from The Downs, off the south coast of England, on 7 February 1832 bound for New South Wales, where she arrived at Port Jackson the following 8 June. Amongst her complement of 200 male convicts was Edward Rees of Llangurig. There is no evidence to establish that he played any part in the following incident. Correspondence dated 11 March 1832 whilst at sea, between Samuel John Lowe, master of the 'John', James Lawrence surgeon superintendent, R. Campbell and Geo Baldwin, officers 31st Regiment, and John Kinchela, Attorney General's office, give a vivid account of the disturbance aboard the vessel:

the surgeon superintendent having been informed by some of the convicts that a considerable number of their fellow prisoners, were plotting to get possession of the ship, communicated the same to the officers of the guard and captain of the ship, in order to secure the cordial co-operation of these officers, that by their united exertions the most efficient means possible might be taken to prevent the plotters carrying their plans into execution.

The officers of the guard, captain of the ship and surgeon superintendent have therefore made minute enquiry into the circumstances of the case; and are of the opinion from what has been stated by the informers, that the convicts named by them are plotting to obtain possession of the ship; and murder those placed in authority over them; which opinion is corroborated by the circumstances of knives having been found on searching the beds, berths and bags of those accused of being concerned in the plot; not with standing the most positive orders that no prisoner should keep a knife in his possession and for which they were all diligently searched when they embarked. And to avoid bloodshed and prevent the convicts carrying their diabolical intentions into execution, the officers of the guard, the captain of the ship and the surgeon superintendent have agreed, that the most efficient means will be to [shackle] and yoke together by two's, those accused 8 of being concerned in the plot and to separate the ringleaders, who are of particularly bad and vicious . . . from the rest of the convicts.

In further letters dated 8 and 24 June 1832 to the Governor of New South Wales, James Lawrence put forward additional information relevant to the revolt:

I beg leave to acquaint your Excellency that a number of the convicts who are under my superintendence, have been plotting during the passage from England to New South Wales, to obtain possession of the ship, and murder those placed in authority over them; which educed me, in conjunction with the officers of the guard and master of the ship, as a measure of precaution, to put two bezzles connected with a chain on the legs of each suspected convict; one bezzle on each leg and then yoke them together in pairs; as your Excellency will see by the document herewith enclosed; and I beg leave further to acquaint your Excellency that on the night of the 26 March, an attempt was made to kindle a fire in the prison for the purpose it is supposed of setting fire to the ship, which several of the convicts had threatened to do; and that in consequence I next day punished John Clifton, who from some expression which he had used, I suspected of being concerned in kindling the fire, by ordering him to walk the deck with a bed on his back for two hours, which exhausted him a good deal and while in that state he drank unknown to me, about two quarts of cold water, which caused his death. I therefore earnestly beg, should your Excellency deem it fit, that previous to the debarkation of the guard, and while every one is on board who has witnessed my treatment of the convicts, your Excellency will be pleased to order an Inquiry to be made into the particulars herein stated; when I trust your Excellency will find that the comfort of the prisoners under my superintendence has been my principal study and forbearance and humanity towards them, as far as the safety of the ship would allow, the uniform tenor of my conduct.

John Kinchela wrote on 20 June 1832 to the Hon. Alexander McLeay, Colonial Secretary:

I have the honour to acknowledge the receipt of your letter of the 10th instant, trans-mitting to me a letter from the Surgeon Superintendent of the male convict ship 'John', reporting that in consequence of the attempt of some of the prisoners to set fire to the ship on the passage, he punished John Clifton, a party suspected, by placing him in double irons and making him walk the deck for two hours with a bed upon his back; and requesting that as Dr Lawrence states, the prisoner alluded to, died in consequence of drinking two quarts of cold water while under exhaustion from the punishment above mentioned; and his request that an Inquiry may be instituted into his conduct on the occasion, that I would favour you with my opinions to what is proper to be done in this case. In reply I have the honour to state for your information, that as no Inquest was held on the body at the time of the death of the above named convict, the only mode in which an investigation can take place is by lodging information on oath before the Magistrates of the police office, stating the death of the convict, and the Magistrates may then examine such witnesses as they met think necessary respecting the cause of his death, and act as circumstances may require in case they shall, upon such examination, be of the opinion that this man's death was caused by any improper or unfair means. Following an Inquiry, it was the opinion of the court that the conduct of Dr Lawrence towards all the prisoners under his supervision, was one of great kindness and humanity. It was found that the punishment afforded to John Clifton "was very light that no blame can attach to any person on account of the sudden death of the prisoner".[6]

Edward Evans, John Farren, Henry Beastall, Jonathan Roose and David Owen, sailed on the 'Katherine Stewart Forbes' which left London on 26 February 1832. The master of the ship was John Anderson and surgeon John Stephenson. On board were 222 male convicts but during the voyage 13 died and 209 eventually disembarked at Hobart. The surgeon's instructions included the necessity that a medical and surgical journal be maintained between 26 January and 24 July 1832, the time that the ship had been employed in conveying convicts to Van Diemen's Land, and the following extracts include reference to the death of Edward Evans:

January 26th	–	*joined the ship at Deptford.*
February 8th	–	*moved down to Woolwich.*
10th	–	*received 80 convicts from 'Justitia'.*
11th	–	*received 70 convicts from 'Justitia'.*
11th	–	*received 32 convicts from dockyard.*
13th	–	*received 40 convicts from Chatham.*

On March 3rd, three malignant cases were brought in including Edward Evans age 25 who was taken ill March 3rd about noon; had diarrhoea two days previous; excessive prostration of strength; constant vomiting and purging; racking spasm of abdomen and extremities; darning sweat; no pulsation; burning thirst and desire for cold water; face dirty white; tongue red; voice very low; fingers contracted and nails blue; external applications; hot bath; . . . with mustard in the bath; constant . . . with anodyne and stimulating liniments and hot water to the face etc., etc.

At 2 p.m. the same day, it was noted that there was:

Not a shade of alteration for the better; his head appears affected by the brandy; blisters applied to the legs and . . . to the feet; Acct: Morph: . . . form; Plym: stimulants except brandy as before.

By 8 p.m. it was noticeable that:

Pulse perceptible in brachial artery; skin dry; not so cold;.tongue red; vomiting and purging not quite so frequent; alvine discharge frothy mucous and thin white fluid like starch; extremities cold as before; no spasms; rather comatose; feels the blisters, but not the . . .; breathing more free; is anxious for more rum; urine totally suppressed; external stimulants as usual; rum(no brandy on board) in a very small quantity every hour to maintain the present excitement.

By midnight further examination noted that he was:

anxious and very uneasy; burning thirst; likes the spirits; a considerable degree of excitement kept up until this hour; complains of blisters; stools not so frequent; water with white flakes floating in it; no urine.

By 8 a.m. the following morning (4th), it was recorded that:

sinking in spite of everything; extremities dead; fingers blue; eyes sunk, watery and pale pink; tongue red and parched, lips purple; face dirty blue white and dark blue under the eyes; not much vomiting; stools as before; no urine; no pulsation; the strongest stimulants of every description.

At 9 a.m. Edward Evans was:

exactly as at 8 a.m.; no stimulants can affect him; breathing free and slow; apparently suffers no pain; talks incoherently; lies on his back; eyes and mouth half open; voice stronger than when taken ill; treatment as before without . . .

At noon he was:

insensible; stools involuntary; still swallows.

By 3 p.m. on 4 March 1832, Edward Evans died from cholera.

Of the thirteen deaths that occurred on the voyage, at least seven deaths resulted from a Cholera Morbus epidemic, which accounted for 24 cases before 31 March, by which date 16 cases had been discharged and one remained in hospital. The surgeon John Stephens, was intent to ensure that his methods of dealing with cholera should be made available to surgeons for use on future voyages and his account of how he dealt with Edward Evans and others is recorded:

having thus pointed out the very unfavourable circumstances under which I will obliged to cope with this frightful malady, I shall now endeavour to describe it in it's general appearance and progress. The disease usually attacks those who had been labouring under either constipation or diarrhoea, but in two instances it appeared in men, who a few hours before, were in perfect health. It almost invariably commenced with severe pain across the belly, desire to go to stool, sickness of stomach, giddiness of head, feebleness of the limbs, cramp of the abdominal muscles succeeded and shortly after, the hands first and legs were in a strong state of spasm. The muscles of the legs and thighs were drawn into round balls or knots and excruciating painful. The face was deadly pale, eyes sunk and glassy, skin cold as ice, fingers bent and shrivelled, no pulsation at the wrist and very barely in the brachial artery. The vomiting was very distressing, gourging incessant,burning thirst tormented the patient and he was incessantly praying for cold water. In some cases the voice sunk to a whisper and the exhaustion was so great the patient hardly seemed to live. The breathing was generally free but in one or two it was oppressed and slow from the beginning. Some had little or no spasms and in all eased for a time in the bath or very shortly after the patient was taken out. It sometimes happened that six or eight hours from the first attack the skin on the body would become warm and pulsation distinct in the brachial artery, but no stimulants could force the circulation to the extremities. The patient would also appear more alive and describe his feelings, this however did not last long, the same icy coldness returned, the stomach became, if possible, more irritable and every thing swallowed was immediately squirted up again. Spasm returned at irregular intervals and the face and neck were covered with clammy sweat. After about 18 to 20 hours the patient usually became insensible, moaned much and was restless. The eyes were watery and . . . a pale pink colour . . . The cadaverous appearance of the face increased and it usually assumed the colour of new sheet lead, especially under the eyes. After this there was no longer a chance for the patient. The vomiting ceased but the stools were passed in-voluntarily. He lay upon his back with his mouth open, cough saliva exuding from the angles, his eyes were fixed and breathing laboured, his cough and restlessness at this stage only occurred in an instance. All the others for the last four hours appeared as if asleep with eyes open. Death usually took place in 24 or 25 hours, one patient died in thirteen, and others lived about 50 hours after the first attack. In those who survived the state of collapse reaction began to take place at various periods between 24 and 72 hours, generally about the former time or an hour or two sooner. The skin began to get warm on the body and the pulse might be felt in the brachial artery. Very slowly and gradually the heat extended to the extremities, pulsation was discernible at the wrist, which as it increased in strength, was invariably inter swelling. Sometimes from this state, the patient would suddenly recede and exhaustion great as at first come on. In the cases which terminated favourably the following were the usual symptoms. Vomiting and purging not so frequent, discharge unaltered, patient very restless and uneasy eyes dull, watery and reddish, face highly flushed, skin warm and dry, pulse small and hard, not quick pain in abdomen but nothing like spasms. The thirst and desire for cold drink continued. There were followed by headache, stupor and delirium, with a dark brown or black tongue and quick pulse. As none died after reaching this point, I cannot describe the fatal appearances, the favourable were a gradual abatement of all the foregoing. The tongue began to clear, skin to get moist and vomiting to cease. Gripping pain in the bowels was followed by a full and frequent discharge of green or blue slime. The stupor and delirium abated rapidly, the thirst diminished and an extraordinary flow of urine took place. The treatment was the most energetic I could possibly pursue. As soon as the patient was brought into the hospital a hot bath was ordered and in the meantime an emetic was administered, either of mustard or ?? pielv ipraec and tartr antimon. Strong friction was used on all the parts in a state of spasm with a liniment composed of equal parts of leg ammonia . . . or solid opium combined with lard. In the bath, which was always made so hot as to be disagreeable to the feelings of the patient, he was rubbed with leg: ammo and mustard. On coming out of the bath he was put into bed between blankets . . . The friction was continued incessantly, artificial heat was applied to the feet and . . . to the legs, hot punch was pressed upon him but was generally disliked and invariably rejected by the stomach. As the cry for cold water was so constant and pitifully, I returned at first sometimes to indulge the patient, but the draught tho'greedily drank, was never retained for an instant . . . When the spasm returned with severity, the hot bath and friction as at first were repeated. The acc:morph prepared according to the formula of Plymouth hospital, I administered in free doses, but it was so certainly and instantaneously rejected, I soon abandoned it altogether . . ., but nothing so often remained in the stomach as calomel, especially when washed down with a small quantity of raw spirits. Bleeding I attempted. From one patient I obtained somewhat more than an ounce of black viscid matter, and from another rather less, although the orifice in each case was large. In fact, I do not believe blood can be obtained from a patient labouring under malignant cholera. In one peculiar case (J. McNamara), where the symptoms were those of enteritis accompanied by severe spasms and frequent purging of such matter as is discharged in cholera, and where the pulse at the wrist was distinct, I bled freely and successfully. Blisters I used largely and as external stimulants they proved superior to anything else. Internally I used every thing I could procure which I thought likely to the patient or allay the irritability of stomach, but I might just as well have given nothing except perhaps calomel, which was certainly more frequently retained than anything else and which (provided the power of absorption was not lost), was sure sooner or later to produce an alteration in the alvine discharge. In the consecutive fever, I thought the less I did the better, my only object was therefore to keep the patient as quiet as possible. When the stupor or delirium ran high, I shaved the head and kept it constantly wet with spirits. If the pulse became feeble, the tongue black and there was delirious muttering, I gave . . . and applied blisters, but under ordinary circumstances I did nothing save administer calomel in 4 or 5 grain doses every four hours for the purpose of keeping up the discharge from the bowels. On looking back, I perceive I have neglected to say anything of the alvine discharge. At the commencement it was invariably either a fluid resembling very thin starch or clear water with white . . . matter floating in it. In only one instance did the patient complain of tenesmus. At the termination of the disease (in the fatal cases), it was little else than water of a dark brown colour, but in those which ended favourably, large quantities of dark green or blue slime was discharged . . . nor has anyone of the hospital attendants, or persons more immediately employed about the patients when the disease was most rife, suffered in the slightest degree at anytime, except from fatigue or sea sickness.[6]

Between 26 June and 12 October 1836, the 'Elizabeth IV' was at sea conveying 161 female convicts to New South Wales. The surgeon, Robert Espie, was called on 16 July to examine Ann Bennett, a 22-year-old from Montgomeryshire. In his journal he noted that she was taken ill at sea on 18 July suffering from obstipation.

The history, symptoms, treatment and daily progress is recorded as follows:

this patient is a dull phlegmatic welsh woman with little if any intellect. She applied to me the day before yesterday complaining of – saying that she had not had a passage thro' her bowels for the last ten days. Gave her . . . of Colocynth and Calomil six grains of each. Saw her at night, physic had not operated,' skin very cool, pulse not in the least accelerated; finds a heavy dull sensation in her head and Listlessness. Ordered her senna and salts.

On 19 July it was noted that:

. . . not operated, pulse much . . . gave her an enema composed of a quart of lukewarm water with a handful of salts and about four ounces of olive oil. The injection remained up about two hours and then produced a copious evacuation.

By 20 July:

The bowels . . . on properly thro'out the after part of yesterday; she has had a good night, directed cold washings and exercise in the open air.

This patient had a little opening – occasionally and cold bathing daily for some time. This case forms but one out of about ten or twelve which have occurred during the last month; all requiring every means short of enema to produce relaxation of the bowels. I have therefore expended a considerable quantity of pergative medicine without being enabled to produce written cases to show for it. However up to the present time and place . . . July 20 1836, the women are in a very healthy state and not in any bad state of discipline, but nevertheless, "I would I were well [rid] of them".[8]

During this voyage, Robert Espie apparently found that solitary confinement, as punishment, was ineffective. As an alternative means of punishment he had the women whipped over their arms, legs and backs with a stout piece of rope. Although his action must have been brought to the attention of the Authorities, he escaped any formal punishment.[9]

By 1 November 1836, W. Burnett, Physician General, had issued the following amended instructions to surgeons superintendents:

the surgeons superintendent of convict ships are particularly desired to notice, that they will be required to render a regular sick book with the journal and the nosological synopsis now added thereto, in a complete and scientific state, together with a certificate from the medical storekeeper at Deptford, as to the condition and number of their surgical instruments, in all respects the same as if employed in king's ships, agreeably to the new instructions for the service afloat, and that in the event of any failure in these particulars, the certificates necessary from the Department, to entitle them to receive their pay and allowances will be withheld.[10]

From March to September 1838, the 'Lord Lyndock' was required to convey 330 male convicts to New South Wales. Amongst these were two men sentenced in Montgomeryshire, Thomas Bailey and David Lewis. On its arrival at Port Jackson, the surgeon superintendent, Obadiah Pineo, was able to record in his journal that Thomas Bailey required treatment for an inflamed leg on 8 June 1838 but was declared fit for duty by 20 June.

The voyage was not without a degree of panic for during the period spent at sea, 19 had died from various illnesses. Upon arrival, 112 men were sent to the colonial hospital suffering from the effects of scurvy including both Thomas Bailey and David Lewis. The surgeon confirmed that:

the general appearance of the prisoners when they came on board, and several days whilst we lay at Woolwich afterwards, was that of good health. I examined them frequently during this time, neither symptoms of scurvy or any other disease was apparent. They were kept constantly on deck, except at night, when they were locked up at the usual hour of eight. Our first visitation – was smallpox, out of seven I lost one. The next was an accident whereby 16 men were dreadfully scalded by boiling tea, many of them from their shoulders down to their heels. Of these only one died and this was more owing to previous disease(phthisis), than the scald. From this time forward, with the exception of a very few slight cases of scorbutic affection which became convalescent, till we passed the Cape of Good Hope 20 June, we had no cases of consequence. But after this period, symptoms of scurvy began to appear and in the end, that is before the termination of our voyage at Port Jackson, became general. At the period of our arrival at this port, there was upwards of 150 affected, out of which 112 were sent to Sydney hospital, leaving on board 40 to 50, who were but slightly diseased. In my two former voyages, I did not lose a single prisoner. I pursued the same general system in this and if anything more strictly enforced. They were never allowed to go below, after rising in the morning, until sunset and the hour of going to bed at 8 p.m. The ship was dry and so roomy, that from 30 to 40 more prisoners than we actually had might have been accommodated. The prisons were kept dry, clean and well fumigated with hot vinegar, or sprinkled with cold vinegar and the solution of chlorine of lime alternately every day of the week. I have walked through every part of them in the middle of the night, without experiencing the slightest foul smell not ever from the water closets, where a guard was constantly kept, that this part of the prison should not be rendered uncomfortable to any one. The scuttle was kept open most of the time and wind sails used at the different hatchways. The ship's hold, which I examined more than once, was in good condition and her ballast the best I ever saw. The prisoners and comforts for the prisoners, were of excellent quality. The water was better than I had before in one of those ships. I began the general use of lemon juice and sugar, shortly after leaving England and wine sometime afterwards. These two were served out mostly on alternative days. Their food was well cooked, and at the regular hours and I never allowed it to be served out till after I had tasted it. Beside the regular inspection of every prisoner twice a day, I was constantly (almost), amongst them. We had plenty of musicians and some good instruments. Everyday when the weather would allow, we had dancing, gymnastics and trotting exercises all round the decks and forecastle. I cannot account for the general appearance of scurvy, or attribute it to any cause, except that of a peculiar . . . or constitutional temperament of a great portion of these people. It was not only remarked by myself, but frequently by the passengers of this ship, how uncommonly healthy the prisoners appeared. Even when the disease was most general, you could not perceive any symptoms of ill health in the look of most of them. Perhaps the suddenness from a restricted diet as that on board the hulks and plenty of exercise, exchanged for a generous diet and abridged exercise may have some share in producing the disease, added to the slight hope of never returning to their native country and those friends to whom they were still dear, notwithstanding their fallen state. Yet I have had the charge of some whose conduct and kindly feelings would not have thrown discredit on . . . May I take the liberty of requesting that you will use your influence in obtaining an order from the government, making it imperative on all surgeons superintendents, to call at some Port on the voyage to N. S. Wales. I am quite convinced of the necessity, from its great length and the risk of some epidemic arising after passing the Cape of Good Hope, as it happened in my case. Had sufficient cause existed, at the time, I should not have hesitated, but when the execution of orders have been left discretionary with me, I cannot think of making my own private wishes and interest, a pretext for fulfiling them . . . But when I refer to the small number of deaths by scurvy,[8] (some of whom had suffered severely from other diseases), out of 150 afflicted with it, there is matter of consolation.[11]

George T. Moxey, surgeon, on the 'Woodbridge' which left England in October 1839, had a convict complement of 230 men. One hundred and thirty had embarked from the hulks at Woolwich and the remaining 100 from the 'Fortitude' hulk at Chatham. (Amongst these were Lewis Humphreys, James Morris and Abraham Owen, three of the Chartist rioters from Llanidloes and James Corbett convicted of horse stealing at Kerry.) The surgeon was able to report on the voyage:

I was much pleased at their apparent clean and healthy condition on inspecting them previous to their embarkation. They had not however been long on board the ship before I perceived that some amongst them had but recently recovered from sickness, and that others were not even then free from disease. We were fortunate in getting a good start out of the Channel and from the fine state of the weather, the prisoners did not suffer a great deal from sea sickness, which circumstance I always considered as having a material influence on their health during the passage. Many of them had been upwards of twelve months in the hulks, and as I found out on subsequent enquiry, some had laboured under ague, scurvy and cutaneous affections, which diseases they are occasionally liable to. The greater number were said to be labourers, or in other words, brought up to no particular trade or business, loose, idle characters, indolent and lazy habits. Most of the tradesmen manifested an anxious desire to be employed at their respective trades, and managed to keep as many of them at work as possible, light and cheerful occupation proving to be one of the best preventive of scurvy and other diseases. Thirty, who had been soldier deserters from the Army in Canada, were without exception, the best conducted men on board, and the example they set of order and obedience contributed in no small degree to the regularity and good discipline of the whole. Their habits of cleanliness, together with the cheerful state of their minds, as they seemed to place much reliance upon shortly receiving a mitigation of their sentences, were no doubt the principal cause of their especially good health during the voyage out. The only death on board was certainly a soldier, but that man had been convicted of sacrilege and went out of course under very different circumstances. We had no fever of any consequence and most of the patients who were put on the sick list with that disease, were attacked after our anchoring in the harbour of Port Jackson, to be assailed to the excessive heat of the weather at that period, it being then the middle of summer . . . scorbutus first shewed itself . . . after being about seven or eight weeks at sea, and I regret to say that one man died of that malady as we reached the Cape of Good Hope, which port I considered it necessary to order the ship into for the express purpose of obtaining a proper supply of fresh meat and vegetables; the more particularly as the general health of the prisoners seemed to be much impaired. The symptoms denoting scurvy in the commencement were a dry and constricted appearance of the countenance; with a feeling of languor and Lassitude; dependency and want of sleep; flying pains about the thorax; heaviness at epigastrium and sometimes, tho' not always, defective appetite. As to the origin of this disease, I cannot attribute it to anything . . . in their food or in their manner of living; their rations were regularly served out, meals taken at regular hours and victuals properly cooked; the ship was always dry, clean and thoroughly ventilated.

Amongst the prisoners convicted at the Montgomeryshire Assizes whose names are recorded on the sick list whilst at sea were:

7 December 1839: James Morris aged 19 years and suffering from psoriasis.

Following treatment he was discharged as cured 14 December.

9 January 1840: Abraham Owen aged 49 years and suffering from dyspepsia.

Following treatment he was discharged as cured 13 January.[12] John Frost, the Newport Chartist, wrote two letters during the voyage of the 'Mandarin' in 1840. On 4 May he wrote to his friend, Feargus O'Connor, when the ship was at sea near the Cape of Good Hope. In this letter John Frost described that:

. . . we were immediately put upon a barge and clothed in the prison dress, and it being very cold, a piece of an old tarpaulin was thrown over our shoulders. In this

miserable plight and nearly half starved, we were put on board the 'Mandarin'. Our appearance was miserable In the extreme, so much so that many on board thought that a few days would terminate my earthly career. The commander, Doctor A. McKecknie, received us with much kindness. He promised to do all in his power to make us comfortable during the voyage and well has this gentleman redeemed the pledge. I hope the Chartists will not forget this, but that they will show themselves as sensible of kindness as of cruelty. When men are sentenced to transportation for life, they generally know their doom and time is given to adjust their affairs and to see their families, but this usual arrangement was denied us . . . The passage has hitherto been remarkably fine; we are all in excellent health and good spirits . . .

In another letter, dated the same day, Frost wrote to Morgan Williams of George Town, Merthyr Tydfil, stating that:

. . . we sailed from Portsmouth on 25 February and Falmouth on the 28th. For some days we had it rather rough but so far there never was a finer passage. I was apprehensive when I came on board that I shall have a sailor's grave, but I have turned out a better sailor than I expected. We have met with but two men in authority who have treated us unkindly, first the keeper of Monmouth gaol and one in the hulk. We have experienced very kind treatment at the hands of the commander Dr A. McKecknie . . .[13]

The 'Cadet' convict ship left London 9 September 1847, en route to Van Diemen's Land, with female convicts amongst whom was Eliza Thomas of Montgomeryshire who had been sentenced to 10 years transportation. The surgeon superintendent was Charles R. Kinnear, who gives a detailed account of the health of the women during the voyage. In his general remarks he stated that:

The 'Cadet' of 376 tons was chartered to convey female prisoners from England to Hobart Town, and received on board part of the prisoners at Woolwich on the 25 August 1847. It is customary for the surgeon superintendent to examine the convicts in the prison before they embark, but owing to the miscarriage of a letter from the medical inspector of the Millbank penitentiary, I had not that privilege, but I made a hasty examination of them as they came on board and out of 170, I rejected five for bodily infirmities. Along with the prisoners we received a matron and religious instructor from Millbank, and the duties of the surgeon superintendent were lightened considerably by the clothing being all marked and the messes formed previous to embarkation. The women were chiefly young and healthy looking One death occurred in the Channel from fever; The patient complained the day after she came on board and I have no doubt but it was induced by mental anxiety and depression of spirits. Sea sickness prevailed at first to a considerable extent, but they soon recovered and came on deck to enjoy the fresh air and taste a glass of wine, which was denied them if they did not make their appearance. We were detained in the Channel for 10 days by contrary winds, which blew strong from the westward, and it was necessary to use great precaution to keep the prison dry and at the same time to keep up a proper degree of ventilation. The practice of . . . was always adopted in damp weather and having stoves put down during the day. The women were kept on deck when the weather was fine, and the bedding got up every morning as well as their clothes bags. A minute inspection of the prison, every morning as at ten, prevented any accumulation of filth or wet and the prison soon presented the appearance of a clean, wholesome and well regulated establishment, on a mess straining against another for the liberal allowance of tea and sugar awarded daily to the best regulated messes, and it was seldom – that I had to find fault with the appearance of the prison, or the state of the women's persons and I only wish I could say the same as regards their tempers. The synopsis shews the total immunity from disease of any endemic character. A few slight cases of opthalmia appeared at first starting which I attributed to the . . . of the season compared to that of a prison. Two cases of syphilis of old standing were put under treatment, and in one of these cases, I remarked the great use of the chloride of zinc which healed up the sores very speedily after the other remedies, usually adopted, had failed. I recommended this application to the surgeon of the convict hospital at Hobart Town, and he had a case under treatment when I left, but as my stay in the colony was so short, I cannot speak of the results. In the tropics, the women were never allowed to go below during the day, but were kept on the poop, sewing and knitting and it was in these latitudes when I found the benefit of the chloride of zinc as a disinfecting agent. We did not touch at any port on the passage, as we were not in want of any replacements, and we arrived at Hobart Town on 2 January 1848, in a very healthy state. One hundred and sixty four prisoners were embarked at Woolwich, together with 29 children. One death occurred in the Channel and one birth on the passage, so that the total number landed amounted to 163 women and 30 children.

In an accompanying list of ten persons vaccinated on board the 'Cadet', Eliza Thomas had an unsuccessful vaccination on 2 September but by 4 October, a second attempt proved successful.[14]

In 1865, the 'Racehorse' left Portland in May 1865 bound for Western Australia. Amongst her convict complement were ten men: John Baker, James Booth, William Brannan, James Foster, William Jones, David King, Thomas Riley, William Thompson, William Weston and John Wilson, who were by far the greatest number of convicts sentenced in Montgomeryshire to travel together in the same ship to the same location. The superintendent surgeon, Dr A. Watson, aboard the 'Racehorse', does not include the names of any of the Montgomeryshire convicts in his list of those taken ill. The following procedures confirm that he was able to maintain a high level of health amongst the convicts and ensured that firm discipline was the norm throughout the voyage between 8 April and 23 August 1865. The weekly routine probably proved tedious, but the prisoners were better kept to this routine than finding their own pastimes:

Regulations:

> *Prisoners must conduct themselves in a respectful and becoming manner to all the officers on board; they are to strictly obey such orders as I may issue through the wardens on duty or head of messes*
>
> *Prisoners must behave themselves in a decent and becoming manner at all times, but more especially when prayers are read to them or divine service performed, with prayers morning and evening, weather permitting.*
>
> *Cursing and all foul language, quarrelling, fighting or exchanging or giving away clothes, are strictly prohibited.*
>
> *Any person stealing or secreting any of the mess stores, or any article belonging to the mess or to the ship, will be severely punished.*
>
> *Prisoners are on no occasion to hold conversation with the guard or talk through the bars below.*
>
> *Each mess shall have a captain and it will be the business of one man, in his turn, to clean the mess utensils. The latter after each meal are to be taken on deck and thoroughly cleaned and dried before being taken below. The members of each mess are to sit together.*

The captain of messes are warned that they will be held responsible for the good order and cleanliness of their messes. They are to see that the men wash themselves every morning, and that they attend to their hair; that there are no stragglers at night and no one sleeping with his clothes on.

Smoking tobacco or striking lights of any kind in the prison; washing clothes or attempting to dry them below, will not be allowed under any pretence.

The captain of messes will receive their provisions in the order of their messes; they are to tally the pieces of meat and to deliver them to the cooks; they are also to receive water for their messes.

The bedding is to be taken on deck every morning when the weather will permit. Wardens on duty are to see the beds neatly rolled up by 5.30 a.m., after which they are to be handed through the prison gate to the upper deck crew to be stowed by them, and when they are ordered down, they are to be received by the same party.

If at any time a prisoner has reason to complain of provoking language, or treatment from the ship's company or guard, he is hereby strictly enjoined not to retaliate, but to make the same known to me that the complaint may be investigated.

The surgeon superintendent has to impress upon the minds of the prisoners that their future prosperity and happiness will depend upon their good conduct on board and the report he shall have to make to the Governor of the colony on arrival.

Weekly Routine:

4.30 a.m. – *prisoners cooks (2 in number), admitted on deck.*

5.30 a.m. – *upper deck crew admitted on deck for the purpose of filling washing tubs. Prisoners at the same time to commence lashing up their beds and STEE hammocks.*

6.00 a.m. – *half the prisoners admitted on deck for the purpose of washing their persons under the superintendence of the warder on duty, half an hour being allowed for this purpose.*

7.30 a.m. – *down all prisoners, ship's company to commence washing upper deck and water closets.*

8.00 a.m. – *breakfast.*

8.30 a.m. – *one man from each mess admitted on deck for the purpose of washing up their mess utensils.*

9.00 a.m. – *all the prisoners admitted on deck, with the exception of two men in each mess, who, in rotation, will clean and scrape dry the prison deck and their berths, the bottom boards of the latter being removed during which time I will attend the surgery and seek the sick.*

9.30 a.m. – *prison inspected, after which all prisoners will be assembled for prayers.*

10.00 a.m. – *one half of the prisoners sent on deck for the purpose of exercise, the other half being arranged in schools under the superintendence of the religious instructor, assisted by monitors.*

11.30 a.m. – *school to break up; one warder and inspector of provisions to be present at the issuing of lime juice.*

noon – *dinner.*

12.30 p.m. – *one man from each mess to be admitted on deck for the purpose of washing mess utensils.*

1.20 p.m. – *deck to be swept up.*

1.30 p.m. – *half the prisoners admitted on deck for exercise the other half remaining below to be arranged in schools as in the forenoon.*

4.00 p.m. – *down all beds and hammocks.*

4.30 p.m. – *supper.*

5.00 p.m. – one man from each mess admitted on deck to wash mess utensils.
6.00 p.m. – prayers.
9.00 p.m. – rounds.

This daily routine was supplemented on Tuesdays by shaving, on Wednesdays and Thursdays by the washing of clothes, on Saturdays by the closure of the schools, bottom boards to be scrubbed and dried on deck, prisoners to be shaved and employed in mending. On Sundays, divine service was held at 11.00 a.m. and those prisoners who professed the Roman Catholic faith were allowed to have one of their number to read prayers to them. It was expected that all would assemble in a clean and orderly manner for the worship of Almighty God.[15]

During the same year (1865), one journal of William Crawford RN, surgeon superintendent on board the 'Vimeira', listed a set of regulations which included decent behaviour, no foul language, no secreting of stores, no talking to the guards, no smoking in prison and bedding to be taken on deck each morning. Amongst the provisions were slates, slate pencils and books for the use of John Williams, religious instructor. He maintained a log of the voyage between 15 September and 24 December 1865:

15 Sep	–	*Left East India dock*
16 Sep	–	*Some children suffering from scarlet fever*
17 Sep	–	*Left for Chatham*
18 Sep	–	*92 convicts arrived from Chatham*
20 Sep	–	*94 prisoners embarked*
21 Sep	–	*Left for Portland*
23 Sep	–	*95 convicts embarked*
27 Sep	–	*95 convicts embarked*
30 Sep	–	*Sailed with several children having died by this time*
4 Oct	–	*Squally and sea sickness*
28 Oct	–	*Wife of Private Williamson had a female child and there was much rain during the last two days*
4 Dec	–	*Northerly gale's and rain*
22 Dec	–	*Anchored at Fremantle*
23 Dec	–	*110 convicts disembarked*
24 Dec	–	*110 convicts disembarked*

Amongst the convict complement on the 'Vimeira' were five men from Montgomeryshire: Thomas Brown, George Fox, William Johnson, John Kirkman and John MacIntyre.[16]

It would be amiss not to make reference to the last convict ship that sailed to Australia with James Robinson on board. He had the distinction of being the last convict sentenced in Montgomeryshire to penal servitude, leading to transportation, and, with 279 other male convicts, including Irish Fenians, embarked on the 'Hougoumont'. In the journal of John Casey, surgeon superintendent, the voyage passed as follows:

12 Oct 1867	–	*Sailed from Portland*
27 Oct	–	*Passed Madeira*
6 Nov	–	*Passed Cape Verde Islands*
22 Nov	–	*Nearly shipwrecked in storm near Trinidad*
2 Dec	–	*Passed Tristan da Cunha*

> 12 Dec   – *Passed south of Cape of Good Hope*
> 25 Dec   – *Storms*
> 26 Dec   – *Storms*
> 9 Jan 1868 – *Arrived Fremantle*
> 10 Jan   – *Landed.*[17]

The arrival of a convict ship in New South Wales and Van Diemen's Land, especially during the early years, would have aroused considerable interest. Not only did the ships bring more convicts, but emigration had begun. In addition, much needed stores of equipment and food were on board and news from home brought much needed support. Local newspapers of the day ensured that they published details of all arrivals and departures. On 13 April 1806 *The Sydney Gazette and New South Wales Advertiser* in its article 'Ship News' confirmed:

> *on Friday arrived the 'William Pitt', with female prisoners (including Jane Owen of Montgomeryshire), in a general state of good health. She sailed from England on the first of September last; made the island of Madeira the first of October and stopped three days. In company with an outward bound East India convoy, she reached the Cape of Good Hope early in January, and from thence sailed for this port.*[18]

The following week (20 April), the newspaper included additional information about the 'William Pitt':

> *the 'William Pitt,' brought 117 female prisoners, three having died on the passage, as did also three children, one of whom died of the smallpox, that infection having prevailed with much malignancy for the considerable space of two months. When she left England bread was at 13d. the quartern loaf, beef 10d. to 1s. per lb, mutton 8d. and pork is ??. per lb. On Thursday, the quantity of tea landed from the 'William Pitt', reduced the price of a commodity to ten shillings per pound, that had a day or two before, with little exception as to quality, sold at forty-eight. On Thursday a draft was made to Parramatta of 46 of the female prisoners arrived by the 'William Pitt'.*[19]

By 1 June the paper was able to review a previous report:

> *our report of the arrival of the 'William Pitt', stated the death of three female prisoners during the passage, having landed 117 out of 120 women received on board. This account was not perfectly correct, as out of the above number received, only two were lost, the third having been discharged the vessel shortly prior to her departure.*[20]

Following similar reporting of news, *The Hobart Town Gazette and Southern Reporter* ensured that the inhabitants of the island kept in touch with the outside world. On 13 June 1818 it was able to report:

> *on Thursday (11 June), arrived the 'Lady Castlereagh' of 842 tons; Captain Welden with 261 male prisoners (including William Cook, Edward Edwards and John Jones from Montgomeryshire), all in good health from England, last from Port Jackson (39 convicts had been landed in New South Wales out of the ship's complement of 300 convicts) The remainder of the 48th Regiment, under command of Major Bell, destined for the relief of this station, came by the 'Lady Castlereagh'.*[21]

On 19 December 1818, the same paper reported:

yesterday morning arrived the ship 'Lord Melville' Captain Wetherell from England which she left on 18 July; having on board 149 male prisoners (including Hugh Davies from Montgomeryshire), all in good health, one only having died on the voyage. She touched at the Cape of Good Hope. Surgeon: Superintendent John McMillan RN. The guard consists of 31 men, 10 of whom belong to the 48th and 21 to the 30th Regiments, under the command of Lieut A. Waddell 48th Regt.[22]

By 2 January 1819, the paper was able to confirm the further movement of the prisoners following disembarkation from the 'Lord Melville':

the prisoners brought by the 'Lord Melville', 149 in number, were landed on the 24 ult; 50 at Kangaroo Point, which body went on direct for Port Dalrymple; the remainder at this settlement. The prisoners arrived very healthy and it is satisfactory to state that they conducted themselves in the most orderly manner on the voyage; and that they expressed themselves very grateful for the good treatment which they had experienced from the officers under whose charge they came out.[23]

As soon as a convict ship landed at its destination, a day was appointed when a government official went on board the ship with the intention of holding a muster of all convicts be carried out. This would take the form of a complete physical record so that any further discretion or abscondment on the part of an individual would enable the authorities to apprehend the offender by publishing the relevant description. Prior to the arrival of a convict ship, a notice was placed in a local newspaper to that effect and one such advertisement dated 24 August 1811 confirmed that:

a ship being expected to arrive here shortly with female convicts from England, such settlers and free persons of good character as may wish to obtain the services of one or more of those females, are hereby instructed to make their applications without loss of time to the several magistrates within whose District they may reside, and to hold themselves in readiness to attend on the magistrates to execute the usual bonds for the retaining of them in their service and treating them with justice and humanity.[24]

On 12 October, the newspaper was able to report that:

on Thursday arrived the 'Friends' transport, Capt. Ralph, from England, having on board 100 female prisoners, all of whom are arrived in a healthy state.[25]

Amongst these female convicts was Ann Evans from Montgomeryshire and it is possible that she was selected as a servant. In the 1814 Muster she is shown to be in the employ of a Mrs King at Parramatta. In addition to recording the medical and physical conditions of patients whilst on board convict ships, surgeons were required to give an account of the number of convicts classed according to their ages and abilities to read and write. On board the 'Racehorse' which left England in May 1865, were ten men sentenced in Montgomeryshire. In accordance with regulations, the ship surgeon, Dr A. Watson, compiled the following information, although there is no indication as to which category those men from Montgomeryshire belonged:

Total number of convicts who embarked: 280

On embarkation from England number who could

Read and Write	163
Read only	72
Neither	45

On arrival in Australia number who could

Read and Write	206
Read only	74
Neither	nil

Is is therefore evident that educational instruction throughout the sea voyage proved to be beneficial to the convicts, and would be to their advantage in a strange land.[26] It has been stated elsewhere that, upon arrival in Australia, a muster was taken of all convicts prior to dis-embarkation. Included in the evidence obtained from each individual was the state of their education. The following table summarizes the response of those convicted in Montgomeryshire:

EDUCATION ATTAINMENT UPON ARRIVAL IN AUSTRALIA

	NSW		TAS		WA	NI	PP	Total	
	Male	Female	Male	Female	Male	Male	Male	Male	Female
Read and Write	9	2	8	3				17	5
Read only	7	3	13	1	4			24	4
Read/Write Part	4		20	4	23			47	4
Read/Write Unable	6		8	2	10			24	2
Not Known	35	8	29	1		2	6	72	9
Total	**61**	**13**	**78**	**11**	**37**	**2**	**6**	**184**	**24**

The arrival of a convict ship in harbour was a most welcomed sight for the local inhabitants. Clothing formed an important part of the ship's indent and, as soon as convenient, government orders were issued to advise the convict population that they would be issued with new clothing. One such order, placed in the local Sydney newspaper, followed the arrival of the 'William Pitt', amongst whose convict complement had been Jane Owen of Montgomeryshire. The paper noted:

A supply of slop clothing being received by the 'William Pitt' . . . the following proportion to be issued from the public store on Friday 2 May at Sydney and Parramatta, and on Monday 5 May at Castle Hill:

male convicts – two shirts; one waistcoat; one jacket; one pair of trousers; one pair of breeches; one pair of shoes and one hat . . . The former orders respecting the care of the slops and selling or bartering them being forbidden, remain in force. (It would appear that female clothing was not issued at this time).[27]

By 1807, an order was issued concerning the level of food that should be distributed:

The following is what to be considered and issued as the established ration to government servants in NSW and its Dependancies to be lessened according to circumstances, as the Governor, may deem proper:

10 lbs. of wheat or 8 lbs. of flour; 3 lbs. of maize or 3 pts. of pea se; 7 lbs. of beef or 4 lbs. of salt pork; 6 ozs. of sugar or 1 lb. of rice.[28]

The arrival of the 'Lady Castlereagh' at Hobart with 261 male convicts, including William Cooke, Edward Edwards and John Jones from Montgomeryshire, (having left 39 at Sydney), once again gave the authorities an opportunity to issue clothing.

A public notice, signed by Thomas Archer, Acting Deputy Assistant Commissary General, Hobart Town, and dated 20 June 1818 stated that:

A supply of winter clothing, having been received from headquarters per the 'Lady Castlereagh', an issue thereof will take place on Friday next the 26 inst, to the whole of the crown servants victualled from the king's stores (excepting those lately arrived per the ships 'Lady Castlereagh' and 'Minerva', who received theirs on landing). One cloth jacket, one cap; one pair shoes; one pair cloth trousers; one cotton shirt and one palisade each to complete their suit of bedding.

In conclusion, the harrowing experiences suffered by those on the sea voyage were, following the appalling conditions of the second fleet's departure from England in 1790, much improved by the authorities. In particular, the responsibility for the care of the convicts during the voyage was transferred from the naval agent, master and naval surgeon to the superintendent surgeon and, from 1801, "an improvement in the conditions in the convict ships" was noted.[29] Additionally, the authorities introduced and enforced various rules for discipline and conduct which mitigated the problems associated with sea travel and sickness.

CHAPTER SIX

Convict Colonial Life

With the ever increasing influx of settlers to the colony, it soon became apparent to the British Government that the expense of looking after all the convicts could be eased by a system of assignment, whereby settlers could avail themselves of the services of convicts by agreeing to feed and clothe the convict and in return freely receive their labour. Whilst male convicts were expected to labour in the fields, female convicts generally remained in the home of a settler and undertook the position of servant. For a number of reasons, convicts found it necessary to place petitions before the appropriate authorities in order that their personal desire to better themselves could be achieved. In a letter dated 18 December 1829 from the Superintendent of Convicts Office to the Colonial Secretary, an application for assignment was made on behalf of Esther Ogden, sentenced to seven years transportation for stealing calico from a shop at Welshpool:

> *with reference to that part of your letter of the 16th instant which directs that the prisoner named in the margin (Esther Ogden 'Louisa'), may be assigned to Elizabeth Brisbane, provided her husband be free, I have the honour to acquaint you that she is the wife of Richard Brisbane ('Neptune'), and holding a ticket of leave No. 27/396, and request therefore that I may be favoured with your further instructions on the subject.*[1]

Esther Ogden had already been assigned in 1827, as the muster of that year confirmed that she had been in the employ of John Barber of Parramatta and that she was accompanied by her 10 month old daughter named Catherine.[2]

Inevitably both male and female convicts sought marriage either with another convict or settler. Whilst still carrying out the remainder of their sentence, convicts were required to obtain permission from the authorities before they could proceed with their wishes. There was the vexed concern that bigamous marriages would be entered into. Many were already married prior to leaving for the colony, and as a result committed bigamy, although following a determined period without any contact from their spouse, it was recognized that they were either widows or widowers. It is evident from the following table that this aspect of relationships must have caused great concern to the authorities and that official permission might create a bigamous act.

CONVICTS KNOWN TO HAVE BEEN MARRIED
PRIOR TO LEAVING ENGLAND

Name	Children	Native Place
NEW SOUTH WALES		
Thomas Bailey	nk	Staffordshire
Richard Barrett widower	1	nk
Richard Bliss	4	nk
Benjamin Davies	4	nk
Hannah Fox	3	Somersetshire
Edward Goodwin	2	Montgomery

Name	Children	Native Place
John Griffiths	5	Churchstoke
David Hughes	2	nk
John Humphreys	9	Llanwnog
Lewis Humphreys	1	Llanidloes
David Lewis	nk	Carno
Esther Ogden	2	Macclesfield
Abraham Owen widower	4	Llanidloes
Joseph Parry	1	Llandrinio
Robert Poppett	nk	Shropshire
Edward Rees	5	nk
Margaret Richards	1	nk
Watkin Watkins	1	Brecknock

VAN DIEMEN'S LAND

Name	Children	Native Place
Evan Astley	nk	Newtown
Mary Ann Aubrey	2	Bristol
John Bumford	1	Newtown
Edward Evans	nk	nk
John Evans	4	Carmarthenshire
John Farren	1	Halesowen
Edward Griffiths	2	Llanwnog
Richard Ingram	nk	nk
Margaret Insell widow	1	Oswestry
John James	4	Merthyr Tydfil
David Miles	3	Merionethshire
Henry Mottram	1	St Albans
David Owen	1	Llanidloes
Evan Owen widower	2	Newtown
William Owen	1	Welshpool
John Price	nk	Montgomery
John Pryce widower	2	Beguildy
Evan Rees	5	Llangurig
Louisa Roberts (Madden)	1	Liverpool
Mary Rogers (Thorn)	nk	Hanwood
Robert Scott	nk	East Haddington
George White	3	Loughborough
Elizabeth Williams widow	3	Montgomeryshire

WESTERN AUSTRALIA

Name	Children	Native Place
Ishmael Jones widower	5	Llanfair Caereinion
John Owen widower	3	Wolverhampton
Edward Roberts	1	Llansantffraid
James Robinson	nk	Stockport
James Watson	2	nk

PORT PHILLIP

Name	Children	Native Place
Frederick Thorn	nk	nk

ENGLAND

Name	Children	Native Place
Thomas Hughes	nk	nk

Whilst the desires of a convict to marry were achievable, it would have had a profound effect on a spouse and family left behind in Great Britain together with the problems of the authorities in Australia doing all they could to avoid bigamous marriages. Problems also existed in Montgomeryshire, with each member of a marriage being at opposite ends of the globe. The authorities found themselves in difficulties due to their respective remoteness. For the family of Edward Goodwin of Montgomery correspondence clearly confirms the difficulties that they faced in proving to the authorities the distressed state they were in due to the transportation of the husband and father. The Rev. Walter Davies, Vicar of Manafon, in a letter dated 28 January 1836 to the Home Secretary and Francis

Allen Esq, of Maes Fron, Trewern, a solicitor and senior official of the Montgomeryshire Assizes, stated:

> *I humbly beg your attention to the following statement. At the Montgomeryshire August Assizes in the year 1830, Edward Goodwin was tried and convicted of sheep stealing and sentenced to be transported for the term of fourteen years, leaving a wife and three (two shown elsewhere) children, chargeable to the parish of Montgomery. Ann Goodwin (the wife), on 4 May 1835, in the parish church Aberdare Glamorgan, after publication of banns, married Richard Owen, whose settlement is in the parish of Berriew Montgomeryshire. Since that time, she and two children by the said Richard Owen have become chargeable owing to casual residence, to the parish of Newtown Montgomeryshire, which parish the overseers of the Poor Law processed an Order of Removal of the said Ann Goodwin and her said two children, to Montgomery, the parish of Edward Goodwin, her transported husband. Whether she actually belongs to the parish of Montgomery depends entirely on this point, whether Edward Goodwin was alive on the 4 May 1835, when his wife, the said Ann Goodwin, married the said Richard Owen. This may be ascertained from the periodical returns from New South Wales to the Minister of State's office . . . The pauper (Ann Goodwin), in her examination stated that to the best of her knowledge and belief, he (Edward Goodwin), was serving the terms of his transportation. Do not these words, and on which the removal is grounded, beg as it were the question of Settlement, there being no sort of proof but the bare belief of the pauper; that Edward Goodwin was alive somewhere at the time of her examination (Goodwin was transported in 1830 . . . If the onus can be thrown upon Manafon, could information be obtained through the Secretary of State's office, whether Goodwin in May last was dead or alive in Australia. Goodwin's mother received a letter from him some two years ago. She lives on Mr Gough's road to Berriew and he shall call for the letter to be brought to you. Manafon is not for running risks in Appeals notwithstanding the old toast. The noble uncertainty of the law if it will be necessary to apply for information from abroad, notice of appeal should be given and the court moved for postponement of the hearing.*

In an accompanying letter the Rev. Walter Davies confirmed:

> *That Mr Gough now waits upon you, by the advice and with the compliments of Mr Williams of Pennant, with a copy of the Examination and Order of Removal of Ann Goodwin, from the parish of Newtown to that of Manafon. The Order is dated 19 January, and sent by post by the wise permission of the new act. It did not reach Manafon till the 26th inset, so that seven out of the twenty one days were lost to Manafon. Your advice is required, whether Manafon would better submit to the Order (such as it is), or Appeal against it; whether the marriage of Ann Goodwin with Richard Owen on the 4th of May last, was valid or not, depends upon a fact difficult to be known; whether Edward Goodwin, the transported felon, was on that day dead or alive . . .[3]*

The outcome of this investigation is not known but, according to the 1837 Muster, Edward Goodwin was employed in Liverwort district and obtained his ticket of leave 26 September 1838. Records are not available to determine the actual incidence of bigamy, but from available evidence it has been possible to establish that, as shown in the following table, at least eight individuals committed this offence.

MARRIED PRIOR TO TRANSPORTATION
AND COMMITTED BIGAMY

Name of Convict	Husband/Wife	Children
NEW SOUTH WALES		
Hannah Fox (Dainty)	John Dainty	3
Esther Ogden	Abraham Ogden	2
VAN DIEMEN'S LAND		
Evan Astley	Martha Astley	nk
Mary Ann Aubrey	nk	2
John Bumford	Mary Bumford	1
Louisa Roberts (Madden)	nk	1
Robert Scott	nk	nk
Elizabeth Williams	nk	3

A number of convicts indicated their intention to marry, even going as far as to obtain permission, but declined to take the final betrothal. As the following table confirms, five took place in New South Wales and eleven in Van Diemen's Land:

GRANTED PERMISSION TO MARRY IN AUSTRALIA
BUT WHICH DID NOT TAKE PLACE

Name of Convict	Name of Intended Spouse	Class	Date Granted
NEW SOUTH WALES			
George Davies	Mary Richardson	F	20 Aug 1838
Hannah Fox (Dainty)	Watkin Watkins	F	6 Feb 1828
Sarah Games	Andrew Croneen	C	1836
Elizabeth Jones	John Sinnott	F	2 Dec 1834
Thomas Newton (Ellis)	Margaret Sullivan	F	2 May 1821
VAN DIEMENS LAND			
Mary Ann Aubrey	William Simmons	F	23 Jan 1845
Mary Ann Aubrey	Dennis Hoigan	C	10 Feb 1845
John Brown	Mary Ann Assen	F	28 Mar 1853
John Bumford	Ann Burrows	F	2 May 1853
Henry Fisher	Rachel Sinclair	F	6 Oct 1853
Ann Roberts	William Uttley	C	Aug 1839
Louisa Roberts	Ralph Culley	F	May 1836
Louisa Roberts	John Armstrong	C	10 May 1836
Mary Rogers (Thorn)	Peter Cooke	F	20 May 1851
Mary Rogers (Thom)	Marshall Cook	F	26 Nov 1851
William Thompson	Anna Selling	C	5 May 1853

Abbreviations – F = Free; C = Convict

It will be noted that Mary Ann Aubrey reached this point on two occasions, January and February 1845, but, by Christmas 1847, she had married her third choice James Chamberlain. Louisa Roberts and Mary Rogers (Thorn) faced a similar course of action, Roberts marrying in September 1836 but Rogers remaining faithful to her husband Frederick Thorn who had been transported to Port Phillip. Whether they were eventually reunited is not known. Amongst a list of convicts applying for the Publication of Banns at St James's Church, Sydney, was the following application dated 6 February 1828 and examined on the 15th of the same month:

Name	Watkin Watkins	Hannah Fox
Age	49	34
State	Widower	Widow
Ship	Neptune 3rd	Louisa
Sentence	14 years	7 years
Arrived	1820	1827
Present		
Service	Ticket of Leave	Assigned to Mr Dobbs, Park Street
Character	Good	Good
Remarks	Nil	Master given consent

A note signed by Richard Hill, Assistant Chaplain, confirmed that Hannah Fox had married John Dainty in Denbighshire, North Wales, leaving three children. As a result of this knowledge that Fox would be committing bigamy, the Authorities declined their permission, but by 1834, Fox once again took the opportunity to obtain permission to marry, this time with Elias Jones of Carmarthenshire, Wales. In the following Petition to the Colonial Secretary, dated 30 April 1834, it is clear that both Jones and Fox lied about their respective matrimonial circumstances and by so doing were granted permission to marry:

> The enclosed Petition from the convict named in the margin (Elias Jones, ship 'Mellish' – life), hereof to the Governor was received by me this morning in a Banns list from the Revd Cowper. The prayer of it is that His Excellency will sanction petitioner's marriage with a free woman of Sydney (Hannah Fox), his former wife being "long since dead" and the proof of the latter circumstances enclosing a letter from his "affectionate" brother Solomon Jones of some misspelt place in Shropshire, England. This letter bears a date 12 September 1831, and being rather a suspicious looking voucher to have travelled some thousands of miles in the pocket of an immigrant pensioner; I was induced to examine it a little closely and I find that the very paper upon which the "affectionate" effusion of his most loving brother was written in 1831, bears the manufacturer's mark of 1832. Attempts at imposture of this kind are unhappily common enough in this Colony, and would be unworthy of serious notice were it not for the issues contained in their detection. The bona fide (if I may so use the phrase), business of the convict population has too great a demand upon the time of this Office to be able to spare any of it to vagabonds of this kind, without injustice to others. I submit therefore for the consideration of His Excellency, whether some means should not be devised to check such practices, which of late are becoming too frequent and whether the convict in question is not deserving of punishment.

An appended note dated 2 May 1834 states:

> Let this case be brought before the Hyde Park Bench on the charge of dishonest conduct and in addition to such punishment as the Bench shall adjudge upon conviction, let Jones be discharged from his present service in Sydney and assigned in a remote District.[4]

The outcome of this deliberate act of dishonesty is not known, although the actual Banns Application dated 29 April 1834 and submitted by the Revd Mr Cowper of St Phillip's Church, Sydney, indicated that Hannah Fox deliberately lied by stating that she had arrived as a free person on the ship 'Lord Holmes' in 1827; there was no such emigrant ship of that name which arrived in that year. Elias Jones had left behind in Carmarthenshire, his wife and one child. Both he and Fox had hoodwinked the Authorities and as a result they were married on 15 September 1834.

As the following table indicates, it has been possible to trace twenty who married in New South Wales, twenty-three in Van Diemen's Land and one in Western Australia:

CONVICTS KNOWN TO HAVE MARRIED
AFTER ARRIVAL IN AUSTRALIA

Name of Convict	Name of Spouse	Date Married	Location	Class of Spouse
NEW SOUTH WALES				
Ann Bennett	Jesse Millard	24 Apl 1841	NK	C
Jeremiah Buffy	Mary Thorpe	1817	Parramatta	C
George Davies	Sarah Robinson	11 May 1840	Windsor	BC
Ann Evans	Lochlan Monoghan	30 May 1814	Parramatta	C
Charles Evans	Mary Browne	24 July 1896	Sydney	C
Rowland Evans	Elizabeth Leonard	1859	Rylestone	NK
John Flitches	Mary J. Wright	1852	NK	NK
Hannah Fox	Elias Jones	15 Sept 1834	Sydney	C
Sarah Gane	William Perry	28 Nov 1836	Sydney	C
Mary Hughes	William Cmwe	23 Oct 1820	Parramatta	C
Lewis Humphreys	Rose Newman	30 Oct 1846	Sydney	NK
Elizabeth Jones	Isaac Newton	16 July 1838	Newcastle	C
Maria Jones	George Jilkes	26 Feb 1821	Sydney	C
Edward Lewis	Mary Andrews	31 July 1852	Sydney	NK
Richard Lloyd	Mary Clifford	15 Jan 1831	Campbelltown	C
Pryce Morris	Mary Croft	1818	Windsor	BC
Esther Ogden	Robert Simpson	27 July 1846	Wollongong	C
Jane Owen	William Davis	7 Jun 1824	Castlereagh	C
John Rogers	Ann Keefe	28 Mar 1831	Sutton Forest	C
Joseph Slater	Ellen Crawford	1836	NK	NK
VAN DIEMEN'S LAND				
Evan Astley	Agnes Robe	20 Aug 1851	Hobart	C
Mary Ann Aubrey	James Chamberlain	27 Dec 1847	Hobart	NK
Fanny Bennett	John Phillips	17 Sept 1855	Hobart	C
Fanny Phillips	Andrew Dumkley	17 Mar 1806	Hobart	NK
John Bumford	Mary Ann Burton	3 May 1853	Hobart	NK
Elizabeth Davies (Grist)	Moses Linton	12 Apl 1852	Hamilton	C
Edward Edwards	Caroline Shillinglaw	29 May 1843	Melbourne	BC
Edward Hancox	Catherine Stewart	6 Nov 1854	Darlington	C
John Hancox	Eliza Thompson	7 Oct 1853	Hobart	NK
John Hartell	Jane Georgina Laing	23 Mar 1848	Swansea	NK
Michael Kelly	Margaret Ryan	26 July 1853	Launceston	C
Margaret Insell	Robert Boyast	14 Mar 1846	New Norfolk	C
David Oliver	Elizabeth Sims	17 Dec 1849	Hobart	C
Rosetta Oliver	George Hill	19 May 1845	Hobart	C
Evan Owen	Janette Paterson	22 Nov 1843	Launceston	C
John Riley	Ann Kelly	5 Apl 1837	Launceston	NK
Edward Roberts	Sarah Ann Edwards	15 Feb 1836	Sorell	NK
Louisa Roberts	John Jacobs	12 Sept 1836	Campbelltown	NK
Jonathan Roose	Ann Weston Sproson	26 Dec 1850	Newtown	NK
William Rowlands	Mary Ann Neale	14 Mar 1859	Rokebeny	NK
Robert Scott	Catherine Collins	12 Aug 1832	Brighton	C
Eliza Thomas	James Castles	14 Nov 1848	Swansea	C
Elizabeth Williams	William Lewis	5 Oct 1829	Clyde	C
WESTERN AUSTRALIA				
Thomas Brown	Bridget Rock	4 Oct 1863	NK	NK

Abbreviations – C = Convict; BC = Born in Colony; NK = Not Known

It is evident that the majority of marriages took place in Hobart (8), Sydney (6), followed by 3 each in Parramatta and Launceston. The origins of convict spouses (25) indicate that the convict population generally took recourse only within its own ranks and relationships with those born in the colony were in the minority.

Following the death of her husband, James Chamberlain, Mary Ann Chamberlain (Aubrey) met John Bunnford and, on 2 May 1853, a licence for the marriage of John Bunnford of Ross Bridge, wheelwright, and Mary Ann Burton of Hobart Town, widow, in the Church of Saint George in the City of Hobart Town was issued.[5]

In some instances the authorities required an affidavit to be sworn to confirm the unmarried status of the applicant before a marriage licence or banns be allowed. This was the case for John Hancock, sentenced to 10 years transportation for housebreaking at Montgomery. In 1853, Hancock was required to swear before Charles Simson, appointed by the Reverend the Moderator of the Presbytery of Van Diemen's Land, that he was above twenty-one years of age, free and unmarried; also that Eliza Thompson of O'Brien's Bridge, spinster, whom he wished to marry in accordance with the rites and ceremonies of the Church of Scotland, was also above twenty-one years of age and unmarried. Additionally, Hancock had to declare that there was no impediment of kindred or alliance or of any other lawful cause, nor any suit commenced in any ecclesiastical court, to bar or hinder the intended marriage. Hancock finally had to declare that he had, for the space of fifteen days immediately preceding 7 October 1853, his usual place of residence within the parish or district of Hobart.[6]

Who were some of the spouses of those convicts transported from Montgomeryshire? As indicated previously, the majority were themselves convicts from all parts of England and Wales.

George Jilkes, the husband of Maria Jones, who had disembarked from the 'Mariner', was by 18 October 1816 sent to Liverpool New South Wales.[7] By 31 March 1823 he was employed at the police office Sydney, having been appointed 5 March 1821,[8] and was still, carrying out the duties of a constable by 31 December 1824.[9] Following their marriage 26 February 1821, their first daughter Jane Jilkes was born the same year and on 8 September 1821 she is included in a list of those being fed from HM Magazines.[10]

Robert Simpson husband of Esther Ogden, arrived on the 'Lord Eldon', 30 September 1817, having been convicted at Bury St Edmunds Assizes 8 August 1816 and sentenced to 7 years transportation. He was a labourer aged 24 years, 5'7½" tall, of fair and ruddy complexion with brown hair and hazel eyes and had originated from Suffolk. The 1822 Muster states that he was a Government servant with William Hayes at Appin and by the 1828 Census he was noted free from servitude and a tenant and partner with Richard Burke of Illawarra.[11] On 18 June 1835, Robert Simpson of Woollongong submitted an application to purchase 100 acres of forest land belonging to the Government near Kiama, part of the Illawarra district.[12] By a letter dated 14 December 1836 he was allowed to purchase 102 acres near Dapto, Co. Camden, for twenty pounds ten shillings.[13] William Crowe, husband of Mary Hughes, is included on a list of convicts who disembarked from the 'Minerva' on 30 December 1819 and was forwarded to Parramatta.[14] Shortly after, on 7 August 1820, he applied for permission to marry at Parramatta.[15] By 22 July 1822 he was attached to a Lumber Yard but was due to be sent to the prisoners' Barracks for 3 months.[16] Within a week he was to be sent to Emu Plains.[17] By 30 December 1822 he was discharged with other convicts from the convict establishment at Emu Plains to Mr Hawkins of Bathurst.[18] Following which he began to commit various offences. By December 1823 he is included in a return of settlers punished in the County of Westmorland[19] and was sentenced to spend a period at Port Macquarie. On 24 December 1823, he petitioned for his wife to accompany him.[20] On Christmas Day, he was listed as a prisoner on board the 'Sally' for transportation to Port Macquarie.[21] In 1825 he was still a prisoner at Port Macquarie and petitioned for mitigation of sentence.[22] Whether this was allowed is not known but the 1828 Census confirmed that he was resident in Sydney gaol. Elias Jones, husband of Hannah Fox, had arrived on the 'Mellish' on 18 April 1829 when he was 29 years of age, being unable to read or write, married with one child at Carmarthen. He had been a miner and ploughman and was tried at Cardiff on 14 April 1828 for shopbreaking and was sentenced to life transportation. He was 5'5¾" in. height, of ruddy/pockpitted complexion with brown hair and grey eyes. The point of his left middle finger was bruised and he had a scar on his upper lip and blue marks on back of his right hand. On arrival he was sent to the Mineral Surveyors Department.[23] His ticket of leave was issued 14 February 1840 in Maitland District, but it was cancelled on 25 July 1840, because had stolen a wheelbarrow. His TL was restored to him in 1841,[24] followed by a Conditional Pardon in June 1846.[25]

Drunkenness also played a part in the day to day lives of some convicts. Janet Paterson who married Evan Owen of Montgomeryshire, was found drunk in 1842 and sentenced to one month hard labour.[26] James Castle who had married Eliza Thomas from Montgomeryshire was convicted on three occasions between 1854 and 1856 for drunkenness.[27]

Some convicts, as a result of their individual trade or calling, took advantage of their experience and applied to the authorities for permission to build their own house. One such case concerned Morgan Miles, who, following his arrival in 1822, made application in 1830 to be granted permission to erect a dwelling house on a third class allotment in Ross, Van Diemen's Land. His letter, dated 26 July 1830, addressed to George Frankland Esq, Surveyor General Hobart Town, states:

> I have the honour to request, that I may be allowed a third class allotment, in the township of Ross, Van Diemen's Land, on which I will engage to erect a weather boarded house as a dwelling house of 2 suitable rooms, 20 feet in front and 15 feet deep, and fence it with a good pailing fence; and make other suitable improvements, agreeably to the Government Regulations. I beg leave at the same time to state that I have at present no allotment but that I have built a blacksmiths shop and am at this present, prepared for building a house as above described, and in order to afford satisfactory proof of my ability to perform what I have above undertaken, I beg leave to refer to the certificates of . . . Simpson Esq police . . . and B. Home Esq JP annexed, and herewith transmitted.

The supporting certificates noted that Morgan Miles was possessed of the means . . . to erect (according to the Government Regulations) a house and to make other suitable improvements in the township of Ross, Van Diemen's Land . . .

The application was approved by George Frankland 3 August.[28]

In a Report of the Select Committee on Transportation in 1837-38, the issue of Tickets of Leave was clarified as follows:

> Your Committee will now turn to the condition, in the penal colonies, of those offenders against the laws of this country, who have either become free by the expiration of their sentence, or have obtained conditional pardons, or what is tended a ticket of leave.

A convict, transported for seven years, obtains at the end of four years; for fourteen years, the end of six years; and for life, at the end of eight years, as a matter of course, unless his conduct has been very bad, a ticket of leave, which enables him, according to certain regulations, to work on his own account. Ticket of Leave men find no difficulty in obtaining work at high wages and have acquired expedience in the colony, and are frequently preferred to lately arrived emigrants. They fill many situations of trust in both colonies: as constables in the police, overseers of mad parties and chain gangs; the better educated have been employed as superintendents of estates, clerks to bankers, to lawyers and to shopkeepers. Some have married free women and have even become wealthy. The mode of applying for tickets of leave, and the rules for granting them to female convicts, are in all respect exactly the same except for a period of probation whereby uninterrupted periods of good behaviour in service; in the married state, or as monitoress in the factory; a female under sentence of seven years, after two years; for fourteen years, after three years; and for life, after four years. Women returned to the first class of the factory will not be considered as having forfeited their claim to a ticket of leave as a return to this class implies that the individual has not been guilty of any fault.

Regulations for Ticket of Leave holders issued by J. S. Hampton, Comptroller General, Van Diemen's Land, dated 17 April 1849, include the following:

On arrival in a District they must register their residence at the Police Office and any change of address whilst in that District.

They must obtain a pass from a Police Magistrate should they wish to move to another District.

They must not be absent from their registered place of residence between the hours of ten o'clock at night and daybreak, except in actual attendance on their employers or by a pass.

In December and June each year, they must personally report themselves at the Police Office of the District in which they are residing, or forward a medical certificate showing that they are prevented doing so by sickness. The indulgence of any ticket holder failing to comply will invariably be revoked and in no case restored in less than one year. They are prohibited from entering any Theatre or Billiard Room. Destitute holders, unable to obtain their own livelihood, will be received into any of the Hiring Depots and maintained at the expense of the government until they can find employment.

They are allowed to hold personal property and that good conduct is the condition upon which their ticket of leave is held.

The procurement of a Ticket of Leave, enabled a prisoner to have a certain degree of freedom without supervision and some took advantage of this. James Evans received his ticket on 16 July 1829, and the following information noted with it:

Name	*James Evans*
Ship	*Elizabeth 3*
Master	*Ostler*
Year	*1820*
Native Place	*Montgomery*
Trade or Calling	*Labourer*

Offence

Place of Trial	*Montgomery Great Sessions*

Date of Trial	*18 Mar 1820*
Sentence	*Life*
Year of Birth	*1791*
Height	*5 feet 9½ inches*
Complexion	*Dark*
Hair	*Black*
Eyes	*Hazel*

General Remarks

He was allowed to remain in the district of Bathurst on the recommendation of the Bathurst Bench dated 28 February 1829 but also written upon the TL was permission to travel between Bathurst and Sydney. He was not to remain in Sydney.[29] *Unfortunately across the ticket is written "cancelled for seducing and cohabiting with the wife of Dennis Begley", and to the side of the ticket is written "This man it is said by Mr O. Davis, has taken away the wife of Dennis Begley, Eastern Creek Prospect about 6 weeks ago. 7 March 1836.". At the bottom of the ticket are the initials 'C.P' (Conditional Pardon) June 1844.*[30]

In 1832, His Excellency Major General Richard Bourke Governor, Captain General and Commander in Chief of the Territory of New South Wales and dependencies, received two petitions. The first from Thomas Ellis (Newton) dated 19 June 1832 stated:

> *That memorialist arrived in the colony per ship 'Fanny' in 1816, a prisoner for life, and having served the probationary time, His Excellency Sir Thomas Brisbane was pleased to grant him a ticket of leave in July 1823 for the district of Sydney which indulgence memorialist held until May 1831; memorialist having at that time done dealing with a man who endeavoured to swindle memorialist out of a considerable part of his property; upon his . . . a most malicious and charge of memorialist having criminal intercourse with his wife, which charge memorialist was most honourably acquitted by the bench of magistrates, but upon reference to His Excellency the late Governor; he was pleased to cancel memorialist ticket of leave, since which time memorialist had been in the service of Government, and having undergone much provocation, most earnestly solicits the removal of his former indulgence Memorialist most earnestly wishes to represent to His Excellency that since the time of his arrival in the Colony, his conduct has been such as not to warrant any punishment, which memorialist most earnestly . . . His Excellency will be pleased to . . . and grant him the boon he do earnestly . . .*

Supporting this petition were statements from a local Justice, Mr Perry, and an officer in charge of the road branch office respectively:

> *In consideration of the abandoned character of the woman to whom the accompanying petition refers, and as the encouragement afforded by her husband who it appears entrusted the petitioner with the management of his affairs; the case was dismissed, but the question whether under all the circumstances Ellis was a fit person to be allowed the indulgence of a ticket of leave was submitted for His Excellency the Governor's consideration.*
> *and*
> *I certify that the within named petitioner joined the road branch survey on general department May 1831. Since that period his conduct has been good.*

As a result of this petition, Thomas Ellis was granted a ticket of leave in December 1832 for Bathurst district.[31] The second petition was from Joseph James, and he also was successful in his application:

> *That your Excellency's petitioner arrived per the ship 'Baring' in the year 1819, and on his arrival he entered the service of Government and continued therein during 10 years, giving satisfaction to the different persons under whom he was placed; That Your Excellency's petitioner . . . in good conduct during that period and his character was never impurged except in the following instance, which in some measure disqualifies petitioner from making application for the indulgence prayed for, in the usual manner; viz in the year 1828 petitioner was sentenced by the bench at Penrith, to three months with No 10 iron gang, for purchasing a stolen shirt. With this solitary exception, petitioner's honestly, sobriety, industry and good conduct has never once been questioned. After petitioner . . . Government employment he was transferred to the service of Charles Marsden Esq of South Creek, where petitioner remains; that being anxious to obtain the indulgence of a ticket of leave, petitioner most respectfully solicits Your Excellency's favourable consideration to the foregoing particulars and humbly implore that Your Excellency will be graciously pleased to concede that indulgence to him, and petitioner as is duly bound will ever pray.*
>
> *A note on his Application states "The petitioner has been in my service ten years during which prisoner has behaved to my satisfaction."*

He received his ticket of leave 28 April 1832.[32]

The withdrawal of a ticket of leave warranted official authorization as seen in a letter dated 26th October 1838 from the principal superintendent of convicts office to the Colonial Secretary:

> *I have the honour to enclose, as per annexed list, letters recommending the cancellation of certain tickets of leave, which I beg may be submitted at your earliest convenience, for the commands of His Excellency the Governor.*

The list included the following entry concerning a Montgomeryshire transportee:

Number	Name	Reason for Recommending the Cancellation and by whom
38/1487	Mary (also Elizabeth) Jones	Attempt at Imposition by gross falsehood.

Entered by Police Magistrate Parramatta.[33]

John Humphries, also a Montgomeryshire transportee, applied for a ticket of leave passport,and this was granted 21 January 1842:

Name	John Humphries
Ship	Camden
Year of Arrival	1833
Where Tried	Montgomery
When Tried	10 March 1832
Sentence	Life

Allowed to proceed to New England in the service of Mr Gregory Blaxland for 12 months. On the recommendation Mr G. Blaxland the Cassiles Bench dated 23 December 1841.[34]

In a letter dated 6 December 1844, from the Principal Superintendent of Convicts office to the Honourable The Colonial Secretary, the following application was put forward in respect of James Morris, one of the transported Llanidloes Chartists, and two other men:

> *In reply to the inquiries contained in you letter of the 4th instant, respecting the cases of the convicts named in the margin James Morris 'Woodbridge' John Mangam 'Couder' and William Kelly, I have the honour to acquaint you, that in the case of Kelly, it became necessary to write to D. MacIntosh at Liverpool Plains which I did on the 29th of October last, and now waiting his reply, I may observe that I have again applied to him on the subject and will furnish my report immediately on receipt of his recommendation. I have the honour further to report, with respect to the case of the two men recommended by Mr Commissioner Hunter that His Excellency the Governor has approved of their having tickets of leave for the capture of Hefferman, and as the letter of Mr Hunter did not contain any request from you for its return, I did not consider it necessary to do so, but if you desire it I will forward that document to you when the tickets are prepared.*[35]

An accompanying note dated 7 December 1844, states that Commissioner Hunter on 10 November, recommended a reward to Morris and Mangam for the recapture of Hefferman. As a result of the above recommendation James Morris received a ticket of leave.[36] Also added to the letter, was a note that the case concerning Kelly had since been disposed of and nothing further was required.[37] James Mangam was a military convict who had arrived on the 'Courier' in 1833 from Mauritius, The nature of the circumstances surrounding the recapture of Hefferman is not recorded.

Another avenue open to convicts was to petition for a Conditional Pardon. James Evans, who arrived on the 'Elizabeth' in December 1820, forwarded the following Petition to Major General Richard Bourke, Governor and Commander in Chief:

> *that Your Excellency's petitioner was tried at Montgomery Quarter Sessions in March 1820 for horse stealing and sentenced to transportation for life and arrived in this Colony in the year 1821; that Your petitioner had the indulgence of a ticket of leave conferred on him in the month of July 1829, which he has continued to hold until the present time, being a period of six years without having been charged with any offence of misdemeanour whatever, and that during the whole time he has been in the Colony upwards of fourteen years, he has uniformly endeavoured so to conduct himself as to merit the approbation of those placed in authority over him. Your petitioner therefore most humbly prays Your Excellency, taking into consideration the number of years he has been in the Colony, and his having held a ticket of leave for six years of that time, will deem him deserving of being recommended for a Conditional Pardon.*

As James Evans was living at the time in Bathurst, his Petition was accompanied by a note from a Justice of the Peace at Bathurst Police Station dated 14 October 1835 which recommended the Petitioner be considered. A further note, dated 28 December 1835, confirmed that there was "nothing recorded" against the petitioner, but a final note dated 1 January 1836, stated "no sufficient claim to a Conditional Pardon appears to be established". James Evans had to wait until 1844 before his Conditional Pardon was issued.[38]

In a letter dated 15th May 1838, Richard Evans who resided at Sutton Forest applied for a Conditional Pardon, having held a ticket of leave since 24 March 1832 viz:

> *that petitioner came to this Colony by the ship 'Elizabeth' in the year 1820 having been convicted at Montgomery 18th March same year and sentenced to transportation for life; that petitioner has held the indulgence of a ticket of leave 6 years and 2 months, being over the time prescribed by the Government Regulations as a recommendation for further indulgence. Petitioner therefore submissively implores Your Excellency will take his unfortunate case into your favour.*[39]

Richard Evans had to wait until 1841 before receiving a Conditional Pardon. Joseph James, received his Conditional Pardon on 1 November 1838, and the official notification to this effect was made in the following terms:

> *Whereas His late Most Excellent King George the Third, by Commission under the Great Seal of Great Britain bearing the date the eighth day of November in the thirty first year of His Majesty's reign, was graciously pleased to give and grant full power and authority to the Governor (or, in the case of his death or absence, the Lieutenant Governor) for the time being of His Majesty's Territory of the Eastern Coast of New South Wales and the Islands there unto adjacent; by an Instrument or Instruments in writing under the Seal of the Government of the said Territory, or as he or they respectively should think fit and convenient for His Majesty's service, to remit either absolutely or conditionally the whole or any part of the term or time for which persons convicted of felony, misdemeanour, or other offences, amenable to the laws of Great Britain, should have been, or should thereafter be respectively conveyed or transported to New South Wales, or the Islands there unto adjacent. By virtue of such power and authority so vested as aforesaid', I Sir George Gipps Knight Captain-General and Governor-in-Chief of Her Majesty's said Territory of New South Wales and it's Dependencies, and Vice-Admiral of the same, taking into consideration the good conduct of Joseph James who arrived in the Colony in the ship 'Baring 2' Lamb master in the year one thousand eight hundred and nineteen under sentence of transportation for life and whose description is on the back hereof, do hereby conditionally remit the remainder of the term or time which is yet to come and unexpired of the original sentence or order of transportation passed on the aforesaid Joseph James at Montgomery General Sessions, on the thirteenth day of August one thousand eight hundred and eighteen, provided always, and on condition, that the said Joseph James continue to reside within the limits of this Government for and during the space of his original sentence or order of transportation. Otherwise the said Joseph James shall be subject to all the pains and penalties of re-appearing in Great Britain and Ireland, for and during the term of his original sentence or order of transportation; or, as if this remission had never been granted.*
>
> *Given under my Hand and the Seal of the Territory, at Government House, Sydney, in New South Wales, this first day of November in the year of Our Lord one thousand eight hundred and thirty eight.*

Accompanying the Pardon was the following description of Joseph James:

Name	Joseph James	Ship	Baring 2
Master	Lamb	Year	1819
Native Place	Llangadfan	Calling	Labourer
Offence	Not Known	Sentence	Life

Year of Birth	*1790*	*Height*	*5'9½"*
Complexion	*Dark Sallow*	*Hair*	*Dark Brown*
Eyes	*Hazel*	*Remarks*	*Nil*

and certified as follows:

> *I certify that Her Majesty's gracious approbation and allowance of the within Conditional Pardon, granted to Joseph James has been signified to me by the Right Honourable. The Secretary of State for the Colonies, in his despatch No. 101 dated 26 July 1839. Signed by Geo Gipps and given under my hand, at Government House, Sydney, this seventeenth day of December one thousand eight hundred and thirty-nine. Entered and signed by Deas Thomson, upon record at pages 253/254 Register No. 7 this first day of January one thousand eight hundred and forty.*[40]

Following receipt of a ticket of leave, the next important stage was to obtain a "Certificate of Freedom". This gave the prisoner greater freedom. On 15 July 1834, Hannah Fox (Dainty) was able to successfully apply for this remission, as the following details confirm:

Cert. No.	*34/924*	*Date*	*15 July 1834*
Prisoner No.	*27/2818*	*Ship*	*Louisa*
Name	*Hannah Fox alias Hannah the wife of John Dainty*		
Master	*Smith*	*Year*	*1827*
Native Place	*Somersetshire*	*Calling*	*Servant*
Offence	*Shop-lifting*	*Place of Trial*	*Montgomery*
Date of Trial	*12 July 1827*	*Year of Birth*	*1794*
Height	*5'2"*	*Complexion*	*Fair*
Hair	*Sandy to Grey*	*Eyes*	*Grey*
Remarks	*Cast inward in right eye.*		

Granted Ticket of Leave No. 30/202 dated 1 May 1830

Some clarification can be ascertained from the following table as to what remissions of sentencing the Montgomeryshire convicts were able to obtain from the authorities:

TYPE OF REMISSION OF SENTENCES RECEIVED IN AUSTRALIA

REMISSION	NSW	TAS	WA	PP	NI	TOTAL
Ticket of Leave	14	12	5			31
Certificate of Freedom	20	7				27
Conditional Pardon		6	3	1		10
Free by Servitude	3					3
Ticket of Leave and Certificate of Freedom	11	14				25
Ticket of Leave and Conditional Pardon	7	22	7		1	37
Ticket of Leave and Conditional Pardon and Certificate of Freedom		4				4
Conditional Pardon and Certificate of Freedom		3				3
Ticket of Leave and Free Pardon			18			18
Not Known	19	21	4	5	1	50
TOTAL	**74**	**89**	**37**	**6**	**2**	**208**

The lot of the convict could be relieved by pursuits which had no bearing upon their original sentence. In a letter dated 3 June 1833, the Rev. C. Dickinson, Archdeacon at Parramatta, wrote to Alexander McLeay, Esq., Colonial Secretary, about the vocal qualities that John Fletcher possessed:

> *There is a man named John Fletcher* [he had been sentenced in Montgomery-shire as John Flitches alias John Fletcher], *in the invalid or hospital gang at work near Brush Farm, who I have discovered has a good voice and was in England one of a church choir in Birmingham. I have spoken to the man and I find that he is willing to attend Divine Service as one of the singers at Kipling Point if permitted to do so. I asked Mr Percy Simpson's leave for the man to come on Sundays to the church, but as the distance is more than two miles from the overseer's station, he suggested the propriety of my applying to you. Will you therefore be good enough to grant Fletcher the indulgence wished for, or make, or direct me how to make application to the proper quarter. By 12 June 1833, approval had been given.*[41]

Whilst it is not possible to establish to what extent religion played a part in the lives of Montgomeryshire convicts, the following table identifies that the majority professed to a Christian faith:

RELIGION

DENOMINATION	NSW		TAS		WA	NI	PP	TOTAL	
	M	F	M	F	M	M	M	M	F
Protestant	36	6	37	8	26	2		101	14
Roman Catholic	1	1	4		10			15	1
Not Known	24	6	37	3	1		6	68	9
TOTAL	**61**	**13**	**78**	**11**	**37**	**2**	**6**	**184**	**24**

It must be accepted that a degree of criminal activity would continue in Australia. Some of the Montgomeryshire offenders would have been classified as 'habitual criminals', and, to refrain from this life style, would have been foreign to their normal routine. Given the opportunity, they would take advantage of the situation and act according to their instinct.

Jeremiah and Mary Buffy with Thomas Till, were indicted on a charge of highway robbery on 5 August 1820, by stealing a filly at Llandinam. Each was found guilty only of possessing stolen property and they were sentenced to 7 years trans-portation. Whilst serving his sentence at Newcastle, New South Wales, Jeremiah Buffy was assaulted by a native called 'Devil Devil', so named by his fellow natives because he had a cloven foot, but known as 'Bumblefoot' by the white population. Apparently Jeremiah Buffy was almost decapitated by the attack and it was generally accepted that the native was already accused for murdering a servant to a Mr Dickson of Windsor. The native, following his capture, was placed in Windsor gaol, but, when charged with murder of the servant, he was unable to understand the charge in English, no-one could understand him and as a consequence he was placed on remand. When he eventually was indicted for the attack on Jeremiah Buffy, although found guilty, Devil Devil was never sentenced.[42] By 1826 Jeremiah Buffy was issued with a ticket of leave by the Newcastle Bench, granted apparently in consideration for the attack that he sustained from the native. In a letter dated 12 April 1826, from F. Allman Esq., Commandant, Newcastle to Alexander McLeay Esq., Colonial Secretary, it is noted:

I have the honour to acknowledge the receipt of your letter dated 25th ult, enclosing a copy of the Attorney General's communication relative to Jeremiah Buffy, a prisoner of the Crown, at present in Government employ at this settlement, and requiring any information in my power relative to this man. In compliance with your request, I have the honour to state that Jeremiah Buffy, in company with a person named Joseph Wilkes (at present free), was employed by John Dunn late district constable at Wallia Plains, and in whose service Jeremiah Buffy then was to join search of several strayed cattle, partly belonging to private individuals and partly to the Government. As this transaction took place several months previous to my taking charge of the settlement, I beg to forward a correct copy of the deposition of Joseph Wilkes, as taken before by my predecessor Captain Gillman. In addition to what the testimony of Joseph Wilkes goes to prove as to the injury sustained by Jeremiah Buffy, I have to inform you that when he arrived here from Sydney, after appearing against the native who ill treated him, I personally examined his wounds, and tho' closed up, evidently appeared to me as bearing out the testimony of Joseph Wilkes, altho' a lapse of nine months took place from the time of infliction till I saw them, he being wounded on the 9th September 1824 and appeared before me on the 13th June . . . In consequence, I was induced to allow Jeremiah Buffy's wife (an elderly woman and a prisoner), to attend her husband as her sole government work and employ him in some manner suitable to his infirmities.

As a result he was issued with a ticket of leave.[43]

Whilst employed as a constable in Windsor New South Wales, Thomas Newton was involved in the capture of two criminals. In a letter from the Colonial Secretary's office to Windsor Bench of Magistrates dated 9 August 1822, it was noted:

I am directed by the Governor to request that steps may be immediately taken to levy the penalties incurred under existing Colonial Regulations by Phillip Tully and Patrick Pasting residents in your District, for having harboured and employed one Stephen Hefferon, a runaway from Thompson's road party, lately apprehended by Thomas Newton and William Green.[44]

By December 1822, Thomas Newton was involved in another instance of re-capturing criminals. A letter, dated 4 December 1822, from Windsor court house and subscribed by several Justices of the Peace, to Sir Thomas Brisbane records that they were:

agreeably to your Excellency's instructions we now have the honour to recommend to your Excellency's favourable consideration, the persons whose conduct appears to us to have been most intrepid in the apprehension of the gang of notorious runaways and pirates from Port Macquarie, of whom Thomas Till was executed and the remainder otherwise punished. Waiting the event of a trial of those felons at the Criminal Court, has delayed this Application to your Excellency which design would have been answered by rewards from the Judge Advocate had they been convicted by . . . robbery, so that had this application been previously made, the individuals now recommended might have been twice rewarded. The following persons having displayed the greatest activity and exertion in the aforementioned service, more especially the two former we do respectfully beg leave to recommend them for such rewards as your Excellency may be pleased to bestow on them, namely:

William Gray	–	*native youth aged 17 years.*
Thomas Walsh	–	*sentence 14 year; ticket of leave and town constable.*
Richard Woodbury	–	*free man and district constable of the lower/first branch.*
Thomas Newton	–	*prisoner for life and a town constable.*[45]

Between 14 April and 8 May 1823, Thomas Newton and Thomas Walsh, while executing their duties as constables at Windsor, were assaulted by Henry Fleming and James Davidson. As a result both offenders were found guilty and each required to pay a fine of £50 and bound to be of good behaviour for 2 years.[46] Following such a period of good relationship with authority, Thomas Newton fell by the wayside. On 19 July 1823, (in the name of Ellis), he was convicted by William Cox JP at Windsor for an unknown crime and sentenced to six months imprisonment. On 6 August 1823, he is recorded in General Orders to the effect that he be dismissed for drunkenness and rioting and that John Ruton 'Larkins', be appointed as constable in his place.[47] He was included in a list of prisoners transported on board the colonial cutter 'Sally' to Port Macquarie.[48]

Due to the obvious shortage of criminal and free women in the colony, cases of adultery were a common occurrence. One such case, which was not proven in fact, concerned Thomas Ellis (Newton). At a court of Magistrates held at Hyde Park Barracks, Sydney on 20 April 1831, an indictment was brought against Ellis and a William Myers, both serving life sentences and holding tickets of leave. The following evidence was put forward by John Wheelar attached to Grose Farm, who stated on oath that:

> I am employed at Grose Farm and generally work till three o'clock in the afternoon. Sometimes I stay there and at other times come to Sydney for the purpose of looking after my family. Yesterday (having had some suspicion that there existed an improper intimacy between the prisoner Thomas Ellis and my wife), I came to town to satisfy myself on that point. On entering my house I observed prisoners William Myers and Thomas Ellis (who had been employed by me before I lost my ticket of exemption), and . . . sitting in the room. Nothing took place at this moment. I remained in the house till near sundown when I went out for about half an hour, and on my return I went to the garden and getting over the fence, looked through the back door, when I saw my wife sitting beside prisoner Thomas Ellis, with her hand in his bosom. She then sent prisoner William Myers for a quart of water and clean towel to wash Ellis's face, and I saw her in the act of washing his face. Prisoner Myers asked my wife for a shilling which she refused him. After which he went upstairs with a candle to the room where he and Ellis usually slept. Presently he (Myers), returned and played with my child who was in the lower room, while prisoner Ellis and my wife went upstairs. On hearing which (as I could not see the stairs from the place where I stood), I ran to the other side of the house and with the assistance of a pole observed through an interval between the eaves and the wall, the prisoner Ellis in connection with my wife on the bed which was in the room. The parties were dressed but their clothes loosed. I then ran round to the other side and burst open the outer door, on which prisoner Myers opposed me with a blow which struck me down. I however succeeded in rushing past him and forced my way upstairs, where I saw prisoner Ellis still lying on the bed and my wife rising from it.

The case was adjourned for further evidence but on 2 April 1831 it was decided that the prisoners be dismissed and the case referred to the decision of the Governor. In consequence of this referral the following letter dated 22 April 1831 was sent to the Colonial Secretary:

We have the honour to transmit to you for the purpose of being laid before His Excellency the Governor, a copy of the proceedings of a case of adultery with which the prisoners named in the margin (Thomas Ellis 'Fanny' life and William Myers 'Surry' life), both holding tickets of leave, are charged by John Wheelar, a prisoner employed in the service of Government at Grose Farm, viz, the former with the actual offence, the latter with aiding and assisting, by offering personal violence to the complainant. From the situation in which the prisoners were placed with the sanction of the complainant, as well as from the want of corroborative proof (both stoutly denying the charge, and offering to produce through counsel, evidence to confute it), and from the strong encouragement given by the wife, who appears to be a woman of most abandoned character, we are induced to dismiss the case, at the same time submit to His Excellency's decision whether under all the circumstances prisoners Thomas Ellis and William Myers are proper subjects for the indulgence of tickets of leave, and request His Excellency's further instructions as to the propriety of instituting further proceedings in this case; also whether persons holding tickets of leave and liable to be brought before this court, are entitled to employ counsel.

A note dated 25 April 1831, confirmed that the tickets of leave of both men were remitted.[49]

The only known prisoner from Montgomeryshire, who met his death by hanging, was John Ashton. On 3 January 1835, he, with four accomplices (Thomas Kirkham, John Burke, Charles Nosworthy and William Weston), was indicted for stealing a quantity of superfine blue woollen cloth of the value of twenty pounds and divers other articles from the shop of James Hamilton at Ross and putting Mr James Hope in bodily fear at the time of the crime. It appeared that the five prisoners, together with a Mr James Rice, who turned King's Evidence, went two days prior to the offence taking place, to Mr Hamilton's house. On the night of the 24th they returned armed. Ashton had blackened both his own and accomplices' faces from a box of blacking. Dogs in the neighbourhood, having started barking, disturbed the family and, when a boy rushed out to see what had disturbed the dogs, the four men went in whilst Rice kept guard with a gun. They tied up Mr Hope and two boys, before proceeding to plunder the store of a considerable quantity of goods. As a result of the alarm being raised, a constable, named Peel, apprehended Rice near New Norfolk upon another charge; during his spell in custody, Rice confessed to the robbery and gave details as to the whereabouts of his fellow conspirators. Constable Peel with other constables, went to the house of Nosworthy and Weston, where they found all in bed together. Upon securing the arms of the prisoners, they took Ashton, Kirkham and Burke on the pretence that they were known runaways. They then returned to the house for Nosworthy and Weston, and by this means ensured violence was kept to a minimum. Following their trial the jury retired but returned within a few minutes with a verdict of guilty against all the prisoners. The judge after passing sentence of death upon each of them, told Ashton, Burke and Kirkham that he could hold out no hope of mercy towards them. On 13 February 1835, John Ashton and the others were executed at Hobart Town.[50]

Richard Lloyd,who had received a 7 year transportation sentence for committing a burglary in Montgomeryshire, led a charmed criminal life in New South Wales. On 1 March 1828, the occurrence book at Campbelltown notes that Richard Lloyd was a blacksmith/labourer, late of Bong Bong, now of Sutton Forest in the Colony of New South Wales. On 1 March 1828, at Bong Bong, he feloniously stole one cattle brand, one currier's knife, one other cattle brand and ten pounds of iron, belonging to a William Bowman.

At Campbelltown Quarter Sessions, he was, however, found not guilty.[51] A further offence, this time committed in Parramatta, resulted in him being charged with stealing a silver coin (pierced dollar) on 3 September 1828, from the person of Thomas Wall who was said to have been in a drunken sleep. One Richard Wright said he saw Lloyd take the coin out of Wall's hand.

The Parramatta Quarter Sessions found him not guilty.[52] It should be noted that in this second indictment, Lloyd was given in charge by William Bowman, the person from whom he was accused of stealing at the first offence. It is possible that Bowman, being grieved by the decision of the Court concerning his case, was in league with Thomas Wall and Richard Wright, in an attempt to ensure that Lloyd was found guilty on the second occasion. For the third time, he was indicted on 3 February 1834 at Parramatta Quarter Sessions, and found guilty of stealing £1.13.0 from John Robins with whom he was lodging. This time the court sentenced him to one year working in irons.[53] Within a short period of being discharged serving his sentence, Lloyd was indicted at Parramatta Quarter Sessions 11 May 1835 of committing three offences:

1. *Charged by John Hodges that on 2 April 1835 he stole property in his possession.*
2. *Charged by Prudence Brown that on 4 April 1835 he committed a felony.*
3. *Charged by Peter Westmacote that on 7 April 1835 he received stolen goods.*

With regard to the first offence John Hodges, shopkeeper of George Street, Parramatta, gave in evidence that:

> *On last Wednesday night he locked up the house and went to bed. On Thursday morning discovered a window in the shop had been forced open. He missed a pair of shoes, quarter chest of tea, six white shirts, one blue shirt, a piece of green gauze, a piece of white calico, six pairs of duck trousers, two beaver hats, two silver spoons, one pewter spoon, a ticket of leave belonging to Thomas Lynch, one pound coloured thread, two handkerchiefs, ¼lb spice and near 1 cwt of soap. He had been informed that part of the above property was offered for sale by the prisoner to Prudence Brown of Parramatta.*

For the second offence, Prudence Brown gave in evidence that:

> *On Thursday about noon, the prisoner came to her house and offered for sale two duck trousers, blue serge shirt etc. She told him that she had heard Hodges was robbed and suspected this was part of the property. The prisoner replied it was. She told him she had no money. He offered the swag for ten shillings on trust. She refused and he tied up the bundle and went away.*

Prudence Brown, for the third offence, stated that:

> *On Saturday 4th she came home from Bedford's public house in company with the prisoner about half past eleven. He stayed half an hour after which she locked up and went to bed. In the morning she found back window open and door not secured. Missing were a pocket knife, gold ring, silk handkerchief and various other property, about forty pounds worth.*

Samuel Horne, the assistant chief constable, stated that:

> *He had searched the prisoner's house last Tuesday and found, about two yards from*

the back door, a quart pot containing articles which since have been identified by Mrs Brown, as those stolen from her. He searched the prisoner's house last Sunday and found some canvas cut up which he believes to be part of a marquee stolen from Captain Westmacote about 5 or 6 weeks ago.

Captain Westmacote examined the canvas and declared it to be part of his marquee. On the second and third charges, Lloyd was found not guilty, but on the first, he was found guilty and sentenced to 10 years transportation at Norfolk Island.[54] His death took place on Norfolk Island, where he was buried 30 November 1836. The record shows him as being "an inoffensive and industrious man".[55]

It must be accepted that a number of convicts took advantage of any opportunity available to abscond from their captivity. In 1852 two instances arose concerning Montgomeryshire men. On 19 January 1852, the following notice was placed in a local newspaper: From the service of Mr Keach, Weobly near Campbelltown on the 11th instant. John Stokes per 'Pestongee Bomangee', tried at Montgomery Q.S. 3 July 1845, 10 years; collier, 5 feet 4, age 24, complexion sallow, hair dark brown, eyes hazel, native place Woolwich, sailor with sword and flag and woman J S on right arm below elbow, rabbit between fore-finger and thumb right hand 1845, mermaid with comb and glass J S below elbow left arm. Reward £2 or such lesser sum as may be determined upon by the convicting magistrate.[56] The outcome of this is unknown.

The second case took place on 19 July 1852, when the following notice was issued: From the service of Captain Dixon, River Isis on 19 instant. John Jones per 'Aboukir', tried at Newtown, Montgomery Q.S. 29 June 1848, 10 years; labourer, 5 feet 3, age 22, complexion swarthy, hair dark brown, eyes brown, native place Manchester, mole right side of nose. Reward £2, or such lesser sum as may be determined upon by the convicting magistrate.

John Jones did not evade recapture for long, was apprehended within a few days and sentenced to 14 days solitary confinement.[57]

At a Police Court in Hobart Town on 23 October 1862, Eliza Thomas (Lewis) who came from Montgomeryshire and John Benjamin Tracey were charged with larceny, having been accused of stealing £2.7.0 and a silk handkerchief belonging to William Miller. They elected to be tried by a jury.

William Miller gave in evidence that:

Tracey was a labourer, and lived now here; he had lately been in the service of Mr Bisdee and came to Hobart Town yesterday morning. About nine o'clock on the night of the same day he was passing Tracey's house in Liverpool Street, when he asked him to come in. The female prisoner was also standing at the door. Tracey, who kept a barber's shop, asked witness to treat them. Witness went to the shop in the morning and was shaved and had his hair cut. They went in the evening to Mr Weare's public house, had something to drink for which witness paid. They went back to Tracey's house and sent for some more drink. Witness had a pound note loose in his pocket and £2.7.0. wrapped up in some rag in the pocket of his jumper. Witness gave Tracey the pound note to get half a pint of rum and he fetched it. Witness asked him for the change and he refused to give it to him. He then drank some rum out of a cup, and immediately felt himself dizzy when he sat down and leaned his head on the table. He had the money in his jumper then, and while he was leaning on the table, he felt the woman's hand in his pocket where the money was. He told her to take her hand out of his pocket as there was nothing there belonging to her. Witness felt in his pocket and found the money was gone. There was no-one else in the house and the male prisoner kept talking all the time. There were only the shop and another room in the house, opening one into the other. There was a back entrance to the house but witness could not say whether the door was open, the shop was not closed. Witness was not drunk but stupid from the effects of the rum. When witness recovered he asked for his money, when they began to abuse him and then turned him out of the house. Witness also lost a handkerchief, and that now produced was the same, the female prisoner took it off his neck. The prisoners were strangers to the witness before he saw them in the morning. He did not change any money at Weare's. Detective Vickers deposed to the apprehension of the prisoners early in the morning at Tracey's house, corner of Harrington and Liverpool streets. He and the female lived together as man and wife. Witness searched Tracey and found in his trousers pocket £1.12.0. in silver and 9d in coppers; the handkerchief (produced), witness found in a jug on the shelf and the prosecutor owned it as his property. Witness then took the prisoners to the watch-house and the female searcher found upon the female prisoner 6½d in coppers.

Following this hearing they were both committed for trial and, on 30 October 1862, appeared at the Supreme Criminal Court. It was stated that:

The prosecutor, who had been in the services of Mr Bisdee of Acton Park, having received his wages, had come down to town to enjoy himself, and being accosted by the prisoner Tracey, who was standing at the door of his shop (a barber's), in Liverpool street, had proceeded firstly to treat him and a woman at the Vine Tavern, next to return to Tracey's place, where he was hocussed, and the money and neckchief taken from him. The prisoner, Tracey, in the course of the examination, appealed to the court that the Solicitor General might not be permitted to make his questions such leading ones. His Honour considered that perhaps they were a little open to that objection. Tracey then cross-examined the witness at length with some skill, with a view to elicit some discrepancies in his statements, and requesting the reading of his deposition at the police court. The witness made some variation as to the time, now stating it was a little after 5 p.m. when he went to the house, whereas his former deposition made it about 9 p.m.

Eliza Thomas also cross-examined to endeavour to prove that they were all drunk together.

The jury took just under two hours to reach a verdict of guilty against both prisoners, coupling it with a recommendation that they might be dealt with leniently. Following remand for sentence, they attended the court the following day, when Tracey emphasized the nature and discrepancies of the evidence and Thomas (Lewis) urged the Court to have mercy as she was in delicate health. The judge, in giving his judgement, declared that:

All these discrepancies appealed to by the male prisoner had been carefully placed before the jury, and therefore having had an impartial trial, the prisoners must abide by the decision arrived at. Tracey had been 20 years in the Colony, having been originally transported for manslaughter; the cause being drink that led him to that crime and drunkenness seemed to have continued it's in fluency. In 1847 he was convicted of stealing under £5; and from the time of arriving in this Colony till 1853, when freed by servitude, he was hardly ever out of punishment. The only favourable point was that since 1853, there was no record against him. The female prisoner was sent here in 1848 for the same offence of which now convicted. In 1855 she obtained her ticket of leave, and in 1857 became free, and drunkenness appeared also to be her besetting sin. The class of offence for which they were now charged, viz hocussing, was a very grave one indeed and the Judge was afraid it was only too prevalent here. The jury, however, gave a recommendation of mercy but without giving grounds; but he never disregarded (unless contrary to his sense of duty), such recommendations. They had rendered themselves liable to a very heavy penalty The female prisoner pleaded delicate health and what was the cause? why, drink! If appealed to on the score of health, why for her own sake the Judge might pass severer sentence, as she would thus be kept from drink.

They were both sentenced to 4 years penal servitude.[58]

Evidence supporting the emigration of a convict's family from Montgomeryshire is difficult to establish, and only one instance has been found. John Humphreys arrived on the 'Camden' in 1833, leaving at home his wife Mary (née Edwards) and nine children, John age 23 years, Mary aged 23 years, Ann aged 21 years, Humphrey aged 19 years, Elizabeth aged 17 years, Catherine aged 15 years, Edward aged 13 years, Richard aged 11 years, and Hannah aged 9 years. They lived at Llanfair Caereinion, Montgomeryshire. At the time of application for permission for his family to accompany him, Mary Humphreys was known as a respectable person to the families of William Watkin and Davy Ellis of the same place. A reference was supplied by G. Blaxland, J.P., John's employer.[59] Eleven years were to pass before some members of the family were united. The immigrant ship 'Sarah' arrived at Sydney 14 August 1851, having left Plymouth 19 April 1851. Amongst her passengers were Mary Humphrey, aged 58 years of Carno, Montgomeryshire and daughter of John and E. Rowland (probably Edwards), both now dead. She was a member of the Church of England, able to read, and her husband was John Humphreys living at the Hunter River. With her were Ann aged 32 years and a servant in Trefeglwys, Mary Ann aged 3 years, Richard aged 21 years, also of Trefeglwys, and Caroline aged 9 probably (Catherine).

There are some instances where death is both sudden and tragic.

> *On 21 May 1844 the case against William Henry was held at Clarence River. Henry was indicted for having on 19 May 1844, at the Clarence River, in New South Wales, maliciously stabbed and wounded, in the left side of the belly, one Joseph Perry (Parry), of which wound the said Joseph Perry, on the following day, died. A letter dated 21 May 1844 from Oliver Fry, Esq Commissioner of Convicts, Clarence River, to the Attorney General at Sydney, included not only the depositions from those giving evidence in the case but also a declaration made before him by the deceased ten minuted previous to his death.*

Patrick Donoughoe gave evidence as a witness that:

> *On the evening of Sunday 19 May, after I had my supper, I came down from Mr Hewitt's to Mr Sharp's in a boat with 6 or 7 other men. When I arrived at the wharf I heard a noise up at the public house. This was about 7 or 8 o'clock in the evening. I left the boat with the other men and came up to the public house. On hearing the noise I with the others went to the tap room where I saw the deceased Joseph Perry, the prisoner and a man named Larry. I did not notice if there was a candle lighted, there was a good fire. The prisoner was walking up and down the tap room apparently disposed to fight with someone. William Henry had been drinking but was neither drunk nor sober On my coming into the tap room the prisoner came towards the door in a manner inclined for fighting. I pushed the prisoner inside the tap room in order to keep him quiet. On putting him back into the tap room, I saw the prisoner open a knife and held it in his hand. The deceased Joseph Perry then came towards*

the prisoner and desired him to be quiet. The prisoner turned towards the deceased and said he would "let his bloody entrails out", and immediately stabbed Perry in the belly. Deceased then came towards me with his hand holding to his stomach and said, "Paddy, I am ruined." Deceased opened his trousers and shewed me the wound in his belly when I saw his entrails hanging out. I then went across to the public house to get assistance to secure the prisoner; and to assist the deceased. Craig came over. After the deceased had been attended to, I rushed upon the prisoner; who was sitting in the tap room, and with the assistance of a man named Lesile, I attempted to secure him, and while I was attending the deceased the prisoner attempted to escape. I yelled out to knock him down, and a man named Macdonald ran after him. I with others then secured the prisoner I only saw the prisoner make one stab at the deceased. I had no quarrel with the prisoner, only seeing the prisoner in a bouncing way. I pushed him into the tap room and Craig made no effort to secure the prisoner. To the best of my belief, the knife now produced, is the same with which the prisoner stabbed the deceased Joseph Perry. While they were securing the prisoner, I heard the prisoner say that if he had a chance he would put it (meaning the knife), into a dozen more.

The final sworn evidence came from Joseph Perry, just ten minutes before his death from the stab wound. He stated that:

Whilst at the Clarence Hotel, Clarence River on 20 May 1844, about seven or eight o'clock last night, William Henry was standing by the fireplace in Mr Sharp's tap room. I believe William Henry and some other man had a quarrel outside the door. William Henry rushed at me with a knife saying he would rip my guts out. Henry struck me in the stomach twice with the knife. The first time he cut me deeply. My guts came out of the wound. The second time he did not cut me so much. I ran away the second time he struck me. William Henry, the man now produced, is the man who stabbed me with a knife. I had no quarrel of any sort with the prisoner. He was not drunk. There were several men in the pub when I was wounded.[60]

After five minutes of deliberation, the jury returned a verdict of manslaughter. The judge then gave the sentence that he be transported beyond the seas for the term of his natural life.[61]

William Henry, who had arrived in New South Wales on the ship 'Royal Sovereign' on 19 January 1834, had been tried at Antrim, Ireland on 15 March 1833 and had been sentenced to 7 years transportation. Following his arrival in New South Wales two further offences were recorded against him. On 5 January 1841, he committed a burglary and was sentenced to spend two years in irons in a road gang, and, on 27 November 1841, a case of disobedience resulted in him receiving 50 lashes. His certificate of freedom was issued 17 March 1840.[62]

A coroner's inquest held on 8 February 1860 records the sudden death of Mary Ann Hogan (Aubrey) in the Wheatsheaf Public House, county of Buckingham, Tasmania. She died from drowning having fallen into a well on her property as a result of being under the influence of alcohol.[63]

A coroner's inquest recorded in 1857 the death of Isaac Walton through an unfortunate circumstance. They found that:

On 10 June 1857 at Longford, county of Westmorland, he had been driving on the highway, a dray drawn by eight bullocks laden with flour being at the time much under the influence of liquor, he accidently fell to the ground and the wheel of the dray ran over his body causing his instantaneous death.[64]

A similar fate beset John Price on 24 January 1849, when a coroner's inquest found that:

> *At the Duck Hole in the District of Richmond on 24 January 1849, he accidently died from a cart passing over his body.*[65]

The most distressing death which occurred to a transportee was that of Ann Glossop. Following her arrival in New South Wales on board the 'Pitt' 14 February 1792, she soon became acquainted with William Broughton, who had himself arrived with the First Fleet as servant to the surgeon John White. Following Broughton's appointment as storekeeper at Parramatta, he was transferred in 1800 to Norfolk Island, to carry out duties as acting deputy commissary. Accompanying him was Ann Glossop (also known as Elizabeth Heathorn) and, although there is no record of any marriage, they eventually had five children, namely Mary Ann (c.1793), Sarah (c.1799), William Henry (1802), Rebecca (1804) and Elizabeth Isabella, known as Betsy (1807).

By 1809 Broughton was apprehensive about the view that would be taken by Governor Macquarie who disapproved of illicit relationships. In order to alleviate any problem with his superiors, it is possible that arrangements were made for Ann and Betsy to visit their eldest daughter who had gone to England for schooling.[66] On 22 October 1809, the following notice was placed in a Sydney newspaper:

> *All persons having any claim on Ann Glossop, now about to depart the colony in the ship 'Boyd', Captain John Thompson, Commander are requested to present the same for payment immediately.*[67]

On 12 November 1809, the 'Boyd' sailed on its voyage to England and amongst the passengers were Ann and Betsy (by now 2 years of age). The ship, en route to the Cape of Good Hope, with a cargo of timber, sealskins, coal and oil, was required to call at Wangeroa, Bay of Islands, New Zealand for a further supply of cargo. Prior to leaving Sydney, the captain had taken on board a number of Maori natives with the intention that they supplemented the crew as far as New Zealand. One of their number was named Tara or Te Aara, a son of a chief. In view of his royal birthright, he refused to co-operate with the captain with regard to his carrying out menial tasks and, as a result, was tied to the mast and flogged. Upon arrival in the Bay of Islands, canoes approached the ship and a party of Maoris went on board. This party included the father and brother of Tara and, having discovered how ill treated he had been, they returned ashore. Some days later, the Maoris returned to the ship and invited the captain and members of the crew to accompany them to a place where an abundance of timber was available. Having landed on the shore, the ship's company was escorted deeper into the forest, and, suddenly, the crew were attacked, and killed. In their jubilation, the Maoris celebrated by holding a cannibal feast. The passengers and crew, remaining on board the ship, were unaware of this tragedy and, when a fleet of canoes appeared, welcomed the natives back on board. Immediately the natives attacked and overpowered the ship, killing the remaining crew and all the passengers with the exception of a Mrs Morley and her baby, a young boy named Thomas Davis and young Betsy Broughton, her mother Ann Glossop being amongst those massacred in January 1810.[68]

Epilogue

It is difficult to comprehend today what compulsory emigration meant to these unfortunate men and women. Whilst some originated from other urban and rural areas of England and Wales, there were those who came from humble backgrounds in small Montgomeryshire towns and hamlets.

Arrival in Australia saw them sent to numerous locations, where they were forced to play their part in vital work required to overcome virgin land in such places as Argyle, Bathurst, Berrima, Camden, Cassilis, Emu Plains, Liverpool, Maneroo, Mudgee, Newcastle, Parramatta, Pitt Water, Queanbeyan, Wollongong, Wellington Valley, and Nepean Valley in New South Wales. In Tasmania they reached such locations as Bridgewater, Cleveland, Campbelltown, Darlington on Maria Island, Green Ponds, Hamilton, Impression Bay, Oyster Cove, Pontville, Ross, Rocky Hills, Southport, Saltwater Creek, Wedge Bay. Western Australia saw them sent to Albany, Bunbury, Beverley, Champion Bay, Guilford, Murray, Newcastle, Sussex, Swan, Toodyay, Victoria Plains, Wellington, and York.

It is surely questionable if life in the formative years of a penal colony was more severe for these individuals, who, as a result of having committed various levels of crime, found themselves sent twelve thousand miles from their homes on a sea voyage as unwilling emigrants. They had left behind unemployment, poverty and the consequential severity of the poor laws, the inability to maintain a decent lifestyle for their families, and hardship encountered by the encroachment of common land by the Enclosure Acts. Those who left behind wives and children must have felt a degree of remorse as to the outcome their absence created for their family, which would be faced with the severe hardships permanent separation caused.

Many became resigned to their own plight in Australia, married once again, raising new families, who would become ancestors of present-day descendants. Some continued a life of crime, following completion of their original sentence, but the majority would seem to have accepted their fate and settled down to a better life than that left behind in their original homeland.

It is understandable that these unfortunate people may have had scant consideration that the judiciary would treat them with fairness and due accord for their personal circumstances, which gave them no alternative but to commit a criminal act, in the hope that they would avoid capture and conviction.

The following letter, printed in a Tasmanian newspaper (*Hobart Town Gazette and Southern Reporter*, 14 August 1819) may confirm the burden placed upon the legal profession when empowered to reach an appropriate sentence, that was to determine the fate of offenders who came before them during the transportation era.

> *A gentleman, on an excursion in Wales, being overtaken by a shower of rain, was induced to seek shelter in a large building, the door of which he perceived to be open. On entering, he found it was a court of justice, where the Assizes were then holding. Being much incommoded, after a time, by the increasing pressure of the crowd, he looked for a more convenient berth, and seeing a space before him which was thinly occupied, he stepped over a railing which separated it from the rest of the*

hall, if it might be so called, and took his place very comfortably. He had not been long there when he was addressed by one of those who were nearest to him, and the following curious dialogue ensued.

"Pray Sir, do you think that man guilty? I cannot tell, I did not hear the beginning of the trial. Never mind, you must find him guilty; we find them all guilty here; the Judge knows very well who ought to be hanged."

The gentleman found that he was in the Jury's box, and took the earliest opportunity of making his retreat as secretly as possible.

Perhaps this determination to find offenders guilty emanated from the necessity of the British Government to populate a new colony.

Convicts to New South Wales

BAILEY Thomas (c.1785–)
(M.P.R. 2423.2/8266, p. 465. S.J.R. 3201. R.908 X641).
Convicted at the Assizes 15 July 1837 of larceny by stealing spoons at Newtown. He had no previous convictions and was sentenced to 7 years transportation. He was moved from Montgomery Gaol to the hulk ship, 'Gannymede', from where he was transported on the 'Lord Lyndock', which departed Portsmouth 4 April 1838 and arrived New South Wales 8 August 1838. He was 53 years of age, height 5'8¾", with brown mixed with grey hair and grey eyes. His complexion was dark and sallow. He was married, a whitesmith by trade, native of Staffordshire and a Protestant. He had lost two front upper teeth, scar outside his left eye, diagonal scar on inner corner of his left eyebrow, similar scars on centre of upper lip, another on left side of under lip, a horizontal scar on his chin, a blue mark on back of his right wrist, 2 scars on his left shin, a similar scar on his right shin and the letters 'TB' on the back of his lower left arm. He was unable to read or write. (44/1533). He received his ticket of leave No. 42/2405, from Bathurst Bench in October 1842 (R.945.4/4167), followed by his certificate of freedom No. 44/1533, 17 October 1844 (R.1018.4/4394).

BARRETT Richard (c.1800-8.12.1856)
(M.P.R. 2425. 2/8271, p. 373. S.J.R. 3206. R.906.4/4015).
Convicted at the Great Sessions 15 August 1829 of larceny by stealing 4 sheets, 2 silk handkerchiefs, 2 cotton handkerchiefs, 2 jackets and several other pieces of wearing apparel from Forden 4 July and one pig value £2 from George Barnett also of Forden on 6 June (*Salopian Journal*, August 1829). He had no previous convictions and was sentenced to 14 years transportation (Q/SR 1829). He was transported on the 'Nithsdale', leaving Sheerness 1 January 1830, arriving New South Wales 12 May 1830. He was 30 years of age, height 5'7½", with dark brown hair and hazel eyes. His complexion was dark and ruddy. He was a widower with one child, unable to read or write and a ploughman (including milking and reaping) by trade. He was a Catholic. He is mentioned in the 1837 Muster, employed by Mr McArthur of Camden. He received his ticket of leave No. 42/2273, from Camden Bench on 28 September 1842 (R.945.4/4196). He died 8 December 1856 at Camden Park (56/01961). The informant of his death was James McArthur, Esq. There is no indication that his child followed him to Australia.

BENNETT Ann (c.1815-1866)
(M.P.R. 2421. 2/8257, p. 295. S.J.R. 3194. R.908. X639).
Convicted at the Quarter Sessions 26 February 1836 of larceny by obtaining property under false pretences in Llanllwchaiarn, Newtown, and was sentenced to 14 years transportation. This included a misdemeanour conviction at the same court, but the Judge was of the opinion that the aforementioned sentence was

sufficient on both counts. This followed a previous conviction when she received 3 months imprisonment (Q/SR 1836). She was transported on the 'Elizabeth', leaving London 26 June 1836, arriving New South Wales 12 October 1836. She was 21 years of age, height 5'1", with sandy hair and hazel eyes. She had large features, stoutly built and was of ruddy and freckled complexion. She was single, able to read and write, a dairymaid and a Protestant (Baptist) (43/2446.51/67). The 1837 Muster indicates that she was at the Factory, Port Macquarie. In 1841 she married Jesse Millard, aged 34 years. (He had been transported on the 'Isabella', following a life sentence). He was of the same parish as Ann and the ceremony took place 24 April 1841, with permission from the Governor, obtained 15 March 1841. The marriage was by banns and the officiating clergyman was the Rev. John Cross, the witnesses being Thomas Mars and Frances Tomlin (Reg. No. 651, Vol. 25 and duplicate entry Reg. No. 147. Vol. 44). Ann received her certificate of freedom No. 51/57 13 May 1851 (R.1027.4/4415). A child, Mary Ann, was born of parents Jesse and Ann Millard in 1861 (Reg. No. 13612). Ann Millard apparently died in 1866 (Reg. No. 06872), showing her parents as William R. and Elizabeth Bennett. Her husband died (Reg. No. 08095) 4 April 1874 at Ulladullah and left a will (Reg. No. 1389/2 and 9611/3).

BENNETT John (c.1819–)
(M.P.R. 2424.2/8268, p. l. S.J.R. 3202. R.2662. X642A).
Convicted at the Quarter Sessions 4 July 1839 of burglary by breaking and entering the house of John Pugh, Glyngynwydd, Llangurig, and stealing two £5 notes, 4 gold sovereigns, 1 crown, two half-crowns and 10 sixpences. In addition he took a watch and other articles (NLW B1/17. S.C. 12 July 1839 and S.R.O. S.J. 5 July 1839). He was sentenced to 10 years transportation. He had a previous minor conviction for which he had been sentenced to 13 days imprisonment. He was transported on the 'Maitland' departing Sheerness 22 March 1840 and arriving New South Wales 14 July 1840. He was 21 years of age, height 5'5¼", with brown hair and dark grey eyes. His complexion was ruddy and slightly pock-pitted. He had the mark of a burn and 2 small moles under his right jaw, a scar on the right thumb, a scar on the heel of his left hand, the letters JB, a fish, a heart pierced with 2 fish and a scar on the inside of his lower left arm. He was single, a farm labourer, unable to read or write and a Protestant. He received his certificate of freedom No. 54/97 dated 12 December 1854 (R.1027.4/4416).

BLAKEMORE Mary (c.1798–)
(M.P.R. 2424. 2/8267, p. 343. S.J. R.3201. COD 147).
Convicted at the Quarter Sessions 13 July 1818 of a felony, she was sentenced to 7 years transportation (QS/R 1818). She was transported on the 'Lord Wellington', departed England and Ireland 10 July 1819, and arrived New South Wales 20 January 1820. She was 22 years of age, height 5'2", with sandy hair, hazel eyes with ruddy complexion and was a farm servant. She received a certificate of freedom No. 20/4124, dated August 1825 (R.602.4/4424).

BLISS Richard (c.1806–)
(M.P.R. 2420. 2/8256, p. 79. S.J.R. 3193. R.908. X641).
Convicted at the Quarter Sessions 23 February 1837 of stealing pigs and was sentenced to 7 years transportation. This followed a previous conviction for stealing pigs in 1833 when a true bill was found dated 2 September 1833 for which he received 12 months imprisonment (Q/SR 1837). He was moved from

Montgomery Gaol to the hulk 'Justitia' at London and transported on the 'Earl Grey', leaving Portsmouth 8 August 1838, arriving New South Wales 2 November 1838. He was 32 years of age, height 5'7¾", with dark brown hair and dark eyes. His complexion was dark and pock-pitted. His eyebrows partially met, he had a scar on the left cheekbone, scrofula marks under the chin, a scar on the back of his neck and a small dark mole on his lower left arm (44/647). He was married with children, 3 male and 1 female. Unable to read or write, he was a Protestant, and a farm labourer/groom. He received his ticket of leave No. 43/499 dated 4 March 1843, issued by Braidwood Bench (R.948.4/4174) and his certificate of freedom 44/647 dated 23 April 1844 (R.1017.4/4391).

BLOCKLEY Thomas (c.1802–)
(M.P.R. 1427. 2/8276, p. 253. S.J.R. 3209. R.2662.4/4009A).
Convicted at the Great Sessions 23 March 1824 of burglary (Q/SR 1824) and sentenced to death, commuted to 7 years transportation. Following a period in Montgomery Gaol, he was transferred to the hulk 'Justitia' at London. He was transported on the 'Royal Charlotte' leaving Portsmouth 5 January 1825, arriving New South Wales 29 April 1825. He was 23 years of age, height 5'4", with brown hair, blue eyes, and his complexion was brown. He was a native of Whitehaven and a ploughman by trade. He had a dimple on the chin, a scar on the ball of his left thumb, and his left arm was crooked following it being broken. Soon after his arrival, he received 72 lashes for insubordination, and the 1828 Muster shows that he was at Moreton Bay (Queensland), having been re-transported for 7 years by the Criminal Court, Sydney, 13 July 1826, for robbery. He was issued with his certificate of freedom No. 33/1095 dated 2 October 1833 (R.991.4/4318).

BREEZE John (c.1795–)
(M.P.R. 2427. 2/8277. S.J.R. 3209. COD 142. R.393.4/4005).
Convicted at the Quarter Sessions 11 January 1816 of a felony, by stealing one handkerchief from Richard Pugh of Llanidloes (Q/SR 816). He was sentenced to 7 years transportation. He was transported on the 'Shipley' leaving England 18 December 1816 arriving New South Wales 24 April 1817. He was 22 years of age, height 5'7¼", with light brown hair and hazel eyes. He was single and a labourer/flannel weaver by trade. It is recorded that he obtained his certificate of freedom during the week of 23 January 1823 (R.6039.4/424, p. 131).

BUFFY Jeremiah (c.1791– 5.9.1836 buried)
(M.P.R. 2420. 2/8256, p. 143. COD 140. R.393.4/400).
Convicted at the Great Sessions 1 August 1812 of stealing a brown filly from Thomas Kinsey of Llandinam, and was sentenced to death, commuted to 14 years transportation (Q/SR 1812). He was transported on the 'Earl Spencer' leaving England 2 June 1813 arriving New South Wales 9 October 1813. He was 22 years of age, height 5'5¼", with light brown hair and dark ruddy complexion. He had a large scar on the back of his neck. He was single and a native of Staffordshire. There are no surviving assignment records available. In 1817, he was granted permission to marry Mary Thorp at St John's, Parramatta (R.6005.4/3496, pp. 25-26), the service being conducted by the Rev. Samuel Marsden (Reg. No. 2036, Vol. 3). On 21 January 1818, Jeremiah Buffy was brought to trial, adjourned to 1 February 1818, for a felony, and sentenced to death. On account of some favourable circumstances in mitigation of his offence, he was granted a pardon on the sole and express condition that he remain in New South Wales, as a convict,

for the term of his natural life, and be kept at hard labour (Commutation Warrant R.6070. 4/7020. No. 46). By 13 March 1818, he is shown on the list of convicts to be sent to Newcastle, per the 'Lady Nelson' (R.6006.4/3498, pp. 86-87). His wife applied 13 May 1818, to be granted permission to proceed to Newcastle to re-join her husband (R.6006.4/3498, p. 217). His ticket of leave was altered for the Camden District 9 July 1827, and to the Argyle District 17 November 1828 but this was torn up when he received his certificate of freedom No. 34/1407, dated 20 October 1834. The 1828 Census shows him to be a stock-keeper to a William Scott of Camden District, that he was still married and a Protestant. The death of Jeremiah Buffy is recorded in the Parish of Wollongong, on the farm of a Mr Johnson at Illawarra (Reg. No. 875, Vol. 20). He was buried 5 September 1836, the officiating minister being F. Wilkinson. He left no will, and his wife, Mary, re-married in 1838, the banns application being as follows:

> NORRIS Thomas age 36 'Lord Sidmouth' 1819. T.L. 33/444.
> BUFFY Mary age 50 'Indispendable'? Bond. Widow.

CADMAN Richard (c.1751-9 Apl 1811)
(M.P.R. 2422.2/8261, p. 123. COD 138. R.392. Fiche 631, p. 129).
Convicted at the Great Sessions September 1800 of larceny by stealing flannel, hempen bags and sheep skins from a John Edwards and others. He was sentenced to death, commuted to life transportation. Following a stay at Montgomery Gaol, he was transferred to the hulk 'Captivity', and was transported on the 'Glatton', leaving England 23 September 1802, arriving New South Wales 11 March 1803. The 1806 Muster shows him as a stockman working at Government House and he is mentioned again in the 1811 Muster. He was buried on 9 April 1811, age 60 years (Reg. No. 201, Vol. 5).

CORBETT James (c.1817-11.11.1840)
(M.P.R. 2428. 2/8282, p. 331. S.J.R. 3213. R.2662. X642).
Convicted at the Assizes 14 July 1838 of horse stealing from a farm in Kerry (*Shropshire Journal* 18.7.38). He was sentenced to 10 years transportation, this following no previous convictions. He was transported on the 'Woodbridge' leaving London 16 October 1839, arriving New South Wales 26 February 1840. He was 22 years of age, height 5'11¼", with dark brown hair, brown eyes, and dark, ruddy and pock-pitted complexion. He had a mole on the left cheek and 3 moles in a cluster under the right jaw, the letters 'JC' inside the lower right arm and a scar inside the forefinger of the right hand. There were the letters 'JJ' inside the lower left arm. He was single, able to read and write imperfectly, a top sawyer and carpenter by trade, and a Protestant. He died 11 November 1840 at the Sydney Hospital.

DAVIES Benjamin (c.1797–)
(M.P.R. 2419. 2/8250, p. 49. S.J.R. 3191. R.905.4/4017).
Convicted at the Assizes 10 March 1832 of horse stealing (pony), and was sentenced to death, commuted to life transportation. This followed no previous convictions (Q/SR 1832). He was transported on the 'Camden', leaving Sheerness 22 September 1832 arriving New South Wales 18 February 1833. He was 36 years of age, height 5'10½", with hazel eyes, dark ruddy complexion and dark brown hair, almost bald. He had a scar inside the top of his left forefinger, a scar on the back of his left wrist, and his chest was hairy. He was married with 4 children and a native of Llanwnog, able to read only and a Protestant. He is mentioned in the

1837 Muster as assigned to a Thomas Walker, Sydney, and in 1841 he received his ticket of leave No. 41/1428, dated 18 July 1841, from the Pitt Water Bench, (R.940.4/4152). His conditional pardon No. 48/133 was issued 31 December 1847 (R.785.4/4454).

DAVIES David (c.1779–)
(M.P.R. 2420. 2/8254, p. 233. S.J.R. 3192).
Convicted at the Quarter Sessions 15 January 1824 of larceny, stealing clothes from a servant of Rev. R. Mytton, Garth, Guilsfield (*Shropshire Journal*, 28 January 1824). He was sentenced to 7 years transportation. He was transported on the 'Countess of Harcourt' leaving Downs 23 March 1824, arriving New South Wales 12 July 1824. He was 45 years of age, height 5'4", with dark brown hair, light blue eyes and brown complexion. He had a mole on the left cheek and had some teeth missing from the lower jaw. He was single, native of Carnarvonshire, tinman by trade and a Protestant. On the 1825 Muster he is shown on Government work at Wellington Valley and the 1828 Census shows him still as a Government servant. He received his certificate of freedom No. 31/23 dated 15 January 1831.

DAVIES David (c.1799-16.6.45)
(M.P.R. 2427.2/8278, p. 219. S.J.R. 3210).
Convicted at the Great Sessions 25 March 1826 of larceny, stealing a shawl and other items of clothes, and was sentenced to death, commuted to life transportation. He had no previous convictions. He was transported on the 'Speke', leaving Sheerness 8 August 1826, arriving New South Wales 26 November 1826. He was 27 years of age, height 5'6¼", with brown hair and dark brown eyes. He had a ruddy complexion and a large hairy mole on the lower left arm (R.397. 4/4011 with copy at fiche 662, p. 129). He was single, able to read only, a farm labourer and a Protestant. He is included in the 1828 Census as assigned to Archibald Bell, St Helier's, Segenhoe. His ticket of leave No. 36/242 was granted 7 March 1836, issued by the Invermerin Bench (R.965.4/4101). There is a notation "Cancelled for Larceny per Col Sec Letter 38/728", dated 14 August 1838. His ticket was restored No. 42/1344 dated 11 May 1842. On the 1837 Muster, he is shown to be at Invermerin. His death is recorded 16 June 1845, at Liverpool Hospital. He was buried 18 June 1845 at St Luke's, Liverpool. The officiating minister was a J. Duffus.

DAVIES George (c.1811–)
(M.P.R. 2423. 2/8266, p. 407. R.906.4/4018).
Convicted at the Quarter Sessions 3 January 1833 of larceny, stealing 2 watches, to the value of 20 shillings and 10 shillings respectively, "with force and arms, the goods and chattels", of a John Beavan. The offence took place at Llanidloes. He was sentenced to 7 years transportation, and, after a period in the hulk 'Justitia', he was transported on the 'Lord Lyndock', leaving Sheerness 4 June 1833, arriving New South Wales 18 October 1833. He was 22 years of age, height 5'4", with dark brown hair and brown eyes. His complexion was brown and he had a scar between the forefinger and thumb of the left hand. He was single, able to read and write, and a Protestant. He was a native of London and a carpenter and joiner, being shown as a first rate workman. He was granted his ticket of leave No. 37/1781 dated August 1837 (R.928.4/4115), and he was allowed to remain in the Penrith District on recommendation of that Bench. In the 1837 Muster he is shown in the employ of a H. Shadforth, Penrith. By 1838, he was applying to marry a Mary

Richardson, the banns reading (R.734.4/2390) "DAVIES George 27. Bachelor. 'Lord Lyndoch' 1833, 7 year TL.37/1781, present service in Penrith District and RICHARDSON Mary, 27, single 'Layton' 1834. Came Free. Present Service Sydney." The wedding was due to take place 20 August 1838 when the officiating minister would have been the Rev. John McGarvie, St Andrew's Scottish Church, Sydney. Although the marriage was allowed, it did not take place. By 1840, George Davies had applied to marry Sarah Robinson (R.737.4/2481), the ceremony taking place 11 May 1840. They remained in the Windsor District until at least 1847, followed by a move about 1867 to Burwood Suburb, Sydney. In all, they had 9 children, namely:

Maria Ann. 14. 6.1841-28.12.1869 (1841/1114, Vol. 25)
George Henry. 21.8.1843-3.7.1914 (1843/919, Vol. 54)
Reuben. 17.12.1845-12.1907 (1846/1138, Vol. 31)
Thomas. 1848-(1848/1843, Vol. 34)
John. 1853-1855 (1853/803, Vol. 71)
Sarah. 1856-14.9.1926. (No entry noted)
Joseph. 18.11.1860-(1861/26.)
Emeline L. 1863-(1863/8849, Vol. 121)
Edmund R. 1867–

All the children were registered under the name Davis, the surname Davies apparently having been changed sometime previous. Following the birth of his son, George Davies (Davis) disappeared with no further trace.

EDWARDS John (c.1809–)
(M.P.R. 2417. 2/8240, p. 251. S.J.R. 3187. R.398.4/4014).
Convicted at the Quarter Sessions 16 October 1828 of larceny, stealing 1lb tea, and several knives and forks. He was sentenced to 7 years transportation (Q/SR 1828) and transported on the 'America', leaving Woolwich 8 April 1829, arriving New South Wales 18 August 1829. He was 20 years of age, height 5'1", with brown hair and blue eyes. His complexion was ruddy and he had a small scar on the right cheek and a scar on top of left knee (C37/67). He was single, able to read and write, flannel weaver by trade and a Protestant. He received his certificate of freedom No. 37/67 dated 2 February 1837 (R.998.4/4337). By this time the following additional marks were recorded about his body, namely, his nose inclined on left side, scar inside top of 2nd finger, hump on right shoulder and left breast protruding. On the 1837 Muster, he is recorded working with Messrs Close and Co, Maneroo. On 9 July 1842, he was sentenced to 12 months in the Iron Gang for larceny, and again, 12 June 1845, he was sentenced by Sydney Quarter Sessions to 12 months in the Iron Gang for larceny.

EDWARDS Thomas (c.1793–)
(S.J.R. 3196. COD 148, copy of R.395.4/4007).
Convicted at the Great Sessions 14 August 1819 of larceny, stealing 3 parts of a peck of wheat, the property of a Thomas Smith, Hurdley. He was sentenced to death, commuted to 14 years transportation (Q/SR 1818). He was transported on the 'Shipley', leaving Portsmouth 14 May 1820, arriving New South Wales 26 September 1820. He was 26 years of age, height 5'5¼", with black hair and hazel eyes. His complexion was sickly and he was a labourer. On the 1822 Muster he was a general servant, working for a Thomas Gibbet of Windsor. By 14 April

1824 he was due to be transported to Port Macquarie on the 'Sally', having been sentenced to 3 years by the Windsor Bench 13 March 1824 (no crime noted). His occupation was a ploughman. However, by 30 October 1824, he was received at Sydney Gaol from Newcastle, and it was necessary to issue him with a suit of slop clothing. (Apparently there were 33 convicts present in a state bordering on nudity (R.6019.4/3864, pp. 121 and 472-3). He must have been sent to Newcastle to await his transfer on the 'Sally' to Port Macquarie. Between 30 October and 10 December 1824 he must have reached Port Macquarie because, by the latter date, he had run away from Port Macquarie. Having been caught, he was re-sentenced to be transported to Macquarie Harbour(VDL) (R.6023.4/6671, p. 103). However, by 11 January 1825 he is listed amongst the "Runaways" from Port Macquarie to be sent to Newcastle on the 'Sally' (R.6014.4/3513, p. 229). 38 runaways from Port Macquarie were sent to Newcastle, to be kept at hard labour in double irons at that settlement. It is probable that following his sentence to Macquarie Harbour, he again ran away as no one would willingly want to be sent to that infamous place. On his being captured for the second time, the decision must have been taken to send him to Newcastle instead. On the 1828 Census, he was employed in the 'Iron Cove' gang. He received his certificate of freedom No. 33/995 dated 30 August 1833 (R.991.4/4318).

ELLIS Joseph (c.1803-30.6.1820)

(M.P.R. 2427. 2/8277, p. 243. S.J.R. 3209).
Convicted at the Quarter Sessions 23 October 1818 of larceny, stealing fowls from an Oliver Thomas of Llandrinio. He was sentenced to 7 years transportation (Q/SR 1818). He was transported on the 'Shipley', leaving Portsmouth 15 May 1820, arriving New South Wales 26 September 1820. During the voyage, he was admitted to the hospital 27 June 1820, suffering from pain in the epigastric region, constant inclination to vomit, pulse 120 per minute and fainting twice during the night. His condition continued in this manner, his vomit being like coffee grains, and he developed red patches on his skin. His death is recorded at 10 p.m. 30 June 1820, aged 17 years (Ship's Surgeon, Henry Rye).

EVANS Ann (otherwise Nancy Waters) (c 1768–)

(M.P.R. 1419. 2/8259, p. 65. COD 139, copy of R.392, fiche 615).
Convicted at the Quarter Sessions 11 January 1810 of larceny, receiving sugar, knowing it to be stolen, from a Jane Lloyd of Meifod. She was sentenced to 7 years transportation (Q/SR 1810). She was transported on the 'Friends', leaving England, date unknown, and arriving New South Wales 10 October 1811. In the 1814 Muster she is shown as a servant to a Mrs King at Parramatta. She had married Locklan Monican (Monaghan) 30 May 1814 at St John's, Parramatta, (there were no children of this marriage). She received her certificate of freedom No. 54/2943 dated 18 November 1824 (R.601.4/4423). It is recorded that she was 4'11¼" in height, with grey hair, black eyes and sallow complexion. On the 1825 Muster, they are residing in Liverpool. The 1828 Muster confirms that Ann was a Catholic, aged 60 years, and that, with her husband Lawrence, they were land-owners at Cabramatta, owning 80 acres with wheat and 30 cattle. (Her husband had been transported from Ireland on the 'Tellicherry' in 1806.)

EVANS Charles (c.1755-23.1.1811)

(M.P.R. 2426. 2/8273, p. 229. R.392.4.4003, copy at COD 9).
Convicted at the Great Sessions 22 March 1790 of larceny, stealing a brass pan

from a John Bore (*Shrewsbury Chronicle*, 9 April 1790 and *Wales* 4/194/4). He was sentenced to 7 years transportation. He was transported on the 'Pitt', leaving Yarmouth Roads 17 July 1791, arriving New South Wales 14 February 1792. He married a Mary Browne 24 July 1796 at St Phillip's, Sydney, the clergyman being a Richard Johnson. (His wife, also a convict, had arrived, via the 'Indispensable', in 1796). On the 1806 Muster he is shown as free by servitude and self-employed as a sawyer. He was buried 23 January 1811 at Sydney, aged 56 years. His wife does not appear on any later Musters and it must be assumed that she re-married.

EVANS Edward (c.1763-9th Sep 1790)
(COD 9.4/4003, copy at R.392. Fiche 615, p. 192).
Convicted at the Great Sessions March 1788 of sheep stealing by stealing 3 sheep from Thomas Jones and Edward Ashton of Llanidloes and sentenced to death, commuted to 14 years transportation (*Wales* 4/193/8). He was transported on the 'Surprise', leaving Portsmouth 19 January 1790, arriving New South Wales 28 June 1790. Aged 27 years, he was possibly buried at Rosehill, 9 September 1790.

EVANS James (c.1792-1859)
(M.P.R. 2421.2/8257, p. 233. S.J.E. 3194.
COD 148.4/4007, copy at R.395, fiche 645, p. 282).
Convicted at the Great Sessions 18 March 1820 of a felony by stealing 2 mares from Berriew (*Shrewsbury Journal*, 29 March 1820 and Q/SR 1820). The offence was committed with Richard Evans and it can be assumed that they were related. He was sentenced to death, commuted to life transportation. He was transported on the 'Elizabeth', leaving Downs 18 August 1820 arriving New South Wales 31 December 1820. He was 28 years of age, height 5'9¾", with black hair and hazel eyes. He was single, of ruddy complexion, a farm labourer, and a Protestant. On arrival, he was assigned to a William Redfern of Parramatta, but, by the 1822 Muster, he was a government servant assigned to a T. Wells, Liverpool. The 1828 Muster shows him as a labourer with a Mr J. N. Grant, Bathurst. On 16 July 1829, he received his ticket of leave No. 29/454, issued by the Bathurst Bench (R.912.4/4071). On the certificate was written "Permitted to travel between Bathurst and Sydney, but not to remain in Sydney, per Colonial Secretary letter No. 32/361 dated 25 April 1832". Across this ticket of leave is also written "Cancelled for seducing and cohabiting with the wife (illegible) per Colonial Secretary letter No. 452 dated 11th October 1836". His ticket of leave was renewed No. 37/1313 dated 26 September 1837 and it was stated by a Mr D. Davis that James Evans had taken away the wife of a Dennis Begley of Eastern Creek, Prospect, about 7 March 1836. He received a conditional pardon No. 474 in 1844 (Recommendations for Conditional Pardons, fiche 829), the recommendation being signed by C. Woodward, F. Sinclair and N. H. Sutton, J.P. It is possible that he died in 1859 (No. 04677), aged 68 years, at Penrith.

EVANS Richard (c.1777–)
(M.P.R. 2421.2/8257, p. 233. S.J.R. 3194).
Convicted at the Great Sessions 18 March 1820 of a felony (with his possible brother James Evans), by stealing 2 mares from Berriew (*Shrewsbury Journal*, 29 March 1820 and Q/SR 1820). He was sentenced to death, commuted to life transportation. As with his relative, he was transported on the 'Elizabeth', leaving Downs 18 August 1820, arriving New South Wales 31 December 1820. He was 43 years of age, height 5'7¾", with brown hair and hazel eyes. He had a ruddy

complexion, was single and a farm labourer. He was a Protestant. On arrival he was assigned to J. T. Campbell of Parramatta (R.1031.4/3503). The 1828 Census states that he was a general servant with John Burrows, a Constable of Lower Minto. He received his ticket of leave No. 32/141 dated 24 March 1832, issued by the Liverpool Bench, but this was altered to Sutton Forest, per Colonial Secretary letter No. 36/225 dated 7 May 1836, still within the Minto area (R.916.4/4082). On 5 July 1841, he received his conditional pardon No. 42/159.

EVANS Rowland (c.1814-22.2.1881)
(M.P.R. 2423. 2/8264, p. 209. S.J.R. 3198. R.908. X640).
Convicted at the Quarter Sessions 23 February 1837 of larceny, stealing 66lb lead from a John Edwards, Esq., of Machynlleth. He was sentenced to 14 years transportation, this following a previous offence for which he had served 6 months' imprisonment (Q/SR 1837). He was transported on the 'James Pattison', leaving Sheerness 16 July 1837, arriving New South Wales 25 October 1837. He was 23 years of age, height 5'0¼", with brown hair and dark hazel eyes. His complexion was dark and sallow, with a diagonal scar on the right side of his upper lip. He was single, able to read and write imperfectly, a labourer and a Protestant (Wesleyan). On the 1837 Muster he is shown in the employment of a David Archer of Berrima. He received his ticket of leave No. 44/902 dated 15 March 1844 by the Hartley Bench for the Mudgee District (R.953.4/4189). In 1859 he married Elizabeth Leonard in Rylestone (1859/2885) and the following children were born – Lewis (1860/12040); Robert (1862/13366), male child (1865/14909) and Margaret (1868/16165). His daughter's death is recorded having taken place in 1876 (1876/07854). In all they had 9 children; the remaining 5 children either died within 24 hours or escaped registration. Rowland Evans died 22 February 1881, being a shepherd at Pipe Clay Creek, Mudgee. Cause of death being registered as 'Coup de Soleul' (sunstroke). At the time of his death he was under the care of Doctor F. L. Newton who last attended 19 February. The death was certified by his son Lewis (Louis), of the same location, and burial took place in a cemetery at Mudgee.

FLITCHES John, (c.1793–)
(M.P.R. 2421. 2/8257, p. 63. S.L.R. 3194. COD 147.4/4007, copy of R.395. Fiche 643, p. 45).
Convicted at the Great Sessions 25 March 1819 of uttering a forged banknote. He was sentenced to 14 years transportation. He was transported on the 'Eliza', leaving England 15/16 October 1819, arriving New South Wales 21 January 1820. He was 27 years of age, height 5'8", with flaxen hair, blue eyes and florid complexion. He was single, a master/farm labourer by trade, had lost 2 teeth and bore a scar on his breast. He was a native of Warwickshire and a Protestant (31/745. 33/335). On 13 October 1824 he is included, but giving the name Jacob Fletcher, on a list of convicts discharged from the Emu Plains Establishment. The 1825 Muster shows him to be on board a hulk at Sydney, having probably committed an unknown offence. By the 1828 Census, he is a Government Servant at Rooty Hill Establishment, Melville, Nepean Valley. He received his ticket of leave No. 31/745 dated 29 September 1831, issued by the Goulburn Bench. His certificate of freedom No. 33/335 dated 15 April 1833 followed. In 1852, under the name Jacob Fletcher, he married Mary J. Wright.

FOX Hannah (c.1794-25th April 1849)
(M.P.R. 2424. 2/8267, p. 437. S.J.R. 3201. R.398.4/4013).
Convicted at the County Sessions 12 July 1827 of larceny, by stealing several pieces of calico from the shop of Morris Jones, mercer, Welshpool. This crime was committed with Esther Ogden and James Smith. Esther Ogden was also transported to N.S.W., whilst James Smith went to Bermuda. She was sentenced to 7 years transportation; this followed 2 previous convictions (Q/SR 1827). She was transported on the 'Louisa', leaving Woolwich 24 August 1827, arriving New South Wales 3 November 1827. She was 33 years of age, height 5'2", with dark brown hair and hazel/grey eyes, with an inward cast on one eye. She was married to a John Dainty and had 3 children. She was a native of Somerset, able to read only, a general servant and a Protestant. Soon after her arrival, Hannah Fox (Dainty) is shown on the list of persons applying for the publication of banns at St James's Church, Sydney, dated 6 February 1828, to Watkin Watkins's who had been sentenced to 14 years transportation by a Montgomeryshire court. Both apparently worked for a Mr Dibbs of Park St., Sydney, who confirmed that their conduct was 'Good' and that he gave his consent to this application, but the ceremony did not take place. The 1828 Census shows her as a General Servant in the employ of William Dibbs, wheelwright, Castlereagh Street, Sydney. On 1 May 1830, she received her ticket of leave No. 30/202. issued by the Sydney Bench (R.913.4/4074) and it is recorded on the ticket that it was being granted, in pursuance of a Government Order dated 17 March 1829, after good conduct whilst in service. On 3 July 1832, an illegitimate daughter (Mary) was born to Elias Jones and Hannah Denton (1832?499/18), the father being described as a quarryman of Campbell Street, Sydney. The child was baptised at St James's, Sydney, by a Rev. Hill. Hannah received her certificate of freedom No. 34/924 dated 15 July 1834 (R.993.4/4323). In September 1834 Hannah married Elias Jones, their ages shown as 39 and 38 years respectively. Neither could write; the witnesses were Thomas Jones and Esther Ogden (see Esther Ogden below). They were married by the Rev. John Clelland, a Presbyterian Minister. On the banns application for this wedding (R.726.4/4226.4), Elias Jones is shown as a transported convict via the 'Mellish' in 1829. Mr Thomas Stokes Evans of 5, Campbell Street, Sydney, on the application, states that Hannah is 'sober and industrious', and he confirms his willingness to employ her. He also confirms that Elias Jones 'lives in Campbell Street'; no doubt he was assigned to Mr Evans. Immediately Hannah Fox received her certificate of freedom (15 July 1834), the pair made an approach to Mr Clelland, the Presbyterian Minister, to marry them. In view of the fact that both had been married prior to transportation, they were now committing an offence. Following their marriage, no children were born. Elias Jones died 21 July 1846 at Maitland (age shown as 46 years. Reg. No. 990.31), and it is probable that Hannah herself died 25 April 1849, widow, of Phillip Street, Sydney (Entry 81, Vol. 34).

GANE Sarah (1816-16.1.1861)
(M.P.R. 2425. 2/7272, p. 199. S.J.R. 3206. R.906.4/4018).
Convicted at the County Sessions 17 October 1833 of larceny, assault with intent to rob Edward Swift of Llanfyllin, the offence taking place in the Parish of Llanrhaeadr-ym-Mochnant. (With her, committing this offence, were Elizabeth Jones, Timothy Partridge and Thomas Wilson, all of whom received similar sentences.) She was sentenced to 7 years transportation (*Salopian Journal*, 6 Nov. 1833). She was transported on the 'Numa', leaving Portsmouth 29 Jan 1834,

arriving New South Wales 13 June 1834. She was 18 years of age, height 5'1", with light brown hair and grey eyes. Her complexion was fair and she had 2 small moles on the left cheek near the ear, a scar on the back of her right hand, a scar on the back of her right thumb and a scar inside the left thumb (39/1348. 41/346). She was single, able to read only, a nurse girl by trade and a Protestant. She was a native of Somerset. In 1836, Sarah applied to marry Andrew Croneen or Crenien, who was 33 years of age and had been transported on the 'Guildford', arriving 1829. He was a carpenter of Maitland and at the time Sarah was in Newcastle Gaol from assignment. The marriage did not take place. (Banns recorded for Christ Church, Newcastle R.730. 4/2304.l.) On 18 November 1836, permission to marry was granted to William Perry, age 32 years, 'Countess Harcourt', 7 years, free, and Sarah Gane, age 20 years, 'Numa', 7 years bond. The marriage took place 2 November 1836 in the Parish of St Phillip's, Sydney, by the Rev. William Cowper. Neither could write (Reg. No. 64, Vol. 20). No children were born of the marriage. On 11 July 1839, Sarah received her ticket of leave No. 39/1348, issued by the Parramatta Bench (R.933.4/4131), and on 11 March 1841, her certificate of freedom No. 41/346. (R.1008.4/4364). She apparently died 16 January 1861 at Campbell Street, age 49 years, and was buried the following day in the Parish of Camperdown by the officiating clergy, Charles C. Kemp.

GLOSSOP Ann (– January 1810)
(M.P.R. 2426. 2/8273, p. 229. R.392.4/4003, copy at COD 9).
Convicted at the Great Sessions 28 March 1791 of larceny, shoplifting 9 yards of velvet from the shop of James Moore of Newtown. Pleading not guilty, the Jury, however, found her guilty and she was sentenced to 7 yrs transportation. She was transported on the 'Pitt' convict ship, leaving Yarmouth Roads 17 July 1791 and arriving New South Wales 14 February 1792. The ship was overcrowded, fever raged and out of a complement of 58 female convicts 9 died whilst en route. Thus, Ann, a single woman from an unrecorded origin, had the distinction of being the first female convict to be sentenced to transportation to Australia by a Montgomeryshire court. Following her arrival in Australia she soon became acquainted with a William Broughton, a Government official who had arrived with the First Fleet 20 January 1788. By 1800 they were at Norfolk Island, and, although not married, they had 4 children, namely Mary Ann, Sarah, William and Rebecca. They eventually left Norfolk Island on the ship 'City of Edinburgh' in September 1808 and by now were accompanied by a fifth child, Elizabeth Isabella, born 1807. Still not married to Ann Glossop, William Broughton was apprehensive about this relationship and the view that would be taken by his superior, Governor Macquarie, who disapproved of illicit relationships. In order to alleviate any problem William Broughton arranged for Ann and Betsy (by now 2 years of age) to visit their eldest daughter who had gone to England for schooling. They were put aboard the 'Boyd' en route to the Cape of Good Hope with a cargo of timber, seal skins, coal and oil. The ship left Port Phillip 8 November 1809 to call en route at Whangaroa, New Zealand. Following arrival in the Bay of Islands, an attack by Maoris resulted in many deaths, including that of Ann Glossop (in January 1810).

GOODWIN Edward (c.1804–)
(M.P.R. 2421.2/8258, p. 195. R.905.4/4016).
Convicted at the Great Sessions 12 August 1830 of sheep stealing, with an accomplice, Joseph Swindley, from a Mr Clayton of Llanmerewig (*Shropshire Journal*, 18 August 1830). He was sentenced to death, commuted to 14 years

transportation. He was transported on the 'Exmouth', leaving Woolwich March 1831, arriving New South Wales 28 July 1831. He was 27 years of age, height 5'4½", with brown hair and hazel eyes. His complexion was sallow and he had a blue scar on the right upper lip. He was married to Ann Goodwin with 2 children, native of Montgomery, unable to read or write, a farm labourer and a Protestant. The 1837 Muster indicates that he was employed by Edward Weston of Liverwort District, and he received his ticket of leave No. 38/1552, dated 26 September 1838 issued by the Liverpool Bench.

GRIFFITHS John (c.1731-31st May 1791)
(COD 9.4/4003, copy at R.392 and fiche 615, p. 192).
Convicted at the Great Sessions March 1788 of sheep stealing (3 sheep), from Catherine and Edward Pryce of Llanbadarn Fynydd, Radnorshire, and was sentenced to death, commuted to 7 years transportation. He was 57 years of age (Wales 4/193/8). He was transported on the 'Surprise', leaving Portsmouth 19 January 1790, arriving New South Wales 26 June 1790. The death of a John Griffiths is recorded 31 May 1791, with burial at Rosehill, Parramatta.

GRIFFITHS John (c.1803–)
(M.P.R. 2423. 2/8266, p. l. S.J.R. 3200. R.906.4/4019).
Convicted at the County Sessions 20 February 1834 of larceny, stealing 13 fowls and 2 ducks from a Mr Price, Lower Packhouse, Welshpool. He was sentenced to 7 years transportation. (This offence was committed with Evan Owen, who was sent to Van Diemen's Land) (*Shrewsbury Chronicle*, 28 February 1834. N.L.W. Bl/16). Following a period in the county gaol, he was removed to the hulk 'Gannymede,' from where he was transported on the 'Lady Nugent', leaving Sheerness 4 December 1834, arriving New South Wales 9 April 1835. He was 31 years of age, height 5'6¾", with brown hair and hazel eyes. His complexion was dark and he had a mole on the upper part of his belly, also a scar near the right elbow. He was married with 5 children, able to read only and was a Protestant. He was a native of Churchstoke and a groom/gardener by trade (40/395.42/213). The 1837 Muster shows him employed by Assistant Surgeon J. Smith of the 17th Regiment, in Sydney. He received his ticket of leave No. 40/395 dated 14 February 1840, issued by Parramatta Bench, altered to Stonequarry 13 April 1840 per Police Magistrate's letter dated 21 March 1840, No. 40/2874, issued by Camden District. His certificate of freedom followed No. 42/213 dated 10 February 1842 (R.1010.4/4371).

GRIFFITHS Mary (c.1778– 9.4.1806)
(M.P.R. 2422. 2/8261, p. 123. COD 138. Copy at R.392, fiche 631, p. 123).
Convicted at the Great Sessions 13 August 1801 of 3 charges of larceny and was sentenced to 7 years transportation. She left England 23 September 1802 on the 'Glatton', arriving New South Wales 11 March 1803. No evidence has been found about the eventual outcome on arrival, except her possible death 9 April 1806, at Parramatta, aged 28 years (Reg. No. 2049, Vol. 2). The entry simply states "still a convict".

HODGKINS William (c.1787–)
(M.P.R. 2421. 2/8259, p. 185. S.J.R. 3195. R.398.4/4013).
Convicted at the Great Sessions 29 March 1827 of burglary, stealing a watch in Alberbury. He was sentenced to death, commuted to 14 years transportation.

(*Shropshire Journal*, 4 April 1827 and Q/SR 1827). He was transported on the 'Florentia' leaving England 15 September 1827, arriving New South Wales 3 January 1828. He was 37 years of age, height 5'6", with dark brown hair and brown eyes. His complexion was sallow, he had a small scar in the corner of the right eye and his left forefinger was bruised at the point. He was single, unable to read or write, a Protestant and a native of Shropshire (34/469.42/6424). In the 1828 Census, he was at the Barracks, Newcastle, and, on 26 May 1834, he received his ticket of leave No. 34/469, issued by Maitland Bench (R.921.4/4093). The 1837 Muster confirms that he remained in Maitland.

HUGHES David (c.1805–)

(M.P.R. 2428. 2/8282, p. 371. S.J.R. 3213. R.905.4/4016).
Convicted at the Great Sessions 24 March 1830 of breaking and entering a dwelling house in Llanfihangel and stealing therefrom. He was sentenced to 7 years transportation, this following a previous conviction for which he had been sentenced to 2 years imprisonment (*Shrewsbury Journal*, 7 April 1830). He was sent from the county gaol to the hulk 'Justitia' at Woolwich, from where he was transported on the 'York', leaving Woolwich 8 April 1830 and arriving New South Wales 7 February 1831. He was 26 years of age, height 5'4¼", with brown hair and grey eyes. His complexion was ruddy and freckled. He was married with 2 children, able to read and write and a Protestant. His trade, as a farm labourer, included the ability to plough, sheer, reap, milk, sow and shepherd. On his left arm were the following letters: 'DHMHJGJH' and he wore a ring on the third finger of his left hand (C37/332).

HUGHES Mary (c.1790–)

(M.P.R. 2423. 2/8277, p. 75. COD 147, copy at R.395.4/4007).
Convicted at the Great Sessions 1 March 1818 of a felony, stealing flannel from a tenter. She was sentenced to 7 years transportation (*Shropshire Journal*, 18 March 1818, NLW Q/SR 1818 and NLW 4/200/10). She was transported on the 'Janus', which left Cork, Ireland, 5 December 1819, arriving in New South Wales 3 May 1820. She was about 30 years of age, height 4'10½", with brown hair and dark eyes. Her complexion was fair and ruddy and she was a servant. Assignment records show that of the 104 female convicts landed from this ship, 68 were transferred to Tasmania, but Mary Hughes remained in N.S.W. On 23 October 1820, she married one William Crowe at St John's, Parramatta (Reg. No. 2625, Vol. 3), this having followed permission to marry (R.6007.4/3502, p. 302). Her husband, also a convict, had been transported on the 'Minerva'. The 1822 Muster shows Mary as freed by servitude and living with her husband in Parramatta. On 10 November 1823, William was convicted for riotous and disorderly behaviour, and was moved to Port Macquarie in the Government employ. His sentence was 100 lashes. Mary was in the settlement with her husband (R.6023.4/6671, p. 107). On 12 May 1825, Mary received her certificate of freedom No. 65/3689 (R.601. 4/4423). During 1827, a daughter, Elizabeth, was born (1093, Vol. 125), but this date is questionable, as an entry for the Female Factory, Parramatta, states that 'Elizabeth' was incorrigible and that her Master, to whom she had been sent as a servant, had returned her to the Factory. Following this, the Factory decided to send the child back to her own mother at Port Macquarie (Letter No. 28/ 5316. 4/1985). This method of separating mothers and children at the Factory was a common occurrence and many of these young children, from about 8 years of age and upwards, were sent out into "Service". This was a system com-

parable with the existence of children left in England and Wales, who had to abide by the Old Poor Laws prior to 1834, and the further consequences of the Poor Law Amendment Act of that year. The 1828 Census confirms that William was in Sydney Gaol but Mary and Elizabeth appear to have taken leave of him and no further record can be traced of their eventual lives.

HUMPHREYS John (c.1794–)
(M.P.R. 2419.2/8250, p. 49. S.J.R. 3191).
Convicted at the Assizes 10 March 1832 of sheep stealing from Evan Jones, Llanllugan, Richard Morgan, Carno, John Thomas, Carno and Evan Chapman, Newtown. He was sentenced to death, commuted to life transportation (*Shropshire Journal*, 14 March 1832 and NLW Q/SR 1832). He was transported on the 'Camden,' leaving Sheerness 22 September 1832, arriving New South Wales 18 February 1833. He was 39 years of age, height 5'4", with light brown/grey hair and hazel eyes. His complexion was sallow, he was able to read and write and a Protestant. He was a native of Llanwnog and married with 9 children. His trade was a farm servant/shepherd (41/586. 47/664. R.905.4/4017). The 1837 Muster shows him employed by Gregory Blaxland of Merton. His ticket of leave No. 41/586 dated 5 March 1841 was issued by the Cassilis Bench and his ticket of leave passport No. 42/93 was issued 2 January 1842 by the Cassilis Bench (R.969.4/4243). His conditional pardon No. 47/664 was issued 30 July 1847 (R.784.4/4452).

HUMPHREYS Lewis (c.1810-12.12.1853)
(M.P.R. 2428. 2/8282, p. 331. S.J.R. 3213. R.2662. X642).
Convicted at the Assizes 13 July 1839 of training and drilling, and was sentenced to 7 years transportation. This followed the Chartist outbreak in Llanidloes that took place during April/May 1839. (A detailed account of this uprising can be found in *Chartism in Llanidloes 1838-1839* by E. Ronald Morris, 1989.) His only previous conviction occurred on 10 April 1834, when he was apprehended in the Llanidloes lock up for a violent assault on a Pryce Owen (NLW.Q/506). He was removed from the county gaol during the first week in August 1839 and sent to the hulks at Woolwich. He was transported on the 'Woodbridge', leaving London 16 October 1839, arriving New South Wales 26 February 1840. He was 29 years of age, height 5'8¼", with brown hair and blue eyes. His complexion was sallow. He was married with 1 male child, able to read and a Protestant. He was a native of Llanidloes and a boot and shoemaker by trade. Marks on his body included loss of part of a front upper tooth, mark of a boil inside the right wrist, scar back of right hand, another on back of forefinger right hand, both little fingers contracted, scar on back of forefinger and thumb of left hand and two scars on back of little finger of left hand (46/813). He received his certificate of freedom No. 46/813 dated 27 August 1846 (R.1022.4/4405). He married Rose Newman 30 October 1846 at the Scots Church, Sydney. Witnesses were William Mawley and Margaret Murray, both from Sydney. Lewis Humphreys, being unable to write, made his mark. The Presbyterian minister who officiated was James Fullerton. Two children were born, namely, Edward in 1850 (Reg. 674, Vol. 141) and William in 1852 (Reg. 2429, Vol. 141). Lewis Humphreys died in 1853, the Register showing his name as Umpires, and was buried 12 Feb. 1853, his abode shown as the Sydney suburb known as Newtown.

INGRAM John (c.1804-3.1.1841)

(M.P.R. 2424. 2/8268, p. 1. S.J.R. 3202. R.2662. X642A).
Convicted at the Assizes 13 July 1839 of training and drilling in Newtown. He was sentenced to 7 years transportation and, following a period in the hulks at Woolwich, was transported on the 'Maitland', leaving London 2 March 1840, arriving New South Wales 14 July 1840. He was 36 years of age, height 5'5¾", with dark brown hair and hazel eyes. His complexion was sallow and freckled and marks on his body included eyebrows meeting, small scar on left cheek, scar under left side of chin, nose inclining a little to the right side, three small moles on right side of neck, large scar back of left hand, nail of middle finger of left hand disfigured and a scar on the palm of the right hand. He was single, able to read only and a Protestant. He was a native of Newtown and a labourer/soldier by trade. Not long after his arrival John Ingram died 3 January 1841 at the General Hospital, Sydney. He was 37 years of age and was buried 4 January 1841 in St James's Parish, Sydney (1841/227/25).

JAMES Joseph (c.1795-22.11.1840)

(M.P.R. 2417. 2/8243, pp. 113-123. S.J.R. 3189. COD 146.4/4006, copy at R.394).
Convicted at the Great Sessions 13 August 1818 of a felony, stealing a mare and bridle, value £8, from a William Jones of Llangadfan. He was sentenced to death, commuted to life transportation (N.L.W. Q/SR 1818). He was transported on the 'Baring', leaving Downs 27 January 1819 arriving New South Wales 26 June 1819. He was 25 years of age, height 5'9½", with dark brown hair and hazel eyes. His complexion was dark and sallow. He was single and a labourer. On arrival, he was assigned to Mr William Howe of Liverpool (R.1030.4/3500, pp. 162-3). The 1822 Muster confirms him as a member of the gaol gang, Parramatta, and by the 1825 Muster he is a member of a road party of an unknown location. Again, by the 1828 Muster, he is on the iron gang at Melville. His ticket of leave No. 32/302 dated 28 April 1832 was issued by the South Creek Bench. The 1837 Muster shows him in the Penrith/Melville District. On 1 November 1838 he received his conditional pardon No. 39/377 (R.777.4/4437). He died 22 November 1840 in the Parish of St Mary Magdalene, South Creek, and is shown as a labourer (NSW Death Index, Reg. No. 865, Vol. 124).

JOHN Jonathan (c.1797–)

Convicted at the Great Sessions 29 March 1827 of burglary at Llansantffraid. He was sentenced to death, commuted to 14 years transportation (*Shropshire Journal*, 4 April 1827 and NLW Q/SR1827). He was transported on the 'John', leaving London 22 July 1827, arriving New South Wales 25 November 1827. No further evidence could be found about him.

JONES David (c.1799–)

(M.P.R. 2421. 2/8257, p. 63. S.J. 3194. COD 147.4/4007, copy at R.395, fiche 643, p. 47).
Convicted at the Great Sessions 25 March 1819 of a felony, stealing one mare from an Evan Jones of Newtown. He was sentenced to death, commuted to 14 years transportation (NLW Q/SR 1819). He was transported on the 'Eliza', leaving England 15/16 October 1819 arriving New South Wales 21 January 1820. He was 20 years of age, height 5'5¾", with sandy hair and grey eyes. His complexion was ruddy and freckled. He was single, a Protestant and a shoemaker by trade (33/382). On arrival he was assigned to Lieutenant Lawson of Parramatta (R.1301.4/3501,

pp. 217/8). On 29 August 1821, he was tried by the Liverpool Bench (details of crime not given) and included on the list of prisoners transported to Newcastle on the 'Sally' (R.6008.4/3504A, p. 31). The 1822 Muster confirms that he was still a convict in the employment of the Government at Newcastle but by 1824 he is included on a monthly return of convicts assigned to a George Brookes, who was a magistrate in the counties of Northumberland and Durham (R.6028.2/8283, p. 83). The 1828 Census shows him employed by a William Eckford of Wallis Plains. On 22 April 1833, he received his certificate of freedom No. 33/382 (Reel 990.4/4314).

JONES Elizabeth (c.1809-19.7.1896)
(M.P.R. 2426. 2/8272, p. 199. S.J.R. 3206. R.906. 4/4018).
Convicted at the County Sessions 17 October 1833 of larceny and assault with intent to rob Edward Swift of Llanfyllin, in the parish of Llanrhaeadr-ym-Mochnant. 3 other members of the gang were also sentenced to transportation, namely Sarah Gane, Timothy Partridge and Thomas Wilson. She was sentenced to 7 years transportation, and was transported on the 'Numa', leaving Portsmouth 29 January 1834, arriving New South Wales 13 June 1834. She was 25 years of age, height 5'1¼", with brown hair and brown eyes. Her complexion was fair and freckled and she had a slight scar under the corner of the right eyebrow. She was single, able to read only, a Protestant who undertook Public House work. She was a native of Shropshire and had no previous convictions. On 2 December 1834, she applied to marry John Sinnott, age 35, who had come free to New South Wales as a mariner and it is possible that he was so employed on the 'Numa', whereby they met each other (Banns Application R.725.4/2225.6). On this application she is shown as being in Newcastle Gaol. The marriage did not take place. The 1837 Muster shows her again in Newcastle Gaol and it is probable that, as she was given permission to marry, she was in the Female Factory, awaiting assignment. In 1838, she applied to marry Isaac Newton, age 25 years, transported on the 'Portland' in 1832 and a ticket of leave No. 37/840. The banns record confirms that they were both assigned to Mr W. Sparke of Woodland (R.2210. 4/2444.9). The marriage took place at Christ Church, Newcastle, 16 July 1838, the Rev. C. P. N. Pleydell Wilton officiating (marriage entry 1838/1897, Vol. 22). There do not appear to have been any children of this marriage and, after 58 years of marriage they died within 3 months of each other. Isaac died 16 April 1896 and Elizabeth 19 July 1896, both residing in Hexham. In his will No. 11299/4 he left his property to his wife and in her will No. 11694/4 she left her property to a William Sparke, solicitor of Newcastle and Thomas Conn of Lambton. The will confirmed that there were no children. It is evident that the above William Spark he was a son of the William Sparke to whom both had been assigned in or about 1838 and who, it has been established, was "a good master". It would seem that they both must have appreciated that assignment to have remembered his son in the manner they did.

JONES Maria (c.1799-13.6.1856)
(M.P.R. 2424. 2/8267, p. 343. S.J.R. 3201. COD 147, copy at R.395, fiche 643, p. 31). Convicted at the Great Sessions April 1818 of larceny, breaking into the dwelling house of John Richards of Ffridd, Trefeglwys, and stealing 4 cheeses (10/-), 31b weight of tallow (1/-), 10 qts of flour (2/-), ½ peck wheaten flour (2/-). It is also noted that she stole 1 silver spoon (£l) from Evan Jones. She was sentenced to death, commuted to life transportation (N.L.W. Q/SR 1817. N.L.W.4/200/7.).

She was transported on the 'Lord Wellington', arriving New South Wales 20 January 1820. She was 21 years of age, height 5'3", with brown hair and eyes. Her complexion was ruddy and her occupation a servant/children's maid (30/1831). Her native place was shown as South Wales. On 5 February 1821 a banns application was made between Maria Jones and George Jilks, aged 28 years, a convict who arrived on the 'Mariner' in 1816 (R. 1031.4/3403). The marriage took place 26 February 1821 at St Phillip's Church, Sydney, the Rev. William Cowper officiating. Maria was unable to sign the register (NSW Marriage Index, Reg. No. 128, Vol. 8). Children of the marriage are Jane E. – 1821 (Reg. No. 418, Vol. 8), Margaret – 1822 (Reg. No. 511, Vol. 8), George – 1825 (Reg. No. 809, Vol. 8), Catherine A. – 1828 (Reg. No. 322, Vol. 13) and Martha N. – 1833 (Reg. No. 499, Vol. 17). Both the 1822 and 1825 Musters show Maria as the wife of George Jilks and, in November 1825, she was granted a conditional pardon (Fiche 3292;4/6974, p. 47). The 1828 Census indicates that she is still the wife of George Jilks, a Protestant of Castlereagh Street, Sydney. His occupation is shown as being a Chief Constable. Maria died and was buried 13 June 1856 in Camperdown Cemetery, Sydney, the entry describing her as "wife of a gentleman" (NSW Death Index, Reg. No. 5379, Vol. 122).

JONES Richard alias BULLOCK (c.1813–)
(M.P.R. 2423. 2/8264, p. 209. S.J.R. 3198.R.908. X640).
Convicted at the Quarter Sessions 30 June 1836 of housebreaking, by breaking and entering the dwelling house of a Mr John Williams in the parish of Manafon, and stealing 2 x £5 notes, 1 sovereign and some silver and, in addition, of stealing from Richard Bumford, servant to Mr Williams, a handkerchief and a razor. He was sentenced to 7 years transportation, this following a previous conviction of 4 months (N.L.W. Bl/16. *Shrewsbury Chronicle*, 8 July 1836). He was taken to the hulk 'Justitia' at Woolwich, from where he was transported on the 'James Pattison', leaving Sheerness 16 July 1837, arriving New South Wales 25 October 1837. He was 24 years of age, height 5'6½", with light brown hair and blue eyes. His complexion was fair and ruddy and he had the following marks, a burn mark on the centre of his forehead, scar left side of same, tumour right side of upper lip, light sandy whiskers and a blue ring third finger of the right hand. He was single, unable to read or write, a Protestant and a top sawyer by trade (46/1123). The 1837 Muster shows him employed by the Government at Moreton Bay. He received his ticket of leave No. 41/2365 dated 8 November 1841, issued by the Moreton Bay Bench (R.942.4/4156) and his certificate of freedom No. 46/1123 dated 22 December 1846 (R.1023.4/4407).

JONES William.(c.1762–)
(M.P.R. 2426. 2/8273, p. 229. Reel.392. 4/40033. Copy at fiche 616, p. 252 and COD 9).
Convicted at the Great Sessions 30 March 1789 of horse stealing by taking a gelding (value £3) from Francis Bird and was sentenced to 7 years transportation (N.L.W.4/194/4). He was transported on the 'Pitt', leaving Yarmouth Roads 17 July 1791, arriving New South Wales 14 February 1792. He was 30 years of age but there is no further information about him. The 1806 Muster confirms that he was free by servitude and was employed by a Mr Fitzgerald of an unknown abode. By the 1811 Muster he was still in New South Wales.

LEWIS David (c.1806-30.1.1849)
(M.P.R. 2423. 2/8266, p. 465. S.J.R. 3201. R.908.X641).
Convicted at the Assizes 15 July 1837 of horse stealing from a Mr William Wylde, a farmer from Radnorshire. He was sentenced to life transportation (N.L.W. Bl/17, *Shrewsbury Chronicle*, 21 July 1837 and Q/SR 1837). He was removed to the hulk 'Gannymede' from where he was transported on the 'Lord Lyndock', leaving Portsmouth 4 April 1838 arriving New South Wales 8 August 1838. He was 32 years of age, height 5'2½", with light brown hair and hazel eyes. His complexion was ruddy and freckled. Marks on his body included lost canine tooth right side of under jaw, small raised mole on back of neck, small dark mole on back of lower left arm, scar on knuckles of fore and middle fingers of left hand and a mole on the outside of his left leg. He was married, able to read and write imperfectly, a Protestant (Baptist), and a farm servant. He was a native of Carno. He died 30 January 1849 and was buried the following day in Queanbeyan. He was 44 years of age and a shepherd (Death Reg. No. 838, Vol. 34).

LEWIS Edward (c.1808–)
(M.P.R. 2421. 2/8258, p. 195. S.J.R. 3195. R.905.4/4016).
Convicted at the Great Sessions 1 August 1830 of house breaking in Manafon. He was sentenced to death, commuted to life transportation (*Shropshire Journal*, 18 March 1830). This followed a previous conviction and sentence of 6 months imprisonment. He was removed to the hulk 'Justitia', and transported on the 'Exmouth', leaving Woolwich 2 March 1831, arriving New South Wales 28 July 1831. He was 23 years of age, height 5'5¼", with brown hair and eyes. His complexion was ruddy and pock-marked, and he had a scar on the left eyebrow and under the left eye. He was single, able to read only, a Protestant, and a farm labourer (39/1694). The 1837 Muster confirms his employment with Messrs. Aspinall & Co, Bathurst, and, on 3 September 1839, he received his ticket of leave No. 39/1694, issued by the Bathurst Bench (R.934.4/4132). However, a notation across the document reads "T of L torn up and cancelled, the holder having been tried at the Bathurst Quarter Sessions in June 1840, and sentenced to transportation to a Penal Settlement for life." It is possible that he married a Mary Andrews at Sydney 31 July 1852, with his wife's relatives, namely John and Sarah Andrews of Newtown Sydney, as witnesses (1852 181/85).

LLOYD Richard (c.1799-30.11.1836)
(M.P.R. 2428. 2/8281, p. 55. Surgeon's Journal R.3212. COD 144. Copy at R.394.4/4006).
Convicted at the Great Sessions 9 August 1817 of burglary. He was sentenced to death, commuted to 7 years transportation. He was transported on the 'Tottenham', leaving Spithead 27 March 1818 arriving New South Wales 14 October 1818. He was 19 years of age, height 5'6½", with black hair and hazel eyes. His complexion was florid. He was single and a shoeing smith by trade. On 29 March 1821, he appears on a list of prisoners transported to Newcastle on the 'Elizabeth Henrietta', having been sentenced to 3 years imprisonment 24 March 1821 for a robbery offence (R.6007.4/3503, p. 198, and R.601.4/4423). The 1822 Muster shows him in Government employment at Newcastle. He received his certificate of freedom No. 8/2598, dated 2 September 1824 (R.601.4/4423), and his calling is shown as blacksmith. During 1831, banns for marriage (R.720. 4/2127.2) were recorded for Richard Lloyd age 32 years, 'Tottenham' 1818, free by servitude and employed by a Mr Dixon, and Mary Clifford, age 27 years,

'Sovereign' 1829, bond and employed by Captain Bunker. They were married 15 January 1831 at Narellan, near Campbelltown, by the Rev. Thomas Hassall (BDM Reg. No. 1113, Vol. 15). The records indicate that Mary was single with two children (not Richard's), there being no children of this marriage. On 3 February 1834, Lloyd was described as a blacksmith, free and a lodger in the house of John Robifl. (R.2413.4/8434, p. 71). It would seem that he may have left his wife and her children, as he was now being shown as a lodger. Having committed further crimes in 1835, he was found guilty and sentenced to 14 years transportation (R.2414.4/8435, pp. 345-370). Taken to Norfolk Island, he did not live to see his sentence expire. On 30 November 1836 he died and was buried on Norfolk Island (NSW Death Reg. No. 1473, Vol. 44). The Death Register of convicts at Norfolk Island notes that he "was an inoffensive and industrious man" (COD 226).

MILLER Samuel (c.1794–)
(M.P.R. 2417. 2/8243, p. 195. S.J.R. 3189. COD 146. R4/4006, copy at R.394).
Convicted at the Quarter Sessions 16 July 1818 of an unknown crime. He was sentenced to 7 years transportation. He was transported on the 'Baring', leaving Downs 27 January 1819, arriving New South Wales 26 June 1819. He was 25 years of age, height 5'2½", with brown hair and hazel eyes. His complexion was ruddy. He was single, a native of Nottingham and a silk weaver by trade. On arrival, he was assigned in Windsor District and the 1822 Muster shows him as a Government servant, employed by a D. West of Windsor. On 18 August 1825 he received his certificate of freedom No. 95/4199 (R.602.4/4424). The 1825 Muster shows that he was still employed by D. West.

MORRIS David (c.1768-16th July 1790)
(COD 9. 4/4003).
Convicted at the Great Sessions March 1788 of sheep stealing by taking 1 sheep from Thomas Williams, Llanfair Caereinion, and was sentenced to death, commuted to 7 years transportation. He was 20 years of age (NLW.4/193/8) and was transported on the 'Surprise', leaving Portsmouth 19 January 1790, arriving New South Wales 26 June 1790. He apparently died 16 July 1790 and was buried at Sydney, being one of the many convicts who died as part of the Second Fleet.

MORRIS James (c.1820-27.5.1854)
(M.P.R. 2428. 2/8282, p. 331. S.J.R. 3213. R.2662. X642).
Convicted at the Assizes 13 July 1839 of feloniously stabbing with intent to do bodily harm at Llanidloes during the Chartist riots and was sentenced to 15 years transportation. He was taken to the hulks at Woolwich by 8 August 1839, from where he was transported on the 'Woodbridge', leaving London 16 October 1839, arriving New South Wales 26 February 1840 and was treated for psoriasis on the voyage. He was 20 years of age, height 5'8½", with light brown hair and hazel eyes. His complexion was fair and ruddy whilst marks on his body included a scar on the inside of his right thumb. He was single, able to read only, a Protestant and a weaver by trade. He was a native of Llanidloes. He received a ticket of leave in 1844 No. 44/2872, issued by the Mudgee Bench, but this was altered to Cassilis on 10 December 1846 (see letter 46/84222). His conditional pardon No. 47/738 was issued 30 July 1847 (R.784.4/4452). He died 27 May 1854 and was buried the following day in the Parish of Christchurch, Newcastle, his occupation shown as a miner (Reg. No. 1558, Vol. 41).

MORRIS Pryce (c.1781-1867)

(M.P.R. 2422. 2/8261, p. 377).

Convicted at the Great Sessions 7 April 1810 of sheep stealing by taking 11 sheep from an Andrew Davies of Carno. He was sentenced to death commuted to life transportation (Q/SR 1810). He was transported on the 'Guildford', leaving London September 1811, arriving New South Wales 18 January 1812. He was 31 years of age, height 5'5½", with brown to grey hair and grey eyes. His complexion was sallow, he was single, a Protestant and a labourer. The 1814 Muster shows him as a servant to a Mr Johnson, Jnr., of Windsor. On 17 August 1818, he applied to marry Mary Croft at Windsor (R.6006.4/3499, p. 22) and they were married later that year in Windsor (Reg. No. 2250, Vol. 3). In December 1818, he was a servant to Andrew Johnson of Portland Head, in Windsor District, when a petition for mitigation of sentence was not successful (Fiche 3188.4/1855, p. 193). The 1822 Muster shows him "Employed by his Wife" at Windsor but by 1825 the Muster identifies him as a landholder at Wilberforce.

The 1828 Census shows the family group, as being: Pry(i)ce Morris, age 45, ticket of leave, Protestant and a labourer at Lower Portland Head, Mary Morris, age 25, born in colony, children of the marriage up to 1828 including Sarah 25.3.1820, Elizabeth 26.10.1821, Price 2.8.1824, William 26.8.1826 and Mary 16.8.1828, all of whom were born at Portland Head. The family were landholding 30 acres of which 25 acres had been cleared and cultivated. In addition they owned 6 cattle. Further children born included Matilda 1830, Susan 1832, James 1834, Dorothy 1836, Hannah 1842 and Frances 1844.

Pryce Morris received his conditional pardon No. 331/67 dated 6 April 1833; an entry in the New South Wales death index shows that he died in 1867 aged 87 years and that at the time of his death he was at McDonald River (1867/0564).

NEWTON Thomas, alias ELLIS (c.1794-10.10.1836)

(M.P.R. 2421. 2/8259, p. 45. COD 141, copy at R.393.4/4005).

Convicted at the Great Sessions 21 August 1813 of a felony, stealing a horse. He was sentenced to death commuted to life transportation (NLW.Q/SR 1813 and *Salopian Journal*, 1 September 1813). He was transported on the 'Fanny', leaving Downs 25 August 1815, arriving New South Wales 18 January 1816. He was 22 years of age, height 5'8¾", with sandy hair and hazel eyes. His complexion was ruddy, he was a labourer, single and a native of Shropshire, although both North Wales and Wales are recorded elsewhere in his records. On 2 May 1821, he applied for permission to marry Margaret Sullivan who is described as free. There is, however, no record that the marriage took place (R.6006.4/1751 and R.6008. 4/3504, p. 20). Between October 1821 and August 1823, he was employed as a constable in the Windsor District. On 9 August 1822, he apprehended a runaway (R.6009.4/3506, p. 160), and, by 9 December 1822, he was recommended for a reward for helping to capture runaways and pirates from Port Macquarie, resulting in a recommendation for an award by the magistrates of Windsor District (R.6053.4/1756, p. 105; and R.6053.4/1756, p. 105c). On 18 December 1822, he apprehended David Tenant (R.6054.4/1759, p. 37a) and the following day he is included on the list of prisoners victualled at Windsor (R.6053.4/1757, p. 108). On 13 February 1824, he has been assigned under the name Ellis (fiche. 3290.4/4570D, p. 36), as a general servant to William Wells of Sydney and this is confirmed in the 1825 Muster. On 1 July 1825 he received his ticket of leave No. 351/1825 (R.890.4/4060). The 1828 Census shows him still using the name Ellis and by now he was a clerk, lodging with Isaac Wise of Pitt Street, Sydney.

His ticket of leave No. 28/416 dated 20 October 1828 was renewed by Sydney Bench (R.911.4/4068) and over the following 4 years his ticket was renewed twice, No. 30/686 dated 6 October 1830 by Sydney Bench and No. 32/1302 dated 3 December 1832 by Bathurst Bench (R.914.4/4076 and R.918. 4/4087). His death took place 10 October 1836 at Bathurst General Hospital; he was 42 years of age (Death Reg. No. 909, Vol. 20).

OGDEN Esther (c.1802–)

(M.P.R. 2424. 2/8267, p. 437. S.J.R. 3201. R.398.4/4013).

Convicted at the County Sessions 12 July 1827 of larceny, stealing several pieces of calico from the shop of Morris Jones at Welshpool. (She had two accomplices, namely Hannah Fox and James Smith, of whom Hannah Fox went to New South Wales in the same ship as Esther Ogden, and James Smith was transported to Bermuda.) She was sentenced to 7 years transportation (Q/SR 1827), and was transported on the 'Louisa', leaving Woolwich 24 August 1827, arriving New South Wales 3 December 1827. She was 26 years of age, height 5'3", with dark brown hair and brown eyes. Her complexion was ruddy, she was able to read and write, a Protestant and a native of Macclesfield. She was married to an Abraham Ogden and had two children. At the time of the offence her family was at Chester. She was a plain cook and confectioner by trade (R.398.4/4013 and 34/180). Esther Ogden was pregnant prior to her conviction and in January 1828 she was delivered of a female child named Catherine. She indicated on the birth register that Abraham was the father (Reg. No. 22, Vol. 12). The 1828 Muster confirms that she was a servant to John Barber of Parramatta and that Catherine was 10 months old and born in the colony. On 26 April 1834 she received her ticket of leave No. 34/180 from the Illawarra Bench (R.920.4/4092) and her certificate of freedom No. 34/1110 on 7 September 1834. Esther Ogden had taken the trouble to obtain her ticket of leave, although she would have been aware that her certificate of freedom was due within a matter of a few months. On 15 September 1834, Esther Ogden acted as a witness to the marriage of her "compatriot in crime", Hannah Fox, and it is clear that from 1833, she had met a man called Robert Simpson and had arranged to be assigned to him. Eventually, they were married but, in the meantime, 5 children were born including Elizabeth 19 June 1833 and William 26 February 1836, both at Dapto, Robert and Sarah baptized 9 August 1840 at Spring Hill, and John 1 June 1842 at Primrose Farm, all locations being in the Parish of Wollongong.

Whilst Robert Simpson is shown as a farmer up to 1840, by the time of the birth of the last child, he has become a landed proprietor. Esther Ogden married Robert Simpson 27 July 1846, at Wollongong, the witnesses being Henry and Maria Hunt. The minister was the Rev. C. Atchison, and the service was Presbyterian. Both the "Permission to Marry" and the "Refusals to Marry" Register for the period 1831-1846 confirm that neither had made an application prior to 1846. This could well substantiate that Robert Simpson was still a convict, able to farm his own land through being in possession of a ticket of leave but such a ticket did not allow him to marry without permission until he was free. He may well have obtained his freedom in 1846 and decided to marry, following a general pattern after being freed, ensuring that the marriage certificate excluded the fact that he had been a convict. Esther Ogden, on the other hand, could have married without permission after 1834 but she may well have thought that she was still married to Abraham Owen, left behind with her 2 children in England, or word had reached her to confirm that her first husband had died prior to 1846.

OWEN Abraham. (1792-10.7.1870)
(M.P.R. 2428. 2/8282, p. 331. S.J.R. 3213. R.2662. X642).
Convicted at the Assizes 13 July 1839 of training and drilling at Llanidloes during the Chartist outbreak. He was sentenced to 7 years transportation and was taken to the hulks at Woolwich, from where he was transported on the 'Woodbridge', leaving London 26 October 1839, arriving New South Wales 26 February 1840. He was 49 years of age, height 5'7¾", with brown/grey hair and grey eyes. His complexion was ruddy and freckled, with sandy whiskers, scar on back of left cheek, breast and arms hairy, scar on back of right thumb, lower left arm had been fractured at some time, scar on back of 3rd finger of left hand and a broad scar on outside below knee of left leg (46/869). He was a widower with 4 male children, able to read and write imperfectly, a Protestant and a weaver by trade. He was a native of Llanidloes.

He received his ticket of leave No. 43/1839 dated 24 July 1843 issued by Queanbeyan Bench, which was altered to Goulburn on 29 August 1843 per letter from the Queanbeyan Bench No. 43/9884 (R.949.4/4179). His certificate of freedom No. 46/869 was issued on 9 September 1846 and a notation confirms that he was still in the Goulburn District at that time (R.1022.4/4405). He died 10 June 1870, age 80 years, and his occupation was shown as a collector (NSW Death Index 1875/06284).

OWEN Jane (c.1774-5.3.1831)
(M.P.R. 2428. 2/8282, p. 243. COD 139. 4.4004, copy at R.393 and fiche 631, p. 215).
Convicted at the Great Sessions 28 March 1804 of various felonies (*Salopian Journal*, 28 March 1804). She was sentenced to 7 years transportation and was transported on the 'William Pitt', leaving Falmouth 10 August 1805, arriving New South Wales 11 April 1806. She was 32 years of age, height 4'9", with brown/grey hair and hazel eyes. Her complexion was sallow, she was a servant, single, a Protestant and a native of Wales. Following her arrival, she gave birth to an illegitimate female child, named Eleanor, who died the same year. The father was given as Andrew Clark (BDM Reg. No. 3937, Vol. 1). The 1806 Muster shows that she was working for a Mr Cox. On 18 May 1811, she received her certificate of freedom No. 3185 which replaced No. 8/987, issued earlier in 1811. (Apparently when Governor Macquarie arrived in Australia, later in 1811, he immediately recalled all certificates to check their validity; following such check, they were reissued) (COD 18). The 1814 Muster states that her husband was Andrew Clark of Windsor, but in fact they were not married. On the 1822 Muster, she is shown as the wife of an E. Harcourt of Sydney although she was living with Joseph Harcourt, Pitt Street, Sydney, and, once again, she was not married. On 10 May 1824, permission to marry was granted to William Davis and Jane Owen (R.6013.4/3511, p. 70), and on 7 June 1824 the marriage took place at Castlereagh Church (NSW. BDM Reg. No. 228, Vol. 155). On 10 February 1825, an affidavit concerning the loss of her certificate was presented and she was issued with a new one No. 62/3185,in lieu of ticket No. 8/987 (R.601. 4/4423 and R.6026.4/1714, pp. 159-60). On the 1825 Muster, she has two entries, namely Jane Davis, via 'Pitt' free from servitude, husband at Port Macquarie, and Jane Owen, wife of William Davis, at Melville in the Nepean Valley District. The 1828 Census shows the family group, as William Davis, age 54, Government servant, who had arrived on the 'Admiral Gambier' 1808 or 1811, a Protestant and a labourer, Jane Davis, aged 54 years, free by servitude, who had arrived on the 'William Pitt' 1806 and a Protestant. Both were living at

Richmond, Nepean Valley District. Jane Davis died and was buried 5 March 1831 at St Mathew's, Windsor, aged 57 years. The officiating minister was a Rev. Joseph Docker. By now her husband was shown as a farmer (BDM Index Reg. No. 1772, Vol. 15).

PARRY Joseph (c.1805-21.5.1844)
(M.P.R. 2419. 2/8250, p. 49. S.J.R. 3191. R.904.4/4017).
Convicted at the Assizes 10 March 1832 of sheep stealing by taking 4 sheep from Richard Owen of Llanfyllin. He was sentenced to death, commuted to life transportation (NLW Q/SR 1832). He had no previous convictions. He was transported on the 'Camden', leaving Sheerness 22 September 1832, arriving New South Wales 18 February 1833. He was 26 years of age, height 5'10½", with sandy hair and brown eyes. His complexion was ruddy, his right little finger contracted and there was a large scar on the left thumb (41/1458). He was married with one child, able to read and write, a Protestant and a farm servant. He was a native of Llandrinio. The 1837 Muster shows him as employed by a Robert Bonner at Bathurst. He received his ticket of leave No. 41/1458 on 18 July 1841 from Bathurst Bench (R.940.4/4152). On 13 October 1841, he received his ticket of leave passport No. 41/425 upon which was shown "Allowed to remain in the District of Clarence River for 6 months in the service of Mr Surveyor Burrows, on recommendation of Dr Dobie" (R.968.4/4242). On 21 May 1844, Joseph Parry, whilst living in Clarence Town, was murdered by William Henry. He was buried 27 May 1844 in Clarence Town where he had been a labourer (Burial Reg. No. 1038, Vol. 29).

PARTRIDGE Timothy (c.1811–)
(M.P.R. 2423. 2/8266, p. 1. S.J.R. 3200. R.906.4/4019).
Convicted at the County Sessions 17 October 1833 of highway robbery in Llanrhaeadr-ym-Mochnant by assault, with intent to rob Edward Swift of Llanfyllin. His accomplices were Sarah Gane, Elizabeth Jones and Thomas Wilson and he was sentenced to 7 years transportation. He was sent to the hulk 'Justitia', from where he was transported on the 'Lady Nugent', leaving Sheerness 4 December 1834, arriving New South Wales 9 April 1834. He was 24 years of age, height 5'5¼", with light brown hair and hazel eyes. His complexion was ruddy and he had an inward cast in the right eye, mole on the right whisker, mole each side of . . . and a scar on the right knee (41/639). He was single, able to read and write, a Protestant and a skinner/tanner by trade. He had no previous convictions. His native place is shown as Barbados. He is not listed on the 1837 Muster and his ticket of leave cannot be traced. He received his certificate of freedom No. 41/639 on 25 May 1841 (R.1009.4/4366).

POPPETT Robert (c.1803–)
(M.P.R. 2419. 2/8250, p. 37. S.J.R. 3191. R.905.4/4016).
Convicted at the Great Sessions 12 August 1830 of horse stealing from Churchstoke. He was sentenced to death commuted to life transportation (*Salopian Journal*, 18 August 1830). He was sent to the hulk 'Justitia', from where he was transported on the 'Camden', leaving London 28 March 1831, arriving New South Wales 25 July 1831. He was 28 years of age, height 5'9¼", with dark brown hair and hazel/grey eyes. His complexion was ruddy, he had an angular scar in the centre of his upper lip, a small scar at the top of the left thumb and a scar above the left wrist. He was married with no children, able to read and write, a Protestant and

a butcher by trade. His native place was Shropshire. He does not appear in the 1837 Muster and, in a letter No. 42/14540 dated 12 December 1842, he is shown as having been transferred to Cockatoo Island for one year and his ticket of leave cancelled. This would have been as a form of punishment. On 11 December 1844 his ticket of leave was reissued No. 44/3011 at Moreton Bay (Queensland), (R.955. 4/4196). By 1851, he was still in Moreton Bay as his name is included in a directory for that year.

POWELL John (c.1793-19.4.1836)
(M.P.R. 2421. 2/8257, p. 63. S.J.R. 3194. COD 147. 4.4007, copy at R.393, fiche 643, p. 45).
Convicted at the Great Sessions 25 March 1819 of sheep stealing at Guilsfield and sentenced to death commuted to 14 years transportation (NLW Q/SR 1819 and *Salopian Journal*, 31 March 1819). He was transported on the 'Eliza', leaving England 15/16 October 1819, arriving New South Wales 21 January 1820. He was 28 years of age, height 5'7", with dark brown hair and hazel eyes. His complexion was dark ruddy, he had a scar on the upper lip, small mole left side of upper lip, and a scar on the back of the little finger of the right hand. He was single, a Catholic, and a horse doctor by trade (33/1134). On arrival, he was assigned to a Major Antill, Liverpool, and was still with him for the 1822 Muster (R.1031.4/3501, pp. 217/8). By 4 July 1823, he was assigned to William Hutchinson, Sydney, returning from there 29 June 1824 to an unknown destination (COD 467). The 1825 Muster shows him in Government employment at Barren Hills, Parramatta District. (At this time there was a huge undertaking cutting down trees in this area and he was probable involved in some manner, not necessarily the actual task of felling). The 1828 Muster places him in the Field of Mars, Barren Hills, by which time he was employed as a stock keeper. On 19 October 1833 he received his certificate of freedom No. 33.1134 (R.991. 4/4318). He died at Liverpool Hospital and was buried at St Luke's, Liverpool, 19 April 1836, the burial certificate shows his age as 40 years, that he was free and the officiating clergyman was a Rev. Robert Cartwright, Church of England.

PROCTOR Lewis, alias MATTHEWS (c.1758-1790)
(COD 9. 4/4003, copy at R.392 and fiche 615, p. 192).
Convicted at the Lent Great Sessions 1787 of stealing flannel to the value of £10 from William Tibbott of Berriew. He was sentenced to 7 years transportation (NLW 4/193/7). During a period spent on the 'Ceres' hulk at Portsmouth, he became ill and eventually resumed work as a brick moulder (PRO HO/42/15/260). He was 30 years of age and was transported on the 'Surprise', leaving Portsmouth 19 January 1790, arriving New South Wales 26 June 1790. There are no records held in Australia concerning him and he probably died en route.

PUGH Richard (c.1791-c.1825)
(M.P.R. 2427. 2/8277, p. 231. S.J.R. 3209. COD 144, copy at R.394).
Convicted at the Great Sessions 13 March 1818 of larceny by stealing flannel. He was sentenced to 7 years transportation (*Salopian Journal*, 18 March 1818). He was transported on the 'Shipley', leaving Woolwich 18 July 1818, arriving New South Wales 18 November 1818. He was 27 years of age, height 5'6", with dark brown hair and dark eyes. His complexion was dark, sallow and eruptive. He was single and a miller/fuller by trade (3623). In 1822 he was assigned to J. J. Greavy of O'Connell Street, Sydney, and this is confirmed by the 1822 Muster (COD 467. 4/4521). On

30 April 1825 he received his certificate of freedom No. 140/3623, which stated that he had been sent to Port Macquarie 2 April 1823 for the remainder of his sentence as a runaway. Although the 1825 Muster shows that he had died, no record of his death appears in the New South Wales Death Index or the Mutch Index.

REES Edward (c.1792–)

(M.P.R. 2423. 2/8264, p. 365. S.J.R. 3199. R.905.4/4017).

Convicted at the Assizes 19 July 1831 of maliciously wounding cattle in Llangurig. He was sentenced to life transportation; this followed no previous convictions (*Salopian Journal*, 27 July 1831). Following a period on the hulk 'Justitia', he was transported on the 'John', leaving Downs 7 February 1832, arriving New South Wales 8 June 1832. He was 40 years of age, height 5'2¾", with brown hair and grey eyes. His complexion was dark with red whiskers. He was married with 5 children, able to read only, a Protestant and a ploughman/shepherd/ reaper/ sower/milker. The 1837 Muster shows him assigned to Jas Bellamy at Parramatta (the name being spelt Reece). The Recommendation for Conditional Pardons up to 1846, gives no indication that he received a pardon, and records after this date are not indexed.

REVELL Edward (c.1799–)

(M.P.R. 2423. 2/8266, p. 407. S.J.R. 3201. R.906.4/4018).

Convicted at the County Sessions 3 January 1833 of larceny, stealing clothes at Llanidloes. He was sentenced to 7 years transportation and had no previous convictions. Following a period in the hulk 'Justitia', he was transported on the 'Lord Lyndock', leaving Sheerness June 1833, arriving New South Wales 18 October 1833. He was 34 years of age, height 5'7½", with dark brown hair and grey eyes. His complexion was sallow and freckled. He was single, a Protestant, able to read and write and a native of Shrewsbury. He was a mariner/navigator by trade. He had a mole on the left cheek, carroty whiskers and the letters 'GERHPS-G' inside the lower right arm (39/26). The 1837 Muster shows him with H. H. Arthur at Goulburn and on February 1839 he received his ticket of leave No. 39/26 issued by the Goulburn Bench.

RICHARDS Margaret (Senior)

(M.P.R. 2422.2/8261, p. 123. COD 138, copy at R.392.4/4004).

Convicted at the Great Sessions 13 August 1801 of larceny, accepting a length of flannel, knowing it to be stolen. She was sentenced to 14 years transportation (*Shrewsbury Chronicle*, 28 August 1801). She was transported on the 'Glatton', leaving England 23 September 1802, arriving New South Wales 11 March 1803. The Arrival Record confirms that she was married to Thomas Richards. The 1806 Muster states that she had been given her ticket of leave, was living with a Michael Broadherring and there was an illegitimate male child. The 1811 Muster shows her still in New South Wales and that she had a ticket of leave No. 345 issued 27 February 1808 by the Concord District (COD 18). According to the 1814 Muster, she was living with a W. Davis and had 2 children.

ROGERS John (c.1792–)

(M.P.R. 2421. 2/8257, p. 63. S.J.R. 3194. COD 147. 4/4007, copy at R.395).

Convicted at the Great Sessions 25 March 1819 of breaking and entering the house of Edward Evans of Burgedin, Llanymynech, and stealing 1 silver watch, 1 jacket, 1 waistcoat, 1 hat, 1 silk handkerchief and 2 pairs of wollen stockings, all to the value of £5. He was sentenced to death commuted to 14 years transportation (NLW Q/SR 1819). He was transported on the 'Eliza', leaving England 15/16 October 1819, arriving New South Wales 21 January 1820. He was 28 years of age, height 5'6¼", with dark brown hair and dark eyes. His complexion was ruddy, he was single, a collier/labourer by trade, a Protestant and a native of Denbighshire (25/105. 35/1040). The 1822 Muster shows him as a convict with a Mr Oxley of Liverpool, and, by the 1825 Muster, he is still a convict on Government Employment at Longbottom (Liverpool). On 16 May 1828, he received his ticket of leave No. 28/105 issued by the Liverpool Bench (R.910.4/4067). It also confirmed that his ticket of leave had been renewed and renamed No. 29/133 for Argyle (Goulburn) on 24 April 1829. The 1828 Census confirms that he was a servant to William Lees, a sawyer at Petersham. In 1831, John applied to marry Ann Keefe, the banns being Rogers, John, age 39 years on the 'Eliza' 1820, TL. 29/133, and Keefe, Ann, age 27 years on the 'Elizabeth' 1828, bond (still being a convict prior to ticket of leave). John Rogers is stated to be employed by Mr Cole of Goulburn Plains and that his character was very good. The marriage was recommended by Mr L. McAlister, J.P. Ann Keefe, at the time, was assigned to a Major E. Lockyer; her character was good and Major Lockyer was in favour of the marriage (R.720.4/2127.2). This took place 28 March 1831 at Sutton Forest by the Rev. Thomas Hassall. John Roger's usual residence is described as Goulburn Plains and Anne Keefe's as Sutton Forest (NSW Marriage Index Reg. No. 571, Vol. 44). He received his certificate of freedom No. 35/1040, 7 September 1835, at which time it was noted that he was ruddy, had a pock-pitted complexion with sandy hair and bright chestnut eyes.

SLATER Joseph (c.1800-3.7.1882)
(M.P.R. 2417. 2/8243, p. 195. S.J.R. 3189. COD 146. 4/4006, copy at R.394).
Convicted at the Quarter Sessions 16 July 1818 of larceny, stealing linen. He was sentenced to 7 years transportation and was transported on the 'Baring', leaving Downs 27 January 1819, arriving New South Wales 26 June 1819. He was 18 years of age, height 5'6½", with brown hair and hazel eyes. His complexion was fair and ruddy. He was single, a spectacle glass grinder by trade and a native of Birmingham. He was on general distribution for his arrival assignments in the Windsor District (R.1030.4/3500, pp. 162/3). On 20 March 1822, he is included on a list of persons transported to Newcastle by the 'Elizabeth Hentietta', having been convicted and sentenced to two years by the Windsor Bench 11 March 1822. The 1822 Muster confirms that he was still on Government employment at Newcastle. He is then shown to have been a runaway from Newcastle and on 5 November 1822 he is included on a list of prisoners for transportation to Newcastle, having been convicted by the Sydney Bench on 4th November 1822 and sentenced to be returned to Newcastle as being a runaway (R.6009.4/3506, p. 406) By 24 March 1823, he is included on a list of convicts removed from Newcastle to Port Macquarie on the 'Lady Nelson', having been convicted by the Windsor Bench 11 March 1822 and sentenced to 2 years (R.6019.4/3864, pp. 396-7). He is again in trouble with the authorities 13 November 1824, when attached to the lumber yard. On a 'Return of Proceedings of the Bench of Magistrates' at Parramatta, the following entry confirms his offence as being "found coming out of the lumber yard with Government nails, contrary to Orders". He was tried 13 November and sentenced to 50 lashes and to be returned to employment. The 1825 Muster states that he is a labourer in Sydney. On 21 July 1825 he received his certificate of freedom No. 78/4036 (R.601.

4/4423). Due to mutilation,this was replaced by C.F. No. 22/5282. dated 4 May 1826 (R.602.4.4424), and, in turn, this was replaced by C.F. No. 27/1040 dated 26 November 1827 (R. 982/4291), eventually changed to C.F. No. 29/542 issued 8 June 1829 (R.985.4/4299), which again was changed to C.F. No. 39/779 dated 27 May 1839. It is possible that he married an Ellen Crawford in 1836. His death possibly took place at Parramatta 3 July 1882 at the George Street Asylum, when he was 82 years of age (1882/07129).

SMITH Henry (c.1818–)
(M.P.R. 2424. 2/8268, p. 191. S.J.R. 3202. R.2662. X642A).
Convicted at the Quarter Sessions 3 January 1839 of housebreaking by entering the house of William Davies of Llanfihangel and taking a watch and a waistcoat. He was sentenced to 14 years transportation. He had no previous convictions. His accomplice was William Shaw who received a similar sentence, but did not leave this country (NLW. Bl/17, *Shrewsbury Chronicle*, 11 January 1839 and *Salopian Journal*, 9th January 1839). He was transported on the 'Mangles', leaving Portsmouth 29 November 1839, arriving New South Wales 27 April 1840. He was 22 years of age, height 5'7¼", with light brown hair and dark grey eyes. His complexion was sallow and freckled, he had two small scars on the outer corner of the left eyebrow and a scar on the back of his left hand. He was able to read and write, a Protestant and butcher by trade. He was single and a native of Birmingham.

STURGES Jeremiah (c.1800–)
(M.P.R. 2417. 2/8243, p. 195. S.J.R. 3189. COD 146. 4/4006, copy at R.394).
Convicted at the Quarter Sessions 16 July 1818 of an unknown crime. He was sentenced to 7 years transportation and was transported on the 'Baring', leaving Downs 27 January 1819, arriving New South Wales 26 June 1819. He was 18 years of age, height 5'6", with black hair and dark eyes. His complexion was fair and ruddy and he was a tallow chandler by trade. He was single, a Protestant and a native of North America. On arrival, he was assigned for general distribution (R.1030.4/3500, pp.162-3). On 1 September 1825 he received his certificate of freedom No. 860 (R.602.4/4224) and, in the Muster of the same year, he is shown as a carpenter at Campbelltown. On 14 December 1825 he was a member of a Jury at the Inquest on a Francis Blong, held at Upper Minto (R.6063.4/1784, p. 273a). By the time of the 1828 Census, he was employed as a carpenter by a George Coy of Pitt Street, Sydney.

WATKINS Watkin (c.1780-20.7.1835)
(S.J. 3205. COD 147. 4/4007, copy at R.5).
Convicted at the Great Sessions 14 August 1819 of cattle stealing. He was sentenced to death, commuted to 14 years transportation and was transported on the 'Neptune', leaving Downs 23 March 1820, arriving New South Wales 16 July 1820. He was 40 years of age, height 5'6", with brown hair and hazel eyes. His complexion was dark and ruddy. He was a Protestant, a labourer and a native of Brecknock (27/779.33/912). On 8 September 1821, he was employed on the roads and on the list of all persons victualled from H.M. Magazines (R.6016.4/5781, p. 80). Between 30 April and 26 October 1822, he was assigned to various people, including an E. Edwards of Sydney, as confirmed in the 1822 Muster (fiche 3291.4/4580D, pp. 128-9). He received his ticket of leave No. 27/779 on 2 November 1827 from the Sydney Bench, which was renewed by ticket No. 32/434 dated 26 May 1832. The 1828 Census shows him as a labourer with a William Dibbs, wheelwright of

Park Street, Sydney. The Census also shows an infant son named William aged 3 months who was born in the Colony. On 6 February 1828, a banns application on behalf of Watkin Watkins and Hannah Fox (Dainty) was submitted to a Rev. Hill, but as Hannah Fox was already married on arrival, permission for the marriage was not given. On 19 August 1833, he received his certificate of freedom No. 33/912 (R.991.4/4317), but by 20 July 1835 he was buried at St Phillip's, Sydney, age 56 years, the officiating minister being a Rev. William Cowper (NSW Death Index Reg. No. 1837, Vol. 19).

WEAVER John (c.1786-12.3.1825)
(M.P.R. 2427. 2/8277, p. 231. S.J.R. 3209. COD 144, copy at R.394 and fiche 642, p. 450. 4/4006).
Convicted at the Quarter Sessions 2 April 1818 of an unknown crime. He was sentenced to 7 years transportation. He was transported on the 'Shipley', leaving Woolwich 18 July 1818, arriving New South Wales 18 November 1818. He was 32 years of age, height 5'4½", with brown hair and hazel eyes. His complexion was ruddy. He was single, a labourer and a native of Shropshire. No mention is made of him in official records before his death by drowning at Liverpool, 12 March 1825. He was 40 years of age and was buried 14 March at Liverpool where he had resided (NSW Burial Index Reg. No. 6384, Vol. 2).

WILLIAMS Jonah (c.1807–)
(M.P.R. 2417. 2/8242, p. 213. S.J.R. 3187).
Convicted at the Assizes 10 March 1832 of larceny, stealing saddles, bridles and a clarionet. He was sentenced to 7 years transportation, which followed no previous convictions. His accomplice was Samuel Swancott (*Salopian Journal*, 14 March 1832). He was transferred to the hulk 'Cumberland' at Chatham, from where he was transported on the 'Asia', leaving Downs 21 February 1833, arriving New South Wales 27 June 1833. He was 26 years of age, height 5'6¾", with dark brown hair and dark hazel eyes. His complexion was sallow and pock-pitted. He was single, unable to read or write and spoke English badly (possibly because he normally spoke Welsh), a Protestant and a farm servant/shepherd by trade. He received his ticket of leave No. 38/1974, 20 November 1838, from the Dungog Bench and was allowed to stay in the Maitland District.

WILLIAMS William (c.1771-31.10.1819)
(M.P.R. 2419. 2/8250, p. 105. COD 146, copy at R.394. Fiche 641, pp. 41-59. 4/4006).
Convicted at the Great Sessions 13 August 1818 of forgery. He was the local Collector of Taxes at Llanerfyl, and had added the figure 3 to £3, thus showing £33 on his return to the Receiver General; as a result he was overpaid. He told the judge that he was an idiot, but the judge over-ruled his plea. He was sentenced to 14 years transportation (NLW Q/SR 1818 and *Salopian Journal*, 19 August 1818) and was transported on the 'Canada', leaving London 23 April 1819, arriving New South Wales 1 September 1819. He was 44 years of age, height 5'7", with black hair and hazel eyes. His complexion was dark and sallow. He was a shepherd by trade and a native of North Wales. He died on Oct 1819 at Parramatta, aged 48 years and was buried at St John's, Sydney.

WILSON Thomas (c.1813–)
(M.P.R. 2423. 2/8266, p. l. S.J.R. 3200. R.906.4/4019).
Convicted at the Quarter Sessions 17 October 1833 of larceny, assault with intent to rob Edward Swift of Llanfyllin in the Parish of Llanrhaeadr-ym-Mochnant. He was sentenced to 7 years transportation, this following no previous convictions. (His accomplices were Sarah Gane, Elizabeth Jones and Timothy Partridge.) He was sent to the hulk 'Justitia' and then transported on the 'Lady Nugent', leaving Sheerness 4 December 1834, arriving New South Wales 9 April 1835. He was 21 years of age, height 5'4¾", with brown hair and grey eyes. His complexion was ruddy and freckled, he had a scar on the forehead, a red blotch on the lower right arm, a scar on the back of the right thumb, a scar on the 4th finger of the right hand, a sun and moon and "hard" crucifix on the left arm and a scar under the right thumb (39/879). He was single, a skinner/poulterer by trade and a native of Kent. He was employed by a William George at Pitt Water in the 1837 Muster and on 29 May 1839 received his ticket of leave No. 39/879 from the Pitt Water Bench for that District (R.933.4/4129).

Van Diemen's Land

ASHTON John (c.1801 or 1811-13.2.1835)

Convicted at the Great Sessions 14 April 1825 of larceny by house breaking at Llanbrynmair, he was sentenced to 7 years transportation. This followed a previous conviction for shop lifting (CON 31/1; 23/1 and ML5). His conduct at Montgomery Gaol was "bad" and again on the hulk ship 'Euryalus' at Chatham he was "bad" although his final report indicated him as being "good" (CON 31/1). He was transported on the 'William Miles' leaving Downs 24 March 1828 arriving VDL 29 July 1828. He was shown as 17 years of age, height 5'1¼", dark brown hair, brown eyes, fair complexion, farmer's boy by trade and a Protestant. He had a large round scar centre of stomach, blue mark inside right arm and a scar across the nail on end of little finger left hand. He was single and at the time of his crime lived with a Mr Thos Davies in his farmhouse located in Hope Parish, his mother (Elizabeth) lived at Leominster, having remarried (Brown) and was a washer woman. The following offences are noted:

> *29 Nov 1828 – Insolence and Misconduct for which his Master beat him and removed him from his service.*
>
> *Jan 1829 – His new Master (J. Simpson), at St Peter's Pass placed him for 14 days in a chain gang, having neglected his duty and being insolent to the sub overseer (Hodgson).*
>
> *31 Jan 1829 – Neglect of duty, insolence and throwing away stones he was ordered to break in order to save himself having to break them this day and similar offences on numerous other occasions, one month chain gang.*
>
> *On 3 Jan 1835 – John Ashton was convicted of stealing from the dwelling house of Jas Hamilton at Ross, a quantity of superfine blue woollen cloth (value £20) and divers other articles of goods. Four other persons were also involved in this offence and following sentence by the Supreme Court, held at Hobart the last week in January 1835, John Ashton and two of his accomplices were sentenced to death; following execution at Hobart Town on 13 February 1835 he was buried by a William Bedford. John Ashton's age was given as 34 yrs.*

(Conduct 1833 F.C. No. 223, 15 Nov. 1833; Death HGD 34/1 1835 No. 3859 (1505) Hobart Town Parish, and *Hobart Town Courier*, 6 February 1835, p. 4, col. 1).

ASTLEY Evan (c.1816-20.2.1870)

Convicted at the Assizes 9 March 1844 of stealing wool (value £5.16.0) from the warehouse of William Jones, Flannel Maker, Newtown. He was sentenced to 10 years transportation which followed a two month sentence for assaulting the Police. He had no previous convictions (Q/SR 1844). He was transported on the 'Lord Auckland' leaving London 20 July 1844 arriving VDL 15 November 1844. The ship's surgeon confirmed his general conduct as being "good". He was

30 years of age, weaver by trade, height 5'5½", head oval, hair brown, whiskers brown, visage oval, forehead medium height, eyes hazel, eyebrows brown, nose medium, mouth medium, chin large and complexion fair. He was stoutly made with a scar on chin and lower lip. He could read and write a little, a Protestant and was a native of Newtown. He was married to Martha with no issue. His parents (Evan and Hannah), brothers (Richard in the 23rd Regiment, Isaac and John), sisters Mary, Ann Jane resided at Newtown (CON 33/61; CON 14/30; CON 18/38). On arrival in VDL he spent 15 months in a labour gang at Southport under class 3 (employment in the public departments or public works), from where he was discharged 15 February 1845. The following offences are noted:

> *24 June 1846 – Whilst acting as a Constable in Hobart he was convicted of misconduct in improperly taking Mr Reynolds into custody and handcuffing him. It was recommended and approved that he be dismissed the Service.*
>
> *June 1847 – Out after hours from Cascade Factory. Two months imprisonment with hard labour.*
>
> *May 1848 – Misconduct in disturbing the public peace at Bailey, Hobart. 7 days solitary imprisonment.*
>
> *April 1849 – Misconduct in being absent from his sleeping place at night and in the company of male and female passholders. 2 months imprisonment with hard labour.*
>
> *17 July 1849 – Insolence and disobedience of orders 6 months imprisonment and hard labour.* (CON 33/62).

He received a ticket of leave 12 August 1850 but by 28 June 1852 he was fined 5/- for disturbing the peace at Hobart. On 29 March 1853, his T.L. was revoked owing to his absence from Muster. His certificate of freedom was issued 20 March 1854. On 26 March 1851 he had applied for permission to marry Agnes Rob(e) (CON 52/4; CON 52/3 p.6). The marriage took place on 20 August 1851, in the Church of the Holy Trinity Hobart, according to the Rites and Ceremonies of the United Church of England and Ireland, by Banns, in the presence, of the Rural Dean Phillip Palmer. Witnesses were William Whyte and T. J. Taylor. Evan Astley was shown as of full age, tinman and brazier and a widower. He signed his name. Agnes Robe was shown as of full age and a spinster. She made her mark (AOT CPtOM CON 52/4; CON 52/3, p.6; RGD 37/10 1851 No. 393 (Marriages Astley/Rob(e)). His death is recorded at the General Hospital Hobart 20 February 1870 age 54 years and described as a tinsmith; cause of death being "Chr Cystitis". The informant was C. Seagar House Steward General Hospital (RGD 35/7 1870 Hobart No. 9169).

AUBREY Mary Ann (c.1816-8.2.1860)
Convicted at the Quarter Sessions 3 January 1839 of larceny from the person, by stealing sixteen shillings from Owen Jenkins of Newtown (*Salopian Journal*, 9 January 1839). She was sentenced to 10 years transportation. Her gaol report confirmed her to be good with respectable connections. She was transported on the 'Hindostan' leaving London 9 May 1839 arriving VDL 12 September 1839. The Surgeon's Journal stated that she was very good, chaste and most attentive. She was 24 years of age, laundress by trade, able to read and write, height 5'5½", head large oval, hair dark brown, visage oval, forehead medium, eyes dark grey, eyebrows black, nose long, mouth medium, chin medium, complexion sallow with no general marks on the body. Her native place was Bristol and she was married

with 2 children. Her husband was living in Merthyr Tydfil and her father George was a Master of a Vessel. She had 4 brothers and 3 sisters (CON 40/2; CON 15/9; CON 18/24; CON 40/2).

The following offences are noted:

15 Jan 1840 – Absent without leave. 6 days solitary confinement on bread/water.

24 Apl 1840 – Absconding. 14 days cell on bread/water.

19 May 1840 – Absent all night without leave. 4 days cell on bread/water.

7 Aug 1840 – Absent without leave. 6 days cell on bread/water.

28 Aug 1840 – Absconding. 2 months hard labour in cell.

19 Jan 1841 – Refusing to work. 10 days cell on bread/water.

29 Apl 1841 – Larceny under £5. Existing sentence of transportation extended by 2 years. Recommended to be detained 12 months in the Female House of Correction on probation.

1 Sep 1842 – Absent one day/night without leave. 6 months at (difficult to read) and assigned in the Interior only.

18 Apl 1843 – Absent without leave and in a disorderly house. 6 months hard labour in House of Correction.

Feb 1844 – Out after hours. Reprimanded.

22 Nov 1844 – Misconduct, in a state of fornication. 2 months hard labour.

Jan 1845 – Out after hours. 14 days hard labour House of Correction.

Feb 1845 – Drunk. Fined 5/-.

2 Feb 1845 – Not known. 2 months hard labour House of Correction.

22 Apl 1845 – Larceny under £5. 9 months hard labour.

11 May 1846 – Absent without leave. 6 days solitary confinement.

17 Dec 1846 – Absent without leave. 6 months hard labour.

27 Jan 1847 – Absent without leave/Drunk. 14 days solitary confinement.

Sep 1847 – Absconded. 1 month hard labour. (CON 40/2).

A ticket of leave was issued 20/21 November 1848 and a free certificate 29 January 1850. In January 1845 an application for permission to marry was made by Mary Ann Aubrey with William Simmons (free) and this was approved 23 January 1845. Again another application was made by Mary Ann Aubrey to marry Dennis Hoigan (convict on the 'Abercrombie'), which was approved 10 February 1845 (CON 52/2, pp. 370 and 429). Records do not confirm that either marriage took place. On 27 December 1847 Mary Ann Aubrey married James Chamberlain age 37 years and a labourer. The service took place in St George's Church, Hobart (Bethesda). Witnesses were Henry Mottram and Bridget Beedle (Henry Mottram had been convicted by a Montgomeryshire Court in 1833) (RGD 37/6 1847 No. 903). Following the death of her husband, Mary Ann Chamberlain (Aubrey), applied on 2 May 1853 to marry John Bumford of Ross Bridge. Her sudden death took place on 8 February 1860, at which time her name was shown as Mary Ann Hogan.

BEASTALL Henry (c.1796–)

Convicted at the Assizes 19 July 1831 of stealing a bay mare from Dolanog House, Welshpool, the property of Mr David Jones, and a black gelding, the property of Mr Henry Jones, Surgeon. His accomplices were John Farren and Jonathan Roose (*Salopian Journal*, 27 July 1831). He was sentenced to death, commuted to life transportation (CON 31/4; 31/5). His gaol report states that he was of a bad disposition and a member of a gang of horse thieves. His period spent on the hulk 'Justitia' was given as orderly. He was transported on the 'Katherine Stewart Forbes' leaving London 26 February 1832 arriving VDL 16 July 1832. The Ship Surgeon confirmed that he was quiet on board. He was 36 years of age, single, cattle jobber by trade, height 5'4¾", head round, hair dark brown, visage narrow, forehead perpendicular and wrinkled, eyes grey, eyebrows dark brown and meeting; nose long, mouth large, chin short and projecting, complexion dark and he was slightly pockpitted (CON 18/10). The following offences are noted:

> *6 Aug 1832 – Leaving the Barracks without permission. 6 days on Tread Wheel.*
> *22 May 1840 – Drunk. Fined 5/-.*
> *26 Apl 1844 – Drunk. Fined 5/-.* (CON 31/4-5).

He received a conditional pardon No. 11 on 1 January 1842 having held a ticket of leave for 5 years and a Police character shown as good (HO 10/57).

BEBB John (c.1791–)

Convicted at the Quarter Sessions 7 January 1841 of burglary by stealing 40 lbs bacon from his brother Evan Bebb at Meifod. He had also been indicted for arson by setting fire to his brother's haystack, but was acquitted of this second offence. He was sentenced to 10 yrs transportation (Q/SR 1841). His gaol report confirmed him to be of bad character with respectable connections, although the hulk report stated that his conduct was good. He was transported on the 'Tortoise' leaving Plymouth 26 October 1841 arriving VDL 19 February 1842. On the ship the Surgeon recorded his conduct as orderly. He was 51 years of age, single, Protestant, a farm labourer, able to read and write a little, height 5'3½", head small, hair brown to grey, whiskers dark brown to grey, visage oval, forehead high broad, eyes hazel, eyebrows black, nose long and thin, mouth medium, chin broad, complexion sallow with a wrinkled face and a scar on back of left hand. He had 5 brothers (CON 33/17; CON 14/13; CON 18/30). There are no offences recorded against him and his ticket of leave was issued 2 March 1847, to be followed by a conditional pardon 4 July 1848, it being noted that his conduct had been good and he had completed 7½ years of a 10 year sentence. A free certificate was allowed him 23 August 1852 (CON 33/17; HO 10/61, Despatch No. 212 of 21 October 1848).

BENNETT Fanny (c.1833–)

Convicted at the Quarter Sessions 19 October 1848 of larceny. She was sentenced to 7 years transportation and was transported on the 'Stately' leaving Plymouth 5 June 1849 arriving VDL 2 September 1849. Records in this Country show her age as 13 years, but the Tasmanian Archives on her arrival show her to be 16 years of age. She was single, Protestant, housemaid by calling and able to read only. Height 4'10¼", head round, hair sandy brown, visage round, forehead high, eyes grey, eyebrows sandy brown, nose and mouth small, chin round and of fresh complexion (CON 41/23; CON 15/5; CON 19/7). By 9 January 1850 she had been placed in Convict Class 3. The following offences are noted:

> *9 Aug 1851– Larceny under £5. 6 months hard labour.*
> *9 Aug 1852 – Absconded.*
> *7 Sep 1853 – Absconded. 12 months hard labour.*

Application for a ticket of leave was refused 22 June 1852 but approved by 3

April 1853. On 17th September 1855 she married John Phillips at the Cathedral Church of St David Hobart Town according to the Rites and Ceremonies of the Church of England and Ireland by Banns, the Officiating Minister being H. E. Drew in the presence of James Doley and Mary Curly. She was shown to be 20 years of age and a spinster whilst her husband was 23 years of age and a fisherman (CON 52/7, p. 362; NS/282/10/4; RGD 37/14 No. 186/1855). Records show that she was remarried on 17 March 1906 to an Andrew Dumkley at Hobart when she must have been about 73 years of age (RGD 1/16/605).

BRADBURY John (c.1819–)

Convicted at the Quarter Sessions 6 April 1843 of housebreaking by entering the house of Mrs Ann Davies Welshpool and stealing 1 gold watch, 1 gold key, 1 watch guard, 1 scarf and 1 silk handkerchief. From the same house, the property of Rev. Joseph McIntosh, was stolen 1 top coat, 1 black coat, 1 waistcoat, 1 dressing gown and 1 silk handkerchief. His accomplices were John Hartell, John Walden and Eliza Paskin of Dudley (who was sentenced to 12 months hard labour in Montgomery Gaol, the men being sentenced to transportation) (*Shrewsbury Chronicle*, NLW B1/19; Q/SR 1843E; *Eddoes Journal*, 15 March 1843). He was sentenced to 15 years transportation. The gaol report confirms him as bad in every respect with bad connections. At the hulk his behaviour was good. He was transported on the 'Lord Petre' leaving London 7 July 1843 arriving VDL 15 October 1843. The Surgeon confirmed that he had committed no offences whilst on board, that he was a useful blacksmith and his conduct good. He was 24 years of age, single, a cable chain maker and blacksmith by trade, could read only, height 5'4¼", head oval, hair dark brown, whiskers dark brown, visage oval, forehead medium height, eyes hazel, eyebrows dark brown, nose medium, mouth medium, chin medium and pale complexion. Marks included 3 small blue marks and foul anchor upper part right arm, 2 pipes bottle and glass below elbow right arm, foul anchor and star FE heart and blue mark upper part left arm, mermaid with comb and glass, AG 2 star and 3 below elbow left arm, Ring on 4th finger left hand, blue dots on all fingers. He was a native of Wolverhampton where his stepfather Jno, mother Jane, brother Alfred? and sisters Eliza and one other resided (CON 33/45; CON 14/24; CON 18/34). He served 18 months probationary service in a gang based on the Black River as class PPH 3rd being released from the first stage of Probation 15 April 1845.

The following offences are noted:

> *June 1845 – Misconduct at Hobart. Discharged.*
> *July 1847 – Drunk, out after hours and falsely presenting himself as Free at Hobart. 2 months hard labour.*
> *7 March 1848 – Out after hours and absent without leave in Pontville. Admonished.*
> *22 May 1848 – Misconduct by being in the Township on a Sunday without a pass and under the influence of liquor in Pontville. 3 months hard labour.*
> *20 April 1850 – Misconduct by being out after hours in Hobart. 3 months hard labour and to be hired for the Interior upon discharge.*
> *Same date – Burglary. Discharged.*
> *23 July 1850 – Absent without leave in Hobart. 6 months hard labour and then to reside in the Interior.*

His ticket of leave was refused 6 May 1851 but was granted 28 October 1851 with the proviso that he did not reside in Hobart Town. Owing to being absent from a Muster his Ticket was revoked 29 March 1853. There is no record as to when he regained his freedom (CON 33/45; AOT Correspondence File No. 57).

BROWN John (c.1821–)

Convicted at the Quarter Sessions 2 July 1845 of housebreaking and stealing a piece of cheese, 1 silk handkerchief, 1 pr trousers and 1 piece of velvet from John Lloyd of Meifod, of stealing 4 handkerchiefs from house of Andrew Gittins, 1 razor (value 1/-) and 1 pocket knife (value 5d) the property of Jane Haynes of Meifod. His accomplice was Michael Kelly (NLW Q/SR 1845 and NLW Bl/19, *Shrewsbury Chronicle*, 11 July 45). He was sentenced to 10 years transportation. His gaol report found him to be incorrigible and bad in every respect, although the Surgeon stated that he was good. He was transported on the 'Rodney 2' leaving Queenstown 24 September 1851 arriving VDL 20 December 1851. He was 30 years of age, single, miner by calling and a native of Plymouth, where his father (John), mother (Mary) and sister (Mary) lived, height 5'6¾", able to read only, head large, hair black, whiskers black, visage large, forehead low, eyes hazel, eyebrows black, nose mouth and chin large and complexion dark. He was slightly pockpitted (CON 33/105; CON 14/44).

The following offences are noted:

14 May 1853 – Absent without leave. 2 months hard labour.
16 Mar 1855 – Absconded. (CON 33/105)

He was placed on Probation for 21 months at Old Wharf. An Application for Permission to Marry was received from John Brown to marry Mary Ann Assen (free) on 28 March 1853 but the marriage is not confirmed (CON 52/6).

BUMFORD John (alias BOOMFORD: BOONFORD: BURNFORD: BOUNFORD: BOUMFORD) (c.1808-6th Nov 1890)

Convicted at the Great Sessions 24 March 1830 of larceny, stealing from the house of Evan Chapman Llanllwchaiarn two £5 banknotes, one £1 note, 30 sovereigns and a bankers receipt for £30. His statement of offence confirmed that he had stolen the money from his Uncle. He was sentenced to death, commuted to 14 years transportation (Q/SR 1830). His gaol and hulk 'Justita' reports confirm that he was good, orderly with respectable connections. He was transported on the 'Red Rover' leaving Portsmouth 18 November 1830 arriving VDL 25 March 1831. He was 23 years of age, married with one child (his wife Mary and child resided at Bettws), native of Newtown, sawyer and ploughman by trade, Protestant, height 5'3½", head round, hair brown, whiskers none, forehead perpendicular, eyes light brown, eyebrows brown, nose medium large, mouth medium wide, chin medium large, complexion fair with no bodily marks (CON 31/4; ML13; CON 13/5; CON 18/22). An Appropriation List shows him as a pitt sawyer and ploughman by trade (CSO 1/512/11203). There are no offences shown against him (CON 31/4). He received a conditional pardon No. 1945 on 26 January 1839 and a free certificate 30 January 1852. He obtained a Licence to Marry Ann Burrows at St George's Hobart on 2 May 1853 but the marriage is not recorded (NS 373/1 No. 911). Under the name Bamford he apparently married Mary Ann Burton, a 50-year-old widow at St George's, Hobart, according to the rites and ceremonies of the Church of England. The Service was performed by the Rev. H. P. Fry and the witnesses were Richard and Jane Bury. John Bumford died on November 1890, his age being shown as 95 years and burial took place at Ross General Cemetery. His wife predeceased him on 20 Feb 1875 aged 74 years and was buried at the same location as her husband (TAMIOTI ROOS/1000611-2).

CANE Charles (c.1822–)

Convicted at the Quarter Sessions 2 July 1845 of housebreaking and stealing 1 sovereign, one half sovereign, one shilling and sixpence and other articles from the dwelling house of John Owens of Llanwrin. His accomplices were Edward Simmonds and William Storey. He was sentenced to 10 years transportation (NLW Q/SR 1845 and NLW Bl/19, *Shropshire Chronicle*, 11 July 1845). The Surgeon reported that he was good and well behaved. He was transported on the 'Pestongee Bomangee' leaving Plymouth 22 September 1845 arriving VDL 30 December 1845. He was single, butcher by calling and possibly native of Dover, he had a brother (John) who was a tailor, height 5'2¾", 23 years of age, able to read and write and a Protestant, head oval, hair brown, visage oval, medium height, eyes grey, eyebrows brown, nose and mouth medium, chin small and complexion fresh. He was deeply pockpitted and had 3 small marks on the left arm below the elbow (CON 33/74; CON 14/34). He spent 15 months in the Rocky Hills class 1 gang. The following of fences are noted:

> *8 August 1846 – Misconduct. 2 days imprisonment with hard labour.*
> *8 March 1847 – Disobedience of an Order Probation extended by 1 month.*
> *16 December 1847 – Misconduct. Admonished.*
> *20 January 1848 – Misconduct by falsely stating that his contract had expired thereby obtaining his discharge 3 months imprisonment with hard labour.*
> *24 – Misconduct in feigning sickness. 4 days solitary.*

COOK William (c.1777-28.2.1820)

Convicted at the Great Sessions 3 March 1817 of burglary, breaking and entering, and stealing from the house of Mr Richard Pryce of Forden, 1 pr boots (£1), 1 pr shoes (4/-), 1 pr shoes (2/-), 1 shoe brush (6d), 1 jug (3d), 2lb butter (2/-), 1 qtr milk (ld) and 1 cheesebag (1/-). Found not guilty for the first two offences but guilty of stealing and taking away the above items, he was sentenced to 7 years transportation. His accomplice George Chambers received the same sentence (NLW Wales 4/200/6). He was transported on the 'Lady Castlereagh' leaving England 2 December 1817 arriving VDL 11 June 1818. He was a native of Shropshire, age 41 years, labourer and wagoner by trade, height 5'1" or 5'3", eyes grey, hair brown, complexion fair, pale and pockpitted marks. General remarks state that he was well behaved although an invalid (CON 31/6; 13/1, p. 173; CON 23/l; CSO 1/562/12465). His death is recorded on 28 February 1820, with burial the following day (RGD 34/1 1820 No. 377).

DAVIES Elizabeth (alias GRIST) (c.1831–)

Convicted at the Quarter Sessions 4 January 1849 of larceny by a Servant in that she stole clothing whilst working for her employer (NLW B1/22, *Shrewsbury Chronicle*, 1849/50NLW Q/SR 1848). Sentenced to 7 years transportation she was transported on the 'St Vincent' leaving London 19 December 1849 arriving VDL 4 April 1850. The Surgeon reported that her general conduct had been very good. She was 19 years of age, single and lived with her mother (Elizabeth) and brother (Samuel) possibly at Abermule. Country servant by calling, Protestant and unable to read or write, height 5'1½", head small, hair dark brown, visage small, eyes hazel, eyebrows dark brown, nose and mouth small, chin medium and complexion fresh. There were no distinguishable marks (CON 41/25; CON 15/6; CON 19/8). No offences are recorded and she received her ticket of leave 10 August 1852. On 12 April 1852, and in the name of Elizabeth Davis, she married Moses Linton, age 45 years and a shopkeeper. The marriage took place in the Parish Church of St Peters in the District of Hamilton, according to the Rites and Ceremonies of the United Church of England and Ireland by Banns, the officiating clergyman being George Wright in the presence of Joseph Exley and Ellen Howard (RGD 37/11 No. 115 1852).

DAVIES Hugh (c.1790–)

Convicted at the Great Sessions 9 August 1817 of burglary. He was sentenced to 7 years transportation (Q/SR 1817). The gaol report shows him to have been orderly. He was transported on the 'Lord Melville' leaving England July 1818 arriving VDL 17 December 1818. He was a native of Montgomeryshire, aged 28 years, of unknown marital status, farmer's labourer by trade, height 5'8", eyes hazel, hair dark brown, and complexion fresh (CON 31/9; CON 23/1; CSO 1/95/2278). It is possible that he departed Launceston, Tasmania, 4 March 1840 on the 'Paul Pry' (*Launceston Advertiser*, 5 March 1840).

DAVIES John (c.1820–)

Convicted at the Quarter Sessions 10 April 1845 of housebreaking and larceny, having feloniously entered the house of Richard Matthews at Broniarth and stole money and other articles. He had also stolen 1 pair boots value 5/- from John Jones, 4 loaves of bread and 6lb bacon from Elizabeth Harris, for which he had been sentenced to 3 months and 6 months respectively. He was sentenced to 15 years transportation (NLW Bl/19, *Shrewsbury Chronicle*, 18 April 1845). He was transported on the 'Pestongee Bomangee' leaving Plymouth 22 September 1845 arriving VDL 30 December 1845. He was 25 years of age, single, native of Berriew and lived with his father (Thomas) and brothers (Thomas and Andrew), farm labourer by calling, unable to read and write and a Protestant, height 5'1¼", head oval, hair light brown, visage oval, medium height, eyes blue, eyebrows brown, nose and mouth medium, chin large and complexion fresh. He was pockpitted and had 2 scars on right eyebrow (CON 33/74; CON 14/34; CON 33/61; CON 18/46). He was placed in the Salt Water River Gang for twenty-four months in Class 2nd PPH 3rd. The following offences are noted:

> *13 June 1846 – Absconding. 14 days solitary confinement.*
> *26 January 1848 – Idleness and neglect of duty. 3 months imprisonment with hard labour.*
> *9 February 1850 – Misconduct by stating that he could not remain in his Master's service. 10 days solitary confinement.*
> *11 April 1854 – Misconduct in representing himself as freeman and having firearms. Reprimanded.* (CON 33/74).

His ticket of leave was issued 16 November 1852 but this was revoked 10 October 1854 due to his absence from muster. On 5 October 1865 he was tried at Launceston and sentenced to 8 years reconviction in that he had broken into a store (CON 37/10, p. 5606). This sentence was remitted by 2 months 13 June 1871, and the remainder of his sentence remitted by the Governor in Council, 4 September 1871.

DAVIES Thomas (alias CORN) (c.1804–)

Convicted at the Great Sessions 23 March 1829 of stealing 4 pigs. He was sentenced to 7 years transportation (Q/SR 1829). His gaol report stated that he was a thief by habit and repute and the hulk report confirmed that although he had been orderly it had been necessary to punish him. He was transported on the 'Bussorah Merchant' leaving Downs 6 October 1829 arriving VDL 18 January 1830. He was a native of Shropshire, single and lived with his father (Thomas Davies) and mother, ploughman and able to reap, mow, milk and shear by trade, able to read and write, height 5'4¾", hair brown, eyes brown, with no marks on the body (CON 23/1; ML 10; CON 31). Only one offence is recorded against him when on 13 August 1831 he was found guilty of being drunk and neglecting his duty for which he was sentenced to receive 25 lashes (COD 31/9; F.C. No. 122 25 March 1836 (CON 23/1).

DAVIES William (c.1810–)

Convicted at the Quarter Sessions 17 October 1833 of housebreaking and larceny at Guilsfield. He was sentenced to 14 years transportation. The gaol report stated that he was a plundering tramp of violent disposition and the hulk report 'Justitia' confirmed him to be orderly. He was transported on the 'William Metcalfe' leaving Portsmouth 23 May 1834 arriving VDL 4 September 1834. The Surgeon reported that he had been orderly. He was 23 years of age, ploughman by trade and a native of Newport, height 5'7", head oval, hair brown, whiskers none, visage long, forehead high, eyes grey, eyebrows brown, nose medium length, mouth medium width, chin large, complexion sallow with star WGD on left wrist, anchor WD cross on same hand and ring on finger (CON 31/10; CON 18/22; CSO 1/746/16103; The Appropriation List shows that he was employed by Thos Betts at Coal River, to plough, reap, sow, mow, milk and make butter (ML 33/6; CSO 1/746/16103). The following offences are noted:

> *19 December 1835 – Drunk and absent from work without leave. Sentence unknown and he returned to Government work.*
>
> *28 February 1836 – Assaulting a fellow prisoner (Wicks). 6 months hard labour in chains at Spring Hill Road Party.*
>
> *28 April 1836 – Absconded. Existing sentence to Spring Hill extended by 6 months.*
>
> *7 May 1836 – Absconded. 18 months prison with hard labour at a Chain Gang, Bridgewater.*
>
> *22 November 1836 – Repeated idling in Chain Gang. 25 lashes.*
>
> *14 July 1837 – Absconded. 50 lashes and existing sentence in chains extended by 6 months.*
>
> *7 October 1837 – Refusing to work and saying that he would never work more on that ground for any person. 14 days solitary confinement with bread/water.*
>
> *23 October 1837 – . . . to work. Sentence in irons extended by 6 months.*
>
> *25 October 1837 – Refusing to work. 3 weeks solitary confinement with bread/water.*
>
> *28 October 1837 – Gross misconduct by destroying his blankets and pulling down the lining of his . . . which he was confined. Also some of the brick work with the intention of making his escape. To be removed to Port Arthur for 12 months under severe discipline and to be kept in close confinement until he can be removed.*
>
> *31 January 1838 – Absent from gang, getting firewood without permission. 48 hrs solitary confinement on bread/water at Port Arthur.*

> *9 February 1838 – Using oil in a hut contrary to orders. 14 days No. 3 chain gang at Port Arthur.*
>
> *26 February 1838 – Making use of improper language. 48 hrs solitary confinement on bread/water at Port Arthur.*
>
> *7 December 1839 – Idleness, insolence and absent without leave. Text not visible.*
>
> *18 July 1840 – Insolence and gross misconduct. 6 months hard labour out of chains in the Cleveland Road Party and to be returned to his master's service only.*
>
> *11 August 1840 – This man's punishment sentence is ordered to be remitted by His Excellency the Lieutenant Governor 11th August 1840. (CON 31/10).*

He was issued with a ticket of leave 6 September 1844.

DAVIES William (alias Maurice JONES) (c.1824-7.8.1896)

Convicted at the Quarter Sessions 2 October 1841 of larceny by stealing clothes from William Davies and Thomas Williams of Montgomery (*Salopian Journal*, 27 October 1841). This followed a previous conviction of one month imprisonment when he committed a felony by stealing a timber chain. He was sentenced to 7 years transportation. His character whilst in gaol was bad and with bad connections, and on the Hulk it was very bad. He was transported on the 'Eden 2' leaving Woolwich 22 March 1842 arriving VDL 5 July 1842. The Surgeon reported that his general conduct had been good and that he was known as William Davies the First in order to distinguish him from another of the same name on the same ship. He was 18 years of age; single; native of Forden (There is no mention of any near relatives except an uncle living in Cornwall by the name of Richard Wilcock.) Protestant, able to read only and a labourer by trade, height 5'2½", head large, hair light brown, whiskers none, visage round, forehead medium height, eyes blue, eyebrows brown, nose long, mouth medium, chin medium and complexion fresh. He had 2 scars on the left thumb. It is also recorded that his proper name was Maurice Jones (CON 33/22; CON 14/12; CON 28/1). Upon arrival he was placed on 2 year probation at Salt Water Creek Station (SWC). The following extensive list of offences committed by him confirm the gaol and hulk reports:

> *19 October 1842 – Absent from work without leave at SWC. Existing period in the primary gangs to be extended by 3 months.*
>
> *1 February 1843 – Disobedience of Orders in refusing to work at SWC. 24 stripes on the back.*
>
> *21 March 1843 – Refusing to work at SWC. 7 days solitary confinement.*
>
> *13 April 1843 – Misconduct in making away with Goat boots at SWC. 10 days solitary confinement.*
>
> *29 April 1843 – Insolent to his Overseer at SWC. 30 lashes.*
>
> *9 May 1843 – Absent from SWC without leave. 8 days solitary confinement.*
>
> *14 May 1843 – Misconduct in losing or making away with his boots and shirt at SWC. 36 lashes.*
>
> *7 August 1843 – Misconduct being absent from work at SWC. 5 days solitary confinement.*
>
> *6 September 1843 – Misconduct by ill-using another prisoner at the Coal Mines (CM). Admonished.*
>
> *23 November 1843 – Disobedient and Insolent at CM. 6 weeks hard labour in chains.*
>
> *17 February 1844 – Misconduct by losing a Goat bed tick at CM. Admonished.*

21 February 1844 – Idleness at CM. 4 days solitary confinement.

1 March 1844 – Indecent language at CM. 4 days solitary confinement.

13 March 1844 – Misconduct by tearing the number out of his Goat blanket or allowing it to be done at CM. 7 days solitary confinement.

4 April 1844 – Disobedience of Orders at CM. 36 stripes.

9 April 1844 – Disobedience of Orders at CM. 6 days solitary confinement.

18 April 1844 – Disobedience of Orders at CM. 6 weeks hard labour in chains.

16 May 1844 – Disobedience of Orders at CM. 36 stripes.

15 June 1844 – Insolence at CM. 14 days solitary confinement.

23 July 1844 – Misconduct in losing or taking away his Goat bed tick at CM. 14 days solitary confinement.

19 August 1844 – Disobedience of Orders at CM. 5 days solitary confinement.

23 December 1844 – Gross misconduct in behaving irreverently in Church during Divine Service at CM. 11 days solitary confinement.

8 January 1845 – Insolence at CM. 2 days hard labour in chains.

17 January 1845 – Misconduct in tampering with his irons at CM. 14 days solitary confinement.

1 February 1845 – Assaulting the Assistant Superintendent at CM. 75 lashes.

14 February 1845 – Refusing to work at CM. 10 days solitary confinement.

7 March 1845 – Misconduct in losing or taking away his Goat boots at CM. 7 days solitary confinement.

1 April 1845 – Insolence at CM. 36 lashes.

19 April 1845 – Insubordination at CM. 18 months hard labour in chains.

21 April 1845 – Refusing to work at CM. 36 lashes.

30 April 1845 – Insubordination at CM. 3 months hard labour two of which will be in solitary confinement at ? Impression Bay.

12 June 1845 – Absent from Muster at CM. 10 weeks added to previous sentence.

2 August 1845 – Misconduct in losing or making away with his Goat bed tick and rug at CM. Admonished.

5 September 1845 – Misconduct in losing or making away with his Goat waist-coat at CM. 6 days solitary confinement.

27 September 1845 – Misconduct in damaging one of the separate apartments at CM. 36 lashes.

16 October 1845 – Insubordination at CM. 30 days solitary confinement.

22 November 1845 – Absent from work without leave at CM. 24 lashes.

3 December 1845 – Insubordination at CM. 100 lashes and recommended to be transferred to Port Arthur (PA).

13 December 1845 – Disobedience of Orders at CM. 14 days solitary confinement.

Following this offence the decision that he be removed to Port Arthur took place and his calendar of offences continued:

19 January 1846 – Refusing to work at PA. 36 lashes.

20 January 1846 – Refusing to work at PA. 14 days solitary confinement.

16 June 1846 – Misconduct in making use of threatening language at PA. 8 days solitary confinement.

4 August 1846 – Insolence at PA. 11 months added to existing sentence of hard labour in chains.

2 October 1846 – Misconduct in feigning sickness at PA. 2 months hard labour in chains.

24 October 1846 – Disobedience of Orders at PA. 24 lashes.

26 October 1846 – Disobedience of Orders in altering his clothing at PA. 14 days solitary confinement.

22 December 1846 – Disorderly conduct at PA. 10 days solitary confinement.

1 July 1947 – Refusing to work at PA. 10 days solitary confinement.

21 July 1847 – Misconduct in having tobacco in his possession at PA. 7 days solitary confinement.

27 August 1857 – Misconduct in the same cell with another man at PA. 4 months hard labour in chains.

4 October 1847 – Misconduct having tobacco . . . in his possession at PA. 7 days solitary confinement.

21 October 1847 – Making use of threatening language at PA. 14 days solitary confinement.

l December 1847 – Making use of improper language and answering to his name at Muster in an impertinent manner at PA. 7 days solitary confinement.

18 December 1847 – Making use of improper language at PA. 4 days solitary confinement.

10 January 1848 – Assaulting his Overseer at PA. 30 days solitary confinement.

26 February 1848 – Refusing to work at PA. 7 days solitary confinement.

10 March 1848 – Misconduct in making use of threatening and improper language at PA. 7 days solitary confinement.

31 March 1848 – Disorderly conduct in striking a fellow prisoner at PA. 6 months hard labour in chains.

11 April 1848 – Disorderly conduct. 14 days added to existing sentence.

27 April 1848 – Misconduct in attempting to strike a fellow prisoner at PA. 3 months added to existing sentence of hard labour in chains.

Between 1842 and 1848, William Davies committed 59 offences, received 529 lashes, spent 315 days in solitary confinement and a total of 4 years and 5 months hard labour in chains. It is recorded that he "be removed to Norfolk Island" dated 19 April 1848 and on 20 December 1848, it is noted 'If conn has been good to be forwarded to VDL', but he is not at Norfolk Island on 31 December 1853. His possible death may have taken place on 7 August 1896 (CON 33/22).

DODD Edward (c.1797-31 Jan 1845)
Convicted at the Quarter Sessions 16 October 1834 of larceny, stealing 1 gun and 1 jacket from Mr Gill, Rhiwargoer Llanwddyn, where he had been employed as a butler. This followed a previous conviction of stealing fowls for which he had been sentenced to 6 weeks imprisonment in July 1832. He was sentenced to 7 years transportation (NLW Q/SR 1834). His gaol report states that he was dishonest, while the period he spent on the hulk 'Gannymede' notes that he was a working man, of peaceful disposition and decent connections. He was transported on the 'Layton 2' leaving Sheerness 29 August 1835 arriving VDL 10 December 1835 and the Surgeon reported that his conduct had been good. He was single, native of much Wenlock, Shropshire, age 34/38 years, gent's servant, butler and groom by trade, having been so employed all his life, height 5'3¼", head oval, hair black, whiskers black, visage oval, forehead high, eyes blue, eyebrows dark brown, nose long, mouth wide, chin medium length and complexion fresh. He had a scar on the inside of his right arm below the elbow. The Appropriation List confirms his trade as above and that he had been appointed to Doctor Ross Hobart Town (HT) (CON 31/10; CON 27/2; CSO 1/839/17773; CON 18/13).
    The following offences are noted:

> *January 1837 – Neglect of duty at HT. 4 days solitary confinement.*
> *13 March 1840 – Drunk and out after hours. Admonished.*
> *6 March 1844 – Misconduct. 14 days hard labour.*
> *7 May 1844 – Felony. Committed for Trial.*

His ticket of leave issued 24 February 1840 was followed by a free certificate No. 731 in 1841. His death took place in hospital 31 January 1845 (CON 31/10).

EDWARDS Edward (c.1794 – buried 13 August 1828)

Convicted at the Great Sessions 31 March 1817 of an unknown crime. He was sentenced to 7 years transportation and transported on the 'Lady Castlereagh' leaving England 22 December 1818 arriving VDL 11 June 1818. He was 24 years of age, native of Radnorshire, labourer, height 5'7¼", eyes hazel/dark grey, hair brown, with fresh dark sallow complexion. He was well behaved (CON 31/9; CON 13/1, p. 173; CON 23/1, p. 62). He was assigned to a Mr Yate.

The following offences are noted:

> *11 November 1822 – Riding in a cart without reins, etc. Fined 10/-.*
> *16 July 1827 – Drunk/Disorderly. Fined 5/-.*
> *1 August 1827 – Drunk/Disorderly. Fined 5/-.*
> *2 January 1828 – Drunk/Disorderly on the street. Fined 5/-. (CON 31/9).*

He received a free certificate 30 April 1824. His death is recorded at Port Dalrymple in the Parish of St John's, Launceston, County of Cornwall. The burial took place 13 August 1828, the service was conducted by Mr James Norman, Chaplain. Cause of death attributed to apoplexy occasioned by drinking an unusual quantity of wine (RGD 34/1 No. 1837 1828).

EDWARDS Edward (c.1811–)

Convicted at the Quarter Sessions 14 January 1830 of larceny by stealing a quantity of sugar from the warehouse belonging to David Davies Grocer of Newtown. His accomplices were Richard Thomas and Owen Parry. He was sentenced to 7 years transportation (NLW Q/SR 1829). He had one previous conviction and a 2 year sentence for stealing ten gallons of porter, one barrel and two glasses. His gaol report stated that he was quarrelsome with bad connections although the hulk report found him orderly. He was transported on the 'Manlius' leaving London 6 April 1830 arriving VDL 12 August 1830. He was 19 years of age, single and a native of Newtown, Protestant, farm labourer/weaver by trade and able to read and write, height 5'6¼", hair red, eyes grey with a scar right side cheek close to the ear. The Appropriation List shows him with G. Thompson Esq. (CON 31/11; CON 23/1; MGS ML 11).

The following offences are noted:

> *1 December 1830 – Extreme insolence and neglect of duty. 14 days Treadwheel.*
> *Same date – Gross insubordination in telling the Chief Police Magistrate that he would not obey his orders and he would sooner have his head cut off. 25 lashes.*
> *29 April 1831 – Disobedience of orders. 1 month imprisonment with hard labour, and as it appears that his Master cannot manage him it is recommended he should be assigned a considerable distance from Hobart Town.*
> *7 December 1835 – Absent without leave from his Master's place. 3 weeks in cell (at night doing his own work).*

8 December 1835 – Disorderly conduct by beating his fellow servants and for losing some property. 14 days treadwheel and to be kept in a cell at night. This sentence to take effect at the expiration of the sentence passed yesterday.

His free certificate No. 21 was issued 14 Jan 1836 (CON31/11;CON 23/1).

EVANS Edward (c 1807 – 1.3.1832)

Convicted at the Assizes 19 July 1831 of maliciously wounding cattle. He was sentenced to 7 years transportation. The gaol report found him of a peaceable disposition whilst the report on the hulk 'Gannymede' found him to be orderly. He was transported on the 'Katherine Stewart Forbes' leaving London 26 February 1832 arriving VDL 16 July 1832. He was married but no other information is available (CON 31/11; 13/5). He died about 14 March 1832 of cholera whilst on the sea passage (CON 18/10; ML 14; ADM 101/40 Reel No. 3199).

EVANS John (c.1795–)

Convicted at the Great Sessions 4 August 1823 of stealing from the person. He was sentenced to 7 years transportation. This followed a previous offence of stealing money from the person at High Temple, Carmarthenshire. During his stay on the hulk 'Justitia' his conduct was orderly. He was transported on the 'Lady East' leaving Falmouth 16 December 1824 arriving VDL 9 April 1825. He was 30 years of age, married with 4 children who were living in Carmarthen, Protestant and a shopkeeper/labourer by trade, height 5'7", hair dark brown, eyes grey. He had a scar on the right cheek near the nose and lip which was preceded by the words 'High Temple' ie possibly his home. The Appropriation List shows him with a Mr Feat at Risdon Creek (CON 31/9; CON 14/1A; CON 69/1; MM 33/10).

The following offences are noted:

16 June 1825 – Defrauding his Master of 4 Spanish Dollars. 25 lashes.
27 December 1830 – Drunk. Fined 5/-.
2 May 1831 – Drunk. Fined 5/-.
4 May 1831 – Stealing a shawl at Hobart Town the property of Wm Cowley. Dismissed.
11 May 1832 – Drunk. Fined 5/-.
10 May 1833 – Breach of No. 8. Fined £2 and costs. 2 years in the Green Ponds Road Party and conduct to be reported vide Lieut Gov.
28 February 1845 – Assault. Committed for Trial. (CON 31/9).

His pardon was issued vide Colonial Secretary Memo, 29 November 1838.

EVANS William (c.1825–)

Convicted at the Quarter Sessions 2 January 1845 of larceny, stealing 120 yds of flannel from Edward Clayton of Welshpool. He was sentenced to 7 years transportation (NLW Q/SR 1845). He was transported on the 'Bangalore' leaving Bermuda 11 April 1848 arriving VDL 14 July 1848. He was 23 years of age, single, possibly native of Newtown and lived with his father (William), mother (Jane), brother (George) and Sisters (Mary, Jane, Elizabeth and Sarah). Engineer/ Millwright by trade, able to read and write and a Protestant, height 5'5¼", head oval, hair black, whiskers black, visage oval, forehead medium, eyes hazel, eyebrows black, nose small mouth and chin medium and complexion fresh. He had a scar in the corner of the right eye (CON 33/90; CON 14/39). On 24 January 1851 he was discharged from an offence of being in the company of another man who had committed a felony. His free certificate was issued 30 January 1852.

FARREN John (c.1807–)

Convicted at the Assizes 19 July 1831 of horse stealing with Henry Beastall above. He was sentenced to death, commuted to life transportation. His gaol report stated that he was of a bad disposition and belonged to a gang of horse stealers. He was orderly during his time on the hulk 'Justitia'. He was transported on the 'Katherine Stewart Forbes' leaving London 26 February 1832 arriving VDL 16 July 1832. The Surgeon reported that he was quiet on board the ship. He was 25 years of age, native of Halesowen, a horse dealer by trade and married with one child. His wife Rossetta lived at Newcastle . . ., height 5'4¾", head large, hair dark brown, whiskers dark brown and small, visage oval, forehead high and retreating, eyes dark brown, eyebrows dark brown, nose long, mouth medium width, chin medium size with florid complexion. Marks on his body included an anchor on the right arm (CON 31/14; CON 13/5; CON 18/10).

The following of fences are noted:

> *27 November 1834 – Preparing a frivolous complaint against his Master. 6 days confinement on bread/water.*
> *7 April 1836 – Neglect of duty. 7 days in cell with bread/water.*
> *19 July 1836 – Insolence. 2 months hard labour out of chains in the Ford Road Party.*
> *24 January 1837 – Absent without leave. 6 months hard labour out of chains in the Ford Road Party.*
> *22 December 1841 – Drunk and negligence in driving. Fined 15/-.*
> *23 January 1843 – Disobedience of Orders. 14 days hard labour.* (CON 31/14).

He received his ticket of leave 11 September 1840, a conditional pardon No. 725 on 27 September 1843 and a Pardon to move about the Australian Colonies, 29 July 1845.

FISHER Henry (c.1824–)

Convicted at the Quarter Sessions 2 July 1845 of housebreaking and stealing 1 silver watch, 1 waistcoat, 1 snuffbox and a pair of shoes from a Thomas Davies of Buttington. His accomplice was John Stokes. He was sentenced to 10 years transportation (NLW Bl/19, *Shrewsbury Chronicle*, 11 July 1845). He was transported on the 'Pestongee Bomangee' leaving Plymouth 22 September 1845 arriving VDL December 1845. The Surgeon's Report states that he was good and well behaved. He was single, native of Liverpool, Roman Catholic and 21 years of age. He was able to read and write and had been a labourer/servant and was probably a sailor by calling. Height 5'1½", head and visage oval, hair sandy, forehead medium height, eyes hazel, eyebrows brown, nose, mouth and chin medium with complexion ruddy. He was freckled with the following tatoos – IHS and crucifix/anchor on right arm below elbow; hull of a ship, glass cross pipes, brig 'Hero Quebec' 1844 on left arm below elbow (CON 33/74; CON 14/34). He spent 15 months in the Lymington gang in class 1st PPH 3rd.

The following offences are noted:

5 March 1846 – Insolence. 7 days solitary confinement.
21 March 1846 – Absent without leave. 36 lashes.
do – Disobedience of Orders and Insolence. 25 lashes.
15 February 1847 – Idleness and Insolence. 7 days solitary confinement.
30 March 1847 – Absent without leave. Reprimanded.
1 November 1848 – Drunk and Disorderly. 10 days solitary confinement.
4 May 1849 – Misconduct in giving a ticket of leave to a woman in the surgery of the hospital for an immoral purpose and being in an improper position with her. 6 months imprisonment with hard labour.
26 April 1850 – Absconding. 18 months imprisonment with hard labour in chains.
1 May 1850 – Disobedience of Orders by refusing to work. 14 days solitary confinement.
5 June 1850 – Refusing to work. Existing sentence of imprisonment with hard labour in chains to be extended by 2 months.

In view of his criminal record it was recommended 3 May 1850 that he be taken to Norfolk Island where he arrived 28 June 1850. His life of crime continued there.

17 January 1851 – Idleness and Insolence. 1 month hard labour in chains.
1 May 1851 – Disobedience. 2 months hard labour in chains.
27 October 1851 – Disobedience. 14 days hard labour in chains.
17 November 1851 – Idleness. 2 months hard labour in chains.
9 December 1851 – Idleness. 2 months hard labour in chains.
26 January 1852 – Absent. 14 days hard labour in chains.
5 April 1852 – Falsely accusing fellow prisoner of writing improper verses. ? or 6 months hard labour in chains.
19 April 1852 – Disobedience. 4 days solitary confinement.

He was returned to VDL on the 'Seppings' during October 1852.

8 February 1854 – Using violent language to the Constable. 6 months hard labour.
30 August 1854 – Insolence. Admonished.
21 February 1855 – Uttering a forged order for payment of money amounting to £8.12s.8d. with intent to defraud Emmanuel Moses Myers.
5 June 1855 – Fully committed for trial at Hobart Town Supreme Court for above offence. Life Transportation sentence approved 6 years probation to Port Arthur.
4 December 1857 – 3 months remitted for meritorious conduct.
19 February 1858 – 4 months remitted for services rendered by him to the Persian emigrants at Impression Bay.
3 December 1858 – Absconded and apprehended at Hobart Town. Not shown.
16 January 1859 – Absconded from the Coal Mines Tasman Peninsula. 16 days solitary confinement and recommended to 4 months separate treatment. To serve 2 years on Probation for a ticket of leave.
7 March 1860 – Drunk. 14 days solitary confinement.
24 October 1860 – 3 months hard labour. (CON 33/74).

He received his ticket of leave 9 March 1853 and again on 9 October 1860 but this was revoked about 3 September 1862. An Application for Permission to Marry was received 26 September 1853 in respect of Henry Fisher and Rachel Sinclair (free). This was approved 6 October 1853 but does not appear to have taken place (CON 52/6).

GRIFFITHS Edward (c.1810-18.5.1879)
Convicted at the Assizes 13 July 1844 of larceny having broken into the factory of William Jones, Newtown, and stolen wool to the value of five pounds. He was sentenced to 7 years transportation (NLW Q/SR 1844). He was transported on the 'Sir Robert Peel' leaving London 9 September 1844 arriving VDL 26 December 1844. He was 34 years of age, married to his wife C(K)atherine and had two children Mary (born 1837) and David (born 1841). He also had brothers (David and Richard) and sisters (Elizabeth and Sarah), all living at Llanwnog. Weaver/labourer by calling; Protestant (Methodist) by religion and able to read a little. Height 5'8½", head long, hair black, whiskers brown to red, visage long, forehead medium height, eyes hazel, eyebrows black, nose medium, mouth and chin large with complexion fresh. He was pockpitted and had a hairy mole on right arm below the elbow (CON 33/63; CON 14/28; CON 18/43). Following his conviction it was necessary for his wife and children to be admitted into the Newtown and Llanidloes Union Workhouse at Caersws during the quarter ended 24 March 1845 as result of destitution. Their discharge also took place during the same quarter (Workhouse Admission Register 18441847). He spent 12 months in the Browns River Labour Gang in Class 3 from where he emerged 26 December 1845. The following offences are noted:

> *20 July 1848 – Larceny by stealing oats and barley in the straw and fully committed for trial.*
> *30 August 1848 – Tried at Hobart Town Quarter Sessions for the above offence. 7 years transportation and to be sent to Port Arthur for 2 years.*
> *27 February 1849 – Misconduct in holding communication with another prisoner in solitary confinement. Reprimanded.*
> *29 May 1849 – Misconduct. Reprimanded.*
> *6 August 1849 – Neglect of duty as watchman in being asleep on his feet. 14 days added to his probation. (CON 33/63).*

His ticket of leave was issued 7 October 1851 and a conditional pardon refused 21 April 1852. This was approved 18 January 1863. His possible death took place on 18 May 1879 when an Edward Griffiths aged 76 years died from senility, and was buried in Cypress Street, Launceston (RGD 35/48 No. 551/1879 Launceston; TAMIOT LNO3/0).

GWYNNE Thomas (Taylor) (c.1823–)
Convicted at the Assizes 15 March 1847 of robbery with violence in that he stole 17 sovereigns and other monies from John Wozencroft. His accomplice was William Bradley. He was sentence to 15 years transportation. His gaol report stated that he was good and was transported on the 'Rodney 2', leaving Queenstown 24 September 1851 arriving VDL 20 December 1851, and the Surgeon reported that his general conduct had been good. He was 28 years of age, native of Brosely, single with an uncle Thomas Evans living in Bilston. A Protestant, labourer by calling and able to read a little, height 5'1½", head medium, hair light to dark brown, visage oval, forehead medium, eyes hazel, eyebrows black, nose, mouth and chin medium with complexion sallow. He had an anchor GT on left arm, heart in dots and circle of dots on right arm (CON 33/105; CON 14/44; CON 18/56).
The following offences are noted:

> *11 February 1852 – Misconduct in leaving his Master's house. 1 month hard labour.*
>
> *3 April 1852 – Drunk. 3 months hard labour.*
>
> *28 October 1852 – Misconduct in not obeying orders. Reprimanded.*
>
> *22 December 1852 – Refusing to obey orders. 6 months hard labour in chains.*
>
> *16 August 1853 – Misconduct in refusing to hire in service of Mr Bromley. 2 days hard labour.*
>
> *31 August 1853 – Disobedience of orders in refusing to go to his Master's farm when ordered. 6 months hard labour.*
>
> *7 January 1854 – Misconduct in breaking a night tub and throwing it into the creek. 1 month added to existing sentence of hard labour.*
>
> *21 June 1854 – Disobedience of orders and insolence. 6 months hard labour.*
>
> *28 December 1854 – Insolence and neglect of duty. Reprimanded.*
>
> *6 August 1855 – Insolence and neglect of duty. Discharged to service of the Crown.*
>
> *22 December 1855 – Absent. 14 days hard labour.* (CON 33/105).

He received his ticket of leave 14 August 1855 and a conditional pardon 28 April 1857. On 15 October 1861 at Swansea Petty Sessions he was given one year's imprisonment and hard labour for a larceny offence.

HANCOX Edward (c.1826-30.12.1892)

Convicted at the Assizes 9 March 1848 of housebreaking in that he and his brother John Hancox, entered the house of Samuel Brown Ironmonger and Blacksmith of Montgomery (NLW Bl/21, *Shrewsbury Chronicle*, 15 March 1848 and NLW Q/SR 1848). He was sentenced to 10 years transportation and was transported on the 'Rodney 1' leaving Portland 23 August 1850 arriving VDL 28 November 1850. The Surgeon stated that his general conduct had been good. He was 24 years of age, single, native of the Tenbury or Ludlow area and family as shown for his brother John Hancox. He was a blacksmith and farrier by calling; Protestant (Church of England) and able to read and write imperfectly. Height 5'5½"; head medium, hair dark brown, visage oval, forehead medium, eyes grey, eyebrows dark brown, nose, mouth and chin medium with complexion sallow. He had a small scar right side of the chin and a hair mole right side of throat (CON 33/99; CON 14/41).

The following offences are noted:

> *11 May 1861 – Stealing a pair of wagon arms. 6 months hard labour.*
> *15 September 1862 – Larceny under £5. 12 months hard labour.* (CON 33/99).

He received his ticket of leave 20 July 1852, a recommendation for his conditional pardon 27 July 1852 which was approved 14 June 1853. On 3 October 1854 he applied to marry Catherine Stewart, who had arrived on the 'Sir Robert Seppings' (CON 52/7, p. 179), the ceremony taking place 6 November 1854 at Darlington Church, Lincoln, in the District of Campbelltown. His wife was 24 years of age. The service was conducted by the Chaplain Rev. Thos B. Garlick according to the Rites and Ceremonies of the Church of England by Banns in the presence of David Fulton and Mary Bolton (RGD 37/133 No. 88 1854). His possible death took place on 30 December 1892 the cause being "inflammation of the kidneys". He was buried at Latrobe General Cemetery (TAMIOT/R/LT? 04/00224/2; RGD 35/61 No. 439/1892).

HANCOX John (c.1816 – 14.5.1877)

Convicted at the Assizes 9 March 1848 of housebreaking in that he and his brother Edward Hancox, entered the house of Samuel Brown Ironmonger and Blacksmith of Montgomery (NLW Bl/21, *Shrewsbury Chronicle*, 15 March 1848 and NLW Q/SR 1848). He was sentenced to 10 years transportation and transported on the 'Rodney 1' leaving Portland, Dorset 23 August 1850 arriving VDL 28 November 1850. The Surgeon stated that his general conduct had been good. He was 34 years of age; lived with his father (John), sisters (Elizabeth, Hannah and Ann) and brothers (Thomas, Charles and Edward) in the Tenbury/Ludlow area. He was single, carpenter by calling, Protestant (Church of England) and able to read and write imperfectly. Height 5'7"; head medium, hair brown, whiskers brown, visage oval, forehead medium, eyes grey, eyebrows dark brown, nose, mouth and chin medium with complexion sallow. The end of his right thumb had been cut and there were two scars on his right cheek (CON 33/99; CON 14/41).

The following offences are noted:

> *13 December 1852 – Misconduct in being out after hours. Admonished.*
> *1 February 1853 – Disturbing the peace. Fined five shillings.* (CON 33/99).

He received a ticket of leave 27 July 1852 and a conditional pardon was approved 21 June 1853. On 7 October 1853 he married Eliza Thompson aged 21 years, both of them living at O'Brien's Bridge. The ceremony took place in the house of Rev. C. Simson in the Parish of Hobart, according to the Rites and Ceremonies of the Church of Scotland by Banns in the presence of Ann Lovell (?Lovett) and John? Tormill (RGD 37/12 No. 636 1853 and NS 435/1/390). A John Hancock(x) carpenter died 14 May 1877 at Bathurst Street, Hobart, of "malignant disease of stomach". He had been born in England. The informant was the undertaker (RGD 35/9 No. 488/1877 Hobart). There is no evidence to confirm whether or not the brothers were able to keep in touch with each other. John committed his offences in Hobart Town whilst Edward carried out his crimes in Campbell Town. At the time of their marriages they were living at O'Brien's Bridge and Lincoln respectively.

HARTELL John (c.1819–)

Convicted at the Quarter Sessions 6 April 1843 of housebreaking and stealing handkerchiefs etc at the house of Mrs S. Davies of Welshpool. He was sentenced to 15 years transportation. His accomplices Jno Bradbury and John Walden. His gaol report confirms him to be of bad character with respectable connections and the hulk report stated that he was good. He was transported on the 'Lord Petre', leaving London 7 July 1843 arriving VDL 15 October 1843. He had not been employed on the journey, committed no offences and the Surgeon confirmed his conduct as good. He was 24 years of age, single and a native of Birmingham. His step father was Richard Meredith, mother Sarah, brother Jas and 4 sisters Emma, Caroline, Margaret and Jane. Protestant, carpenter/joiner by trade and able to read and write, height 5'7", head oval, hair dark brown, whiskers dark brown and small, visage oval, forehead medium height, eyes grey, eyebrows dark brown, nose medium, mouth medium, chin medium with fresh complexion. Marks AP 6 HMB on left arm, APX 6 1843 ten dots pipe and dot on left hand, blue marks on all fingers left hand (CON 33/45; CON 14/24; CON 14/12; CON 18/34). He spent 18 months in a primary gang as a Class 3 PPH located at Rock Hills and was released from the first stage of Probation 15 April 1845. The only offence noted was on 5 February 1847 when he was admonished for being on the Township at night without a pass (CON 33/45). His ticket of leave was issued 2 February 1847 followed by a recommendation for a conditional pardon September 1848 which was approved 27 November 1849. He applied for permission to marry Jane Laing (free) in December 1847 (CON 52/2, p. 383; *Hobart Town Gazette*, 28 December 1847) and on 23 March 1848 the marriage took place in the Parish Church, Swansea, in the District of Swan Port according to the Rites and Ceremonies of the United Church of England and Ireland by the Minister Joseph Mayson. He married under the name of John Hartell, alias Richard Meredith (i.e. the name of his stepfather). Witnesses to the marriage were John Franklin and E. M. Lewis.

HARVEY James (c.1810–)

Convicted at the Quarter Sessions 7 March 1848 of housebreaking at the house of Evan Price of Kerry on 13 February 1848 and stealing bread, bacon and clothes. His accomplice was William Thompson. He was sentenced to 10 years transportation (NLW Bl/21, *Shrewsbury Chronicle*, 17 March 1848; NLW Q/SR 1848). He was transported on the 'Rodney 1' leaving Portland 23 August 1850 arriving VDL 28 November 1850. The Surgeon reported that his general conduct was good. He was single, native of County Donegal, Ireland where his sister (Catherine) lived. It is possible that other members of his family had emigrated to America. He was 40 years of age, Roman Catholic, able to read and write a little, and a sailor by calling, height 5'3¾", head medium, hair and whiskers grey, visage oval, eyes grey, eyebrows dark brown, nose, mouth and chin medium with complexion dark. He had scars on the left shin, a small scar inside the left arm and was blind in the left eye (CON 14/41; C0N33/99).

The following offences are noted:

29 May 1851 – Making use of indecent language. 7 days solitary confinement.
13 March 1852 – Misconduct by not returning to his Depot. 1 month hard labour.
24 March 1852 – Drunk. 2 months hard labour.
26 August 1852 – Misconduct in representing himself as Free. 3 months hard labour.
7 January 1853 – Drunk and disorderly.
28 January 1853 – Insolence. 3 months hard labour added to existing sentence.
10 February 1854 – Drunk. 5 days solitary confinement.
17 February 1854 – Disobedience of orders in refusing to do his work. 4 months hard labour.
14 March 1855 – Drunk. Fined £1.
30 March 1855 – Drunk and being out after hours. 3 months hard labour.
9 July 1855 – Drunk. Fined £1.
10 August 1855 – Drunk. Fined £2.
31 August 1855 – Drunk and being out after hours. 3 months hard labour.
14 April 1856 – Drunk (at Hobart). Fined £1.
14 April 1856 – Drunk (at Franklin). Fined £1.
29 May 1856 – Drunk. Fined £1.
10 September 1856 – Drunk. 14 days solitary confinement.
8 December 1856 – Drunk. 6 months hard labour.
28 December 1857 – Drunk. Fined £1.
12 February 1858 – Drunk. Fined 5 shillings. (CON 33/99).

His ticket of leave was issued 26 December 1854 and revoked 10 June 1856. A further ticket of leave was issued 11 August 1857.

HOLLOWAY John (c.1810–)

Convicted at the Quarter Sessions 16 October 1834 of larceny, robbing a house near The Welsh Harp, Long Mountain, Welshpool, and stealing 20 sovereigns and a silver watch, the property having been found on his person and was committed to the county gaol by Rev. G. A. Evors. He was sentenced to 7 years transportation. The gaol report states that he was sober, of quiet disposition and had never before been convicted or imprisoned. Whilst being on the hulk 'Gannymede' his record shows him as good. He was transported on the 'Layton 2' leaving Sheerness 29 August 1835 arriving VDL 10 December 1835. The Surgeon confirmed that he was good. He was 25 years of age, native of Newtown and single, able to plough, reap, mow, thatch, shear and milk, height 5'5", head oval, hair black, whiskers black, visage long, forehead high, eyes light blue, eyebrows black, nose medium length, mouth medium width, chin long, complexion pale with no body marks. The Appropriation List confirms that he was appointed to Mr Joseph Morgan and Mr Josh Morgan, both of whom were Chief Constables, to perform his trade as above (CON 31/21; CON 23/2; CON 27/2; CSO 1/839/17773; CON 18/13).

The following offences are noted:

> 21 October 1837 – Stealing ¾ cwt of potatoes value 8/- the property of Charles Harrison. 12 months added to existing transportation sentence and to be sent to PB till further notice.
> 17 November 1838 – Disobedience of Orders and neglect of duty. 25 lashes.
>
> (COD 31/21).

His ticket of leave was issued 3 September 1840 and a free certificate issued 10 January 1852.

HOOD James (c.1810-24.12.1866)

Convicted at the Quarter Sessions 2 January 1840 of housebreaking the house of Edward Howells and stealing various goods. He was sentenced to 10 years transportation (Q/SR 1840). The gaol report indicates that he was a bad character with non respectable connections, but the hulk Report shows him to have been good. He was transported on the 'Lady Raffles' leaving Portsmouth 2 December 1840, arriving VDL 17 March 1841 and the Surgeon confirmed that he was good. A native of Stroud, Gloucestershire, there is conflicting evidence as to his marital state. He was approx 31 years of age, able to read and write imperfectly and his mother (Sarah) a laundress and sister (Elizabeth) both resided at Stroud Water. Ploughman/farm labourer by trade, height 5'7", head round, whiskers dark, visage round, forehead round, eyes blue, eyebrows black, nose straight, mouth medium, chin bread and dark complexion. He had a scar on the left side of the throat (CON 33/6; CON 14/8).

The following offences are noted:

> April 18 – Misconduct in conveying ? spears for other persons in his Master's coach wagon without permission. Reprimanded.
> 10 February 1848 – Refusing to work. 2/10 days hard labour in House of Correction and to forfeit 10% of his wages.

24 February 1848 – Drunk. Fined 5/-.
10 May 1848 – Drunk. Fined 5/-. (CON 33/6).

A ticket of leave was issued 24 March 1846. He died at Port Arthur 24 December 1866 of paralysis, aged 56 years and a farm labourer. The informant was P. Geo Duicham, Senior Medical Officer in the District of Tasman's Peninsula (RGD 35/35 No. 500 dated 26 December 1866).

HUMPHRIES George (c.1811–)

Convicted at the Assizes 2 March 1833 of passing eight forged Bank of England £5 notes to William Edwards of Machynlleth, knowing them to be forged. He was sentenced to life transportation (NLW Q/SR 1833). Following a period on the hulk 'Discovery', where his report was good, he was transported on the 'Emperor Alexander' leaving Downs 12 April 1833 arriving VDL 12 August 1833. The Surgeon confirmed that he had been reported once for disobedience but was subsequently orderly and very quiet. He was 22 years of age, single and a native of Dilton Priors, Shropshire. A horse dealer/ploughman by trade, height 5'4¼", hair red, eyes dark hazel, complexion and no marks on the body (CON 31/20; CON 23/2; CON 13/6).

The following offences are noted and it should be noted that the first 3 offences took place while he was carrying out the duties of a constable:

> *3 November 1835 – Gross neglect of duty in allowing George Priest, who had been apprehended by him by Warrant and charged with Felony, to enter a Public House unhandcuffed and thereby escaping from custody. 36 lashes.*
>
> *7 November 1835 – On suspicion of having received a bribe to discharge George Priest. Discharged with an admonition as to his future conduct, there being no positive proof.*
>
> *26 December 1835 – Repeated neglect of duty and disobedience of orders. Recommended to be dismissed the Police and to spend 6 months in the Green Point road Part.vide Lieut Governor~s decision Jan 1836.*
>
> *20 December 1836 – Absconding from Road Party. 12 mths imprisonment and hard labour.*

On 13 January 1837, an entry confirms that he had run away and evaded recapture.

INGRAM Edward (c.1815–)

Convicted at the Quarter Sessions 7 April 1837 of highway robbery by stealing a sovereign from a shoemaker at Tregynon. He had, at the same Sessions, acted as a witness against an accomplice John James (NLW, *Shrewsbury Chronicle*, Bl/17 dated 14 April 1837). He was sentenced to 7 years transportation. The hulk report on the 'Gannymede' confirms that he was good. He was transported on the 'Neptune 1' leaving London 7 October 1837 arriving VDL 18 January 1838. He was 23 years of age, single and a native of Llanllwchaiarn, Newtown. He was able to read and write imperfectly and a labourer/spinner by trade, height 5'8½", hair black, eyes dark grey, complexion pale with pockpitted marks (CON 31/24; CON 23/2).

The following offences are noted:

> *1 June 1838 – Absent from duty without leave. 6 weeks hard labour on the roads with ? Reibey's Ford Party then to be returned to Launceston Prison Barracks.*

13 February 1839 – Gross carelessness. 3 months hard labour in chains.
17 May 1839 – Neglect of duty. 2 months hard labour in chains with Launceston Chain Gang. (CON 31/24).

He received his ticket of leave 15 July 1842, a conditional pardon No. 186 23 February 1843 and a free certificate No. 364 in 1844.

INGRAM Richard (c.1784-4.9.1842)
Convicted at the Quarter Sessions 6 January 1842 of sheep stealing 1 lamb from John Wood, Llanerfyl. He was sentenced to 10 years transportation (NLW Bl/18, *Salopian Journal*, 12 January 1842, and *Shrewsbury Chronicle*, 14 January 1842). His gaol report states that he was bad in every respect and hulk report found him to be good. He was 58 years of age, married and unable to read or write. He was transported on the 'Emily' leaving London 28 June 1842 arrived VDL 24 November 1842. His death is recorded on board the ship 4 September 1842.

INSELL Margaret (c.1810–)
Convicted at the Quarter Sessions 22 February 1844 of larceny from the person in that she stole from John Lewis at Welshpool, 1 sovereign, 1 half sovereign and 10/6d in silver. Her accomplices were Samuel Bennett age 22 years, a bricker by trade and native of Alfracton and Mary Ann Booth age 19 years, a hawker by trade and native of London. Margaret Insell was sentenced to 7 years transportation (NLW Q/SR 1844), and transported on the 'Tasmania' leaving London 8 September 1844 arriving VDL 20 December 1844. Her gaol report stated that this was her first offence whilst the Ship Surgeon confirmed her conduct on board ship as quiet. She was 35 years of age, widowed with one child, native of Oswestry, Shropshire, where her father Richard, mother Sarah, brothers Richard, Edward, James, sisters Elizabeth, Sarah, Mary, Sophia and Ann lived. She was able to read and write imperfectly and a house servant/laundress by trade, height 5'0½", head small, hair grey, visage round, forehead medium height, eyes blue, eyebrows brown, nose medium size, mouth small, chin small and complexion brown. She had a scar behind the left ear (CON 41/4; CON 15/3; CON 19/4). In January 1846 an application for permission to marry was made by Margaret Insell and Robert Boyash (T) age 40 years, widower and a farming man (Emancipist) (CON 52/2, p. 289). The marriage took place at St Matthew's Church, New Norfolk, in the District of Hobart on 14 March 1846 according to the Rites and Ceremonies of the United Church of England and Ireland. The service was performed by the Chaplain W. Garrard in the presence of William Gale Lambert and Harriet Gale Lambert (RGD 37/5 1846 No. 126 (Marriage Insell/Boyast).

JAMES John (c.1806–)
Convicted at the Quarter Sessions 6 April 1837 of highway robbery by stealing a sovereign from the person of Edward Watkin of Tregynon on 28 March at Newtown Fair (NLW Bl/17 14 April 1837). He was sentenced to 7 years transportation. His record on the hulk 'Gannymede' was good. He was transported on the 'Moffatt 2' leaving Woolwich 27 October 1837 arriving VDL 1 April 1838. The Surgeon stated that he was quiet and orderly. He was 32 years of age, married (Margaret) with 4 children who resided at his native place Myrtha Fidwelil (Merthyr Tydfil), Glamorganshire. Unable to read or write he was a collier/miner by trade, height 5'4½", hair dark brown, eyes light blue and complexion fresh. There were no marks on his body (CON 31/25; 23/2; CSO 5/114/2615). On 15

September 1838 he was afforded a "meritorious conduct" in his favour, having saved a child from drowning in the Rubble Stone Quarry.

The following offences are noted:

> *2 December 1838 – Drunk. Reprimanded.*
> *8 April 1839 – Drunk. Reprimanded.*
> *3 September 1839 – Absconded. Existing term of Probation extended by 6 months.*
> *28 September 1840 – Drunk at the Slaughter House. 2 months imprisonment with hard labour on the roads.*
> *17 May 1843 – Drunk. Fined 5/-.*
> *10 Mar 1844 – Drunk. Fined 5/-. (CON 31/24).*

His ticket of leave was issued 5 January 1843 and a free certificate No. 1014 in 1844.

JONES Humphrey (c.1810–)

Convicted at the Assizes 8 March 1834 of housebreaking at Maengwyn, Machynlleth, the property of Hugh Owen Esq. Solicitor and stealing plate and other articles. He was sentenced to life transportation. This followed a previous conviction in 1828 when he was also sentenced to transportation. His accomplice was John Thomas (NLW Bl/16, *Shrewsbury Chronicle*, 14 March 1834). The gaol report stated that he was a bad character with quiet disposition. On the hulk 'Gannymede' his conduct was good. He was transported on the 'Norfolk' leaving Woolwich 10 June 1834 and proceeded to Cork via Portsmouth (30 June). Due to sickness on the 'Neptune', the remainder of the journey was undertaken by the 'Lady Kennaway' leaving Cork 27 October 1834 arriving VDL 13 February 1835 (Bateson, p. 273). The Surgeon confirmed that he had been very good. He was 24 years of age, single and a native of Mathon Hugh (Machynlleth), height 5'5", hair brown, eyes grey and complexion brown. The letters HJ were inside his right arm. The Appropriation List shows that his trade was groom/house servant and it was ordered by the Secretary of State that he be worked in chains and placed in Class 2 (CON 31/26; CON 23/2; CSO 1/785/16764).

The following offences are noted:

> *11 May 1835 – Absconded from Chain Gang. 24 lashes and recommendation that he be removed to the Hulk Chain Gang.*
> *1 December 1836 – Insolence. 6 hours in the stocks.*
> *21 February 1837 – Absconded. 6 months hard labour in chains with Launceston Chain Gang.*
> *3 May 1837 – Repeated Idleness in Chain Gang. 1 month added to existing sentence of 21 February.*
> *31 August 1837 – Idleness in Chain Gang. 1 month added to existing sentence of 21 February and 3rd May.*
> *29 January 1838 – Gross Insolence. Admonished.*
> *6 August 1838 – Absent without leave and being in a house on Windmill Hill. Admonished.*
> *23 April 1839 – Drunk and absent without leave. 11 months hard labour.*
> *4 December 1839 – Absconded. 2 months imprisonment with hard labour of which 3 weeks to be in solitary confinement.*
> *16 July 1841 – Refusal to work. 1 month hard labour. (CON 31/26).*

His ticket of leave was issued 7 September 1843 and he was recommended for a conditional pardon 28 December 1845. This was approved 31 October 1846 (This was a 2nd class C.P. in view of the fact that "only one slight record having been made against him during the last six years and the testimonials of character produced by him being good") (PRO HO 10/59).

JONES John (c.1774-14 September 1818)

He was convicted at the Great Sessions April 1817 of an unknown crime and sentenced to 7 years transportation. He was transported on the 'Lady Castlereagh' leaving England 22 December 1817 arriving VDL 11 June 1818. He was 44 years of age, sawyer/carpenter by trade and a native of Montgomeryshire, height 5'9¼", eyes grey, hair black and complexion dark and pale. He was generally well behaved (CON 31/23; CON 13/1; CSO 1/562/12464). His possible death took place in the Parish of St David's, Hobart, on 14 September 1818 with burial the following day (RGD 34/1 No. 294 1818).

JONES John (c.1802–)

Convicted at the Quarter Sessions 10 April 1823 of a felony by stealing money at Llanfair Caereinion. He was sentenced to 7 years transportation. The hulk report 'Justitia' found him to be orderly. He was transported on the 'Lady East' leaving Falmouth 16 December 1824 arriving VDL 9 April 1825. He was 23 years of age, Protestant, single, able to read and a native of Worthen, Shropshire. Ploughman/farmer's labourer, height 5'7", head small, hair dark brown in 1825 changing to black inclined to grey by 1848, whiskers dark brown, visage small, forehead low, eyes dark brown, eyebrows dark brown, nose short, mouth medium, chin medium and complexion ruddy. He had a scar over the right eyebrow, a scar between the eyebrows down left side of nose and his left leg had been broken above the ankle. The Appropriation List shows him as a ploughman (CON 14/1A; CON 31/23; CON 69/1; CON 37/4, p. 1076).

The following offences are noted:

17 November 1827 – Absconding into the woods. 50 remitted to 25 lashes.

24 January 1828 – Shoving a fellow prisoner off the jetty of a small island. 35 lashes.

26 January 1828 – Tearing his shirt to pieces. 25 lashes.

6 June 1828 – Remaining behind the small island gang boat and stealing bread from a fellow prisoner. 25 lashes.

17 January 1829 – Cutting his bed tick. 18 lashes.

23 June 1830 – Neglecting his work. 6 days solitary confinement on bread/ water and turned into gangs – 2 days remitted.

17 January 1848 – Larceny by stealing apparel from a cart. 7 years transportation by Richmond Quarter Sessions.

12 December 1848 – Misconduct in smoking in the penitentiary. 3 days solitary confinement.

He was placed in Port Arthur Probation Gang Class 3 from 9 March 1848 to 22 May 1849.

JONES John (c.1830–)

Convicted at the Quarter Sessions 29 June 1848 of housebreaking and larceny in that he entered the house of Mr William Owen Farmer of Aberhafesp on 30

April 1848 and stole £1.3s.6d. and 1 pair of shoes. His accomplice was George Wilson. They had been caught the same night that the offence took place having been apprehended at Llanidloes by Constable Robert Williams of Caersws. John Jones was also indicted for stealing 1 pair of shoes from John Harris of Montgomery (Could it be that having only been able to steal one pair of shoes as they passed through Montgomery, it was necessary that they obtained another pair and as a result carried out the offence at Aberhafesp?) (NLW Bl/21, *Shrewsbury Chronicle*, 7 July 1848; NLW Q/SR 1848). He was sentenced to 10 years transportation. The hulk report shows him to be very good. He was transported on the 'Aboukir' leaving London 7 December 1851 arriving VDL 20 March 1852 and the Surgeon confirmed that he had been well behaved. He was 22 years of age, single, native of Manchester where his uncle (David Wilson) lived. He was a Roman Catholic, labourer by calling and able to read and write a little, height 5'3", head oval, hair dark brown, visage oval, forehead high, eyes brown, eyebrows dark, nose and chin medium, mouth wide and complexion swarthy. He had a mole right side of nose (CON 33/106; CON 14/31).

The following offences are noted:

> *28 July 1852 – Absconding. 14 days solitary confinement.*
> *14 January 1853 – Disobedience of Orders. Insolent and using threatening language. 6 months hard labour.*
> *15 March 1853 – Absent without leave and fighting. 7 days solitary confinement.*
> *3 May 1853 – Neglect of duty. 1 month hard labour added to existing sentence of hard labour. (CON 33/106).*

He received a conditional pardon 19 December 1854.

KELLY Michael (c.1826–)
Convicted at the Quarter Sessions 2 July 1845 of housebreaking at the house of Andrew Gittins and stealing 4 silk handkerchiefs; at the house of John Lloyd of Meifod a piece of cheese, 1 silk handkerchief, 1 pair trousers and 1 piece of velvet, at the house of Jane Haynes of Meifod 1 razor (value 1/-) and 1 pocket knife (value Sd). His accomplice was John Brown. He was sentenced to 10 years transportation (NLW Bl/19, *Shrewsbury Chronicle*, 11 July 1845; NLW Q/SR 1845). He was transported on the 'Cornwall' leaving Portsmouth 25 February 1851 arriving VDL 11 June 1851. He was 25 years of age, single, and his mother (Mary) lived in Manchester although his native place was County Antrim, Ireland. A Roman Catholic, farm labourer by calling and able to read and write a little, height 5'2½", head medium, hair brown, visage oval, forehead medium, eyes light brown eyebrows dark brown, nose, mouth and chin medium with complexion fair. The nail on his left little finger had been split (CON 33/103; CON 14/41). No offences appear against him and he received his ticket of leave 14 December 1852 followed by a conditional pardon 29 November 1853. His possible marriage to Margaret Ryan, aged 20 years, free and a spinster, took place on 26 July 1853 at St Joseph's Church, Launceston, according to the Rites and Ceremonies of the Roman Catholic Church by Banns. The service being carried out by Rev. Butler in the presence of Joshua Beaumont and Ellen Mcnamara (RGD 37/12 No. 1115 1853).

KIMBERLIN Richard (c.1812–)
Convicted at the Quarter Sessions 8 April 1841 of larceny from the person by

picking the pocket of David Lloyd at Llanidloes Fair and stealing 17 sovereigns, two £5 notes and small pieces of silver. He was sentenced to 10 years transportation. His accomplice was Isaac Walton (NLW Q/SR 1841). His gaol report confirmed that he was believed to have been a member of a pickpocket gang, of quiet disposition and well behaved. The hulk report stated that he was good. He was transported on the 'Somersetshire' leaving Plymouth 19 December 1841 arriving VDL 13 May 1842. He was 29 years of age; single and a native of Faseley (Paisley), Stafford. His father (Richard), mother (Dorothy), 3 brothers and 1 sister lived in Warwickshire. Protestant, unable to read or write and a glass cutter/ labourer by trade, height 5'5¼", head large, hair black, whiskers black, visage broad, forehead high/broad, eyes light hazel, eyebrows brown, nose large, mouth medium, chin medium double and complexion ruddy. His forehead was pimpled and there were marks of punishment on his neck (CON 33/21; CON 14/13; CON 18/32; CON 28/1). He spent 18 months Probation at Saltwater Creek and appeared to have committed no offences as by 30 November 1843 his original term of Probation expired and he was issued with his ticket of leave 8 June 1847. A conditional pardon was recommended 4 July 1848, and approved 4 December 1849, it being noted in the application that he 'has completed upwards of 7 years of a 10 year sentence without offence on record' (Despatch No. 212, 21 October 1848). A free certificate was issued 11 April 1851 (PRO HO 10/61; CON 33/21; CON 28/1).

MILES David (c.1812–)

Convicted at the Quarter Sessions 11 April 1844 of housebreaking by entering the house of David Arthur at Llanfechain and stealing 20 lb bacon, 10 lb beef and clothes. This was his second conviction having previously been convicted of a felony by stealing coals, for which he received 4 weeks imprisonment at North Wales. He was sentenced to 10 years transportation (NLW Q/SR 1844). He was transported on the 'William Jardine 1' leaving London 11 August 1844 arriving VDL 20 November 1844. The Surgeon confirmed his general conduct as good. He was 32 years of age, married to Elizabeth with 3 children, mother Jane, brother John and sisters Jane and Nancy. Protestant, farm labourer/ploughman by trade and a native of Merionethshire, able to read and write imperfectly, height 5'9", head long, hair dark brown, whiskers black, visage oval, forehead medium height, eyes hazel, eyebrows dark brown, nose long, mouth medium, chin medium and sallow complexion.he was pockpitted with a scar on the forefinger right hand (CON 33/62; CON 14/30; CON 18/43). He spent 18 months in the Oyster Cove gang as a Class PPH 3 and was discharged from same 20 May 1846. A ticket of leave was issued 14 May 1850 but revoked 1 October 1850 due to his absence from Muster. It was restored 4 March 1851. A recommendation for a conditional pardon was granted after 6 years 11 months in the Colony including 11 months holding a ticket of leave (Despatch No. 84 dated 2 July 1851). Approval to the CP was given 13 July 1852 (PRO HO 10/61; CON 33/62). It is possible that following his death, date unknown, he was buried in Ulverstone General Cemetery (TAMIOT ULlO/G0259/0).

MILES Morgan (c.1792 – 2 or 29.9.1853)

Convicted at the Great Sessions 23 March 1822 of an unknown crime and sentenced to life commuted to 14 years transportation. He was transported on the 'Caledonia' leaving Portsmouth 19 June 1822 arriving VDL 6 November 1822. The Surgeon reported that he was orderly on board. He was 30 years of age, single, native of

South Wales where probably his parents lived. Blacksmith by trade, height 5'1", eyes grey and hair brown (CON 31/29; CON 13/2 p.367; CSO 1/96/2284).

The following offences are noted:

21 December 1825 – Attempting to take some iron from the Lumber Yard without permission. 25 lashes and PB 3rd Class.

l November 1834 – Stealing from a dwelling house occupied by him and John Weaver, four Promissory Notes of the value of £5 each belonging to John Weaver. Committed for Trial.

22 November 1834 – Stealing two Bullock chains to the value of 14s each, the goods of Chas Sutton. Committed for Trial.

30 May 1835 – Drunk. 10 days solitary confinement on bread/water.

24 July 1835 – Having released himself from the Government irons and substituted a pair of light link irons. 50 lashes in presence of the Blacksmiths of the Kings Yard.

29 July 1836 – Drunk. 6 days in cell on bread/water.

22 April 1837 – Neglect of Duty. Reprimand.

5 June 1837 – Drunk. Reprimanded.

23 August 1837 – Drunk. 2 months hard labour on the roads and to be returned to the Royal Engineer Depot.

27 June 1838 – Drunk. Reprimand.

21 September 1838 – Disobedience of Orders by making a hammer head for his own private advantage in the King's Yard. 6 Saturday afternoon hard labour on the Tread wheel.

24 December 1838 – Drunk. 6 days in cell on bread/water.

19 March 1839 – Drunk. 6 days in cell on bread/water.

24 September 1839 – Drunk. Reprimanded and deprived of half day on Sat.

26 December 1839 – Drunk. 6 months hard labour in chains in Launceston Chain Gang.

20 July 1840 – Drunk. Reprimanded and deprived of half day on Sat.

2 February 1841 – Drunk. Deprived of a pass and work for his own benefit on Saturday afternoon.

16 May 1842 – Misconduct. Reprimanded.

His ticket of leave was issued 29 July 1841 and a Recommendation to the Queen for a conditional pardon 28 February 1844. This was granted 14 May 1844 after 22 years in the Colony, "having served so many years in the Colony and there being but one trivial offence recorded against him for the last three years", and Approved March 1845 (PRO HO 10/58). He died at Prosser Plains and Sorell on 2 or 29 September 1853, about 73 years of age and a labourer. The informant was District Constable Buckland (RGD 35/22 No. 111 1853).

MORRIS Richard (c.1818-12th June 1872)
Convicted at the Assizes 7 March 1843 of burglary in that he entered the home of Edward Middleton of Newtown and stole a coat and other wearing apparel. His accomplice was John Williams For a previous offence of assault he had received a 2 month sentence of imprisonment and now was given 10 years transportation (NLW Q/SR 1842). He was transported on the 'Sir George Seymour' leaving London 21 November 1844 arriving VDL 27 February 1845 and the Surgeon confirmed that his general conduct had been very good. He was 27 years of age, single, native of Llanerchymedd, Anglesey, where his father (John) and sisters

(Sarah, Elizabeth, Anne, Susan, Jane and Kate lived). Protestant and a bricklayer by calling, he was able to read and write a little, height 5'7¾", head long, hair and whiskers brown, visage oval, eyes grey, eyebrows brown, mouth large, nose and chin medium with complexion sallow. He had a scar on the left thumb, scar on 2nd and 3rd finger, scar on back of left hand, slight scar on right cheek (CON 33/64; CON 14/26; CON 18/44).

The following offences are noted:

> *12 April 1845 – Out after hours and creating a disturbance. 3 months hard labour.*
> *23 March 1846 – Neglect of duty. Reprimanded.*
> *6 August 1846 – Embezzlement under value of £5. Hard labour.*
> *12 October 1849 – Drunk. Solitary confinement. (CON 33/64).*

His application for a ticket of leave was refused 23 March 1849 but was granted during October 1850. A certificate of freedom was issued 8 March 1853. There is no record that he married and his possible death took place in Launceston 12 June 1872 when a Richard William Morris, aged 50 years and a bricklayer, died of "Pneumonia", the informant being William Hills undertaker (RGD 35/41 No. 1777/1872 Launceston). He was buried 15 June 1872 at Cypress Street, Launceston (TAMIOT A?LNO3/0).

MOTTRAM Henry (Henry Jackson MOTTRAM) (c.1809–)

Convicted at the Assizes 2 March 1833 of horse stealing one mare from Edward Weaver, Innkeeper of Montgomery, and one mare from John Evans of Kerry. He was sentenced to life transportation (NLW Q/SR 1833). The gaol report stated that he was a very bad character and had been concerned in robberies for many years. His hulk report 'Discovery' at Woolwich, found him to be orderly. He was transported on the 'Emperor Alexander' leaving Downs 12 April 1833 arriving VDL 12 August 1833 and the Surgeon confirmed that he was most refractory and insubordinate. He was 24 years of age, married with one child who with his wife (Jane) lived with his father (William Jackson) at Cheltenham. He was native of St Albans and a silk dyer/labourer by calling, height 5'5¼", hair reddish, eyes dark hazel and complexion fair. There were no marks on his body (CON 31/30; CON 23/2; CON 13/6).

The following offences are noted:

> *3 October 1833 – Drunk and Insolent at Muster. 7 days imprisonment with hard labour.*
> *29 October 1833 – Absent from his Constable post and laying on the floor of the Watch house. Fined 10/-.*
> *2 November 1833 – Gross Misconduct as a Constable in attempting to extort money. 3 years imprisonment with hard labour in the Hulk Chain Gang.*
> *7 December 1833 – Absconding from the Hulk Chain Gang. 100 lashes in front of gang.*
> *6 May 1835 – Gambling. 1 dozen lashes.*
> *13 May 1837 – Absconding. 12 months hard labour in chains.*
> *10 October 1837 – Idleness and smoking. 1 month added to existing sentence.*
> *9 November 1838 – Absent from his home between 6 p.m. and 11 p.m. Reprimanded and returned to the Crown.*
> *20 December 1838 – Disobedience of Orders. 7 days in cell.*

10 January 1839 – Absconding. 2 years hard labour at Port Arthur.
18 February 1839 – Endeavouring to abscond from the Constables at Snake Banks
party with attempt at murder. Charge dismissed.
25 September 1840 – Misconduct. 7 days solitary confinement.
18 February 1841 – Insolence. 30 lashes.
5 April 1841 – Drunk on roads. 3 months hard labour.
16 April 1842 – Gross insolence. 14 days solitary confinement and returned to his
service. (CON 31/30).

Following his offence on 16 April 1842 it was recommended that his ticket of leave be postponed for a period of 12 months and this was an irregular recommendation when forming any part of the legal sentence. His ticket of leave was eventually granted 10 November 1843 and a recommendation for a conditional pardon for the Australian Colonies was put forward 26 August 1845. This was granted in 1846 after 12 years and 1 month in the Colony including 1 year and 10 months holding a ticket of leave. The recommendation stated that "No record having been made against him during the last three years, nearly two of which period he has held a ticket of leave" (PRO HO 10/59; CON 31/30).

OLIVER David (c.1821–)

Convicted at the Quarter Sessions 2 July 1840 of horse stealing by taking a mare, 1 saddle and 1 bridle from Mary Goodwin of Berriew. He had two previous convictions for stealing bread (imprisonment 14 days) and stealing a sovereign (3 days). He was sentenced to 10 years transportation (NLW Q/SR 1840, *Salopian Journal*, 8 July 1840). The gaol report stated that he was not an honest character, whilst the hulk report found him to be good. He was transported on the 'David Clarke' leaving Plymouth 7 June 1841 arriving VDL 4 October 1841. The Surgeon stated that his conduct was orderly. He was 20 years of age, single and native of Berriew/Montgomery where he probably lived with his mother Sarah ("I am a chance child") and sister Eliza. Protestant, labourer by trade and unable to read or write, height 5'4¾", head large, hair brown, whiskers none, visage oval, forehead medium height, eyes hazel, eyebrows black, nose medium, mouth medium, chin long and complexion ruddy. He was freckled and had two scars on the forehead (CON 33/13; CON 14/9; CON 18/29). He spent 18 months from 16 November 1841 on Probation between Browns River and South Fort Station Gangs as a Class 3 1st P.P.H.

The following offences are noted:

9 December 1843 – Being drunk at Hobart. 14 days solitary confinement.
31 August 1847 – Misconduct in leaving his horse and cart without proper control. 8 days solitary confinement. (CON 33/13).

His ticket of leave was issued 17 November 1846, a conditional pardon granted 19 January 1848 and approved 14 November 1848 (PRO HO 10/60). He applied for permission 20 November 1849 to marry Elizabeth Sims, who had been transported on the 'Asia'. The marriage took place 17 December 1849 at St George's, Hobart, by F. Brownrigg according to the Rites and Ceremonies of the Church of England, in the presence of James and Alice Weir (CON 52/3, p. 337; RGD 37/8 No. 794).

OLIVER Edward (c.1814–)

Convicted at the Quarter Sessions 29 October 1836 of housebreaking and stealing

2 guineas from the desk of Mr John Jones of Llanfyllin (NLW Bl/16, *Shrewsbury Chronicle*, 28 October 1836). He had a previous conviction for stealing a bag for which he had been sentenced to 12 months imprisonment. He was sentenced to 14 years transportation. The gaol report states that he was a regular thief and a very dishonest character but the hulk report 'Gannymede' confirms that he was good. He was transported on the 'Elphinstone' leaving London 29 May 1837 arriving VDL 2 October 1837. Possibly a native of Llanfyllin, he was 23 years of age, single, lath render/splitter and groom by trade and able to read and write imperfectly, height 5'7½", head oval, hair brown, whiskers none, visage oval and long, forehead high, eyes grey, eyebrows brown, nose, mouth and chin medium with swarthy complexion. He had two brown moles above the elbow left arm (CON 31/33; CON 23/2; CON 18/7; CSO 5/73/1603).

The following offences are noted:

> *30 December 1839 – Insolent to his Master. Admonished.*
> *22 February 1840 – Disorderly conduct regarding Pass. Admonished.*
> *8 July 1844 – Exposing his person ? Fined 5/-.*
> *3 June 1845 – Stealing pigs. Committed for Trial.*

To be deprived of his ticket of leave (issued 27 September 1843) 27 July 1845 and sent to Glenorchy for a term of imprisonment (vide memo of Col Sec dated July 1845). A free certificate was issued 12 November 1850 or 1851 (CON 31/33). 17 April 1851, he departed from Launceston for Melbourne on the 'Shamrock' as a steerage passenger freed by servitude (POL 20/9/1, p.362).

OLIVER Rossetta (c.1815-23 November 1876)
Convicted at the Quarter Sessions 5 January 1843 of larceny, stealing 2/6d from R. Harris. This followed a previous conviction in 1837 when she picked the pocket of Watkin Watkins and stole 3 sovereigns and was sentenced to 1 month imprisonment. She was sentenced to 7 years transportation. The gaol report confirms that she had bad connections although the Chaplain speaks well of her conduct as a devout woman. She was transported on the 'Emma Eugenia 2' leaving London 30 November 1843 arriving VDL 2 April 1844. She was 28 years of age, native of Llandwellen (possibly Llanfyllin), single and able to read and write imperfectly. Her father John Oliver, brothers Edward and Thomas and sisters Mary Sarah and Elizabeth resided at her native place whilst another brother, Griffith, lived in Liverpool. She was a house servant/pastry cook/laundress by calling, height 5'1½", head small, hair brown, visage small, forehead small, eyes grey, eyebrows brown, nose small, mouth medium width, chin round and complexion swarthy. There were no marks on her body (CON 41/1; CON 15/2; CON 19/4). She spent 6 months Probation class 2 from 12 April 1844 and Class 3 from 27 January 1845.

The following offences are noted:

> *2 January 1845 – Drunk. 14 days solitary confinement.*
> *24 April 1846 – Harbouring a female absconder. 4 months hard labour but the remainder of this sentence was remitted 13th July 1846.* (CON 41/1).

Her ticket of leave was issued 26 September 1846 and a free certificate 5 January 1850. An application for permission to marry was made in April 1845 between Rossetta Oliver and George Hill (free) aged 32 years and a groom by trade (CON 52/2, p. 371), the marriage taking place in the District of Hobart 19 May

1845 in St George's Church according to the Rites and Ceremonies of the Church of England. The Minister was H. P. Fry and the witnesses Eliza Hill and Eliza Morgan (RGD 37/4 No. 1604 1845). 23 November 1876 Rossetta Hill died in New Norfolk Hospital for the Insane from "softening of the brain with heart disease", certified by Jno A. Moore Acting Supt and Medical Officer. She was a pauper and her age shown as 66 years (RGD 35/45 New Norfolk No. 476 1876).

OWEN David (c.1810-1833 or 1855)

Convicted at the Assizes 19 July 1831 of maliciously wounding cattle/cutting and maiming horses. He was sentenced to 7 years transportation. The gaol report found him of savage disposition and the hulk report 'Gannymede' shows him to be orderly. He was transported on the 'Katherine Stewart Forbes' leaving London 26 February 1832 arriving VDL 16 July 1832. He was a 22-year-old ploughman, married with one child and his wife Hannah lived near his native place Llanhidlas (Llanidloes). Height 5'8", head large, hair dark brown, whiskers dark brown, visage long, forehead high/retreating, eyes hazel, eyebrows brown, nose short/sharp, mouth medium width, chin small and complexion fresh. He was pock-pitted (CON 31/33; CON 13/5; CON 1810). There is no further information except a note to say that in November 1833, he was at New Norfolk and off the stores (CON 31/33). The burial of a David Owen is noted on a tombstone (not now in existence) at New Norfolk which read Owen David d.1833 (which could be read as 1855) aged 33 Native Place Llaniglos (Llanidloes) Montgomeryshire North Wales (*The Mercury* newspaper c.1915 – NS/544/1, p. 184). The RGD does not record the 1833 death as it was pre-civil registration but there is a record of a David Owen, 49 year old farm overseer from 'The Plenty' who died and was buried at New Norfolk 12 December 1855 from "concussion of the brain caused by fall from a horse" (AOT General Index Inquest 13 December 1855 No. 3643 SC 195/37; RGD 35/26 No. 577 1857). Although this death occurred as above the Coroner did not register it until 24 June 1857.

OWEN Evan (c.1798-3.11.1873)

Convicted at the Quarter Sessions 20 February 1834 of larceny of stealing a quantity of oak spokes from John Sparrow of Welshpool and, with John Griffiths, of stealing 13 fowls and 2 ducks from Mr Price, Lower Packhouse, Welshpool. He was sentenced to 14 years transportation (NLW B/1, *Shrewsbury Chronicle*, 28 February 1834). The gaol report found that he was suspicious, of good disposition and decent connections. His conduct on the hulk was good. He was transported on the 'Norfolk' which was delayed at Ireland and as a consequence the remainder of the journey was carried out by the 'Lady Kennaway' leaving Cork 10 June 1834 arriving VDL 13 February 1835. The Surgeon found his conduct to be very good. He was 37 years of age, widower with 2 children, native of Newtown and possibly resident in Churchstoke or vice versa. Height 5'5½", head medium, hair dark brown, whiskers dark brown, visage oval/long, forehead high, eyes grey, eyebrows dark brown, nose long, mouth wide, chin medium and complexion pale. The first joint, forefinger, left hand was crippled. He was a Top Sawyer/Ploughman by trade and placed in Public Works (CON 31/33; CON 18/10; CSO 1/785/16764, p. 277-8).

The following offences are noted:

> *11 May 1835 – . . . a Public House on Saturday last having a pass from Mount Lewis. 6 days Tread Wheel.*

7 December 1838 – Drunk. 4 days Tread Wheel
23 March 1839 – Disorderly conduct. Discharged.
22 October 1839 – Disobedience of Orders. 7 days Tread Wheel.
19 February 1841 – Disorderly conduct. 6 days Tread Wheel.
18 October 1841 – Drunk. Fined 5/-. (CON 31/33).

His ticket of leave was issued 3 March 1841 and a recommendation to the Queen was made 15 December 1843, that he be granted a conditional pardon. This was approved vide *Gazette* 14 January 1845. An Application for permission to marry was applied for in September 1843 between Evan Owen and Janet Patterson ('Rajah 1', age 22 years, single and a prisoner) (CON 52/2, p. 140). The marriage took place in the District of Launceston 22 November 1843 in St John's Church, Launceston. The service was conducted by the Rev. W. H. Browne LLB according to the rites and ceremonies of the United Church of England by Banns with consent of Government and in the presence of George Wilson and William Jones (RGD 37/3 No. 196 1843). 25 March 1852, Evan Owen departed from Launceston for Melbourne on the 'Mariposa' with the status of being 'free by servitude'. There is no mention that his wife accompanied him but this is probable (AOT Departure Index POL 20/9/1, p. 632). There is no entry in the AOT Free Arrivals Index to show that they ever returned to Tasmania but the following details of deaths and burials in Tasmania may relate. Evan Owen age 88 years and a woodcarver in the District of Launceston died 3 November 1873 from "retention of urine" and was buried 4 November 1873 in the Cypress Street cemetery, Launceston. The informant was Thomas J. Doolan, undertaker (TAMIOT A/LNO3/0; RGD 35/42 No. 2200 1873 Launceston). Janet Owen died 14 March 1881 being 69 years of age and a widow living in the District of Launceston. Cause of death shown as "senility" and informant being Thomas J. Doolan. It would appear that they had no children (RGD 35/50 No. 263 1881 Launceston).

OWEN Thomas (c.1823–)
Convicted at the Assizes 7 March 1843 of burglary by entering the house of Rev. Charles Wingfield and stealing 3 desks, 1 loaf of sugar (10/-), 1 tea chest (£1) and a gun; from the house of Thomas Morgan 1 Fustian jacket (5/-), and from the house of Edward Bumford 2 prs boots (10/-) and 2 loaves of bread (1/-). His previous record included 2 convictions for Rioting for which her had been imprisoned for 2 months and 1 month respectively. He was sentenced to 10 years transportation (NLW Q/SR 1842). He was transported on the 'Sir George Seymour' leaving London 21 November 1844 arriving VDL 27 February 1845. He was 22 years of age, single and lived at Llanllwchaiarn with his father (James), mother (Mary), brothers (Samuel and John) and sisters (Jane and Mary). He was a Protestant, a shoemaker by calling and able to read a little, height 5'8", head oval, hair dark brown, visage oval, eyes and eyebrows dark brown, nose, mouth and chin medium with complexion fresh (CON 33/64; CON 14/26).
   The following offences are noted:

> *16 May 1845 – Misconduct as a Constable in being in barracks when on duty and challenging the watch house keeper to fight. 2 months hard labour and recommended dismissal from the Police.*
> *2 February 1846 – Wilfully destroying a sheet in the Medical Department and the property of the Crown. 10 days solitary confinement.*

3 July 1846 – Neglect of duty in employing his Master's time in working for himself. Text of sentence faded.

4 December 1846 – Absent without leave. 4 days solitary confinement.

10 June 1847 – Robbing James Mcdonald of a coat. Fully committed for trial at Hobart Supreme Court on ???.

21 July 1847 – For assaulting James Mcdonald, putting him in bodily fear and stealing one coat, 10/- and other articles, his property from his person. Guilty of larceny only. 7 years transportation and to be sent to Port Arthur on probation for 2 years.

19 August 1847 – Disorderly conduct in striking a fellow prisoner. 7 days solitary confinement.

21 February 1848 – Refusing to go to work. 7 days solitary confinement.

24 March 1848 – Refusing to work and misconduct in refusing to be searched. 6 months hard labour in chains

25 March 1849 – Neglect of duty. 1 month imprisonment.

2 August 1851 – Absent from his authorised residence without leave and entering the house of Elizabeth Evans with a felonious intent. Discharged.

30 July 1853 – Absconding. 18 months added to existing sentence of transportation. Approved to undergo 3 years probation at Port Arthur and to be worked in heavy irons in the Quarry Gang during the first year. (CON 33/64).

He received Tickets of Leave 1 December 1846 and 11 February 1851, a conditional pardon was approved 14 June 1853 and a certificate of freedom issued at Launceston, 15 March 1856.

OWEN William (c.1778-18.4.1845)

Convicted at the Quarter Sessions 22 February 1844 of larceny, stealing 6 lbs of Brass from John Owen of Welshpool. This followed a previous conviction of a felony by stealing metal for which he was convicted and sentenced to 12 months imprisonment. He was sentenced to 7 years transportation (NLW Q/SR 1844). He was transported on the 'Lord Auckland' leaving London 20 July 1844 arriving VDL 15 November 1844. The Surgeon found his conduct good. He was 66 years of age, married (Martha) with one child, brothers Edward and Richard, sisters Elizabeth and Mary, who all lived at Welshpool. He was a Protestant, dealer by trade and unable to read and write, height 5'1", head oval, hair dark brown/grey, whiskers dark brown/grey, visage broad, forehead broad/high, eyes hazel, eyebrows brown, nose medium, mouth large, chin medium and complexion fresh. His face was wrinkled and he had a small scar on 2nd finger right hand (CON 33/61; CON 14/30; CON 18/38). He was due to spend 15 months labour at Wedge Bay Probation Station where his death is recorded 18 April 1845 (CON 33/61; Hobart Country Burials 1845).

PARRY Owen (c.1809–)

Convicted at the Quarter Sessions 14 January 1830 of larceny, stealing sugar from the warehouse of David Davies shopkeeper of Newtown. His accomplices were Edward Edwards and Richard Thomas. He was sentenced to 7 years transportation having had previous convictions for receiving stolen goods (6 months imprisonment), stealing wood (6 weeks House of Correction, where he had been seen as a bad character) and had spent a period in the hulks (NLW Q/SR 1829). He was transported on the 'Manlius 2' leaving London 6 April 1830 arriving VDL 12 August 1830. He was 21 years of age, single and a ploughman/able to milk and understand sheep, height 5'5¾", hair black and eyes hazel (CON 31/35; CON 23/3; ML 11). The Appropriation List shows that he was sent as ploughman to work for Mr Thos Wells.

The following offences are noted:

> *20 ??? 1831 – Violently assaulting a fellow prisoner and severely bruising his arm with a stick. 50 lashes.*
>
> *20 ??? 1832 – Neglect of duties and complaining about his provisions without a cause. 50 lashes.*
>
> *14 November 18?? – Obtaining £2 by false pretences. Charge dismissed, appeared to be a mistake.*
>
> *18 April 1836 – Out after hours and representing himself to be free. Admonished.*
>
> *??? July ??? – Neglecting to attend Muster and Church. Admonished.*

(CON 31/35).

He received a free certificate No. 413 on 19 August 1837 (CON 23/3).

PETERS John (c.1823–)

Convicted at the Quarter Sessions 3 July 1845 of larceny from the person and larceny in that he stole £15 from Mary Dawson at Pool Farm Welshpool. He was sentenced to 10 years transportation (NLW Bl/19, *Shrewsbury Chronicle*, 11 July 1845, NLW Q/SR 1845). This followed a previous conviction of stealing money from a Mrs Davis at Bristol. He was transportedon the 'Pestongee Bomangee' leaving Plymouth 22 September 1845 arriving VDL 30 December 1845 and the Surgeon found his general conduct to be indifferent. He was 22 years of age, single, native of Sheffield with no relatives. A Protestant and a weaver/labourer/hawker by calling, he could read and write a little, height 5'5¾", head oval, hair and whiskers dark brown, visage oval, forehead medium height, eyes hazel, eyebrows dark brown, nose, mouth and chin large with fresh complexion. He was pockpitted with a small scar on right cheek (CON 33/74; CON 14/34; CON 18/46). He spent 15 months at Salt Water River in gang class 2 PPH 3rd and the following offences are noted:

> *15 May 1846 – Misconduct in having Government property in his possession. One month added to probation.*
>
> *3 September 1847 – Selling bread from the bakehouse without permission. 3 months imprisonment with hard labour.*

His ticket of leave was issued 14 February 1851, revoked 14 September 1852 for being absent from a muster and restored 28 September 1852, as he had been able to account for his absence from the muster. A recommendation that he be issued with a conditional pardon was passed 14 October 1851 and this was duly issued 11 January 1853 (CON 33/74).

POWELL David (c.1809–)

Convicted at the Great Sessions 24 March 1828 of housebreaking and stealing a piece of flannel from an Edward Hughes. He was sentenced to life transportation. His gaol report shows him as a disorderly and bad character, and his period on the hulks as orderly. He was transported on the 'Manlius 1' leaving London 29 July 1828 arriving VDL 9 November 1828. He was 19 years of age, single and a native of Llanydlas (Llanidloes) where his mother and father (Evan Powell) resided and worked as a mason. David Powell had last worked with his uncle, also as a mason. A Protestant, the only personal note concerned his height 5'7½" (CON 31/34; ML 6).

The following offences are noted:

> *2 March 1829 – Absent from his Master and afterwards being found drunk. 10 days treadwheel.*
>
> *1 May 1829 – Intoxicated. Reprimanded.*
>
> *14 March 1831 – Drunk in the Thistle Ground at the Ship Launch Public House. 5 days treadwheel.*
>
> *19 September 1831 – Absent from Muster without leave. Admonished.*
>
> *11 April 1832 – Absent from duty without leave. To be confined in the cell for the next three Saturday afternoons.*
>
> *15 November 1832 – Throwing a bundle of things over the wall of the Female House of Correction and assaulting Jas Bidey the Constable at the Female House of Correction when taking him into custody. 12 months imprisonment with hard labour at Bridgewater and 24 lashes for the 2nd offence.*
>
> *10 April 1834 – Absent from duty. Reprimanded.*
>
> *26 September 1834 – Absent from his work without permission. To be locked up for the next three Saturday afternoons.*
>
> *2 January 1835 – Absent from Muster. 3 days treadwheel.*
>
> *13 January 1835 – Absent from his duty without leave. 3 Saturday afternoons on treadwheel.*
>
> *27 January 1835 – Absent from his hut and found at a house. Reprimanded.*
>
> *27 June 1835 – Found in a Public House after hours. Reprimanded.*
>
> *26 April 1838 – Being in Town and overstaying his Pass. 48 hours hard labour on treadwheel.*
>
> *29 April 1839 – Misconduct by being in a Public House on a Sunday. 48 hours treadwheel.*
>
> *2 March 1840 – Out after hours. Reprimanded.*
>
> *26 December 1840 – Out after hours. 48 hours hard labour.* (CON 31/34)

A conditional pardon No. 3033 was issued 24 May 1841 and extended 24 March 1846.

PRICE John (c.1815-24.1.1849)

Convicted at the Quarter Sessions 27 February 1840 of housebreaking at the house of Mr C. Cadwallader of Welshpool but there is no record that he actually stole anything. He had a previous conviction of 6 days imprisonment for assault. He was sentenced to 10 years transportation (NLW Bl/18, *Shrewsbury Chronicle*, 6 March 1840). The gaol report confirmed that he was of a quiet disposition, sober, behaved well whilst in gaol and had a good character given him on trial. The hulk report stated that he had been good. He was transported on the 'Duncan' leaving Sheerness 16 December 1840 arriving VDL 18 April 1841. He was 25 years of age and married to Elizabeth who lived at Welshpool. He was a native of Montgomery where his father David, brother David and sister Elizabeth still lived. A Protestant/ Church of England calling and pit sawyer/ ploughman/farm labourer by trade. Able to read but cannot write, height 5'6", head round, hair black, whiskers black, visage round, forehead low, eyes grey, eyebrows dark brown, nose medium, mouth medium, chin medium and complexion ruddy. There was a scar on middle finger left hand (CON 33/8; CON 14/5; CON 18/27).

The following offences are noted:

> *15 January 1842 – Absent from work without leave. 7 days solitary confinement.*
>
> *12 November 1842 – Misconduct, that whilst acting as a constable in Hobart, he allowed some female prisoners in his charge to behave in a disorderly manner and giving them pipes to smoke in the female House of Correction. 14 days solitary confinement.*
>
> *21 January 1843 – Misconduct in being drunk whilst off duty as a constable at Hamilton. 14 days solitary confinement.*
>
> *22 March 1843 – Disobedience of orders as a constable at Hamilton. Fined 10/-.*
>
> *25 March 1843 – Drunk when on special constable duties at Hamilton. 4 months hard labour in chains and recommended to be dismissed from the police which was approved.*
>
> *23 March 1847 – Out after hours at Richmond. 6 days imprisonment with hard labour.*
>
> *25 June 1847 – Misconduct in being absent from his authorised residence at Richmond and on the premises of Mr Butcher and making a disturbance. 21 days imprisonment with hard labour.*
>
> *11 November 1848 – Misconduct in being absent from his authorised residence at Richmond. Admonished. (CON 33/8).*

He was accidently killed by a cart running over his body at Richmond 24 January 1849 (Memo of Police Magistrate, 26 January 1849, Inquest No. 2011 SC 195/23).

PRYCE John (c.1791-26.4.1847)

Convicted at the Quarter Sessions 21 October 1841 of larceny, stealing 7 fowls from Edward Powell of Kerry. This followed a previous conviction of poaching/horse stealing for which he received 2 years imprisonment. He was sentenced to 7 years transportation (*Salopian Journal*, 27 October 1841). The hulk report found him indifferent. He was transported on the 'Eden 2' leaving Woolwich 22 March 1842 arriving VDL 5 July 1842. He was 50 years of age, a widower with 2 children (unnamed), 2 brothers, Edward and Thomas and a sister, Ann Elizabeth Catherine. He was a native of Beguildy, Radnorshire. Protestant by religion, a farm labourer/ploughman by trade and able to read only, height 5'4", head oval, hair grey, whiskers grey, visage oval, forehead high, eyes brown, eyebrows black, nose large and inclined to the right, mouth medium, chin medium and complexion fresh. He had 2 scars on the left hand, a scar on the left wrist and a scar over the left eye. He spent 2 years probation as a farm labourer at Rocky Hills station (CON 33/22; CON 14/12; CON 28/1).

The following offences are noted:

> *4 January 1844 – Misconduct in using tobacco. Existing period of probation extended by 1 month.*
>
> *14 November 1844 – Absent without leave. Existing period of probation extended by 3 months.*
>
> *5 November 1844 – Released from first stage of Probation.*
>
> *24 September 1845 – Misconduct in having a pair of new boots in his possession that had been issued to another man and removing the Gov. mark upon them. 6 months hard labour.*
>
> *22 December 1845 – Absent without leave at Launceston. 10 days hard labour/tread wheel. (CON 33/22).*

He died in Launceston Hospital, 26 April 1847 (CON 33/22).

PUGH Micah (alias Michael) (c.1825–)

Convicted at the Quarter Sessions 4 January 1844 of larceny, stealing 5 packets of thread to the value of £3 from William Pail of Newtown and 1 comb from some person unknown. He was sentenced to 7 years transportation, this having followed a previous felony conviction when he served 6 months for stealing a quantity of lead (NLW Q/SR 1844). By 8 February 1844 he was at Millbank Prison and was transported on the 'Theresa' leaving 1 April 1845 arriving VDL 4 July 1845. He was single and lived at Newtown with his father Lewis, brothers Thomas, John and David and sisters Mary, Jane Catherine and Ann. He was a Protestant, a weaver/servant by calling and able to read and write imperfectly, height 5'7½", of stout build, head oval, hair dark brown, visage broad, forehead medium height, eyes and eyebrows brown, nose and mouth medium with broad chin. His complexion was fresh and pockpitted with a circular scar on the left thumb (CON 33/67; CON 14/29).

The following offences are noted:

15 July 1845 – Drunk. 10 days solitary confinement.

22 April 1847 – Whilst acting as a constable in Hobart he committed misconduct by being absent from his beat. Fined 5 shillings.

28 July 1847 – Whilst acting as a constable in Hobart he committed a misconduct by being in the company with a common prostitute in the watchouse. 4 months imprisonment with hard labour and recommended to be dismissed the Police.

8 May 1848 – Whilst acting as a constable in Hobart (he appears to have been reinstated), he committed a misconduct by being absent from duty without leave. 14 days solitary confinement and recommended to be dismissed the Police.

5 December 1848 – Misconduct by idling about the streets of Hobart. 3 months imprisonment with hard labour and recommended that he afterwards resides in the Interior.

?? June 1849 – Misconduct in being absent from his authorised residence in Hobart Town contrary to the orders of the Lieutenant Governor. 6 months imprisonment with hard labour and afterwards to reside in the Interior and not in Hobart or Launceston.

7 September 1850 – Misconduct in being out after hours at New Norfolk. 3 months imprisonment with hard labour.

He was issued with a free certificate 22 January 1851 (CON 33/67; CON 18/40).

REES Evan (c.1793–)

Convicted at the Assizes 5 March 1831 of larceny by stealing 2 fowls. He had a previous conviction having committed a felony by sheep stealing, with his brother Richard Rees. On 24 March 1821, he was sentenced to death commuted to 7 years transportation, but was discharged 27 July 1824. For his latest offence he was sentenced to 7 years transportation. His period on the hulk 'Justitia' is noted as of an orderly manner. He was transported on the 'Larkins' leaving Downs 18 June 1831 arriving VDL 19 October 1831. He was 38 years of age, married to Hannah with 5 children. His native place was Llangennich/Llangyrich (Llangurig), where his family including his 4 brothers and 1 sister lived nearby. Protestant, a labourer by calling and able to read and write imperfectly, height 5'1¼", head round, hair dark brown, whiskers brown, visage small and furrowed, forehead perpendicular, eyes light grey, eyebrows dark brown/overhanging eyebrows, nose medium length, mouth medium width, chin medium length and complexion dark. He was slightly pockpitted (CON 31/37; CON 14/3; CON 13/5; CON 18/12).

The following offences are noted:

> *15 July 1836 – Neglecting to attend a Muster ever since holding a ticket of leave. Admonished-appearing he has acted under a mistake.*
> *25 January 1838 – Pilfering a waistcoat the property of Nathaniel Hodgets to the value of 15/-. Discharged.*

It would seem that Hannah and three children followed Evan to Tasmania. On 29 January 1846 an Evan Rees and wife with three children embarked at Launceston on the 'Julia' (*Launceston Examiner*, 31 January 1846) leaving for Adelaide, 1 February 1846 (CSO 20/23).

RILEY John (also RYLEY) (c.1800–)

Convicted at the Great Sessions 8 August 1825 of horse stealing and was sentenced to death commuted to life transportation. His gaol report found him good whilst the hulk report 'Justitia' confirmed him as being orderly. He was transported on the 'Chapman 2' leaving London 10 April 1826 arriving VDL 7 October 1826. He was 26 years of age, single, native of Staffordshire and a farm labourer/ploughman by calling. Height 5'10", hair dark brown, eyed blue and complexion dark. He had a scar on the back of the little finger left hand (CON 31/34; CON 23/3; CON 13/3, p. 297; ML 2). The Appropriation List shows that he was employed as a ploughman with a Mr Crawley (MM 33/10). There are no offences recorded and he received a conditional pardon No. 1951 28 January 1839 and a free pardon No. 27 on 28 February 1842, the latter being granted 15 April 1842, after 16 years in the Colony including 3 years holding a conditional pardon (CON 31/34 and PRO HO 10/57). Permission to marry was granted January 1837 between John Riley and Ann Kelly (Free) (CON 52/1 p.167), the marriage taking place in the Parish Church of Launceston, County of Cornwall, the Service conducted by the Chaplain W. H. Browne LL.D. with the consent of the Government. Witnesses were John Lamant and William Jones both from Launceston (RGD 36/3 No. 2837 1837).

ROBERTS Ann (c.1815–)

Convicted at the Quarter Sessions 3 July 1834 of larceny; breaking and entering the house of Richard Harris, Berriew, and stealing 1 cotton gown, a silk handkerchief and several other articles. She was sentenced to 7 years transportation. Her gaol report shows her to be a sober and industrious girl. She was transported on the 'Arab 3' leaving London 26 December 1835 arriving VDL 25 April 1836 (NLW Q/SR 1834). She was 21 years of age, single, native of Meliden, Flintshire and a farm servant by calling. Height 4'11¾", head oval, hair dark brown, visage oval and full, forehead high, eyes hazel, eyebrows black, nose medium length, mouth small, chin large and complexion fresh. There were no marks on her body (CON 40/8; CON 18/23).

The following offences are noted:

> *21 June 1836 – Absent without leave. Admonished.*
> *27 September 1836 – Absent without leave and gross disorderly conduct. 4 months Crime class 4.*
> *12 August 1837 – Absent without leave. 3 months House of Correction 2nd class.*
> *21 December 1837 – Absent without leave. 2 months wash/work tub.*
> *6 August 1839 – Drunk. Admonished.*

18 March 1840 – Misconduct in being out after hours and abusing a constable. 6 weeks hard labour in Hobart Factory.
29 March 1840 – Using obscene language. Fined 5/-.
26 August 1840 – Misconduct in raising a false and malicious rumour against Mr James Jackson and with being a ?????? character. 3 months hard labour and ticket of leave suspended. (CON 40/8).

Her ticket of leave was granted 17 July 1839 and a free certificate No. 495 July 1841. Permission to marry was granted to Ann Roberts and William Uttley (John Barry) in August 1839 but the marriage does not appear to have taken place (CON 52/1, p. 205). The death of William Uttley, aged 51 years and a labourer, took place in the General Hospital, Hobart, 2 December 1851, the cause of death being a "tumour". The informant was the Hospital Superintendent (RGD 35/3 No. 468/1851 Hobart).

ROBERTS Edward (c.1800-12.3.1876)
Convicted at the Great Sessions 5 August 1820 of house breaking and stealing wearing apparel. He was sentenced to death commuted to life transportation (NLW Q/SR 1821; 4/201/3). His conduct was orderly on the hulk. He was transported on the 'Lord Hungerford' leaving July 1821 arriving VDL 26 December 1821. He was 22 years of age, single, lived with his parents at ?Bworgo, Montgomeryshire and a farm labourer/ploughman by calling, height 4'11¼", eyes dark grey and hair dark brown (CON 23/3; CSO1/403/9106, p. 238; CON 31/34). He received a conditional pardon No. 614 21 August 1834 and a free pardon No. 133, 20 October 1842 (CON 31/34).

ROBERTS John (c.1802–)
Convicted at the Great Sessions 24 March 1821 of burglary and sentenced to death commuted to life transportation. The hulk report states that he was orderly. He was transported on the 'Lord Hungerford' leaving July 1821 arriving VDL 26 December 1821. He was 19 years of age, single, his sisters lived at his native place (either Worthen Shropshire or Worthing, Hertfordshire) and he was a farm labourer/ploughman by calling. Height 5'2¼", eyes grey, hair brown, upper jaw greatly projecting over the lower jaw and a ship/anchor tattoo on the left arm (CON 23/3; CON 13/2, p. 243; CSO1/403/9106, p. 238; CON 31/34).
The following offences are noted:

27 December 1827 – Drunk and Disorderly. Reprimanded.
31 October 1831 – Drunk. Fined 5/-.

He received a conditional pardon No. 788 15 December 1835 which was extended to all countries except Great Britain and Ireland (CON 31/34).

ROBERTS Louisa (real name Louisa MADDEN) (c.1810–)
Convicted at the Great Sessions 15 August 1829 of stealing a silk shawl from Frances Collings, Shopkeeper, of Newtown. She was sentenced to 7 years transportation (NLW Q/SR 1829). Her gaol report confirmed that she was bad and had left her husband and one child on the grounds that she had been ill-used and was travelling the country. She was transported on the 'Eliza 1' leaving London 7 November 1829 arriving VDL 24 February 1830. She was 20 years of age, married with one child, native place Liverpool and able to read and write

A Protestant and a dressmaker/cap maker/nursery maid who understood the care of children by calling. Height 5'2", head round, hair dark brown, visage oval, forehead perpendicular, eyes dark hazel, eyebrows dark brown, nose broad, mouth wide, chin medium and complexion pale. She had no marks on her body (CON 40/7; ML 10; CON 18/23).

The following offences are noted:

> *11 October 1831 – Refusing to work. Placed in crime class.*
> *23 May 1832 – Remaining absent from her service the whole of Monday night. Placed in crime class.*
> *16 September 1833 – Out after hours. Reprimanded.*
> *16 October 1833 – Found in an indecent situation after dark. 3 months crime class. (CON 40/7).*

The following permission to marry applications were made but no marriage appears to have taken place. In May 1831 between Louisa Roberts and Ralph Cully (Free) (CON 45/1) and 10 May 1836 between Louisa Roberts and John Armstrong (David Lyon) (CON 52/1, p. 2). On 12 September 1836 in the District of Campbell Town, County Somerset, the marriage took place between Louisa Roberts and John Jacobs. The service was conducted by the Chaplain William Bedford Jnr in the schoolhouse by Banns and witnessed by John and Mary Johnston both of Campbell Town District (RGD 36/3 No. 3577 1836). A free certificate No. 29 was issued in 1841.

ROGERS Mary (proper name THORN) (c.1826–)

Convicted at the Quarter Sessions 8 January 1846 of housebreaking and larceny when she enterered the house of Richard Corbett and stole one silk handkerchief and other articles, and several articles from the house of John Stephens. The location of these houses may have been in the Llandyssil and Llanfair Caereinion areas. She was sentenced to 7 years transportation. Her accomplice on both occasion was her husband Frederick Thorn (NLW Q/SR 1846). Her conduct whilst in prison was good. She was transported on the 'Sea Queen' leaving Woolwich 12 May 1846 arriving VDL 29 August 1846. The Surgeon confirmed that she was a good mess woman. She was 20 years of age; married to Frederick Thorn, her mother was Mary, brothers John, David, Richard and Edward, sisters Elizabeth, Ellen and Ann who lived at Hanwood, Shropshire. She was a Protestant, country servant/dairymaid by calling and able to read and write indifferently, height 5'0½", head large, hair brown, visage oval, forehead high, eyes light blue, eyebrows brown, nose small and turned up, mouth small and a round chin. Her complexion was fresh (CON 41/10; CON 15/3; CON 19/5). She was placed on 6 months Probation class 3 with the Huon gang.

The following offences are noted:

> *2 June 1847 – Insolence and neglect of duty. 3 months hard labour in the factory Hobart and following this sentence she was to be moved to Launceston.*
> *7 March 1849 – Assault. 14 days cells.*
> *24 September 1849 – Insolence and disobedience of orders. 14 days cells.*
> *7 June 1851 – Larceny under five pounds. Original term of 7 years transportation to be extended by 12 months and her ticket of leave revoked. To serve 6 months probation in the factory Launceston.*
> *12 December 1853 – The unexpired portion of her extended sentence of transportation remitted.*

Her ticket of leave was issued 16 April 1850 and revoked 8 July 1851. By 13 July 1852 she was not recommended for her ticket but by 22 February 1853 she was to be allowed to apply in 4 months time for a new ticket. A certificate of freedom was issued 8 December 1853 (CON 41/10). The permission to marry Register shows that a Mary Rogers of the 'Sea Queen' applied to marry two men namely Peter Cooke (free) on 20 May 1851 (CON 52/4; CON 52/3) and Marshall Cook (free) on 26 November 1851 (CON 52/4). Neither wedding appears to have taken place. There is no evidence to suggest that her first husband Frederick Thorn was re-united with her as he had been sent to Port Phillip (Victoria) to serve out his 10 year sentence.

ROOSE Jonathan (c.1800–)

Convicted at the Assizes 19 July 1831 of horse stealing by taking a bay mare from Dolanog House in Welshpool, the property of Mr David Jones and a black gelding the property of Mr Henry Jones, Surgeon, Welshpool. His accomplices were Henry Beastall and John Farren. He was sentenced to death commuted to life transportation. His gaol report stated that he was of a bad disposition and belonged to a gang of horse stealers. His report whilst on the hulk 'Justitia' shows that he was orderly. He was transported on the 'Katherine Stewart Forbes' leaving London 26 February 1832 arriving VDL 16 July 1832. He was 32 years of age, single, native of Elton?, Warwickshire, and a ploughman by calling, height 5'10¼", head round and bald on top of forehead, hair dark brown, whiskers dark brown, visage long and narrow, forehead high and retreating, eyes blue, eyebrows dark brown, nose long, mouth small, chin long and complexion dark. There were no bodily marks (CON 31/37; CON 13/5; CON 18/10). Only one offence is noted:

5 December 1837 – Disobedience. 25 lashes. (CON 31/37).

His ticket of leave was issued 2 July 1840 and a conditional pardon No. 773 5 October 1843, being granted 1 March 1844 after 11 years in the Colony "having held ticket of leave for the prescribed time with good character" (PRO HO 10/58). On 23 December 1850 an application to marry by Licence was made by Jonathan Roose (aged 50 years, bachelor and carrier by calling), to marry Anne Western Sproson (49 years and a widow) (AOT General Index NS 373/1 No. 536). On 26 December 1850 the marriage took place at St John's Church, Newtown in the District of Newtown. The service was in accordance with the Rites and Ceremonies of the Church of England by Licence by Thos J. Ewing in the presence of Thomas Shuword and A. Griffiths (RGD 37/9 No. 416 1850 and *Hobart Town Courier*, 28 December 1850). Jonathan Roose is also mentioned in relation to "The Maypole Inn, Newtown" (*Hobart Town Gazette*, 5 October 1852, p. 810).

ROWLANDS William (c.1813-4.6.1895)

Convicted at the Quarter Sessions 18 April 1833 of horse stealing by stealing a mare from John Ellis, farmer, of Cemmaes. He was sentenced to Life transportation (NLW Q/SR 1833). His gaol report found him being of good character while his period on the hulk 'Justitia' was orderly. He was transported on the 'Moffatt' leaving Plymouth 29 January 1834 arriving VDL 9 May 1834. The Surgeon stated that he had behaved well on route. He was 21 years of age, single, native of ? Llanecill, Merionethshire, and a ploughman by calling. Height 5'6", head small, hair dark brown, whiskers dark brown, visage broad, forehead low, eyes dark hazel, eyebrows dark brown, nose medium, mouth large, chin large and complexion dark. He was stoutly made (CON 31/37; CON 18/15).

The following offences are noted:

> *18 September 1837 – Disobedience of orders. 3 days/nights solitary confinement.*
> *4 June 1839 – Disobedience of orders. 4 days/nights cell on bread/water.*
> *20 June 1839 – Larceny. 12 months hard labour in chains.*
> *28 April 1841 – Gross misconduct in being absent from his Master's farm after dark and strong suspicion of having killed a steer and made away with the meat. 12 months hard labour in chains with strong recommendation that he be sent to Port Arthur subject to severe discipline. (CON 31/37).*

His ticket of leave was issued 4 April 1844 and a recommendation for a conditional pardon 2 October 1845. This was approved November 1846 after 11 years 6 months in the Colony including almost 2 years holding a ticket of leave. The record stated that "Only four offences have been recorded against him since his arrival, the last of which was committed more than 4½ years ago and a servitude of 11½ years having been completed by him in the Colony" (PRO HO 10/59). An Application to Marry by Licence was granted 14 March 1859 between William Rowland(s) aged 46 years, a farmer, and Mary Ann Neale aged 19 years and a Spinster(AOT General Index NS 373/2 No. 2070).The marriage took place 14 March 1859 at St Matthew's Church Rokeby in the District of Clarence Plains according to the Rites and Ceremonies of the Church of England in the presence of John and Ellen Pearce (RGD 37/18 No. 67 1859). William Rowlands died 4 June 1895 aged 84 years and was resident at 20 Melbourne Street, Hobart. Cause of death being "senile decay", the informant being the undertaker (RGD 35/14 No. 153/1895 Hobart). He was buried at Queenborough Cemetery, Hobart (TAMIOT H013/00085/2). Mary Ann Rowlands died 1898 and was buried with her husband (TAMIOT H013/00085/3). An incomplete list of children is noted including on 18 March 1869 a female child Mary Ann (RGD 33/10 No. 238/1869 Hobart), on 7 December 1870 a male child Alfred Henry (RGD 33/10 No. 1523/1871 Hobart) and on 2 May 1873 a male child Walter Albert (RGD 33/11 No. 3316/1873 Hobart). On 3 July 1883, Mary Ann Rowlands, a 14-year-old servant, died of "pericarditis" at the General Hospital, Hobart (RGD 35/10 No. 1038/1883 Hobart). She was buried in Queenborough Cemetery and her parents were eventually placed in the same grave.

SCOTT Robert (c.1796–)

Convicted at the Great Sessions 23 March 1822 of horse stealing possibly at Welshpool. He was sentenced to death commuted to life transportation. He was transported on the 'Caledonia' leaving Portsmouth 19 June 1822 arriving VDL 6 November 1822, his conduct on board being orderly. He was 26 years of age, married with a wife at Welshpool, native of East Haddington, Durham, and a farm labourer by calling. Height 5'9½", eyes blue and hair light brown (CON 23/3; CON 13/2, p. 367; CSO 1/9161/2284; CON 31/38). The only offence recorded against him was:

> *14 October 1833 – Refusing to pay for damages to 10 head of cattle. Ordered to pay the sum of 2d per head.*

A conditional pardon No. 658 was granted 1 January 1835 (CON 31/38) and again on 10 February 1835 (CON 23/3).

In June 1832 permission to marry was granted to Robert Scott and Catherine Collins 'Mary'. He is shown as a bachelor and she as a spinster, both of the Parish of Black Brush in the District of Green Ponds (CON 45/1). The marriage by Banns took place 12 August 1832 at Brighton, the Minister being R. C. Drought LL.D. and the Witnesses Wm ? Gell Brighton, Police Clerk, and Alfred Thrupp, Brighton Parish Clerk (RGD 36/2 No. 2043 1832).

SIMMONDS Edward (c.1825–)

Convicted at the Quarter Sessions 2 July 1845 of housebreaking and stealing 30 shillings and a handkerchief from a house in Llanwrin. He was sentenced to 10 years transportation. His accomplice was Charles Cane. He was transported on the 'Pestongee Bomangee' leaving Plymouth 22 September 1845 arriving VDL 30 December 1845. The Surgeon stated that he had been well behaved on the voyage. He was 20 years of age, native of Kings Lynn, Norfolk and his mother Sarah, brother Charles and sister Sarah, lived at Yarmouth. He was a Protestant, labourer by calling and able to read and write indifferently, height 5'4¼", head oval, hair light brown, whiskers none, visage oval, forehead medium height, eyes grey, eyebrows brown, nose large, mouth small, chin medium and sallow complexion. His face was pimpled; there were 2 moles on the right arm; the letter E on the left arm below the elbow; a blue dot on the back of the left wrist and a ring on the 3rd finger left hand (CON 33/74; CON 14/34; CON 18/46). He spent 15 months with the Salt Water River Gang in class 1st PPH 3rd.

The following offences are noted:

> *8 February 1847 – Neglect of duty. Admonished.*
> *19 June 1851 – Misconduct in being in a disorderly house. Reprimanded.*

His ticket of leave was issued 14 February 1851 and a recommendation for a conditional pardon was made 10 February 1852, approved 31 May 1853.

STOKES John (c.1827-?27.9.1899)

Convicted at the Quarter Sessions 2 July 1845 of housebreaking by entering the house of Thomas Davies of Buttington and stealing a watch, shoes and other articles. He was sentenced to 10 years transportation. His accomplice was Henry Fisher. He was transported on the 'Pestongee Bomangee' leaving Plymouth 22 September 1845 arriving VDL 30 December 1845. The Surgeon found him to be of an indifferent conduct on the journey. He was 18 years of age, a native of Woolwich, London, where he lived with his mother Margaret, brothers Walter and Joseph and sisters Mary Ann, Margaret and Emma. He was a Protestant, ship collier by calling and unable to read or write, height 5'4", head large, hair dark brown, whiskers none, forehead medium height, visage oval, eyes hazel, eyebrows dark brown, nose, mouth and chin medium. His complexion was sallow and there was a sailor with a sword/flag and woman JS on right arm below elbow; Rabbit between forefinger and thumb right hand, 1845 and mermaid with comb and glass JS below elbow left arm (CON 33/74; CON 14/34; CON 18/46). He spent 15 months in the Coal Mines Gang in class 1st PPH 3rd.

The following offences are noted:

> *7 June 1847 – Drunk and out after hours. Reprimanded.*

23 March 1848 – Absconded, 3 months imprisonment with hard labour.

29 October 1850 – Being out all night. 6 months imprisonment with hard labour.

28 December 1850 – Absconded. 3 months hard labour in chains.

7 January 1851 – Absconded from the Cocked Hat, Campell Town. 21 days solitary confinement.

17 February 1851 – Idleness. 14 days solitary confinement.

3 September 1851 – Felony for assaulting Joseph Darling and putting him in bodily fear and stealing money from his person. Not Guilty.

His ticket of leave was issued 19 November 1850 and revoked 7 January 1851. His death probably took place 27 September 1899 at Bathurst Street, Launceston, from "gastritis". His age was however shown as 84 years, a labourer and that he was born in England. The informant was the undertaker (TAMIOT LNO3/0; RGD 35/68 No. 285/1899 Launceston).

STOREY (STORY) William (c.1825–)

Convicted at the Quarter Sessions 2 July 1845 of housebreaking by entering the house of John Owens of Llanwrin and stealing 1 sovereign, 1 half sovereign, one shilling and sixpence including a handkerchief. He was sentenced to 10 years transportation. His accomplices were Charles Cane and Edward Simmonds. He was transported on the 'Pestongee Bomangee' leaving Plymouth 22 September 1845 arriving VDL 30 December 1845 and the Surgeon reported that he had been well behaved. He was 20 years of age and was a native of Edgware, London, where his mother Sarah, sister Elizabeth and brother James lived. He was single, a Protestant, farm labourer by calling and able to read imperfectly, height 5'2½", head oval, hair light brown, whiskers none, visage broad, forehead medium height, eyes grey, eyebrows brown, nose, mouth and chin medium. His complexion was fresh and there was a scar between the forefinger and thumb right hand, scar on left thumb and two faint letters on left arm below elbow (CON 33/74; CON 14/34; CON 18/46). He spent 15 months with the Salt Water River Gang in class 1 PPH 3rd.

The following offences are noted:

6 November 1846 – Throwing bones over barrack wall. Admonished

11 September 1848 – Neglect of duty and absent without leave. 4 months imprisonment and hard labour.

7 November 1848 – Having tobacco and money improperly in his possession. 1 month imprisonment and hard labour added to the previous sentence.

On 22 August 1850 he was advised to apply for a ticket of leave in 4 months time and this may have been issued 14 February 1851. By 1 October 1852 his ticket had been revoked. On 9 August 1852 he apparently absconded and was possibly apprehended 24 August 1852.

THOMAS Eliza (c.1826–)

Convicted at the Quarter Sessions 8 January 1847 of stealing from the person and larceny in that she accosted Thomas Davies of the Birches, Guilsfield, on the highway and stole sixteen pounds (She was accompanied by a man when the offence took place but there is no evidence concerning him.) She was sentenced to 10 years transportation, this sentence following a previous conviction concerning a felony committed at Chester (NLW Q/SR 1847). She was transported on the 'Cadet' leaving London 9 September 1847 arriving VDL 2 January 1848 and the Surgeon had cause to report her conduct as bad. She was 22 years of age, native of North Wales where her mother Margaret and sisters Mary, Emma, Sarah Ann and another lived. Single and it was also noted that she had spent two years "on the town", i.e. prostitution, she was a housemaid/laundress by calling, Protestant and able to read and write, height 4'11¾", head round, hair light brown, visage oval, forehead high, eyes grey, eyebrows brown, mouth large, chin and nose small with fair complexion (CON 41/15; CON 15/4; CON 19/6). She spent 6 months with the Anson gang in class 3rd as at 30 June 1848.

The following offences are noted:

> *21 April 1851 – Drunk. 10 days cells.*
> *29 October 1851 – Creating a disturbance. 3 days cells.*
> *5 December 1852*
> *and*
> *17 December 1852 – Absconded. 6 months hard labour.*
> *12 December 1853 – Being found in bed with a man not her husband. 6 months hard labour.*
> *19 October 1854 – Drunk. 3 months hard labour.*
> *7 August 1855 – Drunk. Fined one pound.*
> *2 October 1855 – Drunk. Fined one pound.*
> *22 August 1856 – Misconduct. 7 days solitary confinement.*
> *28 October 1862 – Stealing from the person. 4 years penal servitude by Supreme Court Hobart Town.*

A ticket of leave was issued 25 October 1853 and revoked 10 January 1854. A further ticket of leave was issued 26 June 1855 and a certificate of freedom 9 January 1857. Permission to marry was granted 24 October 1848 between Eliza Thomas and James Castles 'Westmorland' (CON 52/3, p. 68) and the marriage took place 14 November 1848 at the Parish Church, Swansea, in the District of Swan Port. Eliza Thomas was shown as a spinster and James Castles as a 37 year old farm servant and he made his mark. The service was conducted by the Minister Joseph Mayson in the presence of James and Harriet House according to the Rites and Ceremonies of the United Church of England and Ireland (RGD 37/7 No. 1497 of 1848).

THOMAS John (c.1812–)

Convicted at the Assizes 8 March 1834 of housebreaking and stealing plate at Machynlleth. His accomplice was Humphrey Jones. He had a previous offence of stealing a jacket when he received a 6 week prison sentence. He was sentenced to life transportation. His gaol report confirmed that he had a previous conviction, of quiet disposition but bad character. The hulk report 'Gannymede' found him to be good. He was transported on the 'Lady Kennaway' leaving Cork 27 October 1834 arriving VDL 13 February 1835. The ship Surgeon stated that his conduct had been very good. He was 23 years of age, single and a groom/coachman by calling, height 5'5", head round, hair dark brown, whiskers dark brown, visage oval, forehead high, eyes hazel, eyebrows dark brown, nose medium length, mouth medium width, chin medium length and complexion fresh. The letter JT were inside the right arm and a mermaid inside the left arm (CON 31/43; CON 18/10; CSO 1/785/16764). The Appropriation List shows that he was employed by a Mr Hobler at Launceston (CSO 1/785/16764).

The following offences are noted:

> *28 December 1835 – Absent from his Master's premises and in a house of bad*
> *character. 25 lashes.*
> *11 July 1836 – Drunk. 6 hours in the Stocks.*
> *3 October 1836 – Disobedience of orders. 20 days in the cells.*
> *5 December 1837 – Absent all day and thereby neglecting his work. 25 lashes.*
> *18 August 1840 – Absent without leave. 14 days hard labour on the tread wheel.*
> *22 April 1843 – Absconding. 12 months hard labour in chains. (CON 31/43).*

His ticket of leave was issued 5 July 1844 and a recommendation for a conditional pardon for the Australian Colonies, 22 April 1845. This was approved 12 May 1845, after 10 years 5 months in the Colony including 1 year 1 month holding a ticket of leave as "his general conduct being satisfactory and his behaviour as a ticket of leave holder having shown that he can be trusted with more extended indulgence" (PRO HO 10/59).

THOMAS Richard (c.1812–)

Convicted at the Quarter Sessions 11 December 1829 of larceny, stealing a quantity of sugar from the warehouse of David Davies, Grocer, Newtown. His accomplices were Edward Edwards and Owen Parry. He had been accused of stealing a pound note but was acquitted. NLW Q/SR 1829). The gaol report states that he was bad, the hulk report 'Justitia' that he was orderly. He was transported on the 'Manlius' leaving London 6 April 1830 arriving VDL 12 August 1830. He was 18 years of age, single, Protestant and a ploughman by calling. He was able to read only, height 5'6", hair brown, eyes dark blue and was pockpitted (CON 31/43; CON 23/3; M111). The appropriation list shows that he was employed by Mr H. Grant as a ploughman (M111). There appears to be no offences shown against him and he received a free certificate No. 745, 20 January 1837 (CON 23/3).

THOMAS William (c.1821–)

Convicted at the Quarter Sessions 29 June 1843 of larceny in that he stole watches from James Dudley and Edward Williams and illegally pawning same. He was sentenced to 7 years transportation. His accomplice was his 18-year-old brother Edward, a boatman by calling, who was convicted of larceny and sentenced to 4 months imprisonment (NLW B1/19, *Shrewsbury Chronicle*, 7 July 1843). His gaol report stated that he was of a bad character and had been imprisoned once at Shrewsbury for 12 months having committed a felony, while his period on a hulk ship appeared to have warranted a good report. He was transported on the 'Marion 1' leaving London 9 December 1843 arriving VDL 4 April 1844, when the Surgeon confirmed that he was a good waterman. He was single, 22 years of age and resided at his native place Llandrinio with his father William, mother Catherine, brothers Jno and Hy, sisters Betsy and Ann. He was a Protestant, a rope maker by calling and able to read only, height 5'11", head large, hair black, whiskers none, visage round, forehead medium height, eyes hazel, eyebrows black, nose medium, mouth large upper lip thick, chin large with ruddy complexion. He had 2 scars on upper lip right side, woman SW and 5 plus anchor on right arm WFJ and 791 on left arm; was freckled and stoutly made (CON 33/53; CON 14/27: CON 18/39). He spent 15 months probation in the Jericho Gang in class PPH 3rd.

The following offences are noted:

24 May 1844 – Absconded. 12 months added to existing 7 year transportation sentence and 6 mths added to his period of probation.

20 July 1844 – Absconded. 9 months hard labour in chains and added to his period of probation.

30 October 1844 – Insubordination by breaking out of confinement whilst awaiting trial for absconding 3 months hard labour in chains added to his existing sentence of hard labour and period of probation.

9 November 1844 – Absconded. 75 lashes.

6 December 1844 – Insubordination with others in endeavouring to occasion a riot and breaking out of confinement at night. 18 months hard labour in chains which was to be added to his existing term of probation and that he be removed to Tasman Peninsula.

28 August 1845 – Misconduct in having potatoes improperly in his possession. 24 lashes.

9 March 1846 – Misconduct in losing or making away with his Government trousers. 7 days solitary confinement.

8 March 1847 – Misconduct in having a quantity of soap improperly in his berth. 3 months hard labour in chains and added to his probation.

28 May 1847 – Misconduct in endeavouring to deceive the Supt with regard to his sentence in chains. 3 months added to existing sentence of probation.

2 February 1848 – Misconduct in the Sleeping Ward. 1 month added to existing sentence of probation.

His ticket of leave was refused 21 November 1848 but on 23 September 1851 he received a free certificate.

THOM(P)SON William (c.1824–)

Convicted at the Quarter Sessions 7 March 1848 of housebreaking in that he entered the house of Evan Price of Kerry on 13 February 1848 and stole bread, bacon and clothes. He was sentenced to 10 years transportation. His accomplice was James Harvey (NLW B1/21, *Shrewsbury Chronicle*, 17 March 1848; NLW Q/SR 1848). He was transported on the 'Rodney' leaving Portland 23 August 1850 arriving VDL 28 November 1850 and the Surgeon confirmed that his conduct had been good. He was 26 years of age, single, and native of Salford Manchester where his mother Martha lived. A saddler by calling, Protestant and able to read and write a little, height 5'4¼", head medium, hair brown, whiskers brown, visage oval, forehead medium, eyes grey, eyebrows brown, mouth small, nose and chin medium with fair complexion. He had a heart on the inside of the left arm (CON 33/99; CON 14/41). On 23 December 1850 he was returned to Government service by a Mr Harris who apparently found him as "not being a saddler". The only offence recorded against him was on 6 December 1852 when he was fined five shillings for being drunk at Hobart. A ticket of leave was issued 25 May 1852 followed by a conditional pardon 21 June 1853. He obtained permission to marry on 5 May 1853 Anna Selling ('Anna Maria') (CON 52/6) but there is no record that this marriage took place.

WALDEN John (c.1815-4.9.1853)

Convicted at the Quarter Sessions 6 April 1843 of housebreaking by entering the house of Miss Davies of Welshpool and stealing various articles. His accomplices were John Bradbury and John Hartell above. He had a previous conviction for assault and received 6 weeks imprisonment. He was sentenced to 15 years transportation (NLW Q/SR 1843). The gaol report found him bad in every respect with connexions as bad as possible, although the hulk report found him good. He was transported on the 'Lord Petre' leaving London July 1843 arriving VDL 15 October 1843, the Surgeon reporting that he had been good. He was 28 years of age, single, native of Hagley, Birmingham, and his mother, Mary, lived at ? Bromsgrove, Worcestershire. He was able to read and write imperfectly, Protestant and a nail maker by trade, height 5'7¼", head oval, hair dark brown, whiskers dark brown, visage oval, forehead medium height, eyes grey, eyebrows dark brown, nose large, mouth medium, chin medium and complexion sallow. He had a scar on the back right hand, the letters EJ.JW and APC on left arm and EJ between thumb and forefinger left hand. He had an impediment of speech (CON 33/45; CON 14/24; CON 18/34). He spent 18 months probation at Lovely Banks as a PPH 3rd. There were no offences noted against him. He was released from the first stage of probation 1 April 1845 and his ticket of leave refused 9 October 1849 by being not eligible. This was granted 15 October 1850 and a recommendation for a conditional pardon 27 January 1852 was approved 14 December 1852. He was in Impression Bay hospital 9 March and 3 May 1852, where he died 4 September 1853 (CON 33/45 vide Report of G. Drew Esq. 5 September 1853). He was buried in the Parish of Tasman's Peninsula 7 September 1853, the ceremony carried out by Samuel Brookes Clerk (RGD 34/2 No. 2104 1853).

WALTON Isaac (c.1818-10.6.1857)
Convicted at the Quarter Sessions 8 April 1841 of larceny from the person by stealing 17 sovereigns, two £5 notes and several pieces of silver coins from David Lloyd of Llanidloes. His accomplice was Richard Kimberlin. He was sentenced to 10 years transportation (NLW Q/SR 1841). The gaol report states that he was believed to have belonged to a gang of pickpockets, was of quiet disposition, sober habits and had behaved well in gaol. The hulk report found him good. He was transported on the 'Somersetshire' leaving Plymouth 19 December 1841 arriving VDL 13 May 1842. The surgeon also finding him to be good. He was 24 years of age, single, native of Abingdon Berkshire, and his Uncle Joshua lived at Denton, Lancashire. He was a Protestant, able to read and write and a labourer/ hawker by calling, height 5'4", head oval, hair brown, whiskers black, visage oval, forehead high and broad, eyes hazel, eyebrows brown, nose medium, mouth medium, chin broad and complexion fresh. There were no marks on his body (CON 33/21; CON 14/13; CON 28/1; CON 18/32). He spent 18 months probation at Victoria Valley (CON 28/1).

The following offences are noted:

> *5 January 1843 – Misconduct in having a pipe and tobacco in his possession. 7 days solitary confinement.*
> *Same date – Absent from the Station without leave. Existing period of primary labour extended by 1 month.*
> *30 December 1843 – Extended term of probation expired.*
> *12 March 1844 – Misconduct in not proceeding according to his Pass. Admonished.*
> *29 January 1849 – Drunk. Fined 5/-.*
> *3 February 1849 – Drunk. Fined 5/-. (CON 33/21).*

His ticket of leave was issued 18 January 1848 and a free certificate 22 April 1851. He was accidently killed 10 June 1857 at Longford (RGD 35/26 No. 502 1857 Coroner, Charles Arthur, Inquest No. 4012 SC 195/40).

WHITE George (c.1822–)
Convicted at the Quarter Sessions 19 October 1848 of horse stealing by taking a mare (value £30) from John Francis of Penstrowed. He was sentenced to 10 years transportation (NLW Q/SR 1848). He was transported on the 'Fairlie' leaving Plymouth 11 March 1852 arriving VDL 3 July 1852. He was 30 years of age, married with three children and a native of Loughborough where his wife Elizabeth, father John and brothers John and Thomas may have lived. He was a Protestant, able to read and write and a grinder by calling, height 5'8½", head large/round, hair black/dark brown, whiskers black, visage long/broad, forehead medium/low, eyebrows black/dark brown, eyes grey/brown, nose large/ pointed, mouth medium/small, chin medium/long and complexion dark/ sallow. He had several moles on left arm below elbow and a small scar on the left side of the lip/chin (CON 33/107 No. 25773; CON 14/43 No. 25773; CON 18/56).

The following offences are noted:

12 October 1852 – Absent without leave. 3 months hard labour.
26 September 1853 – Absent without leave. 10 days solitary confinement.
23 January 1854 – Misconduct in being Disorderly. Admonished.
22 February 1854 – Drunk and neglect of duty. 14 days solitary confinement.
21 May 1855 – Resisting a Constable. Fined £1. (CON 33/107).

His ticket of leave was issued 10 October 1854, conditional pardon 28 August 1855 and a certificate of freedom at Hobart 26 October 1855.

WHITTAL(L) Thomas (c.1795-18.7.1844)
Convicted at the Quarter Sessions 2 July 1840 of sheep stealing by taking 8 sheep from Richard Probert, 1 saddle and 1 halter from John Turner of Hyssington (*Salopian Journal,* 8 July 1840). He had a previous conviction for horse stealing but was discharged. He was sentenced to 15 years transportation. His gaol report stated that he had been dishonest all his life. His period on the hulk was marred by spending some time in irons having been convicted of stealing biscuits. He was transported on the 'David Clarke' leaving Plymouth 7 June 1841 arriving VDL 4 October 1841. The Surgeon found him to be orderly. He was 46 years of age, single, able to read only, native of the Bishop Castle/Churchstoke area and had one sister, Eleanor. Height 5'2", head long, hair dark brown, whiskers black, visage oval, forehead low/narrow and wrinkled, eyes light grey, eyebrows dark brown, nose large, mouth large, chin large and complexion ruddy (CON 33/13; CON 14/9; CON 18/29). There were no offences recorded against him and on 4 October 1843 his original term of probation expired. On 18 July 1844 he died in Bridgewater Hospital vide report of Supt dated 20 July 1844 (CON 33/13).

WILLIAMS Edward (c.1804 – 28 April 1831)
Convicted at the Quarter Sessions 15 January 1829 of stealing 70 yds in length of flannel value £2.15.0 from the racks or tenter field at Rhiwsaeson, Llanbrynmair, the property of Hugh Francis, as seen by the wife of Hugh Francis. He was sentenced to 7 years transportation (NLW Q/SR 1829). His gaol and hulk reports state that he was orderly. He was transported on the 'Sir Charles Forbes' leaving London 5 March 1830 arriving VDL 27 July 1830. His conduct on board being very bad. He was 26 years of age, single, Protestant, ploughman by trade and able to read only, height 5'4¼", hair black, eyes grey and with a large scar on his breast

(CON 31/46; CON 23/3; ML 11). His death took place on 28 April 1831 in Hobart Town Hospital and burial followed the next day in the Parish of Hobart Town in County Buckingham, the service being taken by Wm Bedford (RGD 34/1 No. 2428 1831; CON 31/46; CON 23/3).

WILLIAMS Elizabeth (c.1791-7.3.1869)

Convicted at the Great Sessions 29 March 1827 of arson by setting fire to a stack of hay belonging to Thomas Davies of Trewern. She was sentenced to death commuted to life transportation following a Royal Pardon 14 May 1827 (NLW Wales 4/203/1, Q/SR 1827). Her gaol report stated that she was a known thief of vindictive disposition. She had married an old man of some property 12 years ago when she was a servant. Soon afterwards, she became a prostitute and connected herself with a man of bad character. She was transported on the 'Borneo' leaving London 11 May 1828 arriving VDL 8 October 1828. She was 37 years of age; widowed with 3 children aged 12, 7 and 3 years approximately. She was a native of ? Llanowthan/Lenalvin, Montgomeryshire, and a farm servant/able to milk and make butter/cheese by calling, height 5'2", head large, hair brown/ grey, visage broad/oval, face full round, eyes dark grey, eyebrows thin of hair, nose small/turned up, mouth large, chin small and complexion fresh/freckled (CON 40/9; CON 18/23; ML 6). She received a conditional pardon No. 1243 10 January 1837 (CON 40/9). In August 1829 permission to marry was granted between Elizabeth Williams and William Lewis (Malabar), both of the Parish of Clyde (CON 45/1), the marriage being solemnised in the Parish Church of New Norfolk, County Buckingham, 5 October 1829. The marriage by Banns was carried out by H. R. Robinson Chaplain in the presence of Henry Goldsmith of the Hollow Tree and W. J. Ring of New Norfolk (RGD 36/1 No. 1368 1829). The following information may well relate to Elizabeth Williams and her family in Tasmania who probably were unaware of her family in Wales and vice versa. Recorded births included Mary Anne Lewis born 22 August 1831 at Green Ponds District, baptised 25 September 1831 (RGD 32/1 No. 4137 1831), and William Lewis born 12 April 1834, baptised 20 April 1834 (RGD 32/1 No. 5901 1834. In both instances the parents are shown as William Lewis a farmer of Bothwel and Elizabeth Lewis. Deaths noted in the District of Bothwell include their son William Lewis on 30 December 1853 aged 19 yrs of a liver complaint. The informant being his mother Elizabeth Lewis (RGD 35/22 No. 101 Bothwell 1853). That of William Lewis took place on 2 June 1861 aged 82 years and a farmer the cause being: "By decay of Nature". The informant was a friend Edward Bowden (RGD 35/30 No. 312 Bothwell 1861). Lastly, the death of Elizabeth Lewis is recorded on 7 March 1869 when her age is given as 72 years. She is shown to be the relict of William Lewis Farm Overseer, and the cause of death being a "Wound on leg accidently caused by the kick of a horse". The Informant again was Edward Bowden and occupier of the house (RGD 35/38 No. 1 Bothwell 1869).

WILLIAMS John (alias John BUTLER) (c.1812–)

Convicted at the Quarter Sessions 17 October 1833 of larceny, stealing 4 shirts at Llandrinio. This followed a previous conviction of housebreaking when he received a 2 year imprisonment sentence. He was sentenced to 7 years transportation. His gaol report states that he was of a savage temper and disposition and the hulk report 'Justitia' found him orderly. He was transported on the 'Norfolk' which had to stop at Cork and transfer its convicts to the 'Lady Kennaway' that had left Woolwich 10 June 1834 and now left Cork 27 October 1834 arriving VDL 13

February 1835. The Surgeon reported that he had received 60 lashes on his bare back for theft and had behaved well thereafter. He was 22 years of age, single, native of Muddle, Shropshire, and a ploughman by calling, height 5'6¾", head large/ round, hair dark brown, visage round, forehead medium height, eyes hazel, eyebrows dark brown, nose short/thick, mouth small, chin small and complexion sallow. He had 2 brown moles on right arm (CON 31/47; CON 18/10; CSO 1/ 785/16764, p. 218). The appropriation list shows that he was employed as a ploughman by Major Gibson New Norfolk (CSO 1/785/16764, p. 218).

The following offences are noted:

> *22 September 1835 – Neglect of Duty. 1 week cell on bread/water.*
> *8 September 1836 – Drunk and Insolent. 25 lashes.*
> *20 October 1837 – Drunk last night in his Master's tap rooms. Admonished.*
> *28 December 1838 – Assaulting Hy Roberts. 14 days cell on bread/water.*

(CON 31/47).

His ticket of leave was issued 22 February 1840 and a free certificate No. 872 the same year.

WILLIAMS Mary (c.1813–)

She was convicted at the Quarter Sessions 5 April 1832 of larceny, stealing 2 pair shoes, 1 silk bonnet, 2 shawls and several other articles of wearing apparel from the house of Edward Evans Guilsfield. She was sentenced to 7 years transportation (NLW Q/SR 1832). Her gaol report stated that she was a bad character but a very peaceable girl. She was transported on the 'Frances Charlotte' leaving Downs 15 September 1832 arriving VDL 10 January 1833, the Surgeon reporting that she had been orderly. She was 19 years of age, single, Protestant, native of Asivestry (Oswestry), unable to read or write and a farm girl by calling, height 4'11", head small, hair dark brown, visage small, forehead perpendicular, eyes dark hazel/grey, eyebrows brown, nose, mouth and chin small, complexion fresh (CON 40/9; CON 13/6; ML 15/16; CON 18/23). No further information was traceable.

WILLIAMS Thomas (c.1800–)

Convicted at the Quarter Sessions 9 April 1835 of larceny, stealing poultry and one pair of quarter boots from Thomas Thomas, Llansantffraid. This followed a previous conviction at Denleigh (Denbigh) when he was imprisoned for 1 week for stealing a goose. He was sentenced to life transportation (NLW Q/SR 1835). His gaol report stated that he had respectable connections and had been 17 years in service. The hulk report 'Gannymede' found him to be good. He was transported on the 'Layton II' leaving Sheerness 29 August 1835 arriving VDL 10 December 1835. It is probable that his conduct on the voyage was indifferent as he appears to have been flogged. He was 35 years of age, single, unable to read or write, native of Llansilin, Denbighshire, and a ploughman/reaper/milker by calling, height 5'6½", head oval, hair black/grey, whiskers dark reddish/brown, visage oval, forehead medium height, eyes light brown, eyebrows black, nose long, mouth wide, chin long and complexion sallow. His face and arms were freckled (CON 31/47; CON 18/13; CSO 1/839/17773). The appropriation list shows that he would be worked on probation for 6 months on the roads (CSO 1/839/17773; CON 27/2).

The following offences are noted:

> *17 December 1835 – 6 months on the roads on probation for improper conduct during the voyage.*
> *1 September 183(8) – Neglect of duty in losing 25 sheep left in his care by his Master. 25 lashes.*

WILSON George (c.1830–)

Convicted at the Quarter Sessions 29 June 1848 of housebreaking by breaking and entering the house of Mr William Owen farmer of Aberhafesp on 30 April 1848 and stealing £1.3s.6d and one pair of shoes. With his accomplice John Jones, they were caught the same night in Llanidloes by constable Robert Williams of Caersws with the property still on their persons. George Wilson was sentenced to 10 years transportation (NLW Bl/21, *Shrewsbury Chronicle*, 7 July 1848, Q/SR 1848). Following a period spent in a hulk, where his conduct was recorded as being very good, he was transported on the 'Aboukir' leaving London 7 December 1851 arriving VDL 20 March 1852. Throughout the voyage the Surgeon stated that he had been of exemplary conduct. He was 22 years of age, native of Reading, single, baker/labourer by trade, only relative appears to be an uncle living at Windsor. He was Church of England and able to read and write a little, height 5'4¾", head oval, whiskers none, visage long, forehead medium, eyes black, eyebrows dark, nose, mouth and chin medium, complexion sallow with no visible marks on the body (CON 33/106; CON 14/31; CON 18/56).

The following offences are noted:

> *11 April 1852 – Misconduct in that he was engaged as cook and baker and found unable to do either. 6 weeks hard labour.*
> *17 August 1853 – Embezzlement under five pounds. 18 months hard labour.*
> (CON 33/106.

His ticket of leave was issued 14 August 1855.

WOOD John (c.1819–)

Convicted at the Quarter Sessions 21 October 1841 of larceny by a servant in that he stole brown sugar, soap, 1 sack, 1 umbrella, 2 linen wrappers 1 qtr measure and various other articles from his employers John Jones and Francis Hallowes of Machynlleth (*Salopian Journal*, 27 October 1841). It is possible that he may have had a previous offence when he stole sugar, soap, etc., the property of Mr Rees shopkeeper at his native place. He was sentenced to 7 years transportation (NLW Q/SR 1841). His gaol report stated that he had received a good character from his Prosecutor and his behaviour in the hulks was good. He was transported on the 'Duchess of Northumberland' leaving Sheerness 2 October 1842 arriving VDL 18 January 1843. The Surgeon reported that he was orderly but subject to despondency. He was 24 years of age, single, farm labourer/ploughman by calling, Protestant and a native of ? Highstone, Montgomeryshire. His mother Elizabeth and brother Richard are named. It is noted that his mother tongue was Welsh. He is shown as being unable to read or write in English but able to read in Welsh, height 5'¾", head medium, hair dark brown, whiskers brown, visage long, forehead medium, eyebrows brown, eyes light brown, nose, mouth and chin medium and complexion fair. He had a scar on the chin. He spent 14 months of primary labour in the St Mary Vale Gang. His ticket of leave was issued 28 July 1846.

WOOD Samuel (c.1820–)

Convicted at the Quarter Sessions 5 January 1843 of larceny by breaking and entering houses and stealing as follows:

> *Parcel of clothes from Mr John Davies, Forden.*
> *Coat from Mr Edward Davies, Forden.*
> *Brush from Mr John Newall, Forden.*
> *Pair of Breeches from Mr John Hughes, Welshpool.*

He was sentenced to 7 years transportation (NLW B1/18, *Shrewsbury Chronicle*, 13 January 1843; NLW Q/SR 1843). He was transported on the 'Sir George Seymour' leaving London 2 November 1844 arriving VDL 27 February 1845. The AOT Convict Index does not have an entry for Samuel Wood; the only available source, but with no additional information, is CON 14/26.

APPENDIX C

Western Australia

BAKER John (c.1844–)

(Acc. 1156/R21B; Acc. 128/33 and 1156/R30; Acc. 1386/5).

Convicted at the Welshpool Assizes 17 December 1863, having committed arson by the burning of hay. Sentenced to 8 years penal servitude, he was moved to Chatham, where his record showed that he had received a good character. He was transported 19 May 1865, on the 'Racehorse'. The ship reached Perth 10 August 1865. Official records indicate that he was 21 years of age, height 5'5", with dark brown hair and hazel eyes. His visage was oval, complexion sallow and appearance stout. He was single and occupation is shown as miner or collier. He was able to read and write imperfectly. On his arms were tattooed the following marks – sailor with cutlass and flags on his left arm and flag and crown, with the letters 'JSD' and date 1863, on the right arm. His religion was Protestant. No next of kin is recorded. He was charged with stealing cabbages on 12 July 1867 at Perth and sentenced to 12 months hard labour in Perth Prison. He was granted his ticket of leave 3 May 1869 and also 7 March 1870, but both were destroyed. He obtained his conditional release 27 February 1871. Between 6 May 1869 and 7 December 1870 he was assigned to work in the Perth District to the employers Messrs J. Sallinger, T. Langoulant and J. Perry and received a wage of 25 shillings. During these years his work is shown as labourer, lime-burner and general servant. No further evidence is available on him and the date of his death cannot be traced.

BARNES Henry (c.1834-16.5.1869)

(AJCP Reel 2844 HO 27/118; Acc. 128/27 and 1156/R7 and R22; Acc. 1156/R21B; Acc. 1386/8; Acc. 1386/15).

Convicted at the Welshpool Quarter Sessions 22 October 1857 for breaking and entering the dwelling house of Robert Pryce, Llanfair Caereinion, and stealing a watch, for a crime committed in the house of Robert Lloyd, Castle Caereinion, and stealing 4 shirts, 2 pr stockings and 1 scissors, and for a crime at the house of Eleanor Morgan, Llangyniew, where he took 1 wedding ring and 1 scissors. He was sentenced to 7 days upon the 1st conviction, 7 days upon the second, and 10 years penal servitude on the last. Following his conviction he must have been transferred, date unknown, to the prison establishment at Bermuda. Eventually, he was transported from Bermuda to Perth on the 'Merchantman', which had left London 10 October 1862, calling at Bermuda. The ship reached Perth 14 February 1863. Official records show that he was 29 years of age, height 5'8¾" and had dark brown hair with blue eyes. He was stout with full visage and sallow complexion. The only mark on his body was the letter 'D' on his left side. He was a labourer, single, unable to read and write and of Protestant religion. No next of kin is recorded. He committed numerous offences including:

> *3 May 1864 – Breach of Regulations. 7 days prison.*

> *2 February 1866 – Burglary. Dismissed.*
> *16 May 1866 – Insubordination. 7 days bread and water.*
> *5 June 1866 – Refusing to work. 3 days bread and water.*
> *10 August 1866 – Insubordination. 3 days bread and water.*
> *8 October 1866 – Idleness. Cautioned.*
> *15 October 1866 – Insubordination. 3 months hard labour in irons.*

He was granted his ticket of leave on 14 March 1863. Between 30 June 1863 and 3 April 1869 he was assigned to work in a number of Districts, including York, Bunbury, Sussex, Vasse, Murray, Swan, Victoria Plains, Northam and Toodyay. Most of this period was spent as a labourer, although he was engaged on striking a well in July 1864. Payment fluctuated between 1 shilling per day, 8 shillings per week and 30 shillings per month. His eventual death is recorded at Toodyay Depot on 16 May 1869, the cause shown as disease of the heart.

BOOTH James (c.1831–)

(Acc. 128/33; 1156/R30; Acc. 1156/R21B; Acc. 1386/5; 1386/10; 1386/12; *Police Gazette*, 1876, p. 4; *Shrewsbury Chronicle*, 25 December 1863).

Convicted at the Welshpool Assizes 17 December 1963, of setting fire to hay at Newtown, this following a previous conviction for felony. He was sentenced to 8 years penal servitude, which was spent initially at Chatham, where his conduct was good. He eventually was transported on the 'Racehorse', leaving on 19 May 1865 and arriving at Perth on 10 August 1965. Official records show that he was 34 years of age, height 5'6¼", with light brown hair and grey eyes. He was middling stout, with thin visage and sallow complexion. Marks on his right arm included two flags, a star and sailor. On his left arm were a woman, crown, wreath, anchor, with the letter 'D' and date 1863. There was a medal on his breast. He was a labourer cum fireman, single, with no next of kin, could read and write imperfectly, and was of Protestant religion. He incurred numerous convictions, as follows:

> *4 December 1865 – Absconding. 6 months in irons.*
> *22 May 1866 – Insubordination. 3 days bread and water.*
> *15 January 1869 – Desertion. 3 months hard labour.*
> *21 June 1869 – Leaving without Pass. 7 days hard labour.*
> *27 July 1869 – Absconding. 3 months hard labour.*
> *17 October 1870 – Absconding. 6 months hard labour.*
> *2 September 1871 – Absconding. Ticket of leave revoked.*
> *18 December 1871 – Refused to work. Cautioned.*
> *5 March 1872 – Insolence. 3 days bread and water.*

He was granted his ticket of leave 11 September 1868, revoked on 2 September 1871. He received a conditional pardon 30 December 1872. He was assigned to work in the following Districts, namely Perth, Bunbury, Wellington, York and Toodyay, between 11 September 1868 and 5 November 1872, and was employed as labourer, sawyer, gardener and general servant, for wages of varying amounts up to 35 shillings per month. In the *Police Gazette*, 1876, it is noted that he had left the Colony on 18 December 1875, and moved to Sydney on the SS 'Clarence'. There is no further information concerning him.

BRANNAN William (c.1843–)

(AJCP Reel 5984 PCOM2/110; Acc. 128/33 and 1156/R30; Acc. 1386/5; *Shrewsbury Chronicle*, 25 July 1863 and NLW Q/SR 1863H).

Convicted at the Newtown Assizes 15 July 1863, of setting fire to a haystack (with Thomas Brown), this following a previous conviction of stealing 24 yards of blue flame serge, from David Hamer, Llanidloes, for which offence he had 19 weeks hard labour in Montgomery Gaol. He now received an 8 years penal servitude sentence and was transferred to Millbank Prison, having spent 2 months and 4 days at Montgomery. During his stay of 4 months and 14 days at Millbank, his character remained good. Eventually he was moved to Portsmouth, where he was used on Public Works throughout his stay of 1 year and 9 days. He was transported on the 'Racehorse', leaving Portland on 26 May 1865, arriving Western Australia on 10 August 1865. On arrival, official records show that he was 22 years of age, height 5'5", with brown hair and blue eyes. He was stout with round visage and sallow complexion. His only mark was a scar on the left leg. He was single, a labourer, able to read and write and was a Roman Catholic. No next of kin are recorded. He appears to have maintained his good character, only two offences being committed, namely Insubordination (14 August 1866), 7 days bread and water, and making away with government property (18 August 1866), for which the case was discharged. He was granted his ticket of leave 7 December 1867, conditional release 8 August 1870 and his full pardon 4 August 1871. He was assigned to work in the following districts, namely Perth, Swan and Toodyay, where he was employed on labouring, cutting sandal wood, teamster and general servant. His wages fluctuated between 25 shillings and 40 shillings per month, during the period 9 December 1867 and 30 June 1870. It is recorded 7 August 1871 that should he be unable to earn his livelihood due to his heart disease, he would become chargeable to Imperial funds. No further information is available following receipt of his full pardon.

BROWN John (c.1824-30.11.1873)

(Acc. 128/29; Acc. 1156/R21B, R27 and R29; AJCP Reel 5983 Pri Com 2/109; NLW Q/SR 1862M).

Convicted at the Newtown Quarter Sessions 3 July 1862 of breaking and entering the house of Thomas Jones, Guilsfield, and stealing 3 pieces of black coborg cloth and 1 piece of alpaca cloth. He was sentenced to 7 years penal servitude. He spent 14 days in Montgomery Gaol, 9 months 2 days at Millbank, and the remainder at Portsmouth. In all, he spent 1 year 2 months and 11 days on public works. His character at Montgomery was bad, at Millbank good, although the Governor of Preston House of Correction stated that this prisoner had been in his custody twice and in every prison in England, Ireland and Scotland. He was transported on the 'Lord Dalhousie', leaving Portland 25 September 1863, arriving Perth 28 December 1863. Official records show that he was 39 years of age, height 5'1¾", with brown hair and hazel eyes. He was stout, with oval visage and sallow complexion. There were no marks on his body. He was single, a labourer (although cigar maker is noted), was unable to read or write and was a Roman Catholic. His next of kin is shown as his father (William Brown of Warrington, Lancashire). On the ship were 270 male convicts, including John Jones, John Macdonough and John Robinson who had also been convicted by Montgomeryshire Courts. His previous bad habits travelled with him, as the following list of convictions confirms:

20 January 1864 – Bad language and refusing to work. 14 days bread and water.

8 February 1864 – Absconding. 6 months hard labour.
15 March 1867 – Not sending in Return. 14 days hard labour.
17 February 1869 – Drunk and bad language. 1 month hard labour.

He was granted his ticket of leave on 22 November 1865, but no further certificate was granted although he was due for his conditional pardon 4 October 1867. All his assignments were in the Swan District, where he was employed either as a labourer or as a general servant. His wages fluctuated between 20 shillings and 30 shillings per month, during the period 3 November 1865 and 30 June 1870. His death is recorded on 30 November 1873.

BROWN Thomas (c.1835–)
(Acc. 128/8; 128/41; Acc. 1156/R21B; AJCP Reel 5977 Pri Com 2/63; Reel 5988 Pri Com 2/136).
Convicted at the Newtown Quarter Sessions 4 July 1850 of sheep stealing. As this followed a previous conviction of stealing cheese, for which he was sentenced to 1 month imprisonment, he was now sentenced to 7 years Penal Servitude. He was returned to Montgomery Gaol but during this period he was placed in solitary confinement for 3 days for an attempt to break out of prison. He was transferred to Millbank on September 1850, his character, on transfer being shown as "Notoriously Bad". Here he remained until a transfer to Pentonville on 29 November 1850. His behaviour had improved at both these large prisons where it was shown as "Good". Once again he was transferred on 6 November 1851 and this time he went to the hulk ship 'York'. By 28 July 1852 he had been moved to Portsmouth Prison where he remained until his transportation on 2 February 1853, on the 'Pyrenees', which arrived in Western Australia on 30 April 1853. Official records show that his crime was committed in Welshpool although his next of kin (Jno Brown) lived at Silver Street, Reading. He was 18 years of age, height 5'5", weight 9st 7lbs, with dark brown hair and grey eyes. He was tolerably stout with oval visage and fair complexion. Marks included crown and wreath on left arm, and scars on back of both hands. He was single, a general labourer, able to read and write indifferently and was of the Wesleyan persuasion. He obtained his ticket of leave on 1 May 1853 and his conditional pardon 12 August 1864. No record is available as to his further life although a man of his name married on 4 October 1863 one Bridget Rock, who had arrived on the 'Mary Harrison', (probable emigrant), on 24 June 1862.

BROWN Thomas (c.1845–)
(AJCP Reel 5984 Pri Com 2/110; Acc. 128/34; Acc. 1156/R13; Acc. 1156/R21B; Acc. 1386/5; *Shrewsbury Chronicle*, 25 July 1863 and NLW Q/SR 1862M).
Convicted at the Newtown Assizes 15 July 1863 of arson, by setting fire to a haystack at Montgomery (with William Brennan). He had previously been convicted for breaking and entering a house at Forden in 1862. Following committal to Montgomery Gaol on 4 April 1863, he was transferred to Millbank 19 September 1863, and finally Portsmouth on 2 May 1864. His conduct at these prisons was good. Having spent 1 year 4 months 18 days on Public Works, he was eventually transported on the 'Vimeira', leaving Portland on 3 September 1865, and arrived Swan River on 22 December 1865. He was 20 years of age, height 5'2¼", with brown hair and dark blue eyes. His appearance was slight with thin visage and dark complexion. He had lost his left eye. He was single, a labourer, able to read and write, and a Roman Catholic. No next of kin was recorded. He appears to have been fond of alcohol, as the following list of offences confirms:

?? February 1866 – Absconding. 2 months in irons.
25 May 1867 – Stealing soap. 2 days bread and water.
24 April 1868 – Drunk. Fine 5 shillings.
22 March 1869 – Drunk and Incapable. 1 month hard labour.
4 June 1869 – Drunk. Remain in depot.
27 December 1869 – Drunk and Incapable. Fine 5 shillings.
1 October 1870 – Drunk. Fine 5 shillings.
1 October 1870 – Breaking pot. Fine 1 shilling & 6p.
1 July 1871 – Drunk and Incapable. Fine 5 shillings.

He was granted his ticket of leave 2 February 1868, and full pardon 19 September 1871. His assignments were in the Swan, Perth, Toodyay and York Districts, where he was employed as a general servant, herdsman, labourer, mason, hut keeper and bark ripper, for which he was paid between 20 shillings and 60 shillings (with rations) per month, during the period from 5 February 1868 to 18 August 1871. It is possible that he died 11 January 1877.

CHIRDEN James (alias SHELDON, alias DUFFY William) (c.1839–)

(AJCP Reel 5983 Pri Com 2/110; Acc. 128/31 Acc. 1156/R2; Acc. 1156/R21B; Acc. 1156/R28).

Convicted at the Welshpool Assizes 11 March 1863 of arson by setting fire to hay, at Montgomery. This followed a previous conviction of stealing clothes in October 1862, for which he was sentenced to 1 month hard labour. He was now sentenced to 10 years penal servitude. Following committal to Montgomery Gaol on 20 December 1862, he was transferred to Millbank 5 April 1863 and Portsmouth 23 January 1864. He spent 1 year 3 months and 10 days on Public Works, and at each location his conduct was good. Eventually, he was transported on the 'Merchantman 2' leaving Portland 1 July 1864 and arriving Swan River 12 September 1864. He was 25 years of age, height 5'3", brown hair and grey eyes. He was middling stout, with fresh complexion and deep sunk eyes. He was single, a labourer, unable to read or write, and a Roman Catholic. No next of kin are recorded. The following offences are recorded against him:

4 December 1864 – Idle on work. Tobacco stopped 1 month.
24 December 1864 – Refusing to work. 3 days bread and water.
24 December 1864 – Having bread improperly included as above.
28 December 1864 – Disobedience. Forfeit Sunday dinner.
18 April 1866 – Gross Insubordination. 1 month hard labour.
17 September 1866 – Idleness and work shy. 3 days bread and water.
16 December 1867 – Absconding. 3 months hard labour.
28 June 1872 – Absent without pass. 2 months hard labour.
22 August 1873 – Refusing orders. 3 months hard labour.
15 January 1874 – Absconding. 3 months hard labour.

He received his ticket of leave 17 January 1867, and a full pardon 11 February 1874. Between 18 January 1867 and 9 December 1873, he was assigned in the Perth and Victoria Districts, working as a rail splitter, labourer, hut keeper shepherd, stock keeper, and general servant, for which he was paid between 20 shillings and 50 shillings per month. Records up to 1905, confirm that he had not married or died.

DAVIES John (alias MILLER) (c 1817–)

(AJCP Reel 5982 Pri Com 2/108; Acc. 128/26; Acc. 1156/R7; Acc. 1156/R21B; Acc. 1156/R22).

Convicted at the Montgomery Assizes 9 March 1859, of burglary at Berriew, which followed previous convictions at Radnor Summer Assizes 1850 (sentenced to 10 years transportation. It would appear that he did not go, but spent part of his sentence in prison before being released) and Cheshire Spring Assizes 1856 (sentenced to 18 months hard labour). Having spent 13 days in Montgomery Gaol, he was transferred to Millbank 23 March 1859, and Portsmouth 2 November 1859, having been sentenced to 6 years penal servitude. His conduct on leaving Portsmouth was exemplary and on 8 October 1862, he left Portland on the ship 'York II', arriving at Swan River 31 December 1862. Official records state that he was 45 years of age, height 5'8", with blue eyes and light brown hair. He was middling stout, with long visage and ruddy complexion. Marks included red whiskers and blue dots on knuckles of his left hand. He was single, able to read and write imperfectly and of Protestant religion. His trade was a labourer cum miller. No next of kin is recorded. No offences are shown against him in Australia. He obtained his ticket of leave 12 February 1863 and his full pardon 20 April 1864. He was assigned in the York District, between 20 June 1863 and 31 December 1863 as a labourer, earning 30 shillings per month. No further record has been found.

DAVIES Thomas (c.1828–)

(Acc. 128/6; Acc. 128/41; Acc. 1156/R21B; NLW Bl/22, *Shrewsbury Chronicle*, 1849/50 and Q/SR 1849).

Convicted at the Assizes 5 April 1849 of stealing 3 sovereigns from Richard Lewis, Sun Inn Llansantffraid, 25 December 1847, from whom he had previously stolen five pounds in January the same year. He was now sentenced to 7 years, but there are no records of his prison movements prior to leaving Portland 2 November 1851 on the 'Marion', arriving at Swan River 30 January 1852. Records show that he was aged 24 years, height 5'3", with dark hair and eyes. His appearance was stout, with long visage and dark complexion. There was a scar on the back of his left hand. Single and a labourer, he was a native of Birmingham, having lived most of his life in Llansantffraid. He obtained his ticket of leave 31 January 1852, and full pardon 14 January 1854. Further record of his life in Australia is missing.

FOSTER James (c.1843–)

(AJCP Reel 5984 Pri Com 2/110; Acc. 128/33; Acc. 1156/R30; Acc. 1156/ R21B; Acc. 1386/5; Acc. 1386/13; *Police Gazette*, 1876, p. 124; *Shrewsbury Chronicle*, 25 December 1863).

Convicted at the Welshpool Assizes 17 December 1863 of arson by burning oats at Leighton, for which he was sentenced to 8 years penal servitude. Having spent 8 months in Montgomery Gaol, he was sent to Millbank 26 December 1863, and then Portsmouth 19 October 1864, having spent 6 months and 22 days on Public Works. His conduct at Montgomery was good but at Millbank he attempted to escape. He was transported on the 'Rachorse', leaving Portland 26 May 1865, and arriving at Swan River 10 August 1865. He was 22 years of age, height 5'3¼", with brown hair and hazel eyes. He was stout, with oval visage and sallow complexion. On his right arm were flags and the date 1.8.1863. On his left arm were an anchor, dart, heart, crown and bracelet. Single and a labourer, he was unable to read and write and was a Roman Catholic. No next of kin is recorded. He was granted his ticket of leave 2 May 1874, but probably due to his conduct, as is evident from the following list of offences, the authorities did not consider him a suitable person to receive a pardon.

7 November 1865 – Spitting on prison floor. Forfeit dinner.
17 May 1866 – Disobedience 2 counts. 6 days bread and water
5 June 1866 – Gross insubordination. 1 month solitary.
21 August 1866 – Larceny. 6 months hard labour.
1 September 1866– Drunk. 6 months hard labour.
26 October 1866 – Insubordination. 6 months hard labour.
26 October 1866 – Absent from camp. 2 months hard labour.
5 February 1867 – Robbing Government store. 12 months hard labour.
22 March 1867 – Sentence remitted.
30 April 1867 – Idle and insolent. 7 days bread and water.
22 May 1867 – Absent from camp. 14 days bread and water.
19 June 1867 – Absconding. 3 months in irons.
2 October 1867 – Having tobacco. Forfeit supper.
13 December 1867 – Malingering. Cautioned.
12 February 1868 – Absconding. 6 months in irons.
12 February 1868 – Larceny of a gun & stores 2 years hard labour.
5 October 1868 – Absconding from Prison. 6 months in irons.
6 October 1868 – For above. Conviction 3 months solitary.
6 October 1868 – Larceny of clothes, etc. 6 months hard labour.
2 December 1868 – Pipe, flint & steel on person. 1 day bread and water.
4 December 1868 – Knife, tobacco etc on person. Caution.
20 February 1869 – Losing scrubbing brush. Purchase new one.
11 December 1869 – Idleness. 3 days bread and water.
14 July 1870 – Gross idleness. 2 days bread and water.
27 September 1870 – Insolent to Chaplain. 3 days bread and water.
28 March 1871 – Drunk & riotous. 28 days bread and water.
28 May 1871 – Larceny tea & sugar. 3 months hard labour.
18 December 1871 – Refusing to work. 1 day bread and water.
10 April 1872 – Absconding. 3 years hard labour.
17 April 1872 – For above conviction. 4 months solitary.
22 May 1872 – Larceny clothes from wash. Not proven.
19 December 1873 – Granted. 3 year remission.
11 September 1874 – Illegally at large & drunk. 1 month hard labour.
28 October 1874 – Destroying pass. 1 month hard labour..
30 November 1874 – Drunk. 2 days in cells.
28 December 1874 – Drunk & incapable. 3 months hard labour.
24 August 1875 – Drunk & incapable. Fine 5 shillings.
4 November 1875 – Drunk & loitering. 7 days hard labour.
14 January 1876 – Drunk & out after hours. Cautioned.

The above periods of extensive confinements were in Fremantle Prison and the minor offences were carried out in the Resident Magistrate areas of Fremantle, Perth, Vasse and Bunbury. In view of his record it is no wonder that his ability to undertake any form of employment was drastically curtailed and during the period 1 June 1874 to 14 January 1876 he was only employed at three locations, namely Perth, Fremantle and Sussex, where he carried out labouring duties, and was paid between four & sixpence per day and five pounds per month. The last record of

James Foster, dated 26 May 1880, confirms that he had finally been successful in his attempt to abscond.

FOX George (c.1844–)

(Acc. 128/34; Acc. 1156/R13; Acc. 1156/R21B; Acc. 1386/5; Acc. 1386/10; Acc. 1386/12; Acc. 1386/13).

Convicted at the Newtown Assizes 19 July 1864, for arson (with William Johnson), for which he was sentenced to 8 years penal servitude. He was eventually admitted to Chatham 22 December 1864 his whereabouts previous to this date being unknown. His character is shown as good, although he received 3 summary convictions whilst in prison. On 30 September 1865 he left Portland on the 'Vimiera', arriving at Swan River, 22 December 1865. Official records show that he was 21 years of age, height 5'6¼", with light hair and blue eyes. His appearance was stout, with full visage and fair complexion. On his left hand were warts and a flower pot whilst on his right arm were fishes and an anchor. He was single, able to read and write, and of Presbyterian religion. No next of kin is recorded. He was granted his ticket of leave 15 January 1869 and full pardon 26 August 1873. Offences committed by him were as follows:

> *2 January 1866 – Absent from Mt Eliza Depot. 2 months hard labour in irons.*
> *28 June 1866 – Disobedience. 7 days forfeit of tobacco.*
> *26 January 1867 – Leather in possession. 21 days bread and water.*
> *2 July 1867 – Concealed soap on body. 7 days bread and water.*
> *2 October 1867 – Refusing to be searched. 1 day bread and water.*
> *11 February 1870 – Drunk, resisting and assault of policeman. 12 months hard labour at Fremantle Prison.*
> *11 February 1871 – Released.*
> *30 November 1871 – Drunk and Incapable. 7 days hard labour.*

Between 15 January 1869 and 9 May 1873 he was assigned in the Perth and Wellington Districts, carrying out general servant, labourer, and ploughing duties, for which he was paid between 30 shillings and 50 shillings per month.

GOUGH Robert (c.1825–)

(Acc. 128/35; Acc. 1156/R14; Acc. 1386/12; AJCP Reel 5991 Pri Com 2/384; NLW Q/SR 1864M).

Convicted at the Welshpool Quarter Sessions 30 November 1864 of breaking and entering the house of Thomas Jones, and stealing, 1 coat, 3 waistcoats, 2 pairs trousers, 1 pair boots, 1 pair stockings, 2 shirts and 1 watch. He was sentenced to 14 years penal servitude. Previous convictions were taken into consideration as follows:

> *Montgomery Q.S. December 1848 – Vagrancy. 1 month hard labour.*
> *Denbigh Ass. July 1849 – Stealing shoes. 1 year hard labour.*
> *Denbigh Ass. July 1852 – Stealing clothes. 7 years hard labour.*
> *Denbigh Q.S. October 1857 – ditto. 4 years penal servitude.*
> *Montgomery Ass. 1862 – ditto. 1 year hard labour.*

With regard to his conviction 31 July 1852 at Denbigh Assizes, he spent his penal servitude at Millbank 9 days, Pentonville 11 months 17 days and Portland where he was admitted 12 September 1853, and remained until his eventual discharge, date unknown. During this period his conduct was good at all establishments. As for his current sentence of 14 years Penal Servitude, during his stay at Montgomery Gaol, Mr R. P. Edwards, gaoler reported on 28 November 1864, "Robert Gough has been transported once . . . sentenced to penal servitude and four times convicted of felony." (His assumption regarding a previous transportation sentence does not appear to be correct). His history following transfer from Montgomery Gaol cannot be traced until his eventual departure from Portland 7 April 1866, on the 'Belgravia', which arrived at Swan River 4 July 1866. Official records show that he was 41 years of age, height 5'6", with dark brown hair and grey eyes. He was stout with round visage and fresh complexion. There were scars on his chin and the 4th finger of his left hand was crooked. He was single, seaman by trade, able to read and write and of Protestant religion. His next of kin was his father, Thomas Gough a collier of Brymbo, Wrexham, Denbighshire. It is recorded that although his character was "very bad", his conduct however was "very good." The following offences are noted:

> *3 July 1868 – Disobedience of Orders. 5 days bread and water.*
> *20 July 1868 – Absent from work party. 7 days bread and water.*
> *8 February 1869 – Drunk and allowing 4 prisoners, in his charge, to be the same. 21 days solitary.*
> *3 September 1870 – Receiving rum from a ticket of leave man. 14 days solitary.*
> *3 November 1870 – Sixpence and copper in his possession, to be forfeited. 3 days bread and water.*
> *21 April 1871 – Idle and disobedient. 3 days bread and water.*
> *24 August 1871 – Refusing to work. 2 days bread and water.*
> *6 April 1874 – Drunk and incapable and out after hours. 7 days hard labour and 5 shillings fine.*
> *5 July 1875 – Drunk and out after hours. 3 days bread and water.*

He received his ticket of leave 10 June 1872 and full pardon 31 January 1879. He was allocated to assignments, between 18 June 1872 and 30 January 1879, in the District of York, working as a labourer or on general service. No further record of his whereabouts available.

GRIFFITH William (c.1828–)
(AJCP Reel 2829 HO 27/93; AJCP Reel 5978 Pri Com 2/31).
Convicted at the Assizes 16 July 1850 of burglary, and sentenced to 10 years transportation. He was moved from Montgomery Gaol 6 September 1850 to Millbank, and then to Pentonville on 29 November 1850, his character shown as "bad". He was transported on the 'Sea Park', leaving London 1 January 1854, arriving Swan River 5 April 1854. He was 26 years of age, single, by trade a labourer and able to read and write imperfectly. Protestant by religion, his next of kin was his father John Griffith, a farmer of Cardiff. He was granted his ticket of leave 5 April 1854 and a conditional pardon 1 May 1856.

HIGGS Thomas (c.1837–)
(AJCP Reel 5982 Pri Com 2/108; Acc. 128/25; Acc. 1156/R7; Acc. 1156/R9; Acc. 1156/R11; Acc. 1156R21B; *Perth Gazette*, 27 June 1862, p. 3a and 4 July 1862, p. 2c; *Eddowes Journal*, 21 July 1858).
Convicted 14 July 1858 at the Newtown Assizes of breaking and entering a dwelling house in Dolfor and stealing 20 lb ham and 6 lb bread. He was sentenced to 8 years penal servitude. He had previous convictions as follows:

1851 – Stealing pair of horses and 25 shillings. 6 months hard labour.
1854 – Breaking and entering a warehouse and stealing. 4 years penal servitade.

With reference to this last conviction, he was in Millbank from 2 August 1854 to 30 June 1857. His conduct was very good but immediately he obtained a license and was discharged he committed the current offence. He now spent 20 days in Montgomery Gaol, followed by transfer to Millbank 4 August 1858, Pentonville 24 August 1858 and Portsmouth 26 May 1859. On 16 Mar 1862 he left Portland on the 'Norwood', arriving at Swan River 9 June 1862. Official records confirm that he was 25 years of age, height 5'7¾", with dark brown hair and eyes. He was middling stout, with long visage and sallow complexion. Marks included an anchor and the letters 'TH' on his left arm; an anchor and the letters 'TH' on his right arm, and blue dots on the back of his right hand. He was single, able to read and write imperfectly, a weaver, and of Protestant religion. It is noted from official records that on 17 November 1859, he was transferred on the 'Sir John Lawrence', to undertake Public Works in the Penal Settlement at Bermuda. There is no record of his eventual return to England and as the 'Norwood', on its journey to Western Australia, did not steam via Bermuda, there would appear to be some inaccuracy in the records. He was granted his ticket of leave 24 July 1862, and his conditional pardon 14 December 1863. In the Perth Gazette dated 27 June 1862, the following entry has some bearing on the granting of his conditional pardon:

> *Last Monday night, about 12 o'clock, a fire broke out at the Convict Establishment in Fremantle. It was confined to the office attached to the Establishment and some distance from the main building. It probably commenced in the office of the Registrar and many valuable convict records were damaged or destroyed. The offices of the Comptroller-General and Commanding Royal Engineer were also injured. An inquiry is to take place. The prisoners behaved well.*

What part, if any, Thomas Higgs played in this incident, is not known, but records show that he was granted "Special Remission" due to his exertions at the fire described above.

He appears to have behaved himself. Only one conviction is recorded against him, namely, that on 17 September 1863, he assaulted and used insubordinate language to Supt. W. Vincent, for which he received 1 month hard labour.

HUTTON Frederick (c.1832–)
(Acc. 128/38; Acc. 1156/R15; Acc. 1386/5; Acc. 1386/12; NLW Q/SR 1864M; *Eddowes Journal*, 7 December 1864).
Convicted at Welshpool Quarter Sessions November 1864 of stealing 2 umbrellas from a Pryce Griffiths of Welshpool. At his trial the learned judge (R. H. Mytton, Esq.), sentenced him to 7 years penal servitude, whereupon Frederick Hutton thanked his Lordship, and nimbly leaped down from the dock. He had previous convictions for larceny committed during 1862, 1863, and 1864. His prison locations in England are unknown, until he embarked on the 'Norwood II', which left Portland on 18 April 1867, and arrived at Swan River 13 July 1867. Official records confirm that he was 35 years of age, height 5'2", with brown hair and grey eyes. He was of strong appearance, with oval visage and fresh complexion. He had no marks other than that his right knee had a stiff joint. Single and by trade a baker, he could read and write and was of Protestant religion. It is of interest to note that his next of kin is shown as H. Habermann, of Halle, Saxony

Province. He was granted his ticket of leave 15 October 1868, and his full pardon 29 November 1871. There are no records to indicate that he misbehaved and during the period 17 October 1868 to 30 June 1870 he was assigned to work in the Perth and Swan Districts, either as a general servant or as a cook. His wages fluctuated between 20 and 30 shillings per month.

JOHNSON William (c.1840-21.12.1866)

(AJCP Reel 5984 Pri Com 2/111; Acc. 128/34; Acc. 1156/R13; Acc. 1156/R21B; Death Reg Fremantle 3374/66).

Convicted at Newtown Assizes 19 July 1864 of arson, namely setting fire to hay at Welshpool. He was sentenced to 8 years penal servitude. He had been summarily convicted for a previous offence. Having spent 1 month 4 days in Montgomery Gaol, he was sent to Millbank on 22 April 1865 and Portsmouth 3 July 1865, his conduct at Montgomery being satisfactory and at Millbank good. On 30 September 1865, he left Portland on the 'Vimiera', arriving at Swan River 22 December 1865. Official records show that he was 26 years of age, height 5'2½", with light brown hair and blue eyes. He was middling stout, thin, slim visage and sallow complexion. Marks included burn marks on right cheek. Single, unable to read or write, and was a Roman Catholic. He was Irish by birth, his next of kin being his father, William Johnson, a gardener of Londonderry, Ireland. During his short stay in Western Australia he was convicted as follows:

22 May 1866 – Insubordination. 3 days bread and water.
15 September 1866 – Disobedience. 1 month tobacco loss.
22 September 1866 – Not recorded. 10 days bread and water.

Soon afterwards, he died at Fremantle on 21 December 1866, the cause shown as "phth:pul", namely pulmonary tuberculosis. His occupation whilst in Wales is shown as a labourer (tramp).

JONES Ishmael (c.1820-28.11. 1892)

(Acc 128/30; Acc 1156/R2; Acc. 1156/R28; Acc. 1156/R31; Acc. 1156/R21B; Death Reg Fremantle 939/92).

Convicted at Montgomery Assizes 10 March 1862, having murdered his wife, thereby having the singular distinction of being the only convicted murderer from Montgomeryshire, sentenced to death, commuted to life penal servitude. On 11 January 1864, he left on the 'Clara II', and arrived at Swan River on 13 April 1864. During his stay in English prisons, his conduct is recorded as very good. Official records state that he was 44 years of age, height 5'4¼", with brown hair and light hazel eyes. He was middling stout, with oval visage and sallow complexion. Marks were scars on his right leg. He was a farm labourer, native of Llanfair Caereinion, and had 5 children, namely John (20), Mary (18), Thomas (16), David (12) and William (7). All children had been born in Llanfair Caereinion but Ann Jones, the unfortunate wife, had been a native of Carno, Montgomeryshire. He was able to read and write imperfectly and of Protestant religion. The only official record regarding his conduct is dated 3 October 1864, when he received a reprimand and caution for being absent at a bathing muster. He was granted his ticket of leave 26 April 1867 and a conditional release 6 April 1877. His assignments during the period 15 May 1867 to 31 December 1876 were in the York and Beverley Districts, where he was employed as a labourer, earning between 16 shillings per week and 60 shillings per month. Little else is known about his remaining life except that records indicate a failing health which was conspicuous by periods spent in York hospital (31 July 1880, 31 March 1851, 30 November 1885 and 31 December 1885.) On 14 January 1886 he was re-admitted suffering from rheumatic and general debility and discharged on 29 January 1886, when he was transferred to the Invalid Depot from where he was finally discharged 10 May 1886. On 28 November 1892 he died at Fremantle Depot.

JONES John (c.1839–)

(Acc. 128/29; Acc. 1156/R27; Acc. 1157R/29; Acc. 1156/R31; Acc. 1156/R21B; Acc. 1386/12; NLW Q/SR 1862E).

Convicted at the Quarter Sessions 7 March 1862 of stealing 20 sheep from Charles James Lloyd, Machynlleth. He was sentenced to 14 years penal servitude. He had two previous convictions, namely in 1858 – stealing a watch – 18 months, and in 1862 – stealing sheets – 6 months. Following a period in prison, he was moved to Portland, and left on the ship 'Lord Dalhousie', 25 September 1863, arriving Swan River 28 December 1863. He was 24 years of age, height 5'2¾", with brown hair and black eyes. He was middling stout, with long visage and ruddy complexion. His only mark was a scar on the left wrist. He was single, french polisher by trade, able to read and write imperfectly and was of Protestant religion. His next of kin was his father, namely James Collins, a weaver of Ludgate Hill, Manchester. Although his character from the English prisons is recorded as "good", it is evident from the following list that this did not continue.

> *21 March 1863 –Destroying prison towels. 3 days bread and water.*
> *31 December 1863 –Remission for good conduct on voyage.*
> *21 June 1865 – Fighting-1st offence. Admoni and water.*
> *28 July 1865 – Special remission. Not known.*
> *6 October 1865 – Absconding from Perth. 3 months in irons.*
> *18 April 1866 – Special remission. 15 days.*
> *18 April 1866 – Damaging prison property. 3 days bread and water.*
> *15 June 1866 – Turning file into knife. 2 days bread and water.*
> *26 June 1866 – Disobedient. 3 days bread and water.*
> *6 May 1867 – Larceny. 3 months hard labour.*
> *29 February 1868 – Bad language and work shy. 3 days bread and water.*
> *3 May 1868 – Idle and making chess men. 7 days bread and water.*
> *29 July 1868 – Holding party-not approved. 3 days bread and water.*
> *19 August 1868 – Selling 2 blankets. 3 months hard labour.*
> *17 September 1868 – Leaving camp-not approved. 10 days bread and water.*
> *15 October 1868 – Stealing flour. 12 months hard labour at Fremantle Prison.*
> *30 October 1869 – Idleness at work. 1 day bread and water.*
> *12 January 1870 – Insolent to Supt. 3 days bread and water.*
> *20 July 1870 – Threatening E. Banon. 2 days bread and water.*
> *28 October 1870 – Money in possession. 3 days bread and water and forfeit money.*
> *1 October 1871 – Admitted Fremantle Prison.*
> *19 October 1872 – Discharged.*
> *19 December 1872 – Abusive and threatening language. 3 months Perth Prison.*
> *26 February 1875 – Stealing timber. 18 months Fremantle Prison.*
> *13 June 1876 – Remission. 2 months.*
> *9 June 1879 – Unlawfully on premises. 6 weeks hard labour Fremantle Prison.*

Irrespective of the above offences, he was employed on assignments, between

28 December 1866 and 31 December 1881 when he was employed as a labourer, carpenter, general servant, sawyer and polisher and his earnings fluctuated between 4 shillings per day and 40 shillings per month. This work was carried out in the Fremantle, Perth, Wellington and Swan Districts. He received his ticket of leave 19 December 1866, and full pardon 12 January 1882. The final record confirms that he left for Adelaide 16 January 1882.

JONES William (c.1845-11.5.1883)
(Acc. 128/33; Acc. 1156/R30; Acc. 1156/R21B; Acc. 1386/5).
Convicted at Welshpool Assizes 17 December 1863, of arson by setting fire to hay at Montgomery. He was sentenced to 8 years penal servitude. This followed a previous conviction at the Spring Assizes (location unknown), 1863, when he was sentenced to 4 months hard labour for burglary and larceny. He was eventually transported on the 'Racehorse' leaving Portland 26 May 1865, arriving Swan River 10 August 1865. He was 20 years of age, height 5'3¾", with dark brown hair and dark hazel eyes. He was stout, with long visage and dark complexion. Numerous marks were: two anchors, heart and dagger, hope, and star on left arm, ring on 2nd finger of left hand, anchor, date 1863, anchor encircled by a wreath of flower and 2 flags, moon, 'WJ', cross and 'HXH', three stars on right arm and 3 rings on fingers of right hand. He was single, able to read and write, a groom by trade, and of Protestant religion. His next of kin was his mother Sarah Wellings of Great Malvern, Worcestershire. It is recorded that he did use the name William Wellings. He received his ticket of leave 14 May 1868 and his full pardon 27 December 1871. The only offence recorded against him was a serious one of larceny and he was sentenced on 7 October 1874 to 2 years hard labour. His assignments between 21 May 1868 and 31 December 1869 included working as a labourer, general servant and farm servant in the Fremantle and Perth Districts, for which his wages were between 20 and 25 shillings per month. It is shown that he went to Madras on 3 October 1876. The only other possible mention of him was that a William Jones had been found dead on 14 May 1883, having been reported missing from Roebourne, a year previously.

KING David (c.1845–)
(Acc. 128/33; Acc. 1156/R30; Acc. 1156/R2113; Acc. 1386/5; Acc. 1386/12).
Convicted at Welshpool Assizes 17 December 1863 of arson in Montgomeryshire, and was sentenced to 8 years penal servitude. He left Portland 26 May 1865 on the 'Racehorse', arriving Swan River 10 August 1865. He was 20 years of age, height 5'4", with light brown hair and hazel eyes. He was middling stout, with long visage and fair complexion. There were numerous marks on his body, namely cross, flags, anchor, crown and horseshoe, head and arrow, 'NKD 18', and 1863 on right arm, hope, five dots and rings on his right hand, 'NK', anchor and bracelet on his left arm, two flowers and rings on three fingers of his left hand. He was single, a labourer, able to read and write and of Protestant religion. His next of kin is shown as his mother, Agnes King of George Street, Ayr, Scotland. The following offences are recorded during his life in Western Australia:

> *14 August 1866 – Gross Insubordination. 6 months hard labour.*
> *6 September 1866 – Idle on Public Works. 6 months in irons.*
> *3 February 1867 – Released from irons.*
> *4 April 1867 – Money in possession. Reprimand.*
> *29 June 1867 – Insolence. 5 days bread and water.*

17 January 1868 – Good conduct noted and should he remain free from Report for 12 months his case will be reviewed.

6 July 1868 – To be released on ticket of leave due to exemplary conduct.

22 February 1869 – Stealing crowbar wedge, 3 pickaxes and 2 sheets, all Government property, Perth Prison.

From the above date, he was transferred between Perth and Fremantle Prisons, until 31 July 1871. He received his ticket of leave 15 February 1869 and a full pardon on 20 December 1871. From 1 March 1869 to 7 November 1871, he was assigned in the Perth and Newcastle Districts, working as a general servant, teamster, labourer, limeburner and boatman. He was paid between 20 and 25 shillings per month.

KINGTON Henry (c.1830–)

(Acc. 128/19; Acc. 1156/R8; Acc. 1156/R21B; Acc. 1386/4; *Police Gazette*, 1876, pp. 2 and 68; *Police Gazette*, 1877, p. 37).

Convicted at the Assizes 15 July 1856 of arson, by setting fire to hay in an outhouse at Welshpool. He was sentenced to 15 years penal servitude. This followed previous convictions on 25 November 1859 when he received 3 days bread and water and in March 1852 when at Chester Assizes he was acquitted of arson on the grounds of insanity and ordered to be detained at Her Majesty's pleasure but was discharged as sane. During the same year he had made his escape from Chester City Gaol. Following a period of 1 month and 21 days at Montgomery Gaol, he was moved to Millbank where he remained for 8 months and 15 days. He was then moved to Portsmouth and was put on board the 'Nile', which left Plymouth 23 September 1857 and arrived Swan River on 1 January 1858. He was 28 years of age, height 5'9", with sandy hair and dark brown eyes. He was middling stout, with long visage and fresh complexion. The only marks were the letters 'HK' on each arm. He was single, a labourer, unable to read or write, and of Protestant religion. He received his ticket of leave 14 May 1860. His assignments between 30 May 1865 and 10 September 1864 show him as a general servant and a sawyer, in the Guildford and Perth Districts. His wages as a general servant were 20 shillings per week, whilst payment as a sawyer was 2 pounds per week. On 18 December 1865 he was sentenced to 3 years imprisonment and following his eventual discharge it is recorded in the *Police Gazette*, dated 1876, that on 10 October 1868 Henry Kington absconded from a convict party whilst at Point Resolution. There is no further record of him.

KIRKMAN John (c.1844–)

(AJCP Reel 5984 Pri Com 2/110; Acc. 128/34; Acc. 1156/R13; Acc. 1156/R21B; NLW Q/SR 1863M).

Convicted at Newtown Quarter Sessions 9 April 1863 of breaking and entering the dwelling house of David Williams of Welshpool and stealing one ham. He was sentenced to 7 years penal servitude. This followed a previous conviction of housebreaking in Birmingham for which he received 6 months hard labour. He was admitted to Montgomery Gaol and spent 22 days there, followed by transfer to Millbank 30 April 1863, Pentonville 26 May 1863, Chatham 16 June 1864, Portland 1 September 1864 and Portsmouth 31 October 1864. His conduct at Montgomery was not very good but at all the other prisons it was good. In all he spent 1 year 3 months 19 days on Public Works. He was transported on the 'Vimeira', which left Portland 30 September 1864 and arrived Swan River 22

December 1865. Official records show him to be 21 years of age, height 5'4½", with light brown hair and grey eyes. He was stout, with oval visage and fair complexion. On his left arm were a coat of arms and a flag whilst on his right arm were the letter 'J' and an anchor. He was single, able to read and write, a labourer cum cotton weaver and of Protestant religion. His next of kin was his father, namely Thomas Kirkman, sawyer, of Scotland Road, Liverpool. Offences listed against him were:

> *19 October 1868 – Furious riding through street. 5 shillings fine.*
> *4 October 1869 – Obscene language. 7 days hard labour.*
> *Same date – Drunk. 5 shillings fine.*

He received his ticket of leave 1 March 1867 and full pardon 16 April 1870. His assignments were in the Victoria, Albany, Champion Bay and Plantagenet Districts, where he was employed as a labourer, hut keeper, shoemaker, sawyer and general servant. His wages fluctuated between 20 shillings and 3 pounds per month. These duties were carried out between 4 April 1867 and 21 March 1870.

MACDONOUGH John (c.1836–)

(AJCP Reel 5983 Pri Com 2/109; Acc. 128/29; Acc. 1156/R27; Acc. 1156/R29; Acc. 1156/R31; Acc. 1156/R21B; Acc. 1386/5).

Convicted at Newtown Quarter Sessions 3 July 1862 of breaking and entering a dwelling house in Llandinam. He was sentenced to 14 years penal servitude. This followed previous convictions in October 1848 when he committed a felony and received 4 months hard labour, followed in October 1849 by 12 months hard labour for housebreaking. It is noted that the Governor of Cardigan Gaol stated that John Macdonough had previously spent 7 years on Spike Island, Ireland. Having spent 14 days at Montgomery Gaol, he was moved to Millbank 18 July 1862, followed by Portsmouth 20 April 1863. His conduct at Montgomery was very bad and indifferent at Millbank. He left Portland 25 September 1863 on the 'Lord Dalhousie' and arrived Swan River 28 December 1863. It is noted that he was to receive special remission for good conduct on the voyage. He was 27 years of age, height 5'7¼", with brown hair and hazel eyes. He was stout, of ruddy complexion and round visage. He was pock-marked, with scars under his left ear and on the right side of his neck. There was a heart on his right arm. He was single, able to read only, an iron moulder and a Roman Catholic. His next of kin was his father, William Macdonough, farrier of New York, USA. He received his ticket of leave 8 August 1868. The following offences are recorded against him:

> *29 April 1864 – Striking a fellow prisoner. 3 days bread and water.*
> *12 May 1864 – Insolent and disobedient. 3 days bread and water.*
> *2 December 1864 – Assaulting an Officer. 12 months hard labour, 100 lashes.*
> *12 January 1865 – Fighting. 2 days bread and water.*
> *23 February 1865 – Insubordinate, insolent. Caution.*
> *28 February 1865 – Ditto, idle. 14 days bread and water.*
> *8 May 1865 – Assaulting an Officer. 12 months in irons.*
> *3 August 1865 – Fighting. 1 day bread and water.*
> *7 January 1867 – Idle and insolent in cell. 6 days bread and water.*
> *10 January 1867 – Assault, intent to ravish. 12 months hard labour.*
> *5 June 1867 – Concealed library book. Caution.*
> *14 October 1867 – Refused to load lorry. 2 days bread and water.*

> *29 January 1868 – Idle. ditto.*
> *26 February 1868 – Mutinous conduct. 7 days bread and water.*
> *24 March 1869 – Wandering. 1 month hard labour.*
> *11 February 1871 – Absconding. 3 months hard labour.*
> *3 May 1871 – Idle. Caution.*
> *3 October 1871 – Idle. 3 days bread and water.*
> *16 September 1872 – Overstaying pass. Caution.*
> *3 February 1873 – Not reporting himself. 14 days hard labour.*
> *23 January 1874 – Assault, intent to ravish. 5 years hard labour including 1 year in irons & 50 lashes in Fremantle Prison.*
> *11 August 1874 – Disobedience. 3 days bread and water.*
> *3 June 1875 – Fighting. 2 days bread and water.*
> *9 December 1875 – Insolence. 1 day bread and water.*
> *7 August 1876 – Insubordination. 14 days bread and water.*

Between 8 August 1868 and 24 March 1881, he was assigned to work in the Fremantle, Perth, Toodyay, Northam, Victoria Plains, Beverley, York, Wellington and Sussex Districts and was employed as a labourer, general servant, shepherd, sawyer, road worker, fencer, grubber and worker on a vineyard. His wages fluctuated between 20 shillings per week and £4.16.0 per month. He escaped from Toodyay in 1881.

MACINTYRE John (c.1843–)
(AJCP Reel 5984 Pri Com 2/110; Acc. 128/34; Acc. 1156/R13; Acc. 1156/R21B; NLW Q/SR 1864H; *Shrewsbury Chronicle*, 18 March 1864).
Convicted at Welshpool Assizes 16 March 1864 with John Wilson of arson of corn at Pool Quay. He was sentenced to 8 years penal servitude. This followed a previous conviction in January 1864 of stealing a cape, for which he received 2 months hard labour. Following a period of 1 month and 8 days at Montgomery Gaol, he spent 10 days at Pentonville and 12 months and 27 days at Millbank. His character at Montgomery was satisfactory and at Millbank good. He was transported on the 'Vimiera', which left Portland 30 September 1865 and arrived Swan River 22 December 1865. On arrival, he was 22 years of age, height 5'5¼", with dark brown hair and brown eyes. He was middling stout, with oval visage and fresh complexion. The only mark was a mole on the left arm. He was single, a smith's labourer, able to read and write, and a Roman Catholic. His next of kin was his mother, Eliza, from Liverpool. He received his ticket of leave 15 May 1868 and a full pardon 8 May 1872. His character was good as the following list of minor offences confirm:

> *6 July 1869 – Assault. 5 shilling fine.*
> *22 January 1870 – Neglect of official return. 3 days hard labour.*

Between 15 May 1868 and 6 March 1872, he was assigned in the Perth, Wellington and Sussex Districts, where he worked as a labourer or general servant, and received payment between 10 shillings per week and 18 pound per annum. He left the state for Newcastle, New South Wales on 2 March 1875.

OWEN John (c.1817-31.3.1867)
(Acc. 128/30; Acc. 1156/R2; Acc. 1156/R28; Acc. 1156/R21BNLW Q/SR 1862M; *Eddoes Journal*, 22 October 1862).

Convicted at the Montgomery Quarter Sessions 16 October 1862, of stealing 3 heifers from Robert Hughes of Pool Quay and was sentenced to 7 years penal servitude. This followed a previous conviction in 1859, when he received 2 months hard labour for larceny at Condover Sessions. There is no record of his prison life prior to transportation on the 'Clara II', which left London 11 January 1864, arriving at Swan River on 13 April 1864. He was 47 years of age, height 5'6", with dark brown hair and dark hazel eyes. He was middling stout, of long visage and dark complexion. He had a cut on the 4th finger of the left hand. A widower, with 3 children, namely Thomas (13 years), John (10 years), William (6 years), all of whom were placed in the Poor Law Union Workhouse, Wolverhampton. He was a labourer, unable to read and write, and was a Protestant. During a short stay in the Colony, he maintained an unblemished record. Between 11 August 1865 and 31 December 1866, he was assigned in the Toodyay District working as a well-sinker and a labourer, for which he received between 30 shillings, as a labourer and £6 per month as a well-sinker. On 31 March 1867 his death is recorded at Champion Bay, from a compound fracture of the ankle joint. He was 50 years of age.

RICHARDS James (c.1837-23.5.1880)

(Acc. 128/25; Acc. 1156/R7; Acc. 1156/R25; Acc. 1156/R21B; Acc. 1386/4; Acc. 128/43; Acc. 1156/R23; NLW Q/SR 1860J).

Convicted at Newtown Quarter Sessions 5 July 1860 of stealing 2 pairs of boots, the property of Thomas Evans of Welshpool. He was sentenced to 7 years penal servitude. This followed a previous conviction for felony. He must have spent some time on the hulk 'York', followed by a period at Chatham. His conduct was indifferent on the hulk and good on the voyage. He left on the 'Norwood', which embarked from Portland on 16 March 1862, arriving Swan River 9 June 1862. His age was shown as 25 years of age, height 5'3¼", with black hair and dark eyes. He was of slight appearance with long visage and ruddy complexion. Marks were a scar on his left hand, scars on his left thumb and scars on his left eye. He was single, able to read and write, a tailor by trade, and of Protestant religion. No next of kin is recorded. He obtained his ticket of leave 29 August 1863, and full pardon on 14 December 1872. The following offences are recorded against him:

> *16 October 1862 – Damage to watch. 1 pound fine.*
> *22 January 1863 – Absent from school. 1 month tobacco forfeit.*
> *30 April 1863 – Dirty cell. 1 week ditto.*
> *27 June 1863 – Dirty cell. Forfeit Sunday dinner.*
> *31 July 1863 – Disobedience. 1 day bread and water.*
> *31 September 1863 – Neglect of work. 7 days.*
> *18 November 1863 – Stealing 2 blankets, 1 rug and 1 bag. 12 months.*
> *16 February 1865 – Neglecting pass. 6 months.*
> *26 May 1866 – Accusing fellow prisoner of unnatural offence. 6 months hard labour.*
> *31 July 1866 – Stealing butter. 14 days bread and water.*
> *24 August 1866 – Stealing jacket. 3 years hard labour.*
> *24 July 1867 – Trafficking one blue shirt for mutinous conduct. 21 days bread and water.*
> *2 November 1867 – Refusing to work. 1 day bread and water.*
> *6 November 1867 – Throwing bread to prisoner in punishment cell. 2 days bread and water.*

23 December 1867 – Remission. 2 months.

1 July 1869 – Stealing boots. 6 months hard labour.

2 July 1869 – Throwing tobacco to another prisoner. 1 day bread and water.

2 February 1870 – Released.

22 September 1870 – On premises of Mrs Devenish for unlawful purpose. 6 months hard labour Fremantle Prison.

3 November 1870 – Malingering. 3 days bread and water.

25 March 1871 – Released from Fremantle Prison.

28 March 1871 – On premises of Ann Stamp on night of 17th inst. for unlawful purpose. 3 months hard labour.

28 September 1871 – Released.

5 February 1872 – Out after hours. 14 days hard labour.

21 February 1872 – Stealing bottle brandy. 3 months hard labour Fremantle Prison.

27 March 1872 – 18lb flour in his berth. 3 days bread and water.

Between 1 September 1863 and 28 August 1872, he was assigned to work in the Fremantle, Albany, Perth, Swan, York and Sussex Districts, as a servant, baker, general servant, sawyer, and wood cutter. His wages fluctuated between 7 shillings per 100 foot sawed and 40 shillings per month. He was reconvicted for robbery with violence at Perth on 8 January 1874 and sentenced to 4 years hard labour, but after serving 12 months he escaped. Records do not indicate that he was eventually recaptured. His death is recorded on 23 May 1880, at Fremantle Prison hospital, the cause shown as phthisis (tuberculosis).

RICHARDS William (c.1842-17.12.1871)

(AJCP Reel 5984. Pri Com 2/111; Acc. 128/35; Acc. 1156/R14; Death Reg 6063/71 York).

Convicted at Newtown Assizes 19 July 1864 of arson by setting fire to corn at Welshpool. He was sentenced to 8 years penal servitude. He spent 1 month 4 days at Montgomery Gaol, being transferred to Pentonville 22 August 1864 and to Portsmouth 9 July 1865. His character at Montgomery appears to have been of the worst description but at Pentonville he was good. He was transported on the 'Belgravia', leaving Portland on 7 April 1866, arriving Swan River 4 July 1866. He was 24 years of age, height 5'6¾", with brown hair and grey eyes. He was middling stout, with long visage and sallow complexion. He wore bracelets on both wrists. He was single, engine driver by trade, able to read and write and of Protestant religion. His next of kin was his father, Charles Marston, a labourer of Oldham, Lancashire. He received his ticket of leave 16 August 1868. The only offence recorded against him was on 28 January 1867, for being absent from camp, and he received 3 days bread and water. Between 15 August 1868 and 30 June 1871, he was assigned in the Northam, Toodyay and York Districts, as a labourer, teamster, shepherd and general servant. His wages were between 30 and 40 shillings per month.

On 17 December 1871, his death is recorded at York, the cause being shown as "having no marks of violence, but appears to have wasted away".

RILEY Thomas (c.1842–)

(AJCP Reel 5984 Pri Com 2/110; Acc. 128/33; Acc. 1156/R30; Acc. 1156/R21B; Acc. 1386/5; Acc. 1386/12; *Shrewsbury Chronicle*, 25 December 1863).

Convicted at Welshpool Assizes 17 December 1863 of arson by setting fire to oats and barley at Leighton. He was sentenced to 8 years penal servitude. After spending 8 months at Montgomery Gaol, he was transferred to Millbank 26 December 1863 and then Portsmouth 19 October 1864. His character was very good and he spent 6 months 22 days on Public Works. He was transported on the 'Racehorse', which left Portland 26 May 1865, arriving Swan River 10 August 1865. He was 23 years of age, height 5'7", with brown hair and dark hazel eyes. He was stout, with oval visage and fair freckled complexion. His right elbow joint had been broken and was stiff. He was single, a gardener by trade, unable to read or write, and was a Roman Catholic. His next of kin was his sister Mary Riley, of 194, Thomas Street, Dublin, Ireland. He received his ticket of leave 2 January 1868 and a full pardon 16 December 1871. The following offences are recorded against him:

> 19 August 1865 – Dirty Cell. Forfeit Sunday dinner.
> 23 August 1865 – Losing blanket. To pay for it.
> 19 September 1868 – Drunk and disorderly. Fine 7/6d.
> 17 May 1869 – Interfere with police. Fine 5/-.

Between 4 January 1868 and 31 December 1871, he was assigned to work in the York, Perth, Swan, Wellington and Sussex Districts, as a labourer, general servant, grubber and teamster, for which he was paid between 1 shilling per day and £2 per month.

ROBERTS Edward (c.1825–)

(AJCP Reel 2829; HO 27/93; AJCP Reel 5975 Pri Com 2/31; AJCP Reel 5977 Pri Com 2/63; AJCP Reel 5988 Pri Com 2/136; AJCP Reel 5979 Pri Com 2/105; Acc. 128/8; Acc. 128/41; Acc. 1156/R21B).

Convicted at Newtown Quarter Sessions 4 July 1850 of breaking and entering a warehouse and stealing flour. He was sentenced to 7 years transportation. This followed a previous conviction 1 July 1847, when he was sentenced to 2 months imprisonment for stealing a spade. He was transferred from Montgomery Gaol to Millbank September 1850, to Pentonville 29 November 1850, to the hulk ship 'York' 6 November 1851 and to Portsmouth 28 July 1852. During these periods his character was good at each location and in all he spent 30 months 14 days on Public Works. He was transported on the 'Pyrenees', which left England 2 February 1853, arriving at Swan River 30 April 1853. He was 28 years of age, height 5'6½", weight 12st 3lbs, with light brown hair and blue eyes. He was stout, with round visage and fair complexion. He had a scar over the right eye. Married with one child, he was a labourer/sawyer by trade, unable to read or write and was a Protestant. His next of kin is shown to be his father, Richard Roberts of The Gutter, Llansantffraid, a respectable small farmer. There is no mention of his wife. He received his ticket of leave 1 May 1853 and conditional pardon 16 September 1854.

ROBINSON James (c.1837-1890)

(Acc. 128/40; Acc. 1156/R16; Acc. 1386/13 NLW Q/SR 1866J; *Eddoes Journal*, 11 July 1866).

Convicted at Newtown Quarter Sessions 5 July 1866, of stealing a steel watch chain and a watch from Richard Walls of Llanllwchaiarn, Newtown. He was sentenced to 10 years penal servitude. When sentenced by the Judge, the prisoner stated, "You could not have pleased me better". No doubt the sentence took into consideration the following list of offences committed throughout England:

April	1854	Knutsford	Stealing brass	2 months
July	1854		Stealing potatoes and gooseberries	2 months
March	1855		Stealing boots etc	6 months
April	1858		Larceny from person	9 months
June	1859	Derby	Stealing clothes	3 months
	1861	Huntington	ditto	6 weeks
	1861	Gloucester	Obtaining money under false pretences	1 month
	1862	Bodmin	ditto	21 days
October	1862	Doncaster	Stealing sovereign	3 months
	1863	Gloucester	Obtaining money under false pretences	1 month
	1863	Canterbury	ditto	6 weeks
	1863	ditto	ditto	6 weeks
	1865	Warwick	ditto	2 months
	1865	Lewes	ditto	1 month

From the above table it is possible to establish that itinerant vagrants covered a considerable distance in order to obtain relief, either by legitimate or illegitimate means. He was transported on the 'Hougoumont', leaving London 12 October 1867, arriving Swan River 10 January 1868. He had the distinction of being the last convict sentenced by a Montgomeryshire Court to penal servitude, followed by transportation to Western Australia on the last convict ship to the continent of Australia. He was 31 years of age, height 5'5½", with light brown hair and grey eyes. He was of strong appearance, with long visage and swarthy complexion. He had the letter 'D' on his left side, with gun shot wound on his left arm. There were sabre cuts on his right cheek. Married with no children, he was a travelling engraver by trade, able to read and write and a Protestant. His next of kin was his wife, namely E. Adshead, of 25 Lavender Row, Richard, Near Stockport, Lancashire. He received his ticket of leave on 8 October 1872 and his conditional release on 6 March 1875. The following offences are recorded against him:

22 February 1868 – Malingering. Admonished.
11 November 1870 – Neglect of duty. Admonished.
28 November 1870 – Aiding another prisoner to have a quantity of nails in his possession. 12 months hard labour.
25 October 1872 – Illegally at large. Discharged.

Between 21 October 1872 and 31 December 1874, he was assigned in the Albany, Fremantle, Murray and Plantaganet Districts, working as a labourer, general servant and shepherd, being paid between 30 shillings and four pounds per month. It is possible that he died in Perth during 1890 (Pth 269/90).

ROBINSON John (c.1839-1.12.1887)
(AJCP Reel 5983 Pri Corn 2/110; Acc. 128/27; Acc. 1156/R29; Acc. 1156/R21B; Death Reg Murray 751/87).
Convicted at Newtown Quarter Sessions on 3 July 1862, of breaking and entering a house in Llangyniew and stealing therefrom. He was sentenced to 7 years penal

servitude. This followed a previous conviction when he stole clothes and received 14 days hard labour. He was transported on the 'Lord Dalhousie', which left Portland on 25 September 1863, arriving at Swan River on 28 December 1863. He was 24 years of age, height 5'1½", with brown hair and grey eyes. He was middling stout with long visage and sallow complexion. There was a burn mark on his left thigh, an anchor on both his left arm and left thumb, and he had high shoulders. He was single, a labourer, able to read and write imperfectly, and a Protestant. His next of kin was his father, James Williams, a wire worker of Ulverstone, Lancashire. He received his ticket of leave on 30 August 1865 and a conditional pardon 25 August 1868. Only two offences are recorded against him, as follows:

> *21 March 1863 – Absconding. 14 days bread and water.*
> *28 November 1867 – Out after hours. Reprimand.*

During July and August 1863, he spent 30 days in hospital. Between 7 September 1865 and 17 August 1868, he was assigned in the Bunbury District, as a labourer, cook and general servant, for which he was paid between 20 and 40 shillings per month. On 1 December 1887, he was found dead in his bath.

THOMPSON William (c.1827–)

(AJCP Reel 5984 Pri Com 2/110; Acc. 128/33; Acc. 1156/R30; Acc. 1156/R21B; Acc. 1386/5; Acc. 1386/12; NLW Q/SR 1863 *Eddoes Journal*, 28 October 1863).

Convicted at Welshpool Quarter Sessions on 22 October 1863, of breaking and entering the dwelling house of a Richard Sankey at Berriew and stealing 1 knife, 1 piece of bread and 1 rasher of bacon. He was sentenced to 10 years penal servitude. When sentence had been passed, he said to the judge and jury, "Thank you, I will bring you a ring-tailed monkey home". This followed a previous conviction on 11 July 1860, for burglary at Winchester, when he received 3 years penal servitude. Following a period of 21 days at Montgomery Gaol, he was transferred to Millbank 12 November 1863, Pentonville 13 November 1863 (spending only 1 day at Millbank), and Portsmouth 8 November 1864. His health was good during this period, as was his character. He spent 6 months 3 days on Public Works. He was eventually transported on the 'Racehorse', leaving Portland 26 May 1865, arriving Swan River 10 August 1865. He was 38 years of age, height 5'8¾", with brown hair and blue eyes. He was middling stout, with long visage and fresh complexion. There were no marks on his body. He was single, a gardener/farmer by trade, able to read and write, and a Protestant. No next of kin is noted. The following offences are recorded against him:

> *20 April 1866 – Malingering. 3 months hard labour.*
> *3 August 1867 – Trafficking. 4 months hard labour.*
> *6 February 1872 – Stealing fruit from a garden of T. Jackson at Paradise. 6 weeks hard labour in Perth Prison.*

He received his ticket of leave 10 July 1869, conditional release 1 September 1871, cancelled 10 February 1872, and his full pardon 19 December 1873. He was assigned to work in the Swan, Toodyay, Northam, York and Beverley Districts as a general servant, teamster, labourer, ploughman, reaper, and on drainage and sandalwood. His wages were between 12 shillings (reaping), and 40 shillings per month.

WATSON James (c.1838-31.10.1872)
(Acc. 128/26; Acc. 1156/R21B; Acc. 1156/R22; Acc. 1156/R7).
Convicted at Montgomery Assizes 15 July 1861 of arson by setting fire to a stack of oats at Llangurig and of stealing a gun from Llandyssul. He was sentenced to 10 years penal servitude. He was transported on the 'York II', leaving Portland 8 October 1862, arriving Swan River 31 December 1862. He was 24 years of age, height 5'2¾", with brown hair and grey eyes. He was pock-pitted in appearance, with thin visage and sallow complexion. There was a scar on his right arm. He was married with 2 children, a collier by trade, unable to read or write, and a Roman Catholic. There is no record of his next of kin or family. Only two offences are recorded against him:

> *7 January 1867 – Breach of Regulations. 3 months hard labour.*
> *15 January 1867 – Talking whilst on Public Works. 14 days added to above.*

He received his ticket of leave 1 February 1865, and a conditional pardon 12 October 1869. He was assigned to work in the Champion Bay and Victoria Districts, as a general servant, mason, farm labourer, labourer, grubber and clearing land, for which his wages fluctuated between 20 and 72 shillings per month. On 31 October 1872, it was confirmed that the remains of a body found in the bush, was that of James Watson.

WESTON William (c.1845 -?1872)
(Acc. 128/33; Acc. 1156/R30; Acc. 1156/R21B; Acc. 1385/5; Death Reg Perth 6421/72).
Convicted at Welshpool Assizes 17 December 1863 of arson by setting fire to hay. He was sentenced to 8 years penal servitude. This followed a previous conviction in Southampton, when he stole a watch and received 6 months in 1861, and again in 1863 he was reputed to be a thief and was given 10 days hard labour. He was transported on the 'Racehorse', leaving Portland 26 May 1865, arriving Swan River 10 August 1865. He was 20 years of age, height 5'5", with brown hair and grey eyes. He was middling stout, with long visage and sallow complexion. On his left arm were a star, crown, flags, anchor, heart and arrow. He was single, able to read and write, and a Protestant. His next of kin was his brother George Weston, butcher, of East Street, Southampton. The following offences are recorded against him:

> *21 August 1865 – Dirty cell. Admonished.*
> *15 March 1866 – Gross Insubordination. 6 months added to probation.*
> *21 March 1866 – Absconding and taking blanket. 28 days bread and water.*
> *10 September 1866 – In possession of Government property. 12 months hard labour in Fremantle Prison.*
> *27 February 1867 – Insolent to Chief Warder. 3 days bread and water.*
> *26 March 1867 – Malingering and making away with Government property. 21 days bread and water.*
> *17 May 1867 – Refusing to return to his party. 3 days bread and water.*
> *24 January 1868 – Leaving his party without permission. 1 day bread and water.*
> *9 March 1868 – Absent from camp at Causeway. 6 months hard labour in irons. (1st month in solitary, 1st 7 days bread and water).*
> *11 July 1868 – Disobedience. 1 day bread and water.*
> *30 November 1868 – Refusing to go to work. Cautioned.*

16 December 1868 – Being at cell door of a prisoner in separate confinement and conversing. 3 days bread and water.

23 November 1869 – Absent from North Dandalup party. 6 months hard labour in irons at Fremantle Prison.

29 November 1869 – Deficient of clothes. To pay for same.

4 April 1870 – Lurking in his cell. 2 days bread and water.

31 October 1870 – Playing cards. 2 days bread and water.

23 January 1871 – Refusing to fall into party. Deprived tobacco for 1 month.

28 March 1871 – Drunk in Public House. 1 month hard labour at Perth.

1 September 1871 – Refusing to work. 7 days bread and water.

He received his ticket of leave 6 January 1871 and full pardon 16 January 1872. He was assigned to work in the Swan, Wellington, Perth and Fremantle Districts, as a labourer and sawyer. Between 6 January 1871 and 31 December 1871 his wages fluctuated between 4 shillings per day and 85 shillings per month. A William Weston died in Perth during 1872.

WILSON John (c.1840-15.11.1873)
(Acc. 128/33; Acc. 1156/R30; Acc. 1156/R21B; Death Reg Fremantle 6815/73; NLW Q/SR 1864H).
Convicted at Welshpool Assizes 17 December 1863, of breaking and entering the dwelling house of William Lewis of Newtown, and stealing a cape. He was sentenced to 8 years penal servitude. This followed a previous offence of vagrancy 24 October 1863 for which he received 10 days. He was transported on the 'Racehorse', leaving Portland 26 May 1865, arriving at Swan River 10 August 1865. He was 25 years of age, height 5'8¾", with black hair and dark hazel eyes. He was middling stout with long visage and dark complexion. On his right arm was a horseshoe and he wore a bracelet on his right wrist. On his left arm were cross flags, anchor, crucifix, heart and arrow. He wore a ring on his second finger of the left hand. He was single, a servant/gentleman's servant by trade, able to read and write and a Protestant. His next of kin was his father, Thomas Theobold Wilson, of Feltwell, Brandon, Norfolk.

Offences recorded against him were:

25 September 1868 – Stealing quantity of wine. Dismissed.

18 February 1869 – Insolent and threatening language. 14 days bread and water.

11 May 1870 – Stealing sandalwood. 18 months hard labour.

11 November 1871 – Released from Fremantle Prison.

He received his ticket of leave 12 February 1868, and a full pardon 2 July 1873. He was assigned to work in the Wellington, Toodyay and Fremantle Districts, as a boot closer, general servant, labourer, and cook. His wages fluctuated between 20 shillings per week and 60 shillings per month, between 17 February 1868 and 18 February 1873. He died on 15 November 1873 at Fremantle.

WILSON John (c.1836–)
(Acc. 128/37; Acc. 1156/R15).
Convicted at Newtown Assizes 30 June 1864 of breaking and entering a Counting House at Welshpool with intent to commit a felony. He was sentenced to 7 years penal servitude. This followed previous convictions at Montgomery January Sessions 1864, of shoplifting, sentenced 2 months, and at Chester March Sessions

1864, also of shoplifting and sentenced to 2 months. His character in prison was good. He was transported on the 'Corona', leaving Portland 16 October 1866, arriving Swan River 22 December 1866. He was 30 years of age, height 5'5", with light brown hair and grey eyes. He was stout, with round visage and fresh complexion. He had no marks. He was single, a striker by trade, able to read and write, and a Protestant. His next of kin was his father, George Wilson, 30 Bandon Road, Cork, Ireland. There were no offences recorded against him and he was assigned to work in the Wellington District as a general servant and labourer. Between 14 May 1868 and 30 June 1870, his wages were 30 shillings per month. He received his ticket of leave on 15 May 1868 followed by a conditional release 11 October 1870. He left for Adelaide 24 April 1878.

Port Phillip

DAVIES (DAVIS) John (c.1819–)

Convicted at the County Sessions 11 April 1844 of larceny from the person in that he, with four others, stole from John Langford of Newtown one purse containing one £5 note and twelve shillings and from Edward Jones of Newtown one £5 note, one half sovereign, three half crowns, five shillings and one sixpence. He was sentenced to 10 years transportation. (NLW Q/5R1844). He was sent to Millbank and on 2nd September 1844 was removed to Pentonville. He was transported on the 'Maitland' leaving London 29 June 1846 arriving Tasmania 27 October 1846 and Port Phillip 9 November 1846. He was 26 years of age, able to read and write imperfectly, a joiner/carpenter by trade and single. (AONSW Reel 706 4/4546 p.49). Having been recommended for a CP he may have been included in a list which accompanied the following letter dated 23 February 1847 from the Superintendent's Office Melbourne to "The Colonial Secretary":

> *The accounts from the ship 'Maitland' having been delayed, I have not been able hitherto to forward you the information required by your letter of the 27 November 1846. I am now however in a position to do so and enclose returns of the disposal of the 'Exiles' that arrived in that ship and an abstract of the expenses since the arrival. I regret that the disposal lists are not complete which was occasioned by the parties who undertook to record this information respecting the men who were sent to Geelong, having omitted to do so, and which may be excused from the rapid manner in which the men were engaged. Some of these men also did not enter into service, but undertook employment on their own recourses* (CSIL 4/2781 letter 47/1936).

ELLIS Thomas (c.1823–)

Convicted at the County Sessions 8 January 1846 of larceny by stealing a gun to the value of three shillings from Edward Lodwick of Llanwddyn. He was sentenced to 7 years transportation. (NLW Q/SR 1846). Following a period at Millbank he was removed on 16 May 1846 to Pentonville. He was transported on the 'Marion' leaving Spithead 29 September 1847 arriving Tasmania 9 January 1848 and Port Phillip 25 January 1848. He was 25 years of age, single, farm labourer, able to read and write imperfectly and was native of Llandrillo. Following his arrival he was employed as a shepherd by Chermside and Co Geelong for one year at an annual salary of twenty pounds (AONSW Reel 706, 4/4546, p. 87, CSIL 4/2821 letter 48/5787).

HUGHES Lewis (c.1829–)

Convicted at the County Sessions 26 February 1846 of larceny by stealing a padlock and key from Mr E. Davies of Parc (Llanwnog) and various articles from John Kitchen. As these offences followed a previous felony conviction, he was sentenced to 7 years transportation (NLW Q/SR 1846; NLW B1/SO, *Shrewsbury Chronicle*). Following a period spent at Millbank he was transferred on 13 May 1846 to Pentonville. He was transported on the 'Marion' leaving Spithead 29 September

1847 arriving Tasmania 9 January 1848 and Port Phillip 25 January 1848. He was single, age 19 years, able to read and write imperfectly, farm labourer/tailor by trade and native of Llanwnog. Upon arrival at Port Phillip he went ashore at his own request (AONSW Reel 706 4/4546, p. 91, CSIL 4/2821 letter 48/5787).

PRICE John (c.1760-25.11.1803)

Convicted at the spring Great Sessions 1800 of stealing 2 oxen (value £20), the property of Thomas Ashford of Newtown. Aged 40 years, he was sentenced to death commuted to 14 years transportation after evidence for the prosecution was supplied by six persons. Following a period spent on the 'Captivity' hulk at Portsmouth, he was transported on the 'Calcutta' leaving Spithead 24 April 1803 arriving Port Phillip 9 October 1803. On board were 307 convicts who had been transferred from the hulks at Woolwich (120), Portsmouth (100), Langston (80) and Gibraltar (7). The ship complement also included 17 wives of convicts and 8 children. John Price had the distinction of being one of the first convicts to be landed at Port Phillip, but it is evident that his health must have been troubling him as his death is recorded at Port Phillip on 25 November 1803. Had he lived, he would have been included with his fellow prisoners on the 'Calcutta' who were taken to Tasmania early in 1804, who were amongst the first convicts to arrive at Hobart Town. (AOT Correspondence File "Port Phillip Exiles". Extract from *The Victorian Historical Magazine*, Vol. 30, pp. 239-40; Marjorie Tipping, *Convict Unbound: The Story of the Calcutta Convicts and their Settlement in Australia*, pp. 302-303. Penguin, Australia, 1988).

TAYLOR James (c.1818 –)

Convicted at the Quarter Sessions 16 October 1845 of housebreaking and stealing from the house of John Jones at Meifod 9 yards of print and various other items to the value of £2. He was sentenced to 10 years transportation (*Shropshire Journal*, 29 October 1845). His accomplice was James Smith. He was 27 years of age, a labourer and able to read imperfectly. His native place is shown as Hammersmith, London. He was transported on the 'Joseph Somes' leaving London 4 June 1847 arriving Port Phillip 24 September 1847. En route the ship had called at Hobart on 10 September 1847 and disembarked one male prisoner (HO 11/15 Reel 92, p. 186; Charles Bateson, *The Convict Ships*, p. 395).

THORN Frederick (c.1818 –)

Convicted at the County Sessions 8 January 1846 of housebreaking and larceny when he entered the house of Richard Corbett and stole one silk handkerchief and other articles including clothing from the house of John Stephens, both probably from the parishes of Llanfair Caereinion and Llandyssil. His accomplice was his wife who was convicted under the name of Mary Rogers. He was sentenced to 10 years transportation and following a period spent at Millbank was removed to Pentonville 12 March 1846. He was transported on the 'Marion' leaving Spithead 29 September 1847 arriving Tasmania 9 January 1848 and Port Phillip 25 January 1848. He was 30 years of age, able to read and write imperfectly, a gentleman's servant/tailor by profession and native of Southampton. Although his marital state is shown as single, he was married to Mary Rogers who had been transported to Tasmania. There is no confirmatory evidence that they were reunited. Following his arrival he was employed as a butler by Mr E. Curr of St Hiliers for one year at an annual salary of twenty-five pounds. (AONSW Reel 706 4/4546, p. 85, CSIL 4/2821 letter 48/5787).

APPENDIX E

Norfolk Island

HUMPHREYS (HUMPHRIES) Hugh (c.1812–)

Convicted at the Assizes 8 March 1845 for feloniously stabbing in the groin Police Constable Thomas Cowdall at Machynlleth with intent to do bodily harm. He was sentenced to 15 years transportation. This was his first conviction. His accomplice Thomas Morris was acquitted. He was transported on the 'Mayda' leaving Woolwich 29 August 1845, arriving Norfolk Island 8 January 1846. During his stay in Norfolk Island the following offences are noted:

> *4 February 1846 – Misconduct in absenting himself from his gang without leave. Admonished.*
> *3 August 1846 – Abusing his overseer. 2 months hard labour in chains.*

He was eventually removed to Tasmania where he arrived on the 'Pestongee Bomangee' 19 May 1847. Upon his arrival in Tasmania he was single, aged 35 years, native of Montgomeryshire (possibly Machynlleth) where his father John, mother Mary, brothers John and Benjamin, sisters Ann, Mary, Margaret, Elizabeth, Sarah and Catherine lived. He was a Protestant, tanner and currier by trade and able to read, height 5'7¾", head round, hair brown, whiskers black, visage oval, forehead medium, eyes not recorded, eyebrows brown, nose long and thin, mouth and chin small, complexion sallow and a scar on the elbow joint left arm (CON 33/79; CON 17/2; CON 18/49). The following offences are noted:

> *14 August 1847 – Disobedience of Orders. Reprimanded.*
> *15 October 1847 – Disobedience of Orders in refusing to be silent in his separate apartment. 3 days solitary confinement.*
> *23 October 1850 – Misconduct in cohabiting with a free woman who had run away from her husband. Discharged and returned to government work. Recommended that he be hired in the Interior, having formed bad connexions in Hobart.*
> *5 March 1851 – Misconduct in living with a woman named Elizabeth Jones and falsely representing that she was his wife. 9 months imprisonment with hard labour.*
> *17 March 1851 – Misconduct in not performing his tasks. One month added to existing sentence.*
> *26 May 1851 – Absconding. Remainder of hard labour sentence to be carried out in chains.*
> *22 November 1852 – Misconduct in being out after hours. Reprimanded.*
> *27 December 1852 – Drunk. Reprimanded.*
> *11 January 1853 – Misconduct in being in a public house on Sunday tippling. 10 days solitary confinement.*
> *17 May 1853 – Disturbing the peace. Fined five shillings.*
> *30 July 1853 – Disturbing the peace. Fined five shillings.*

1 October 1853 – Misconduct in being out after hours and disturbing the peace. 3 months hard labour.
13 February 1854 – Common Assault upon Jno Smith. 18 months hard labour.
7 April 1856 – Assault. Fined £5 and costs.
30 November 1856 – Drunk. Fined £1.

A ticket of leave was issued 21 December 1852 and revoked 13 December 1853. A second ticket of leave was issued 9 October 1855, revoked 20 May 1856, returned 4 July 1856, followed by a CF 29 September 1857 (CON 33/79).

SMOUT Richard (c.1820-11.7.1849)

Convicted at the Assizes 13 July 1844 of feloniously stabbing with intent to do bodily harm to John Lloyd at a dance held at Buttington Inn by inflicting a knife wound to the neck. He was sentenced to 15 years transportation (SRO, *Shropshire Journal*, 17 July 1844) and was transported on the 'Hyderabad', leaving Downs 21 October 1844, arriving Norfolk Island 19 February 1845. The surgeon reported that he was a steady and good man. Whilst at Norfolk Island he was placed in class PFH 3rd until his removal to Tasmania where he arrived on 1 May 1847. He was 27 years of age, able to read and write, height 5'9", head round, hair brown, whiskers dark brown, visage long, forehead high, eyes hazel, eyebrows dark brown, nose and chin long, mouth large with fresh complexion and no bodily marks. He was a farm labourer by calling, native of Westbury Shropshire, single and a Protestant. His family included his father John, mother Martha Hester, brother Thomas and sisters Margaret/Ann. The only offence noted against him took place on 22 June 1848 when, whilst acting as a constable in Hobart, he neglected his duty and was sentenced to 3 days in solitary confinement. His death is recorded in Hobart hospital on 11 July 1849 and his age shown as 31 years (CON 33/86; CON 14/29: CON 18/55 and CON 63 Register of Convict Deaths No. 19987).

Bermuda

BRADLEY William (c.1825–)
Convicted at the Assizes 15 March 1847 of robbery with violence by stealing 17 sovereigns and other money from a John Woxencroft. This offence was committed with Thomas Gwynne. He was 22 years of age, a native of Shrewsbury, a machine maker by trade and unable to read or write. He was sentenced to 15 years transportation. (NLW B1/20 and Q/SR 1847). Following transfer to Bermuda, he received a Discharge by Licence on 14 April 1855.

EDWARDS Timothy, alias ROGERS (c.1814–)
Convicted at the County Sessions 5 April 1838 of larceny, with a previous conviction. He stole a bridle from a Mr Edwards of Burgedin, Guilsfield. Following his sentence of 7 years transportation, the judge stated that he would censure a witness, namely John Jones, who had purchased the bridle for 5s. as it was worth treble that amount. He was 24 years of age, a labourer and unable to read or write. (NLW Bl/17). Following transfer to the hulk 'Gannymede' at Woolwich, he was sent to the hulk 'Coromandel' at Bermuda in June 1842. He was then transferred to the 'Prince George' transport on 27 April 1844.

EVANS John (– 30.3.1834)
Convicted at the Great Sessions 12 July 1827 of stealing 11s. in money belonging to Arthur Watkins the elder and a silver tea spoon and 2 other spoons belonging to Arthur Watkins the younger, both of Buttington. He was sentenced to 7 years transportation. Following a period in Montgomery gaol, he was transferred to the hulk 'Justitia' at Woolwich, from where he was removed to the hulk 'Coromandel' at Bermuda. He died in the Royal Naval Hospital, Bermuda, 30 March 1834.

GRIFFITHS Edward (c.1804–)
Convicted at the County Sessions 10 April 1823 of larceny in Llangyniew. He was sentenced to 7 years transportation. Aged 19 years, he was a labourer. Following a period in the hulk 'Justitia' at Woolwich, he was transferred to the hulk 'Antelope' at Bermuda. On 17 April 1828 he received a free pardon.

JONES John (c.1812–)
Convicted at the County Sessions 5 July 1838 of larceny by stealing clothes at Trehelig, Welshpool. Whilst working there, he took the clothes from a trunk belonging to another servant called John Davies. The Police were informed and John Jones was caught in Shrewsbury. He was sentenced to 7 years transportation. He was 26 years of age, a labourer and able to read and write imperfectly (NLW B1/17, *Shrewsbury Chronicle*, July 1838). Following a period on the hulk 'Gannymede' at Woolwich, he was transferred to the hulk 'Coromandel' at Bermuda. He was discharged to 'Prince George' transport 27 April 1844.

JONES John (c.1825–)
Convicted at the County Sessions 16 October 1845 of breaking and entering 2 houses and stealing 2 shirts, 1 pair boots, and 3 shirts from Edward and John Pugh, and 3 shirts from Elias and Enoch Mason, all from Llansantffraid. He was sentenced to 10 years transportation. He was 20 years of age, a native of Oswestry, a labourer and was unable to write but could read imperfectly (NLW Bl/19, *Shrewsbury Chronicle*, 31 October 1845 and Q/SR 1845). Having been sent to the 'Coromandel' hulk at Bermuda, he was discharged on 1 August 1850, to be taken on HMS 'Netley' to Halifax, Nova Scotia.

JONES Maurice(c.1811–)
Convicted at the County Sessions 26 February 1846 of larceny by stealing a goose, to the value of 2s. from Martha Williams of Kerry. This followed a previous conviction of a felony. He was sentenced to 7 years transportation. He was 35 years of age, a carpenter and able to read and write imperfectly (NLW Q/SR 1846). He spent part of his sentence on the 'Coromandel' hulk at Bermuda from where he was removed to the brig 'Mayflower' bound for Philadelphia 13 March 1850.

SMITH James (c.1805–)
Convicted at the County Sessions 12 July 1827 of larceny by stealing several pieces of calico from the shop of Morris Jones, Welshpool. He was sentenced to 7 years transportation. His accomplices were Hannah Fox and Esther Ogden. He was 22 years of age and a labourer (NLW Q/SR 1827). Following a period in the hulk 'Justitia' at Woolwich, he was sent to the hulk 'Coromandel' at Bermuda. He returned on HMS 'Racehorse' to the 'York' hulk at Portsmouth in November 1833 and there received a free pardon 12 December 1833.

SMITH James (c.1807–)
Convicted at the County Sessions 16 October 1845 of breaking and entering the house of John Jones of Meifod, and stealing 9 yards of print and various other items to the value of £2. He was sentenced to 10 years transportation. His accomplice was James Taylor. He was 38 years of age, a gardener by trade and able to read and write imperfectly. He was a native of Yeovil (NLW Q/SR 1845 and Bl/19, *Shrewsbury Chronicle*, 31 October 1845). He was taken to the 'Thames' hulk at Bermuda and returned to England on HMS 'James', followed by discharge 16 August 1851.

TURNER Evan (c.1826–)
Convicted at the County Sessions 6 January 1848 of larceny on 3 counts, by stealing 2 pigs from Mary Jones, 3 pigs from Edward Owen and 1 pig from John Lewis, all of Meifod. He was sentenced to 7 years transportation. Aged 22 years, a labourer, he could read imperfectly and was unable to write (NLW Q/SR 1848). He was pardoned whilst on the 'Coromandel' hulk 26 November 1852.

WEBB Francis, alias Thomas WEBB (c.1788–)
Convicted at the Great Sessions 20 March 1823 of a felony by stealing 80 yards of flannel from William Davies of Llanmerewig. He was sentenced to 7 years transportation. Aged 35 years, he was single, a native of Birmingham and an ironmonger by trade (NLW Q/SR 1823 and 4/201/7). He was on the 'Justitia' hulk in 1823, prior to which his gaol report confirmed that he was very orderly and was not previously known (HO7/3). He was eventually transferred to the hulk 'Antelope' at Bermuda from where he was discharged 26 March 1829.

Gibraltar

BEAVAN John (c.1824–)
Convicted at the County Sessions 19 October 1843 of 2 offences by breaking and entering the dwelling houses of Richard Goodwin and stealing 1 cotton gown 5s. and 1 shawl 4s., also of breaking and entering the dwelling house of William Poole and stealing 1 cotton handkerchief 4d. He was 19 years of age, able to read and write imperfectly, a native of Birmingham and a brass founder by trade. He was sentenced to 10 years transportation, having already spent 2 months in prison (NLW Q/SR 1843). He was taken to Millbank prison 8 February 1844 and transferred to Gibraltar 7 January 1845 from where he was discharged on 8 February 1851.

GAD Joseph (c.1808–)
Convicted at the Assizes 8 March 1852 of uttering forged banknotes, i.e. £5 to defraud the Bank of England, £5. to defraud Richard Jones and £5 to defraud John Gwynn. He was sentenced to 10 years transportation. He was 44 years of age, a native of West Bromwich and a pig dealer by trade. He was sent to Pentonville from where he was transferred to Portland prison 27 January 1853 (NLW Q/SR 1853). Eventually being moved to Gibraltar, he was returned to England on board the 'Minden' 12 April 1856 for release on licence.

McNAB Andrew (c.1831–)
Convicted at the Quarter Sessions 16 October 1851 of breaking and entering the dwelling house of John Edwards and stealing 1pair woollen stockings and 2 silk handkerchiefs, and from the dwelling house of Evan Jenkins he stole bread and cheese plus 12s. 6d. in silver. Both offences took place in Cemmaes and his accomplice was John Priest. He was sentenced to 10 years transportation. He was 20 years of age, a native of Hamilton, Scotland, and a labourer (NLW Q/SR 1851). Having been sent to Gibraltar he was returned to England for release on the 'Minden' 12 April 1856.

PRYCE Robert (c.1818–)
Convicted at the County Sessions 7 April 1842 of breaking and entering a house in Guilsfield. His accomplice was John Jones. He was sentenced to 10 years transportation. He was 24 years of age, a labourer and could neither read or write. He was sent to the Hulk 'Warrior' at Woolwich from where he was transferred to the 'Owen Glendower' hulk at Gibraltar. He returned to England 15 June 1849.

ROBERTS John (c.1827-10.9.1852)
Convicted at the Assizes 14 July 1849 of robbery with violence by assaulting Henry Pugh and stealing 2 x £5. notes and other monies. He was sentenced to 20 years transportation. His accomplice was William Jones. He was 22 years of age and a native of Llanymynech. Unable to read or write, he was a labourer (NLW Q/SR 1849). He died at Gibraltar, 10 September 1852.

WILLIAMS John (c.1826–)

Convicted at the County Sessions 17 October 1844 of larceny by stealing 2 ass collars and various other items from Guilsfield. This followed a previous conviction of a felony. He was sentenced to 7 years transportation. He was 18 years of age and a native of Llanwyddelan. He was a labourer and able to read and write imperfectly. He was sent to the hulks at Gibraltar and Bermuda respectively in 1844. He was given a free pardon at Gibraltar 3 September 1849. Following his return to Montgomeryshire it is recorded that he continued his life of crime and received a further sentence warranting detention in Montgomery gaol, on a vagrancy charge, in 1853 (NLW Q/SR 1844).

Not Transported

AUSTIN David (c.1789-9.10.1818)

Convicted at the Quarter Sessions 16 July 1818 of stealing 2 bushels of potatoes value 4s. from the gardens of Powis Castle, Welshpool, 11 July 1818. He was sentenced to 7 years transportation and was 29 years of age (NLW Q/SR 1818). He died on the 'Justitia' hulk, 9 October 1818.

BARRETT Edward

Convicted at the Great Sessions 8 February 1795 of grand larceny but not for burglary, by entering the house of David Davies in the parish of Tregynon and stealing 8 cotton handkerchiefs (value 7s.), 5 pieces of tape (value 3s.), 6 papers of pins (value 2s.), 4lb of sugar (value 2s. 6d.), 1 pair woollen mittens (value 6d.) and ¾lb brimstone (value 1s.). He was sentenced to 7 years transportation (NLW 4/195/6). It is possible that he may have remained or died in Montgomery gaol.

BELLAMY William (c.1776–)

Convicted at the Great Sessions 2 April 1808 of a felony and was sentenced to 7 years transportation. He was 32 years of age (NLW 4/199/1 and Q/SR 1810). He received a pardon whilst on the 'Justitia' hulk, 1 May 1814.

BLISS John (c.1759–)

Convicted at the Great Sessions March 1792 of horse stealing and was sentenced to death, commuted to 7 years transportation. He was 32 years of age (NLW 4//194/7).

CHAMBERS George

Convicted at the Great Sessions spring 1817 of breaking and entering the dwelling house of a Richard Pryce of Forden, stealing 1 pair boots (£1), 1 pair shoes (4s.), 1 pair shoes (2s.), 1 shoe brush (6d.), 1 jug (3d.), 2lb butter (2s.), 1 qtr milk (1d.) and 1 cheese bag (1s.). He was found not guilty of breaking and entering, but guilty of stealing and taking away. His accomplice was William Cooke. He was sentenced to 7 years transportation, but, on 21 April 1817, both with force and arms, he was rescued from Montgomery gaol by Elizabeth Bufton, Sarah Eyton and Richard Griffiths. There is no record that he was re-captured (NLW 4/200/6).

DAVIES Edward (c.1768–)

Convicted at the Great Sessions 28 March 1791 of sheep stealing. He was sentenced to death, commuted to 7 years transportation. He was 23 years of age (NLW 4/194/7).

DAVIES Salisbury (c.1752-10.8.1799)

Convicted at the summer Great Sessions 1792 of a felony by stealing 1 purse containing 12 guineas and 2 half guineas all in gold, the property of a Richard Davies from Llanfyllin. He was sentenced to 7 years transportation. For some unknown reason he remained a prisoner at Montgomery gaol until his death in August 1799 when a fellow prisoner, Aaron Bywater, murdered him. Salisbury Davies would have been about 47 years of age at his untimely death and one can only wonder if he would have enjoyed a better and longer life "Beyond the Seas".

DAVIES William
Convicted at the Great Sessions 28 March 1804 of a felony. He was sentenced to 7 years transportation, but a petition to Her Majesty dated 23 September 1804, asked that he be allowed to serve a life term in either the Army or Navy. On 1 December 1804, the gaoler at Montgomery gaol was given permission to provide the prisoner with 1 coat, 1 pair breeches, 2 shirts and a pair of shoes, prior to his discharge (NLW Q/AG 1).

DAWSON Hugh Leah (c.1800-14.12.1819)
Convicted at the Great Sessions 14 August 1819 of taking from the pocket of Jeremiah Evans of Llanrhaeadr-ym-Mochnant, a pocket book containing £9 in notes. He was 19 years of age and sentenced to 7 years transportation. (NLW Q/SR 1819). He eventually died whilst on the 'Justitia' hulk, 14 December 1819.

DURKIN Michael (c.1828–)
Convicted at the County Sessions 29 June 1848 of larceny, by housebreaking and stealing from David Vaughan of Meifod, wearing apparel, 1 loaf of bread, some sugar and butter. This offence was committed with Henry Williams. He was sentenced to 7 years transportation. He was 20 years of age, a native of Newcastle, Shropshire, a labourer by trade and could neither read or write (NLW Q/SR 1848).

EDWARDS Edward (c.1777-19.1.1826)
Convicted at the County Sessions 13 January 1825 of larceny by stealing a quantity of wheat from John Griffiths of Glanmeheli, Kerry. He was sentenced to 7 years transportation. He was 48 years of age and a labourer (NLW Q/SR 1825). Following transfer to the hulk 'Justitia' at Woolwich, he died there on 19 January 1826.

ELLIS James (c.1783–)
Convicted at the Great Sessions spring 1816 of horse stealing, a bay mare from William Micklewright of Newtown. He was sentenced to death, commuted to life transportation. He was 33 years of age (NLW Q/SR 1816). He received a pardon whilst on the 'Justitia' hulk, 17 June 1823.

EVANS David
Convicted at the Quarter Sessions 15 January 1824 of a felony and was sentenced to 7 years transportation.

EVANS Edward, alias EDWARDS (c.1801–)
Convicted at the Quarter Sessions 28 February 1839 of larceny by stealing a blanket from a Mrs Pryce, Upper Packhouse, Welshpool. This followed a previous conviction. He was sentenced to 7 years transportation. He was 38 years of age, a labourer and able to read and write imperfectly. He was also known as "Neddy Upstairs". Following a period in Montgomery gaol, he was transferred to the hulk 'Justitia' at Woolwich where he received a pardon, 26 December 1842.

EVANS Hannah Maria (c.1820–)
Convicted at the Quarter Sessions 11 May 1837 of larceny by a servant, having stolen wearing apparel from her employer in Berriew. She was sentenced to 7 years transportation, but received the Gracious Pardon of Her Majesty, on condition that she remained in prison for a period of 12 months. She was 17 years of age, a spinster and able to read and write imperfectly.

EVANS John (c.1749–)
Convicted at the Great Sessions 28 July 1785 of stealing a black gelding, value £5, from Thomas Daniel, Llanfechain. He was sentenced to death, commuted to 7 years transportation. He was 37 years of age (NLW 4/193/2). He received a free pardon whilst at Montgomery gaol, 15 September 1788 (NLW 4/193/3).

EVANS John (c.1802–)
Convicted at the Great Sessions 23 March 1822 of stealing £14 in money and a Bill of that value, enclosed in a letter from a Mrs Pryce to John Humphreys (his master), and also a bridle from his master. He was sentenced to 7 years transportation. He was 20 years of age (NLW Q/SR 1822). Following transfer from Montgomery gaol to the hulk 'Gannymede' at Woolwich, he was discharged 21 August 1824.

EVANS Richard, alias Evan RICHARDS (c.1822-24 December 1848)
Convicted at the Assizes 15 March 1847 of larceny, he was sentenced to 7 years transportation. This followed previous convictions in Caernarvonshire and Denbighshire respectively, namely an unrecorded offence in the first place and the stealing of a shawl from a Mary Evans in the second place. For these earlier offences he had received sentences of 10 and 7 years transportation respectively but he escaped without serving the above sentences. A native of Denbighshire, he was 25 years of age, a labourer and able to read and write imperfectly (NLW 61/20 and Shropshire Record Office, *Salopian Journal*, 24 March 1847). Eventually placed aboard the 'Hashemy' due to leave Portsmouth 11 February 1849 for New South Wales, he died of cholera on Christmas Day, 25 December 1848, aged 26 years.

FARMER Joseph (c.1807–)
Convicted at the County Sessions 5 February 1837 of larceny by stealing from the dwelling house of David Morgan, Gungrog, Welshpool, 3 x £10 notes. He was sentenced to life transportation but on 20 February 1837 his sentence was commuted to 7 years. He was 30 years of age, a labourer and able to read and write imperfectly. Following a period in the hulk 'Gannymede' at Woolwich, he was transferred to Millbank penitentiary, June 1837 (NLW Q/SR 1837).

GEORGE Michael (c.1801–)
Convicted at the County Sessions 21 October 1824 of larceny by stealing 1 pistol (5s.), 6 knives and 6 forks (5s.) from Llandinam. He was sentenced to 7 years transportation. He was 23 years of age and a labourer (NLW Q/SR 1824). He received his pardon whilst on the 'Justitia' hulk, 9 February 1830.

GOODWIN Robert (c.1787–)
Convicted at the Great Sessions 7 April 1810 of larceny by stealing 4 cheeses and butter from David Morgan of Llanwnog. He was sentenced to death but received a pardon 14 June 1810, to be followed by a 2 year period in Montgomery gaol before his final discharge. He was 23 years of age (NLW Q/SR 1810).

GOUGH James (c.1780–)
Convicted at the spring Great Sessions 1817 of a felony and was sentenced to 7 years transportation. He was 37 years of age, healthy and orderly. On 11 May 1817, an order was received from His Royal Highness The Prince Regent, that he be confined in the common gaol for the space of 12 months, and then discharged (NLW 4/200/7 and Q/SR 1817).

GREEN John
Convicted at the spring Great Sessions 1806 of a felony and sentenced to 7 years transportation. Following a period in the hulk at Portsmouth, he received a pardon to join the Army and serve abroad.

GRIFFITHS James (c.1808–)
Convicted at the County Sessions 30 June 1836 of larceny by stealing a pocket book from Mr Thomas Owen of Red House, Llanllwchaiarn, Newtown Fair Day. He was sentenced to 14 years transportation. He was 28 years of age, a labourer and able to read and write imperfectly (NLW B1/16). Although it is recorded that he was on the 'Justitia' hulk and listed for transportation, there is no indication that he was sent to Australia.

GUMM Thomas (c.1776-19.2.1815)
Convicted at the Great Sessions spring 1812 of felony. He was sentenced to death which was commuted to 7 years transportation. He was 36 years of age (NLW Q/SR 1812). He died on the 'Justitia' hulk, 19 February 1815.

HANKINSON John (c.1821–)
Convicted at the County Sessions 20 October 1842 of larceny by stealing 1 waistcoat and 1 pair of trousers, to the value of £2, from Griffith Davies Griffiths. He was sentenced to 7 years transportation. He was 21 years of age, a labourer and able to read and write imperfectly. He had a previous conviction of felony and was a native of Oswestry (Shropshire Record Office, *Salopian Journal*, 26 October 1842). He was transferred to the hulk 'Justitia' at Woolwich, and in a return of prisoners held on that ship dated 27 March 1847, he is shown as suffering from defective vision (PP 1847). He received a pardon on the 'Justitia', 30 April 1847.

HILL Samuel (c.1791–)
Convicted at the Great Sessions 25 March 1819 of being in possession of forged notes and paid one. He was sentenced to 14 years transportation, mitigated to 7 years. He was 28 years of age, and was transferred to the hulk 'Justitia' at Woolwich. By September 1824, he was reported as being infirm and was given the Sacrament (NLW Q/SR 1819). He received a pardon on the 'Justitia' hulk, 25 March 1825.

HUGHES Thomas (c.1768–)
Convicted at the summer Great Sessions 1811 of a felony by being bigamously married to another since his first marriage. He was sentenced to 7 years transportation (NLW Q/SR 1811 and 4/199/4). He received a pardon on the 'Justitia' hulk, 2 April 1817.

HUMPHREYS Evan (c.1817–)
Convicted at the Assizes 7 March 1840 of breaking and entering the shop of William Cleaton, mercer, of Llanidloes, and stealing woollen cloth and cotton goods to the value of £40 approximately. He had been seen in the vicinity of the shop in the early hours of Sunday morning, and, the following day, he was seen in Kerry where he was trying to sell the stolen goods. The constable was sent for, but Evan Humphreys escaped over the border into Radnorshire. Following his capture in that county, he was handcuffed but on his return to Newtown, he escaped and hid between two graves in the churchyard. Following recapture he was brought before the Assizes and sentenced to 10 years transportation. Aged 23 years he was able to read and write imperfectly (Shropshire Record Office, *Salopian Journal*, 11 March 1840). He was still in a penitentiary by August 1840.

HUMPHREYS John (c.1816-25.12.1838)
Convicted at the County Sessions 20 October 1836 of breaking and entering the shop of Mr Charles Jones of Llanfyllin and stealing a quantity of copper coins to the value of 2s. 9d. On his own evidence he was also guilty of other burglaries. He was sentenced to 14 years transportation. He was 20 years of age, a currier by trade and able to read and write imperfectly. He was removed to the hulk 'Gannymede' at Woolwich, where he was reported to be ill in June 1837 (NLW 61/16, *Shrewsbury Chronicle*, 28 October 1836). He died on the 'Gannymede', 25 December 1838.

HUMPHREYS Matthew (c.1770–)
Convicted at the County Sessions 16 January 1800 of a felony by stealing 24 fir trees from the grounds of Powis Castle, Welshpool. He was sentenced to 7 years transportation. He was 30 years of age.

JAMES William (c.1782–)
Convicted at the County Sessions 11 May 1837 of larceny by stealing ducks. This followed a previous conviction for a felony. He was sentenced to 14 years transportation. Aged 55 years, he was unable to read or write. His sentence was commuted to one year in Montgomery gaol, 18 July 1837.

JENKS Evan (c.1733–)
Convicted at the Great Sessions 31 March 1788, that with his wife Elizabeth (age 56 years), he aided and abetted Margaret Webster (age 15 years), to steal 3 sheep (value 10s. 6d.), belonging to Edward Turner of Bettws. He was sentenced to death commuted to an unknown period of transportation which was respited during His Majesty's pleasure. Still in Montgomery gaol he received a free pardon 23 June 1791. He was 55 years of age (NLW 4/193/8).

JOHNSON William (c.1831–)
Convicted at the Assizes 13 March 1853 of burglary and sentenced to 7 years transportation. Aged 22 years, he was removed to Millbank prison and eventually discharged from Portland prison, 30 April 1856.

JONES David (c.1799–)
Convicted at the Great Sessions 25 March 1824 of stealing 5 sovereigns and two £1 notes from Evan Roberts and sentenced to 7 years transportation. He was 25 years of age and spent time on two hulks, namely 'Justitia' and 'Gannymede', both at Woolwich (NLW Wales 4/202). He received a free pardon 16 January 1828.

JONES David (c.1785–)
Convicted at the Assizes 10 March 1832 of larceny by stealing 80 yards of flannel from William Lloyd and John Lewis of Llanllwchaiarn, Newtown. He was sentenced to 7 years transportation. He was 47 years of age (NLW Q/SR 1832).

JONES Elizabeth alias EVANS (c.1740–)
Convicted at the Lent Great Sessions 1785 and the Great Sessions March 1788 of house breaking and was sentenced to death commuted to 14 years transportation, which, in turn, was commuted to 3 years hard labour in Montgomery gaol, 16 September 1791. She was 45 years of age (NLW 4/193/7).

JONES Hugh (c.1737–)
Convicted at the Great Sessions 1784, 30 March 1786 and March 1788 of a felony and sentenced to death commuted to 7 years transportation. He was 49 years of age (NLW 4/193/7). He received a free pardon at Montgomery gaol, 15 September 1788.

JONES Humphrey (c.1811–)
Convicted at the Great Sessions 11 August 1828 of larceny by stealing 1 letter or packet out of a mail bag. Aged 17 years he was sentenced to 7 years transportation (NLW Q/SR 1828). He received a pardon whilst on the 'Justitia' hulk, 15 May 1833. This pardon did not deter him from committing further crimes because in 1834 he was indicted once more and received a life sentence of transportation, culminating in his going to Tasmania.

JONES John (c.1789–)
Convicted at the spring Great Sessions 1812 of a felony. He was sentenced to death commuted to 7 years transportation. Prior to leaving Montgomery gaol, he escaped by climbing the wall of the male felon ward on 10 July 1812 and was not seen afterwards. He was 23 years of age (NLW Q/SR 1812 and *Bygones*, 1884, p. 118).

JONES John (c.1822–)
Convicted at the County Sessions 7 April 1842 of breaking and entering the dwelling house of Abraham Breeze and stealing 5 fowls, from the house of Robert Parry a horse halter, a whip and an ousting thong and from the house of George Williams a smock frock. All these offences took place in the Llanfair Caereinion/ Guilsfield area. He was sentenced to 10 years transportation. He was 20 years of age, a labourer and unable to read or write. He spent some time on the hulk 'Warrior' at Woolwich and from a return of convicts held on the 'Warrior' as at 27 March 1847, he is shown to be in good health (NLW Q/SR 1842.PP 1847). Whilst still on the 'Warrior' he received a pardon, 25 June 1847.

JONES John
Convicted at the Quarter Sessions 4 July 1850 of horse stealing at Manafon, following a previous offence of a felony. He was sentenced to 7 years transportation. A labourer, he was transferred to Pentonville prison and received a discharge with licence whilst on the 'Warrior' hulk, 27 December 1853.

JONES John
Convicted at the Assizes 16 July 1850 of burglary and sentenced to 10 years transportation. He was discharged from Millbank penitentiary, 6 June 1851.

JONES Joseph, alias Joshua (c.1788–)
Convicted at the spring Great Sessions 1814 of a felony. He was sentenced to death commuted to life transportation. He was 26 years of age (NLW Q/SR 1814).

JONES Joseph (c.1804–)
Convicted at the Great Sessions 21 March 1825 of sheep stealing from John Hughes of Trefeglwys. He was sentenced to death commuted to 7 years transportation (NLW 4/202/3). He was 21 years of age and spent some time on the hulk 'Justitia' at Woolwich where he received a pardon, 30 July 1829.

JONES Lewis (c.1805–)
Convicted at the County Sessions 7 January 1841 of sheep stealing at Llanidloes. He was sentenced to 7 years transportation. He was 36 years of age, a farmer and able to read and write imperfectly (NLW Q/SR 1841). Having been sent to the 'Justitia' hulk he received a pardon, 9 September 1844.

JONES Owen (c.1807 – 15.9.1829)
Convicted at the Great Sessions 23 March 1829 of burglary at the house of John Oliver of Mochdre and stealing 1 Drab coat (5s.), 1 Blue coat (15s. and 1 tin cannister (6d.). He was sentenced to death commuted to 14 years transportation. He was 22 years of age (NLW Q/SR 1829). His death is recorded on the 'Justitia' hulk, 15 September 1829.

JONES Richard (c.1764–)
Convicted at the Great Sessions 1827 of manslaughter by killing Edward Gardener of Trelystan. At an inquest held on Monday 28 August 1827 it was reported that:

> *On Saturday 26 August at Trelystan, Montgomeryshire, Richard Jones of Leighton in the parish of Worthen, not having the fear of God before his eyes but moved and seduced by the instigation of the Devil, upon the said Edward Gardener, in the peace of God and Our said Lord the King, then and there with force did wickedly and feloniously make and with a certain instrument called a scythe of the value of three pence, a wound upon the temple, the length of one inch and depth of three inches, of the said Edward Gardener, did feloniously inflict of which wound the said Edward Gardener then and there immediately died.*

Pleading not guilty, the jury however found him guilty of manslaughter and he was sentenced to 14 years transportation. (NLW 4/202/7). Aged 63 years he spent 7 years on the 'Justitia' hulk from where he received a pardon, 1 February 1834.

JONES Samuel (c.1804–)
Convicted at the County Sessions 21 October 1824 of larceny by stealing from Forden, 1 pair gaiters (6s.), 1 silk handkerchief (1s.), 2 handkerchieves (2s.), 1 pair breeches (3s.) and 1 smock frock (7s.). He was sentenced to 7 years transportation. He was 20 years of age and a labourer (NLW Q/SR 1824). He received a pardon in January 1828.

JONES Thomas (c.1777–)
Convicted at the Great Sessions 18 March 1820 of larceny. He was sentenced to 7 years transportation (NLW Q/SR 1820). Following a period on the hulk 'Gannymede' at Woolwich, he was discharged 21 August 1824.

JONES William (c.1828–)
Convicted at the Assizes 14 July 1849 of robbery with violence by assaulting Henry Pugh and stealing 2 x £5 notes and other monies. His accomplice was John Roberts. He was sentenced to 15 years transportation. He was 21 years of age, a native of Stourport, a labourer and able to read only (NLW Q/SR 1849). He was sent to Pentonville prison and discharged 18 January 1856.

KINSEY John (c.1803-25.8.1850)
Convicted at the County Sessions 21 October 1847 of breaking and entering the house of Lilian Stephens in that part of the parish of Alberbury that lies in the county of Montgomery, from where he stole several articles of clothing. He was sentenced to 10 years transportation. He was 45 years of age, a native of Llanidloes, a labourer and unable to read or write (NLW Q/SR 1847). He died on the 'Warrior' hulk, 25 August 1850.

LESTER Joseph (c.1823–)
Convicted at the Quarter Sessions 3 July 1851 of breaking and entering a house in Cemmaes. He was sentenced to 10 years transportation. His accomplice was John Smith. He was 28 years of age and a labourer. He was discharged on licence from the 'Stirling Castle', 19 August 1855.

LEWIS Thomas (c.1811–)
Convicted at the Assizes 9 March 1848 of feloniously uttering a forged acceptance to a bill of exchange amounting to £17.5s.0d., with the intent to defraud Anthony Jaundrell. He was sentenced to 10 years transportation. He was 37 years of age and able to read and write imperfectly. He was a flannel manufacturer in Newtown (NLW Q/SR 1848). He received a free pardon, 24 January 1849.

LLOYD Edward
Convicted at the Assizes 16 July 1850 of burglary and sentenced to 10 years transportation. He was sent to Pentonville prison and was discharged from Dartmoor 12 February 1855.

LLOYD Jane (c.1763–)
Convicted at the Quarter Sessions 11 January 1810 of larceny by stealing sugar from a shop to the value of £1. Aged 47 years, she was sentenced to 7 years transportation (NLW Q/SR 1810 and 4/199/1).

LOW Daniel
Convicted at the Great Sessions 1 August 1807 of a felony. He was sentenced to 7 years transportation, but allowed by the court to serve in the Marines.

MACFARLANE James (c.1804–)
Convicted at the Assizes 13 March 1853 of burglary. He was sentenced to 7 years transportation. Aged 49 years, he was sent to Millbank prison and then transferred to Portsmouth prison 30 May 1854 from where he was discharged 27 May 1856.

MEREDITH John
Convicted at the Great Sessions 27 March 1806 of horse stealing. He was sentenced to death, commuted to 7 years transportation but allowed by the court to serve in the Army abroad.

METCALF Thomas (c.1834–)
Convicted at the Quarter Sessions 2 July 1852 of larceny by stealing 2 linen sheets and other articles from David Thomas of Machynlleth. This followed a previous conviction of a felony. He was sentenced to 7 years transportation. He was 18 years of age, a native of York, a labourer and able to read and write (NLW Q/SR 1853). Following a period at Pentonville prison, he was transferred to Portsmouth prison 5 November 1853. His discharge took place on 16 November 1855.

MILES Arthur (c.1837–)
Convicted at the Quarter Sessions 3 March 1854 of larceny by stealing 1 axe from Robert Davies, Tybrith, Guilsfield. This followed a previous conviction of a felony. He was sentenced to 4 years penal servitude (NLW Q/SR 1854). He was still on the 'Warrior' hulk in June 1856.

MORGAN Elizabeth, alias EVANS (c.1745–)
Convicted at the Great Sessions March 1787 for receiving stolen goods, she was sentenced to 14 years transportation (NLW 4/194/3). She was 45 years of age and remained in Montgomery gaol from where she received a free pardon 23 June 1791.

MORRIS Evan
Convicted at the spring Great Sessions 1805 of larceny by stealing a quantity of flannel. He was sentenced to 7 years transportation. Following a period in the hulk at Portsmouth, he was granted a pardon to serve in the Army abroad (Shropshire Record Office, *Salopian Journal*, 17 April 1805 and NLW Q/AG1).

MORRIS John (the Younger) (c.1836–)
Convicted at the Quarter Sessions 1 October 1850 of larceny by stealing 1 silver watch from John Jones of Welshpool. This followed a previous conviction of a felony. He was sentenced to 7 years transportation. He was 14 years of age, native of Welshpool, a labourer and able to read and write imperfectly (NLW QSR 1850). He was taken to Millbank penitentiary in February 1851 and transferred to Reigate farm school 24 March 1851 with a conditional pardon.

MORRIS Richard (c.1787–)
Convicted at the Great Sessions 24 March 1828 of larceny by stealing 1 flannel to the value of £4 from Andrew Jones of Trefeglwys. He was sentenced to 7 years transportation. His accomplice was Edward Williams. He was 41 years of age, a native of Bettws and a staymaker by trade (NLW Q/SR 1828.4/203/1). He received a pardon whilst on the 'Gannymede' hulk, 29 November 1832.

MORRIS Stephen
Convicted at the Great Sessions 23 March 1829 of a felony and sentenced to 7 years transportation. He received a pardon whilst on the 'Gannymede' hulk, 13 May 1834.

NEWALL Thomas (c.1810-8.9.1834)
Convicted at the County Sessions 20 February 1834 of sheep stealing. He was sentenced to life transportation. Aged 24 years, he died on 8 September 1834, soon after being sent to the hulk 'Gannymede' at Woolwich.

OWEN Evan (c.1784–)
Convicted at the County Sessions 17 October 1844 of larceny by stealing 3 geese to the value of 3s. from a John Price of Llanwnnog. This followed a previous conviction of a felony. He was sentenced to 7 years transportation. He was 60 years of age, a labourer and unable to read or write (NLW Q/SR 1844). In a report on the hulks in 1847, his name is included in a list of prisoners held on the hulk 'Justitia' at Woolwich, which confirms that he was asthmatic (PP 1847). He received a pardon whilst on the 'Justitia', 23 December 1847.

OWEN Richard (c.1820–)
Convicted at the Assizes 9 March 1848 of house breaking, having a previous offence of a felony. He was sentenced to 7 years transportation. Aged 28 years, he could read and write imperfectly. He received a free pardon 24 January 1849.

OWEN Thomas (c.1794–)
Convicted at the County Sessions 19 October 1837 of sheep stealing, one ewe and one wether sheep from the Foel, Trefeglwys, the property of Richard Evans. He was sentenced to 15 years transportation. Aged 43 years, he was a yeoman farmer of Trefeglwys and was able to read and write imperfectly. Due to the state of his health it is probable that he was granted a pardon whilst at the County gaol (NLW Q/506).

PARRY Griffith (c.1769–)
Convicted at the spring Great Sessions 1817 of a felony by stealing money. He was sentenced to 7 years transportation. Aged 48 years, he was healthy and orderly (NLW Q/SR 1817). He was pardoned whilst on the 'Justitia' hulk, 19 April 1821.

PARRY Thomas (c.1783–)
Convicted at the Quarter Sessions 16 July 1818 of larceny by stealing 15 hurdles and a quantity of potatoes from the gardens of Edward Herbert (Lord Clive), at Powis Castle. He was sentenced to 7 years transportation. Aged 35 years (NLW Q/SR 1818). He was sent to the hulk at Chatham, from where he received a pardon 17 July 1822.

PASSANT Joseph (c.1785–)
Convicted at the Great Sessions 18 March 1820 of a felony and sentenced to 7 years transportation. He was 35 years of age (NLW Q/SR 1820). He was sent to the hulk 'Discovery' at Deptford, where he received a pardon 31 January 1825.

POWELL John (c.1808-24.4.1828)
Convicted at the County Sessions 14 April 1825 of larceny at Llanbrynmair. He was sentenced to 7 years transportation. Aged 17 years and a labourer, he was taken to the hulk 'Justitia' at Woolwich where he drowned 24 April 1828.

PRICE Eleanor, alias OWEN
Convicted at the Great Sessions 1805 of a felony by stealing 28¼ yards of material. She was sentenced to death, commuted to life transportation (NLW 4/198/10; 4/199/1).

PRICE Evan
Convicted at the spring Great Sessions 1805 of sheep stealing. He was sentenced

to death, commuted to 14 years transportation (Shropshire Record Office, *Salopian Journal*, 17 April 1805).

PRIEST John (c.1832–)
Convicted at the Quarter Sessions 16 October 1851 of house breaking at Cemmaes and stealing therein. This followed a previous conviction for a similar offence. He was sentenced to 10 years transportation. His accomplice was Andrew McNAB. He was 19 years of age, native of Liverpool, a labourer and able to read and write. He was discharged on licence from the 'Stirling Castle', 21 November 1855.

PRYCE Evan (c.1805–)
Convicted at the Great Sessions 18 March 1820 of a felony by stealing from a house. He was sentenced to death, commuted to 2 years imprisonment (NLW Q/SR 1820).

PRYCE John (c.1778-27.10.1820)
Convicted at the Great Sessions 9 August 1817 of burglary at Llandinam and sentenced to 7 years transportation. He was 39 years of age (NLW Q/SR 1817). He died on the 'Justitia' hulk, 27 October 1820.

PRYCE John (c.1831-7.8.1851)
Convicted at the Quarter Sessions 7 March 1850 of larceny by stealing 3 fowls (3s.) from Evan Edwards, 2 ducks from William Bowen and 3 fowls from Maurice Bebb, all of Llanllwchaiarn. This followed a previous conviction. He was sentenced to 7 years transportation. His accomplice was Thomas Morris, aged 20 years, a native of Newtown, a labourer able to read only, sentenced to 6 months hard labour. John Pryce was 19 years of age, a fishmonger by trade, able to read only and a native of Newtown. He died at Pentonville, 7 August 1851.

PUGH Simon (c.1785–)
Convicted at the County Sessions 4 January 1849 of larceny by stealing wearing apparel from John Roberts of Forden. This followed a previous conviction of a felony. He was sentenced to 7 years transportation. He was 64 years of age, a labourer and a native of Chirbury (NLW Q/SR 1849). He received a free pardon 12 August 1850.

PUGH Thomas
Convicted at the Quarter Sessions 15 January 1824 of larceny in Welshpool. He was sentenced to 7 years transportation. Following transfer to the 'Discovery' hulk, he escaped from there May 1824.

REES David (– 22.2.1829)
Convicted at the Great Sessions 11 August 1828 of a felony by stealing flannel, with force and arms from the tenter field of Richard Brown of Llanidloes. He was sentenced to 7 years transportation. He was an itinerant shoemaker by trade (NLW 4/203/2). It is also recorded that he was the last prisoner to be kept in the old 'Crib' at Llanidloes Market Hall (*Montgomeryshire Collections*, Vol. 61). He died on the 'Justitia' hulk, 22 February 1829.

REES Evan (c.1794–)
Convicted at the Assizes 24 March 1821 of sheep stealing by stealing one sheep

from John Owen of Llangurig. He was sentenced to death, commuted to 7 years transportation. His accomplice was his brother Richard Rees. He was 27 years of age (NLW Q/SR 1821). He received his discharge 27 July 1824.

REES Richard (c.1801–)
Convicted at the Assizes 24 March 1821 of sheep stealing by stealing one sheep from John Owen of Llangurig. He was sentenced to death, commuted to 7 years transportation. His accomplice was his brother Evan Rees. He was 20 years of age and in good health (NLW Q/SR 1821). He received his discharge 27 July 1824.

RICHARDS Evan (c.1780–)
Convicted at the Quarter Sessions 16 July 1818 of larceny by stealing a quantity of potatoes and 3 fowls from William Ruff, Esq. Sentenced to 7 years transportation, he was 38 years of age (NLW Q/SR 1818).

RICHARDS John
Convicted at the Assizes 13 March 1853 of perjury. He was sentenced to 7 years transportation.

RICHARDS Rees (c.1769–)
Convicted at the summer Great Sessions 1797 of sheep stealing by taking 1 sheep from Berriew value 10s. and sentenced to death, commuted to 7 years transportation. He was 28 years of age (NLW 4/196/7). Following a period in the hulk 'Captivity' he received his pardon 31 March 1802.

RICHARDS Thomas
Convicted at the spring Great Sessions 1811 of an unknown crime and sentenced to 7 years transportation. He was transported on the 'Glatton', leaving England 23 September 1802, arriving NSW 11 March 1803. Records do not indicate that he arrived at his destination and he may have been re-landed before departure or died enroute.

ROBERTS Jane (c.1746–)
Convicted at the summer Great Sessions 1803 of a felony. She was sentenced to death, commuted to 7 years transportation. She was 57 years of age, healthy and orderly (NLW 4/199/1 and Q/SR 1810).

ROBERTS Owen (c.1799–)
Convicted at the Great Sessions 18 March 1820 of a felony and sentenced to 7 years transportation. He was 21 years of age. He received a pardon whilst on the 'Gannymede' hulk, August 1825.

ROBERTS Thomas (c.1774–)
Convicted at the Great Sessions 24 March 1830 of receiving stolen goods and sentenced to 7 years transportation. He was 56 years of age and following a period in the hulk 'Justitia' at Woolwich he received a pardon on 16 May 1832.

ROWLANDS John (– 25.7.1818)
Convicted at the Great Sessions 13 March 1818 of stealing a heifer, value £4 from David Evans of Llandinam. He was 47 years of age. He was sentenced to death, commuted to life transportation (NLW Wales 4/200/7). He died on the 'Justitia' hulk, 25 July 1818.

SHAW William (c.1814–)
Convicted at the Quarter Sessions 3 January 1839 of breaking and entering the house of William Davies, Llanfihangel, and stealing a watch etc. He was sentenced to 14 years transportation. His accomplice was Henry Smith. He was 25 years of age, a labourer and able to read and write imperfectly (NLW Bl/17). He was sent to the hulk 'Justitia' at Woolwich where he was pardoned 26 March 1844.

SMITH John (c.1831–)
Convicted at the Quarter Sessions 3 July 1851 of breaking and entering a house in Cemmaes. He was sentenced to 10 years transportation. His accomplice was Joseph Lester. He was 20 years of age and a labourer. He was discharged on licence from the 'Stirling Castle', 19 August 1855.

SNEAKSMAN James
Convicted at the Quarter Sessions 4 July 1850 of sheep stealing at Welshpool, this following a previous conviction of a felony. He was sentenced to 7 years transportation. A labourer, he was sent to Pentonville prison and discharged on licence 24 March 1855.

SWAIN Thomas (c.1780–)
Convicted at the Quarter Sessions 23 October 1818 of larceny by stealing 1lb cheese (10d.), 1lb bread (6d.), 4 razors (1s.) and 1 razor case (1d.) from a Thomas Roberts. He was sentenced to 7 years transportation (NLW Q/SR 1818). He was pardoned on the 'Justitia' hulk, 25 July 1823.

SWANCOTT Samuel (c.1806–)
Convicted at the Assizes 10 March 1832 of receiving stolen goods namely saddles, bridles and a clarinet from Jonah Williams. He was sentenced to 7 years transportation (NLW Q/SR 1832 and Shropshire Record Office, *Salopian Journal*, 14 March 1832). Aged 26 years, he was sent to the hulk 'Gannymede' at Woolwich, where he received a pardon 18 May 1837.

TUDOR John
Convicted at the Great Sessions 12 July 1827 of a felony by stealing 3 pigs from Richard Morris of Forden and sentenced to 7 years transportation. He was sent to the hulk 'Leviathan' at Portsmouth, where he received a pardon 4 August 1834.

TURNER Elinor (c.1766–)
Convicted at the spring Great Sessions 1813 of a felony. Aged 47 years, she was sentenced to 7 years transportation (NLW Q/SR 1813).

WAINWRIGHT Richard
Convicted at the Great Sessions 1 August 1807 of an unknown crime and sentenced to 7 years transportation. He was permitted by the court to join and serve in the Marines instead.

WATSON Maria (c.1811–)
Convicted at the Quarter Sessions 30 June 1853 of larceny by stealing from the person of Lewis Jones of Machynlleth, a purse containing £3. 5s. 0d. She was sentenced to 10 years transportation. She was 32 years of age, a single woman and a shoe binder by trade. A native of Exeter, she was unable to read or write

(NLW Q/SR 1853). Her sentence was commuted to 7 years at Brixton prison in December 1855, from where she was released on licence 23 June 1856.

WEBSTER Thomas (c.1776–)

Convicted at the spring Great Sessions 1806 of a felony and sentenced to 7 years transportation. He was 30 years of age and was sent to the hulk at Portsmouth from where he received a pardon to serve in the Army abroad.

WHARTON Richard (c.1785–)

Convicted at the Great Sessions 8 August 1822 of a felony by stealing 1 gown from a Richard Jones. He was sentenced to 7 years transportation. Aged 37 years, he was in good health and behaved in an orderly manner, a whitesmith by trade (NLW Q/SR 1822 and 4/201/6). He was sent to the hulk 'Gannymede' at Woolwich and received his pardon 23 September 1826.

WILKINSON Samuel (c.1827–)

Convicted at the County Sessions 24 January 1845 of larceny by unlawfully obtaining from Thomas Walford of Welshpool by means of false pretence, the sum of £10. 11s. 7d., the monies belonging to the Earl of Powis. This followed a previous conviction of a felony. He was sentenced to 7 years transportation. He was 18 years of age, a labourer and able to read and write imperfectly. He was sent to the hulk 'Warrior' at Woolwich (NLW Q/SR 1845). A return of prisoners kept on the hulk dated 2 March 1847, shows him to be in the hospital ward of the hulk, suffering from a diseased heart (PP 1847). He was given a pardon 21 July 1848.

WILLIAMS Andrew (c.1757-4.5.1832)

Convicted at the Great Sessions 29 March 1827 of stealing a cow value 40s. from Robert Thomas of Llanllwchaiarn. Aged 70 years, he was sentenced to 14 years transportation (NLW 4/202/7). He died on the 'Justitia' hulk, 4 May 1832.

WILLIAMS Edward (c.1803–)

Convicted at the Great Sessions 24 March 1828 of a felony by stealing 1 flannel, to the value of £4, from Andrew Jones of Trefeglwys. He was sentenced to 7 years transportation. He was 25 years of age, a weaver and a native of Llanfair Caereinion (NLW Q/SR 1828 and 4/203/1). His sentence expired on the 'Gannymede' hulk and he was discharged 23 March 1835.

WILLIAMS Edward (c.1821–)

Convicted at the Assizes 7 March 1843 of breaking and entering the house of Edward Lewis. This followed a previous conviction of a felony. He was sentenced to 10 years transportation. He was 22 years of age, a farmer and able to read and write imperfectly. He was a native of Llanystymdwy, Caernarfonshire. He was sent to the hulk 'Warrior' at Woolwich, a return of prisoners kept on the hulk dated 27 March 1847 shows him to be in good health (PP 1847). He was given his pardon 26 February 1848.

WILLIAMS Henry (c.1831–)

Convicted at the County Sessions 29 June 1848 of larceny by breaking and entering the house of David Vaughan of Meifod and stealing wearing apparel, bread, sugar and some butter. His accomplice was Michael Durkin. He was sentenced to 7 years transportation. He was 17 years of age, native of Birmingham, a chimney sweep and able to read and write imperfectly.

WILLIAMS John (c.1822–)

Convicted at the Assizes 7 March 1843 of burglary by entering the house of Edward Middleton and stealing a coat and other clothes. His accomplice was Richard Morris. He was sentenced to 10 years transportation. He was 21 years of age, a machine maker and able to read and write imperfectly (NLW/SR 1842). He was sent to the hulk 'Warrior' at Woolwich. A return of prisoners on the hulk dated 27 March 1847 shows that he was in the hospital ward of the hulk suffering from a broken leg (PP 1847). He was pardoned whilst on the 'Warrior', 25 April 1848.

WILLIAMS Joseph

Convicted at the Quarter Sessions 13 January 1791 of an unknown crime and was sentenced to 7 years transportation. He was transported on the 'Pitt', leaving Yarmouth Roads 17 July 1791, arriving NSW 14 February 1792. Due to overcrowding, some convicts were re-landed and others died. It is probable that Joseph Williams was amongst these.

WILLIAMS Thomas

Convicted at the Great Sessions 4 August 1823 of sheep stealing by stealing a ewe lamb from David Ellis. He was sentenced to death commuted to 7 years transportation. He was a native of Kinnerley, Shropshire, and a shoemaker by trade (NLW 4/201/7). He was sent to the hulk 'Discovery' at Deptford from where he received a pardon in November 1827.

WILSON Charles, alias WILLIAMSON

Convicted at the spring Assizes 1831 of larceny and sentenced to 7 years transportation. He was still on the hulk 'Gannymede' at Woolwich in March 1835 from where he received a pardon 21 November 1835.

WOODING John (c.1820–)

Convicted at the County Sessions 20 October 1842 of larceny by stealing a watch from James Evans of Berriew. He was sentenced to 7 years transportation. He was 22 years of age, a labourer and unable to read or write. (Shropshire Record Office, *Salopian Journal*, 26 October 1842). He received a pardon on the 'Warrior' hulk, 13 July 1846.

APPENDIX I

In Memoriam

The final resting place of all those convicts sent from Montgomeryshire and who eventually were laid to rest in Australia, cannot now be identified. Research has however established that some were placed in graves that, through the diligence of their respective families and others, can be found by inscriptions placed upon grave stones.

Morgan Miles, who had arrived in Tasmania on the ship 'Caledonia', 6 November 1822, lived a full life in the colony. It has not been established that he married, but his death in September 1853, is inscribed on a tombstone located in the churchyard at Buckland, Tasmania. The inscription reads:

> *Erected in Memory of Morgan Miles died September 1853 (date unclear) aged 73 years.*[1]

John Bumford, following his arrival on the 'Red Rover', 25 March 1831, left behind in the village of Bettws, Montgomeryshire, a wife and child. After a period in Tasmania, he married Mary Ann Burton, widow of 50 years of age. having been pre-deceased by his wife, who died 20 February 1875, his eventual death took place on 6 November 1890, when he was 95 years of age. Both were buried in Ross general cemetery, Tasmania, where an inscribed stone has been placed in their memory.[2]

Elizabeth Davies (Grist), following a larceny offence, set foot on Tasmanian soil 4 April 1850. On 12 April 1852 she married Moses Linton (alias George Mason), in St Peter's Church, Hamilton, Tasmania. Linton had been sentenced to 14 years transportation by the Lincolnshire Assizes 4 August 1821 for horse stealing from the countryside of Stanford. The gaol report records that he was a bad lot and an old offender. He arrived in Tasmania on board the ship 'Commodore Hayes', 16 August 1823. Aged about 23 years, his parents were farmers (?Atkinson) living at Benson, Lincolnshire.[3] Whilst in Tasmania, he was charged with Jno Jewell at Rumney with rescuing a flock of sheep when the sheep were being driven to a pound by himself and a servant on 5 March 1830, but was admonished. He was conditionally emancipated 21 August 1833.[4] His death is recorded 9 October 1883, at Hobart, aged 83 years , labourer with the cause of death given as "senilis".[5] He was buried at Queenborough cemetery, Sandy Bay, Hobart.[6] Following his death Elizabeth placed a stone on his grave with the following inscription:

> *Sacred to the memory of Moses Linton, died 9 October 1883, aged 84 years. Let my remembrance often creep across thy mind, but do not weep. But go so live thy death may be such as no friend may weep for thee.*[7]

Elizabeth Williams, having committed arson at Trewern, Montgomeryshire, found herself sent to Tasmania on the ship 'Borneo', which arrived 8 October 1828, leaving behind three children in her native land. On 5 October 1829, at the parish

216

church of New Norfolk, she married William Lewis. He had been tried and found guilty at Hereford Assizes 26 March 1821 of stealing timber and sentenced to seven years transportation. Native of Pudleston, Herefordshire, married and a farm labourer with grey eyes and dark brown hair. In 1831, he applied for a grant of land, stating that he was 44 years of age with capital of £139.8.4d and a wife and two children. Renting a farm at Green Ponds, Kempton, a John Bisdee supported his application by stating that:

> *William Lewis was an assigned servant to him about three years during which period he conducted himself much to my satisfaction.*

His application was approved and he was granted 100 acres of land in the Constitution Hill countryside near Kempton.[8] William Lewis died 2 June 1861, to be followed by his wife 7 March 1869. Both were buried in the graveyard of St Luke's Church, Bothwell, Tasmania, where their headstone is inscribed:

> *The memory of William Lewis, who departed this life June 2 1861, aged 82 years. Also Elizabeth, Relict of the above who departed this life March 7 1869, aged 72 years. Lord now lettest thou thy servants depart in peace.*[9]

William Rowlands was convicted in 1833 of horse stealing at Cemmaes, Montgomeryshire and sentenced to life transportation. Following his arrival in Tasmania on the ship 'Moffatt', 9 May 1834, he met and married Mary Ann Neale on 14 March 1859 at St Matthew's Church, Rokesby. Whilst research has produced no evidence concerning their life together, their respective deaths and that of a young daughter are recorded on a stone erected on their grave at Queenborough Cemetery, Sandy Bay:

> *In memory of Mary Ann Rowlands, died July 3 1883, aged 14 years and 3 months. "Though lost to sight to memory dear."*
> *Also William Rowlands, died 4 June 1895, aged 84 years also Mary Ann, beloved wife of the above, died 1898. Footstone M.A.R and W.R.*[10]

Notes on Chapters and Appendices

CHAPTER ONE – THE PLIGHT OF THE TRANSPORTEES

1. 39 Eliz c4 (1597). An Act for the punishment of rogues, vagabonds and sturdy beggars.
2. 18 Chas 2 c3 (1662). An Act for the better relief of the poor of the Kingdom authorizing the apprehension of any rogue, vagabond or sturdy beggar making it lawful for the Justices of the Peace in any of the counties to cause them to be transported and shall be duly convicted and adjudged to be incorngible.
3. 2 Ann c.l2; 22 Geo 2 c.5; 22/23 Geo 2 c.7.
4. 4 Geo 1 c.11. An Act for the further preventing of robbery, burglary and other felonies and for the more effectual transportation of felons.
5. 24 Geo 3 c.56 (1784). An Act for the effectual transportation of felons and other offenders and to authorise the removal of prisoners in certain cases.
6. PRO HO 31/1.
7. The Assize Courts replaced the Court of Great Sessions in Wales in 1830.
8. 16 Geo 3 c.43 (1776). An Act to authorize, for a limited period, the punishment by hard labour of offenders who, for certain crimes, are or shall become liable to be transported to any of His Majesty's colonies and plantations.
   18 Geo 3 c.62 (1778). An Act to extend the use of the hulks.
   19 Geo 3 c.74 (1779). An Act to consider the expediency of erecting a penitentiary house or penitentiary houses.
9. PP 1837-38 xxii 669.
10. Patrick Colquhoun, *A Treatise on the Police of the Metropolis* (1795).
11. PP 1822 xx 448.
12. PP 1837-38 xxii 669.
13. Duncan and Neil Campbell were contracted by the British Government to make the necessary arrangements for the provision and management of the hulk establishments located at Woolwich. They had previously been engaged in the movement of convicts to the North American colonies; other contractors included Aaron Graham and John Capper.
14. PP 1812 ii 306.
15. PP 1812 ii 306.
16. PP 1837 xix 518.
17. Charles Bateson, *The Convict Ships*, p.141.
18. Bateson p.357.
19. Bateson p.350.
20. Bateson p.356.
21. PP 1822 xx 448.
22. A. G. L. Shaw, *Convicts in the Colonies*, p.100.
23. PP 1812 ii 306.
24. PP 1822 xx 448.
25. PP 1837 xix 518.
26. PP 1837-38 xxii 669.
27. Revd Samuel Marsden, 31 January 1820. 201/118.
28. PP 1819 vii 579; L. Evans and P. Nicholls, *Convicts and Colonial Society 1788-1853*.
29. PP 1837-38 xxii 669.
30. HRA 1 xxii pp.516-522. Stanley to Franklin, 25 November 1842.
31. PP 1837 xix 518.
32. PP 1822 xx 448.
33. PP 1812 ii 306.
34. Sir George Arthur, Lieutenant Governor of Van Diemen's Land from 1824-1836. PP 1836 xix.
35. PP 1838 xxii 669.
36. PP 1838 xxii 669.
37. PP 1838 xxii 669.
38. PP 1838 xxii 669.
39. PP 1838 xxii 669.
40. PP 1838 xxii 669.

41. Captain Alexander Maconochie, RN (1787-1860), was appointed private secretary to the Lieutenant governor in 1836. He was also one time Commandant at Norfolk Island.
42. PP 1838 xxii 669.
43. PP 1838 xxii 669.
44. PP 1838 xxii 669.
45. John West, *The History of Tasmania*, p. 397. Born in England in 1809 and went to Tasmania as a minister of the Congregational Church in 1838.
46. PP 1838 xxii 669.
47. PP 1838 xxii 669.
48. PP 1812 ii 306. Edward Cadogan, *The Roots of Evil*.
49. PP 1838 xxii 669.
50. 30 Geo III c.47. An Act for enabling His Majesty to authorize the Governor or Lieutenant Governor of such places beyond the seas to which felons or other offenders may be transported, to remit the sentences of such offenders.
51. PP 1812 ii 306.
52. PP 1837 xix 518.
53. HRA 1 vii pp.779-780. Despatch from Macquarie to Bathurst, 28 June 1813.
54. HRA 1 xiii pp.3-5. Despatch from Darling to Bathurst, 2 January 1827.
55. PP 1837 xix 518.
56. PP 1838 xxii 669.
57. PP 1838 xxii 669.
58. AOT CO 1/48. Despatch from Stanley to Franklin, 25 November 1842.
59. PP 1838 xxii 669.
60. 16/17 Vict c.99. An Act to substitute in certain cases other punishments in lieu of transportation.
61. PP 1856 xvii 561.
62. PP 1856 xvii 404.

Chapter Two – A Welsh Rural Scene

1. Report by W. A. Miles, Assistant Commissioner to the Royal Commission on the Handloom Weavers 1838.
2. Report of the Commission on the best means of establishing an efficient Constabulary force in the counties of England and Wales.
3. *Mont Coll*, Vol. 4 (1871). Thomas Griffiths Jones, 'A history of the parish of Llansantffraid-ym-Mechain'.
4. *Mont Coll*, Vol. 5 (1872). 'A slight historical and topographical sketch of the parish of Llanfechain' in the county of Montgomeryshire by an unknown author.
5. *Mont Coll*, Vol. 6 (1873). Thomas W. Hancock, 'Llanrhaeadr-ym-Mochnant, its parochial history and antiquities'.

Chapter Three – Crime, Detection and Punishment

1. *Mont Coll*, Vol. 33 C. E. Howells, 'The Association for the Prosecution of Felons in Welshpool.'
2. NLW Great Sessions 4/193/7.
3. NLW 4/193/2; 4/193/3.
4. NLW 4/193/5. Melvin Humphreys, 'Rural Society in 18th century Montgomeryshire'. Unpublished thesis.
5. NLW 4/194/5.
6. SRO/SC 6 July 1792.
7. NLW 4/196/7.
8. NLW Montgomery Parish Register CPD 691 (1782-1812).
9. *Mont Coll*, Vol. 14, Rev. W. V. Lloyd, 'Welshpool – Material for the History of the parish and Borough'.
10. *Welsh Convict Women*, pp.59-60.
11. SRO/SC 28 August 1801.
12. NLW 4/(1806).
13. NLW Q/SO/3.
14. NLW Q/SR/1818/9.
15. NLW 4/202/1.
16. NLW 4/202/7.

17. NLW 4/202/8.
18. NLW 4/202/8.
19. SRO/SJ 27 July 1831.
20. NLW Q/SR 1834.
21. Geo IV c.85 sect 22/23.
22. NLW Q/S06; Q/FA/1; Q/SR 1834.
23. NLW B1/17 14 April 1837; NLW Q/SR 1837; SRO/SC 14 April 1837.
24. SRO/SJ 9 January 1839.
25. *Yr Athraw,* June 1839; 'A Parochial account of Llanidloes 1873'; 'One Hundred Years Ago – The Llanidloes Chartists NLW 12888E; 'Chartism in Mid Wales'; 'Who were the Montgomeryshire Chartists'; 'Chartism in Llanidloes 1838-1839'.
26. 'Chartism in Llanidloes 1838 -1839'.
27. SRO/SJ 11 March 1846.
28. SRO/SC 15 March 1848; NLW Q/SR 1848.
29. NLW Q/SO 4 January 1849.
30. *The Convict Settlers in Australia,* pp. 182-187.
31. NLWQ/5R1848.
32. SRO/SC January 1849; NLWQ/1848; NLWB1/22.
33. SRO/SC 14 March 1862.
34. SRO/SC 25 July 1863; SRO/SC 25 December 1863; SRO/SC 18 March 1864; *Crime, Protest, Community and Police in Nineteenth Century Britain,* p. 205.
35. NLW 4/203; NLW/SR 1827.
36. SRO/SJ 14 April 1843; SRO/EJ 15 March 1843; SRO/EJ 12 April 1843; NLW Bl/19.
37. Records of Board of Guardian minute books for Poor Law Union workhouse at Caersws, Forden, Llanfyllin and Machynlleth are to be found in Powys County Archives. Additional institution records are minimal, the majority having been destroyed.
38. 'A History of the parish of Llanfyllin'.
39. 'Chartism in Mid Wales'.
40. Report of Royal Commission on the Handloom Weavers by Assistant Commissioner W. A. Miles.
41. SRO/SC 25 January l839; NLWB1/17.
42. NLW Q/S0 7 27 May 1840; 'Chartism in Llanidloes 1838-1839'.
43. Between 1839-1848, one hundred and two Chartists were transported from England and Wales. The Montgomeryshire Chartists were the only ones to be sent to New South Wales, the remainder going to Tasmania. *Protest and Punishment,* p. 251.
44. 2/3 Vict c.93; 3/4 Vict c.88.
45. 2/3 Vict c.93. An Act for the establishment of county and district constables by the Authority of the Justices of the Peace.
46. 2/3 Vict c.93; 3/4 Vict c.88.
47. NLW Q/S07 22 October 1840.
48. 'Llanfair Caereinion in early eighteenth century'.
49. NLW Q/S07 22 October 1840.
50. NLW Q/S07 7 January 1841.
51. NLW Q/S08 6 March 1843.
52. NLW Q/S08 4 December 1843.
53. NLW Q/S08 9 April 1845.
54. NLW Q/S08 2 July 1845.
55. NLW Q/S0l0 2 July 1857.
56. NLW Q/S10 8 April 1863.
57. NLW Q/S010 1 July 1863.

CHAPTER FOUR – INCARCERATION

1. *Mont Coll,* Vol. 6, 'Llanidloes Market Hall', C. E. Vaughan Owen.
2. NLW 4/203/2.
3. NLW Q/SR 1843; PRO PP 1847; APT CON 33/64; CON 14/26.
4. 'The State of the Prisons in England and Wales', John Howard.
5. *Mont Coll,* Vol. 46, 'Montgomery Gaol in 1803'.
6. NLW Q/AG1 7 January and 4 February 1819.
7. NLWQ/AG11 7 August 1832.
8. NLW doc 194 'Montgomeryshire Chartists'.
9. NLWQ/SR1853.

10. NLW 4/1788.
11. 'Guide to Woolwich, Kent'. Anon.
12. 'Inquiry into the State of the Convict Establishments at Woolwich'. Appendix A. A Return of every prisoner on the 'Justitia' and 'Warrior' hulks at Woolwich, 27 March 1847.
13. PRO PCOM 2/468.
14. 'Chartism in Llanidloes', E. Ronald Morris; SRO/SC 9 August 1839.
15. NLW Q/S08 15 October 1845; Q/SR 1848M; Q/SR 1849J.
16. *The Criminal Prisons of London* and *Scenes of Prison Life*, Henry Mayhew.
17. NLW 4/191.
18. NLW Q/503.
19. PRO HO 17/117.
20. PRO HO 17/51.
21. PRO HO 17/54.
22. PRO HO 17/101.
23. NLW Q/S06.

CHAPTER FIVE – SEA VOYAGE

1. HRONSW, p. 334.
2.
3. HRONSW, p. 367.
4. HRONSW, pp. 387-389.
5. PRO ADM 101/45/1.
6. AONSW CSIL 32/4441 and 4/2145.
7. PRO ADM 101/40/3199; 'The Convict Ships', pp. 361-388.
8. PRO ADM 101/69/5.
9. PRO ADM 101/24/3194; 'The Convict Ships', p. 76.
10. PRO ADM 101/44.
11. PRO ADM 101/44.
12. PRO ADM 101/75/2.
13. NLW Tredegar MSS 40/1.
14. PRO ADM 101/15/2.
15. PRO MT 32/9; AJCP Reel 3181.
16. PRO MT 32/10; AJCP Reel 3181.
17. *Journal of a Voyage from Portland to Fremantle on board the convict ship 'Hougoumont'*, edited Martin Kevin Cusack, 1989.
18. SG and NSWA 13 April 1806.
19. SG and NSWA 20 April 1806.
20. SG and NSWA 1 June 1806.
21. HT and SR 13 June 1818.
22. HT and SR 19 June 1818.
23. HT and SR 2 January 1819.
24. SG and NSWA 24 August 1811
25. SG and NSWA 12 October 1811.
26. PRO MT 32/9.
27. SG and NSWA 27 April 1806.
28. SG and NSWA 7 June 1807.
29. *The Convict Ships*, p. 48.

CHAPTER SIX – CONVICT COLONIAL LIFE

1. AONSW 4/2077; 30/5005.
2. AONSW 1828 Muster.
3. NLW 29/3; NLW 30/8 'Parochial Records St Asaph and Manafon'.
4. AONSW CSIL 34/2863; 4/2230.
5. AOT NS/373/1 No. 911.
6. AOT NS/435/1 No. 390.
7. AONSW 4/3495 reel 6005, p. 205.
8. AONSW 4/1770 reel 6058, p. 192.
9. AONSW 4/1784 reel 6063, p. 314.

10. AONSW 4/5781 reel 6016, p. 63.
11. AONSW 4/4005 reel 394.
12. AONSW CSIL 2/7971 reel 1182.
13. AONSW 36/10945.
14. AONSW 4/3501 reel 6007, p. 145.
15. AONSW 4/3502 reel 6007, p. 188.
16. AONSW fiche 3297/693, p. 21.
17. AONSW fiche 3297/643, p. 22.
18. AONSW 2/8283 reel 6028, p. 129.
19. AONSW 4/6671 reel 6023, p. 107.
20. AONSW 4/1834 reel 6012, p. 46; 4/3510; fiche 3062/75.
21. AONSW 4/3864 reel 6019, p. 98.
22. AONSW 4/1873 p.45 fiche 4245.
23. AONSW reel 398.
24. AONSW 41/238.
25. AONSW reel 935.
26. AOT CON 40/8.
27. AOT CON 37/8.
28. AOT Gen Index LSD 1/107, pp. 744-747, No. 10447.
29. AOT Col Sec letter No. 32/361 25 April 1832.
30. AOT Col Sec letter No. 36/45 11 October 1836.
31. AONSW 4/2166; 32/2941 reel 2193.
32. AONSW 4/2165; 32/1575 reel 2193.
33. AONSW 4/2396; 38/11462.
34. AONSW 42-93.
35. AONSW 44/8519.
36. AONSW 4/2674; 44/9171 reel 2257.
37. AONSW 44/8519.
38. AONSW 4/2296; 35/10408 reel 2200.
39. AONSW 4/2415; 38/11315 reel 2214.
40. AONSW 4/4437; 39/377 reel 777.
41. AONSW 4/2182; 33/3740 reel 2195.
42. *A Hawkesbury Story*, pp. 25-32, Valerie Ross.
43. AONSW 4/4060.
44. AONSW 4/3506.
45. AONSW 4/1756.
46. AONSW reel 6023/820, p. 97.
47. AONSW 4/424.
48. AONSW 4/3864.
49. AONSW 4/2165 and 4/2941.
50. *Hobart Town Courier*, 6 February 1835.
51. AONSW 4/8383.
52. AONSW 4/8429.
53. AONSW 4/8434.
54. AONSW 4/8435.
55. AOT COD 226.
56. *Hobart Town Gazette*, 20 January 1852.
57. *Hobart Town Gazette*, 27 July 1853; 10 August 1852.
58. *The Mercury*, 24 October, 31 October and 1 November 1862.
59. Archives repository, Kingswood 'Applications for families of convicts'. 4/2550; 40/5982 17 June 1840.
60. 9/6329 21 May 1844.
61. *The Australian Daily Journal*, 2/3 July 1844.
62. AONSW CSIL 4/2641; 44/6114; 40/514.
63. AOT general index inquisition No. 4719; SC 195/43.
64. AOT general index inquisition No. 4012; SC 195/40.
65. AOT general index inquisition No. 2011; SC 195/23.
66. *The Founders of Australia*, pp. 50-51.
67. *Sydney Gazette and NSW Advertiser*, 22 October 1809.
68. *Hobart Town Gazette and Southern Reporter*, 2 August 1818. 'Coasts of Treachery' – The Boyd Massacre. 'William Broughton and the Kennedy Connection'.

Appendix I – In Memoriam

1. Buckland Churchyard, Tasmania.
2. Ross General Cemetery, Tasmania.
3. AOT CON 31/27; CSO 1/403/9100.
4. AOT CON 31/27.
5. AOT RGD 35/10 no 436 (1883).
6. TAMIOT HO 13/00138/0.
7. Queensborough Cemetery, Bothwell, Tasmania.
8. AOT CON 31/27; CSO 1/520/11333.
9. St Luke's Churchyard, Bothwell, Tasmania.
10. Queensborough Cemetery, Sandy Bay, Tasmania. Index to Monumental Inscriptions No. 85.

Sources – Primary

PARLIAMENTARY PAPERS

Year	Paper	Title
1776		SC on Transportation CJ.XI.959.
1778		SC on Hulks CJ.XXXVI.926.
1779		SC on Felons CJ.XXXVI.306.
1784		SC on Penitentiary Act CJ.XXXIX.1040.
1785		SC on Transportation CJ.XI.954/1161.
1810-11	199/207	SC on Penitentiary Houses 111.567/691.
1812	306	SC on Penitentiary Houses 11.363.
1812	341	SC on Transportation 11.573.
1819	579	SC on Gaols VII.l.
1822	448	Bigge Report on the state of NSW xx.539.
1823	33	Bigge Report on Judicial Establishments of NSW and VDL X.515.
1831	276	SC on Secondary Punishment v11.519.
1831-32	547	SC on Secondary Punishment v11.559.
1835	438/41	SC on the State of Gaols XI/XII.
1837	518	SC on Transportation XIX.l.
1837-38	669	SC on Transportation XXII.l.
1837-38	121	Maconochie on Prison Discipline in VDL Xl.237.
1839	169	Royal Commission on Constabulary XIX. 1.
1847	149	Supt of Hulks at Woolwich XLIII.63.
1847	831	Inquiry into the Hulks at Woolwich XVIII. 1.
1856	244/ 296/ 355	SC on Transportation XVII.l.
1856	404	SC on Act substituting other punishments for Transportation xv11.561.
1857-58	2414	Jebb on Penal Servitude and Transportation xxlx.285.
1861	286	SC on Transportation XIII.505.
1863	499	SC on Gaols and Prison Discipline IX.1.
1863	3190	Royal Commission on Penal Servitude XXI.1.

PUBLIC RECORD OFFICE, LONDON

HO	6	Hulk Prison Records.
HO	7	ditto.
HO	7-3	Criminals-Convict-Misc. Bermuda 1823-1828. Register of Convicts on Prison Ships.
HO	8	Quarterly list for Convict Prisons 1824-1876.
HO	9	Misc Register for Convict Prisons 1820-1833.
HO	9-1	Chatham – Gannymede. Dolphin. Cumberland.
HO	9-4	Woolwich – Prudentia 1803-1836. Retribution. Justitia.
HO	9-7	Woolwich – Retribution 1802-1834. Bellerphon.
HO	10-23	Census NSW E–H 1828.
	26	ditto R–S 1828.
	27	ditto T–Z 1828.

	28	Muster NSW 1828.
	30	Arrivals NSW 1833-1834.
	31	Pardons NSW and VDL 1834-1838.
	33	Muster NSW D to J 1837.
	34	ditto L to Q 1837.
	52	Pardons NSW 1838-1841.
	57	Pardons VDL 1841 1842.
	58	ditto 1843-1844.
	59	ditto 1845-1846.
	60	ditto 1847-1848.
	61	ditto 1849-1851.
HO	13	Criminal Papers: Entry Books: Correspondence and Warrants 1782-1849.
HO	17	Criminal Petitions Series One 1819-1839.
HO	18	Criminal Petitions Series Two 1839-1854.
HO	19	Register of Criminal Petitions 1819-1854.
HO	21	Prison Registers – Pentonville Correspondence.
HO	24-1/15	Prison Registers – Millbank 1843.
HO	24-16	Prison Registers – Pentonville 1842-1855.
HO	27-1/151	Criminal Registers.
ADM	37-8304	Muster Book HMS Racehorse 1830-1834.
ADM	101	Ships 'Surgeons' journals.
ADM	102-7	Hospital Muster Book Bermuda 1833-1839.
PCOM	2	Prison Records Series One.
PCOM	2-20	Millbank Registers 1837-1843 (Military only).
PCOM	2-31	Millbank Registers 1850-1851.
PCOM	2-60	Millbank Registers 1816-1826.
PCOM	2-63	Pentonville Registers 1849-1850.
PCOM	2-65	Pentonville Registers 1852-1854.
PCOM	2-106	Portland (Portsmouth) 1852-1853.
PCOM	2-106	Portsmouth 1853-1855.
PCOM	2-108	ditto 1859-1860.
PCOM	2-109	ditto 1860-1862.
PCOM	2-110	ditto 1863-1864.
PCOM	2-111	ditto 1865-1866.
PCOM	2-136	'York' Hulk 1841-1851.
PCOM	2-384	Portland 1851-1853.
PCOM	2-468	Removal of 2 Prisoners from Montg Gaol.
PCOM	6-1/4	Register of Licences.
T	38-317	Treasury Accounts: Departmental: Convict Hulks: Justitia 1814-1818.

NATIONAL LIBRARY OF WALES, ABERYSTWYTH

Court of Great Sessions – Gaol Files
Wales 4/193/7 -4/203/6 1788-1830

Newspapers

Reel Bl/16	–	*Shrewsbury Chronicle*	1834-1836.
Reel Bl/17	–	*Shrewsbury Chronicle*	1837-1839.
Reel Bl/18	–	*Shrewsbury Chronicle*	1840-1842.
Reel Bl/19	–	*Shrewsbury Chronicle*	1843-1845.
Reel Bl/20	–	*Shrewsbury Chronicle*	1846-1847.
Reel Bl/21	–	*Shrewsbury Chronicle*	1848 only.
Reel Bl/22	–	*Shrewsbury Chronicle*	1849-1850.

Quarter Sessions
Q/AG County Gaol

1 –	1804-1837	Order Book.
2 –	1821-1824	House of Correction Account Book.
3 –	1817-1819	Returns (various).
4 –	1818	List of Prisoners.
5 –	1818-1819	Returns (various).

Q/FAg Treasurer's General Annual Accounts
    1-19 1843-1861.

Q/SM   Quarter Session Minute Books
          la – 1848-1852.
          lb – 1852-1863.
          2 – 1857-1863.
          3 – 1868-1878.

Q/SO   Quarter Session Order Books
          3 – 1797-1813.
          4 – 1822-1828.
          5 – 1829-1833.
          6 – 1833-1838.
          7 – 1838-1842.
          8 – 1842-1850.
          9 – 1850-1856.
          10 – 1856-1864.

Q/SR   Quarter Session Rolls
          1788-1868.

*Note – The above Quarter Sessions Records have now been transferred
to the County Archives Office, Llandrindod Wells, Powys.*

COUNTY ARCHIVES OFFICE, SHREWSBURY, SALOP

Eddowes Journal
    25 July 1863
    25 December 1863

Shrewsbury Chronicle.
    21 July 1858.
    12 March 1862.
    22 October 1862.
    28 October 1863.
    7 December 1864.
    11 July 1866.

ARCHIVES OFFICE, PERTH, WESTERN AUSTRALIA

DWA *Dictionary of Western Australia, 1829-1914*, ed. Rica Erickson; Vol. 2, *Bond 1850-1868*,
University of Western Australia Press, 1979.

Australian Joint Copying Project(AJCP)

| 2829 | Home Office | HO 27/93 | Criminal Register. Series Two Millbank Prison 1850. |
| 2844 | do | HO 27/118 | Criminal Register. Series Two Montgomery Prison 1857. |

PCOM 2 1837-1864 Prison Books

5971	Prison Commission	2/21	Millbank	1837-43.
	do	2/22	Millbank	1844.
	do	2/23	Millbank	1844-45.
5972	do	2/23	Millbank	1844-45.
	do	2/24	Millbank	1845.
	do	2/25	Millbank	1845-46.
5973	do	2/25	Milibank	1845-46.
	do	2/26	Millbank	1846-47.
	do	2/27	Millbank	1847.

5974	Prison Commission	2/27	Millbank	1847.
	do	2/28	Millbank	1847-48.
	do	2/29	Millbank	1848-49.
	do	2/30	Millbank	1849-51.
5975	do	2/30	Millbank	1849-51.
	do	2/31	Millbank	1850-51.
	do	2/32	Millbank	1851-52.
5976	do	2/32	Millbank	1851-52.
5977	do	2/60	Pentonville	1816-26.
	do	2/61	Pentonville	1842-47.
	do	2/62	Pentonville	1847-49.
	do	2/63	Pentonville	1849-50.
	do	2/64	Pentonville	1851-52.
5978	do	2/65	Pentonville	1852-54.
	do	2/85	Pentonville	1845-46.
	do	2/86	Pentonville	1846-47.
	do	2/87	Pentonville	1847-48.
5979	do	2/105	Portsmouth	1852-53.
5980	do	2/106	Portsmouth	1853-55.
	do	2/107	Portsmouth	1856-58.
5981	do	2/107	Portsmouth	1856-58.
	do	2/108	Portsmouth	1859-60.
5982	do	2/108	Portsmouth	1859-60.
	do	2/109	Portsmouth	1860-62.
5983	do	2/109	Portsmouth	1860-62.
	do	2/110	Portsmouth	1863-64.
5984	do	2/110	Portsmouth	1863-64.
	do	2/111	Portsmouth	1865-66.
5985	do	2/132	Defence and Stirling Castle Hulks	1843-52.
5986	do	2/132	Defence and Stirling Castle Hulks	1843-52.
	do	2/133	Defence and Stirling Castle Hulks	1849-57.
	do	2/134	Stirling Castle Hulk	1837-49.
5987	do	2/134	Stirling Castle Hulk	1837-49.
	do	2/135	Retribution Hulk	1837-41.
	do	2/136	York Hulk	1841-51.
5988	do	2/136	York Hulk	1841-51.
	do	2/137	Europa Hulk	1840-55.
5989	do	2/190	Newgate Prisoners under sentence of Death	1817-37.
5990	do	2/383	Portland	1848-50.
	do	2/384	Portand	1851-53.
5991	do	2/384	Portand	1851-53.

AJCP Reels **5167-5250**

H08/1-180	–	Convict Prisons – 1824-76.
5206/15	–	Portland Prison 1849-54.
5207/10	–	Shorncliffe Prison 1849-51.
5207/11	–	Justitia Hulk Woolwich 1849-52.
5207/11	–	York Hulk Gosport 1849-52.
5207/12	–	Defence Hulk Gosport 1849-52.
5207/13	–	Coromandel Hulk Bermuda 1849-51.
5207/15	–	Dromedary Hulk Bermuda and Portsmouth 1849-53.
5207/15	–	Medway Hulk Bermuda 1849-54.
5207/15	–	Stirling Castle Hulk Portsmouth 1849-54.
5207/15	–	Tenedos Hospital Hulk Bermuda 1849-54.
5207/15	–	Thames Hulk Bermuda 1849-54.
5207/15	–	Warrior Hulk Woolwich 1849-53.
5207/15	–	Owen Glendower and Eyryalus Hulks Gibraltar and Bermuda 1849-54.

5209/15	–	Dartmoor Penitentiary 1850-54.
5212/15	–	Portsmouth 1852-54.
5213/15	–	Boaz Island Prison 1853.
5218	–	Various Prisons 1854-55.

WESTERN AUSTRALIA STATE ARCHIVES

Accession 128 –
   6; 8; 11; 19; 25 ;26; 27; 29; 30; 31; 33; 34; 35; 37; 38; 40 and 41.

Convict Department – Convict Registers – Shipping Lists:

Accession 1156	–	Convict Department –
	R 2	–	Distribution Book.
	R 6	–	Ticket-of-Leave Register.
	R 7	–	Probationer Prisoner's Register.
	R 8	–	Character Book.
	R 9; 11; 13; 14; 15; 16; 21B; 22; 27; 28; 29; 30 and 31.		
		–	General Registers.
	R43	–	Register of Re-convicted Prisoners.
Accession 1386			
	4	–	Ticket of Leave Register Perth District.
	5		ditto.
	8	–	Perth Police Occurrence Book 4 December 63-26 May 65.
	10	–	ditto 29 April 67-31 December 69.
	12	–	Perth Police Occurrence Book 1 January 70-10 July 72.
	13	–	ditto 11 July 72-12 October 76.
	15	–	Perth Police Account Book 30 September 62 – 3 December 63.
Escaped Convicts	–	10587.
Police Gazette	–	1876/77.
Perth Gazette	–	27 June 1862.
	–	4 July 1862.
	–	1-29 November 1872.

PUBLIC RECORDS OF TASMANIA – CONVICT DEPARTMENT

CON 13	–	Assignment lists and associated papers 1810-1826.
CON 14	–	Indents of male convicts 1841-1853.
CON 15	–	Indent of female convicts 1842-1853.
CON 18	–	Description lists of male convicts 1828-1853.
CON 19	–	Description lists of female convicts 1841-1853.
CON 23	–	Alphabetical registers of male convicts 1804-1839.
CON 27	–	Appropriation lists of convicts.
CON 28	–	Registers of the distribution of male convicts to Probation stations 1842.
CON 31	–	Conduct registers of male convicts arriving in the period of the Assignment system 1803-1843.
CON 33	–	Conduct registers of male convicts arriving in the period of the Probation system 1840-1853.
CON 37	–	Conduct registers of male convicts arriving on non-convict ships or locally convicted 1840-1893.
CON 40	–	Conduct registers of female convicts arriving in the period of the Assignment system 1803-1843.
CON 41	–	Conduct registers of female convicts arriving in the period of the Probation system 1844-1853.
CON 52	–	Registers of applications for permission to marry 1834-1857.
CON 63	–	Registers of convict deaths 1840-1846.
CSO 1	–	Appropriation lists of convicts 1823-1839.
CSO 2	–	ditto.

Ships which Transported the Convicts from Montgomeryshire

Archives Office of New South Wales

New South Wales

Reel	Ship	Arrival Year	Reference 2/	Page
2417	America (1)	1829	8240	251
2417	Asia (1)	1833	8242	231
2417	Baring	1819	8243	195
2419	Camden	1831	8250	37
2419	Camden	1833	8250	49
2419	Canada	1819	8250	105
2420	Countess of Harcourt	1824	8254	233
2420	Earl Grey	1838	8256	79
2420	Earl Spenser	1813	8256	143
2421	Eliza (1)	1820	8257	63
2421	Elizabeth (1)	1820	8257	223
2421	Elizabeth (IV)	1836	8257	295
2421	Exmouth	1831	8258	195
2421	Fanny (1)	1816	8259	45
2421	Florentina	1828	8259	185
2421	Friends	1811	8260	49
2422	Glatton	1803	8261	123
2422	Guilford	1812	8261	377
2423	James Pattison	1837	8264	209
2423	Janus	1820	8264	283
2423	John (1)	1832	8264	365
2423	Lady Nugent	1835	8266	1
2423	Lord Lyndock	1833	8266	407
2423	Lord Lyndock	1838	8266	465
2424	Lord Wellington	1820	8267	343
2424	Louisa	1827	8267	437
2424	Maitland	1840	8268	1
2424	Mangles	1840	8268	191
2425	Nithsdale	1830	8271	373
2426	Numa	1834	8272	199
2426	Pitt	1792	8273	229
2427	Royal Charlotte	1825	8276	253
2427	Shipley	1817	8277	219
2427	Shipley	1818	8277	231
2427	Shipley	1820	8277	243
2427	Speke (II)	1826	8278	219
–	Surprise	1790	–	–
2428	Tottenham	1818	8281	55
2428	William Pitt	1806	8282	243
2428	Woodbridge	1840	8282	331
2428	York (1)	1831	8282	371

Van Diemen's Land

Ship	Arrival	Reference	Page
Aboukir	1852	ML/D12	
Arab (II)	1836	ML/A1059(8)	343
Bangalore	1848	ML/D11/Add 539/111	–
Borneo	1828	ML/A1059(3)	271
Bussorah Merchant	1830	ML/A1059(5)	21
Cadet	1848	ML/D11/Add 539/113	–
Caledonia	1822	COD 151	
Chapman	1826	2/8252/R2419	145

Ship	Arrival	Reference	Page
Cornwall	1851	ML/D12	
David Clarke	1841	ML/DS	
Duchess of Northumberland	1843	ML/D5	
Duncan	1840	ML/D5	
Eden	1842		
Elphinstone	1837	ML/A1059(9)	165
Emily (1)	1842		
Emma Eugenia	1844	ML/D5/D6	
Emperor Alexander	1833		
Eliza	1830	ML/A1059(5)	319
Fairlie	1852	ML/D13	
Frances Charlotte	1833	ML/A1059(6)	521
Hindostan	1839	ML/A1059(10)	225
Katherine Stewart Forbes	1832	ML/A1059(7)	195
Lady Castlereagh	1818	COD 144	
Lady East	1825	ML/A1059(1)	51
Lady Kennaway	1835	ML/A1059(7)	371
Lady Raffles	1841	ML/DS	
Larkins	1831	CSO/1/662/14776	
Layton (II)	1835	ML/A1059(7)	501
Lord Auckland	1844	ML/D7	
Lord Hungerford	1821	COD 149	
Lord Melville (1)	1818	COD 143	
Lord Petrie	1843	ML/D6	
Manlius	1828	ML/A1059(3)	347
Manlius	1830	ML/A1059(6)	37
Marion	1844	ML/D6	
Moffatt	1834	NL/A1059(7)	333
Moffatt	1838	CSO/5/113/2615	–
Neptune (III)	1838	ML/A1059(9)	491
Pestonjee Bomanjee	1845		
Red Rover	1831	ML/A1059(6)	239
Rodney	1850	DL/AddS39/124	–
Rodney	1851	DL/Add539/125	–
Sea Queen	1846		
Sir Charles Forbes	1830	ML/A1059(6)	
Sir George Seymour	1845		
Sir Robert Peel	1844		
Somersetshire	1842		
Stately	1849	DL/Add539/129	
St Vincent	1850	DL/Add539/127	
Tasmania	1844		
Theresa	1845		
Tortoise	1842		
William Jardine	1844	ML/D7	
William Metcalfe	1834	ML/A1059(7)	319
William Miles	1828		

Norfolk Island

Hyderabad	1845		
Mayda	1846		

Port Phillip

Calcutta	1803	COD 138	
Joseph Soames	1847	4/4546	95
Maitland	1846	CSIL 47/1936 in	4/2781
Marion	1848		

Western Australia

Belgravia	1866
Clara	1864
Corona	1866
Hougoumont	1868
Lord Dalhousie	1863
Marion	1852
Merchantman	1863
Merchantman	1864
Nile (II)	1858
Norwood	1862
Norwood	1867
Pyrenees	1853
Racehorse	1865
Sea Park	1854
Vimeira	1865
York (II)	1862

JOURNALS OF SURGEON SUPERINTENDENTS OF CONVICT SHIPS WHICH CONVEYED CONVICTS FROM MONTGOMERYSHIRE

Ship	Year	Reel	ADM 101/	Surgeon
New South Wales				
America (1)	1829	3187	2	J. Dickson
Asia (1)	1833	3188	5	T. Galloway
Baring	1819	3189	7	D. Read
Camden	1831	3191	15	D. Boyter
Camden	1833	3191	15	J. Speret
Canada	1819			
Countess of				
Harcourt	1824	3192	18	J. Dickson
Earl Grey	1838	3193	21	C. A. Browning
Earl Spencer	1813			
Eliza (1)	1820	3194	23	J. M. Brydone
Elizabeth (1)	1820	3194	24	A. Montgomery
Elizabeth (IV)	1836	3194	24	R. Espie
Exmouth	1831	3195	26	W. C. Watt
Fanny (I)	1816			
Florentina	1828	3195	27	J. Dickson
Friends	1811			
Glatton	1803			
Guilford	1812			
James Pattison	1837	3198	37	T. Robertson
John (1)	1827			
John (1)	1832	3199	37	J. Lawrence
Lady Nugent	1835	3200	41	O. Sproule
Lord Lyndock	1833	3201	44	D. Watson
Lord Lyndock	1838	3201	44	O. Pineo
Lord Wellington	1820	3201	45	E. F. Bromley
Louisa	1827			
Maitland	1840	3202	46	P. Toms
Mangles	1840	3202	47	A. Nisbet
Neptune	1820			
Nithsdale	1830	3206	56	R. Malcolm
Numa	1834	3206	57	E. F. Bromley
Pitt	1792			
Royal Charlotte	1825	3209	65	G. Fairfowl
Shipley	1817	3209	67	G. W. Clayton
Shipley	1818	3209	67	R. Espie

Ship	Year	Reel	ADM 101/	Surgeon
Shipley	1820	3209	67	H. Ryan
Speke (II)	1826	3210	69	A. Osborne
Tottenham	1818	3212	72	
Woodbridge	1840	3213	75	G. T. Moxey
York (1)	1831	3213	75	C. France

Van Diemen's Land

Ship	Year	Reel	ADM 101/	Surgeon
Aboukir	1852	3187	1	B. Bynoe
Arab (II)	1836	3188	4	W. Rogers
Bangalore	1848	3189	7	M. H. Morris
Borneo	1828	3190	12	O. Sproule
Bussorah Merchant	1830	3190	14	W. Henderson
Cadet	1848	3191	15	C. R. Kinnear
Caledonia	1822			
Chapman	1826	3191	16	J. H. Hughes
Cornwall	1851	3192	17	D. Geddes
David Clarke	1841	3192	19	E. Jeffrey
Duchess of Northumberland	1843	3192	20	W. West
Duncan	1840	3193	20	W. McDowell
Eden (1)	1842	3193	22	A. Neill
Eliza (III)	1830	3194	23	D. Thomson
Elphinstone	1837	3194	24	C. France
Emily (1)	1842			A. Henderson
Emma Eugenia	1844	3195	25	J. Wilson
Emperor Alexander	1833	3195	25	W. Donnelly
Fairlie	1852	3195	27	E. Nolloth
Frances Charlotte	1833	3196	28	J. Osborne
Hindostan	1839			T. McDonald
Katherine Stewart Forbes	1832	3199	40	J. Stephenson
Lady Castlereagh	1818			J. Craigle
Lady East	1825	3200	40	W. McDowell
Lady Kennaway	1835			T. Bell
Lady Raffles	1841	3200	42	R. Wylie
Larkins	1831	3200	42	W. Evans
Layton (II)	1835	3200	42	G. Birnie
Lord Auckland	1844	3201	43	J. J. Lancaster
Lord Hungerford	1821			M. Dorke
Lord Melville (1)	1818	3201	44	J. McMillan
Lord Petrie	1843	3201	44	D. Deas
Manlius	1828	3202	48	P. McTernan
Manlius	1830	3202	48	E. Johnston
Marion	1844	3202	49	W. H. B. Jones
Moffatt	1834	3205	55	T. B. Wilson
Moffatt	1838	3205	55	G. King
Neptune (III)	1838	3205	56	J. Steret
Pestonjee Bomanjee	1845	3206	59	J. W. Johnston
Red Rover	1831	3208	63	J. Osborne
Rodney	1850	3208	64	F. Le Grand
Rodney	1851	3208	64	H. Morris
Sea Queen	1846	3209	66	T. W. Jewell
Sir Charles Forbes	1830	3210	67	W. Petrie
Sir George Seymour	1845	3210	67	J. S. Hampton
Sir Robert Peel	1844	3210	68	J. A. Mould
Somersetshire	1842	3210	68	T. Gibson
Stately	1849	3210	69	J. W. Elliott
St Vincent	1850			S. Donnelly
Tasmania	1844	3211	71	T. Seaton
Theresa	1845	3211	71	C. A. Browning
Tortoise	1842	3211	71	T. Brownrigg

Ship	Year	Reel	ADM 101/	Surgeon
William Jardine	1844	3212	74	J. Robertson
William Metcalfe	1834	3212	74	H. G. Brock
William Miles	1828	3213	75	E. Johnston

Norfolk Island

Hyderabad	1845	3198	35	J. McWilliam
Mayda	1846	3204	52	A. Kilroy

Port Phillip

Calcutta	1803			
Joseph Soames	1847	3199	39	J. W. Elliott
Maitland	1846	3202	46	J. Robertson
Marion	1846	3203	49	J. Andrews

Western Australia MT 32

Belgravia	1866			
Clara	1864	3181	7	
Corona	1866	3181	11	W. Cranford
Hougoumont	1868			
Lord Dalhousie	1863			
Marion	1852			
Merchantman	1863	3181	5	W. Smith
Merchantman	1864	3181	8	W. Smith
Nile (II)	1858			
Norwood	1862	3181	3	A. Watson
Norwood	1867	3181	12	W. M. Saunders
Pyrenees	1853			
Racehorse	1865	3181	9	A. Watson
Sea Park	1854			J. Caldwell
Vimeira	1865	3181	10	W. Crauford
York (ii) 1862				

Newspapers and Magazines

Shrewsbury Chronicle.
Salopian Journal.
Eddowes Journal.
Bygones.
Yr Athraw.
Family Tree Magazine.
Sydney Gazette and New South Wales Advertiser.
Sydney and New South Wales Advertiser.
Hobart Town Gazette.
Hobart Town Gazette and Southern Reporter.
Hobart Town Courier.
The Mercury.
The Australian Daily Journal.
Perth Gazette.
Police Gazette.

Bibliography

Anderson, C. L. *Lincolnshire Convicts to Australia* (Lincoln 1993).

Archives Authority *Guide to the Convict Records in the Archives Office of New South Wales*, Archives Office of New South Wales (Sydney 1981).

Bateson, Charles *The Convict Ships 1787-1868.* (Sydney 1983; Glasgow 1985).

Barnard, Marjorie *Macquarie's World* (Melbourne 1946).

Beattie's, Studio *The Convict Days of Port Arthur* (Hobart 1990).

Beddoe, Deirdre *Welsh Convict Women.*
A Study of Women Transported from Wales to Australia 1787-1852 (Barry 1979).

Brand, Ian *The Convict Probation System: Van Diemen's Land 1839-1854* (Sandy Bay, Tas 1990).

Brown, Martyn *Australia Bound.The Story of West Country Connections 1688-1888* (Bradford on Avon 1988).

Burrows, Peter *Britain and Australia 1831-1855* (Oxford 1967).

Butler, Richard *The Men that God Forgot* (London 1975).

Cadogan, Edward *The Roots of Evil* (London 1937).

Campbell, Charles *The Intolerable Hulks: British Shipboard Confinement 1776-1857* (Maryland 1994).

Carter, Paul *The Road to Botany Bay* (London 1987).

Carty, Margaret *William Broughton and the Kennedy Connection.* (Adelaide 1987).

Chambers, Jill *Hampshire Machine Breakers: The Story of the 1830 Riots* (Letchworth, 1996);
Wiltshire Machine Breakers (Letchworth 1993).
Buckinghamshire Machine Breakers (2nd. ed. Letchworth 1998).
Rebels of the Fields: Robert Mason and the Convicts of the Eleanor (Letchworth, 1995).

Charlwood, Don *The Long Farewell: Settlers under Sail* (Ringwood, Victoria 1981).

Clark, C. M. H. *A History of Australia:*
Pt. 1 – From the earliest times to the Age of Macquarie (Cambridge 1962).
Pt. 2 – NSW and VDL 1822-1838 (Carlton Vict. 1968).
Pt. 3 – The Beginning of an Australian Civilization, 1824-1851. (Carlton Vict. 1973).

Clark, C. M. H (ed.) *Select Documents in Australian History* 1788-1900 (2 Vol.) (Sydney 1950).

Clarke, Marcus *For the term of his Natural Life* (London 1970, 1st pub 1870).

Clune, Frank *The Norfolk Island Story* (Sydney 1967).

Clune, Frank *Wild Colonial Boys* (London 1952).

Clune, Frank and Stephenson, P. R. *The Pirates of the Brig Cyprus* (London 1962).

Colquhoun, Patrick *A Treatise on the Police of the Metropolis* (London 1795).

Cook, Judith *To Brave Every Danger.* The Epic life of Mary Bryant of Fowey, highwaywoman and convicted felon, her transportation and amazing escape from Botany Bay (London 1993).

Costello, Con *Botany Bay. The Story of the Convicts Transported from Ireland to Australia 1791-1853* (Dublin 1988).

Cox, Philip and Stacey, Wesley *Building Norfolk Island* (Melbourne 1971).

Davies, Dewi *Law and Disorder in Breconshire 1750-1880* (Brecon).

Ekirch, A. Roger *Bound for America: The Transportation of British Convicts to the Colonies 1718-1775* (Oxford 1987).

Eldershaw, M. Barnard *The Life and Times of Captain John Piper* (Sydney 1973).

Eldershaw, M. Barnard *Phillips of Australia. An Account of the Settlement at Sydney Cove* (London 1977).

Eldershaw, P. R. *Guide to the Public Records of Tasmania. Convict Dept. Record Group* (Hobart 1965).

Emsley, Clive and Walvin, James (eds) *Artisans, Peasants and Proletarians 1760-1860* (Beckenham 1985).

Erickson, Rica — *The Brand on His Coat: Biographies of some Western Australian Convicts* (Nedland 1983).

Evans, Lloyd and Nicholls, Paul — *Convicts and Colonial Society 1788-1853.* (Melbourne 1976).

Flynn, Michael — *The Second Fleet: Britain's Great Convict Armada of 1790* (Sydney 1993).

Flynn, Michael — *Settlers and Seditionists. The People of the Convict Ship Surprise 1794* (Australia 1994).

Ford, P and G (eds) — *Crime and Law in Nineteenth Century Britain* (Dublin 1978).

Foss, Michael — *Beyond the Black Stump: Tales of Travellers to Australia 1787-1850* (London 1988).

Gillen, Mollie — *The Founders of Australia: A Biographical Dictionary of the First Fleet* (Sydney 1989).

Goodrick, Joan — *Life in old Van Diemen's Land* (London 1978).

Hamer, Edward — *A Parochial account of Llanidloes* (Llanidloes 1873).

Harding, Christopher Hines, Bill Ireland, Richard and Rawlings, Philip — *Imprisonment in England and Wales* (Beckenham 1985).

Hasluck, Alexandra — *Unwilling Emigrants. A Study of the Convict Period in Western Australia* (London 1959).

Hawkins, David T. — *Bound for Australia* (Chichester 1987).

Hawkins, David T. — *Criminal Ancestors: A Guide to Historical Criminal Records in England and Wales* (Stroud 1992).

Hazzard, Margaret — *Punishment Short of Death. A History of the Penal Settlement at Norfolk Island* (Melbourne 1984).

Heard, Dora (ed.) — *The Journal of Charles O'Hara Booth: Commandant of the Port Arthur Penal Settlement* (Hobart 1981).

Hill-Reid, W. S. — *John Grant's Journey. A Convict's Story 1803-1811* (Melbourne 1957).

Hobsbawm, E. J and Rudé, George — *Captain Swing* (London 1969).

Hopkins, Harry — *The Long Affray. The Poaching Wars in Britain* (London 1986).

Horsfall-Turner, E. R. — *A Municipal History of Llanidloes* (Llanidloes 1908).

Hughes, Robert — *The Fatal Shore: A History of the Transportation of Convicts to Australia 1787-1868* (London 1987).

Humphreys, Melvin — *The Crisis of Community: Montgomeryshire, 1680-1815* (Cardiff, 1996).

Ignatieff, Michael — *A Just Measure of Pain: The Penitentiary in the Industrial Revolution 1750-1850* (London 1989)

Ingleton, G. C. — *True Patriots All: News from Early Australia* (Sydney 1965).

Johnson, W. Branch — *The English Prison Hulks* (Chichester 1970).

Jones, David — *Crime, Protest, Community and Police in Nineteenth Century Britain* (London 1982).

Joy, William — *The Exiles* (Sydney 1972).

Kerr, James Semple — *Design for Convicts: An account of design for Convict Establishments in the Australian Colonies during the Transportation Era* (Sydney 1984).

Kingston, Beverley — *The Oxford History of Australia, Vol. 3, 1860-1900* (Oxford 1988).

Kociumbas, Jan — *The Oxford History of Australia, Vol. 2, 1770-1860* (Oxford 1992).

Lloyd, Lewis — *Australians from Wales* (Caernarfon 1988).

Marlow, Joyce — *The Tolpuddle Martyrs* (London 1971).

Mather, F. C. — *Public Order in the Age of the Chartists* (Connecticut 1984).

Maxwell-Stewart, H. — *Reckoning with Convict Workers in Van Diemen's Land* (London 1990).

Mayhew, Henry and Binny, John — *The Criminal Prisons of London and Scenes of Prison Life.* (London, reprint 1968).

McConville, Sean — *A History of English Prison Administration, Vol. 1, 1750-1877* (London 1981).

McLynn, Frank — *Crime and Punishment in Eighteenth Century England* (Oxford 1989).

Montgomery Civic Society — *The Gaol and the County* (Montgomery 1978).

Moore, John — *The First Fleet Marines 1786-1792* (St Lucia, Queensland, 1987).

Morgan, Kenneth — *English and American Attitudes towards Convict Transportation 1718-1775* (London 1987).

Morris, E. Ronald — *Chartism in Llanidloes 1838-1839* (Llanidloes 1989).

Mortlock, J. F. — *Experiences of a Convict* (Sydney 1965, 1st ed. 1864-65).

Neville, Derek	*Blackburn's Isle* (Suffolk 1975).
Nicholas, Stephen (ed.)	*Convict Workers: Reinterpreting Australia's past* (Cambridge 1988).
Nobbs, Raymond	*Norfolk Island and its Second Settlement 1825-1855* (Sydney 1991).
Oldham, Wilfrid	*Britain's Convicts to the Colonies* (Sydney 1990).
Owen, Hugh J.	*From Merioneth to Botany Bay* (Bala 1952).

Powysland Club

Collections

Vol. 14 (1881) Rev. W. Lloyd, 'Material for the history of the Parish of Montgomeryshire Welshpool'.
Vol. 3 (1870) Rev. R. Williams, 'A History of the Parish of Llanfyllin'.
Vol. 4 (1871) Thomas Griffiths-Jones, 'A History of the Parish of Llan-santffraid-yn-Mechain'.
Vol. 5 (1872) Author unknown, 'A slight historical and topographical sketch of the Parish of Llanfechain in the county of Montgomery-shire'.
Vol. 6 (1873) Thomas W. Hancock, 'Llanrhaeadr-ym-Mochnant'. Its parochial history and antiquities.
Vol. 9 (1876) Edward Woodall, 'Population in Montgomeryshire'.
Vol. 11 (1878) T. G. Jones, 'The Parish of Meifod'.
Vol. 12 (1879) Richard Williams Newtown, 'Its ancient Charter and Town Hall'.
Vol. 18 (1885) 'Extracts from the Diary of Richard Griffithes-Parry of Welshpool'.
Vol. 32 (1902) Richard Williams, 'A Parochial Account of Newtown'.
Vol. 33 (1904) C. E. Howells, 'The Association for the Prosecution of Felons in Welshpool'.
Vol. 37 (1915) J. G. Morris and Mary N. Owen, 'Forden Union during the Napoleonic Wars 1795-1816'.
Vol. 46 (1940) Misc. 'Montgomery Gaol in 1803'.
Vol. 48 (1944) Charles H. Humphreys, 'Llanfair Caereinion in the early eighteenth century'.
Vol. 55 (1957/8) A. R. L. Saul, 'Cloddiau Cochion and the Welsh Quakers'.
Vol. 58 (1963/4) E. Ronald Morris, 'Who were the Montgomeryshire Chartists?'.
Vol. 58 (1963/4) J. D. K. Lloyd, 'Montgomery in the Nineteenth Century'.
Vol. 61 (1969/70) Misc, 'Montgomery Gaol and House of Correction'.
Vol. 61 (1969/70) C. L. Vaughan Owen, 'Llanidloes Market Hall'.
Vol. 62 (1971/2) J. D. K. Lloyd, 'Montgomery Gaol'.
Vol. 62 (1971/2) Owen M. Ashton, 'Chartism in Mid Wales'.
Vol. 65 (1977) J. D. K. Lloyd, 'John Wilkes Poundley'.
Vol. 78 (1990) Brian Owen, 'The Newtown and Llanidloes Poor Law Union Workhouse Caersws 1837-1847'.

Priestley, Philip	*Victorian Prison Lives: English Prison Biography 1830-1914* (London 1985).
'Ralph Rashleigh'	*The Adventures of Ralph Rashleigh. A Penal Exile in Australia 1825-1844* (London 1939). Now believed to be a novel by James Tucker, c.1844-5.
Reece, Bob (ed.)	*Exiles from Erin* (Basingstoke 1991).
Ritchie, John	*Punishment and Profit: The Report of Commissioner John Bigge on the Colonies of New South Wales and Van Diemen's Land 1822-1823; their Origins, Nature and Significance* (Melbourne 1970).
Robson, L. L.	*The Convict Settlers of Australia: An Enquiry into the Origin and Character of the Convicts transported to New South Wales and Van Diemen's Land 1787-1852* (Melbourne 1965).
Roebuck Society	*The Sydney Gazette* and *New South Wales Advertiser*, Vol. 9 (1811) (Canberra 1973).
Ross, Valerie	*A Hawkesbury Story* (Sydney 1981).
Rudé, George	*Protest and Punishment: The Story of the Social and Political Protesters Transported to Australia 1788-1868* (Oxford 1978).
Ryan, R. J.	*The Third Fleet Convicts* (Melbourne 1983).

Sainty, Malcolm. R. and
  Johnston, Keith A.
Census of New South Wales 1828 (Sydney 1985).

Shaw, A. G. L.
Convicts and the Colonies. A Study of Penal Transportation from Great Britain and Ireland to Australia and other parts of the British Empire (Melbourne 1978).

Smee, C. J.
Fourth Fleet Families of Australia (Artarmon NSW 1992).

Smith, Coultman
Tales of Old Tasmania. The First Fifty Years (Adelaide 1978).

Smith, Coultman
Shadow over Tasmania: The Whole Story of the Convicts (Hobart 1973).

Steedman, Carolyn
Policing the Victorian Community. The formation of English Provincial Police Forces 1856-1880 (London 1984).

Stevens, John
England's Last Revolution.Pentrich 1817 (Buxton 1971).

Sturma, Michael
Vice in a Victorian Society: Crime and Convicts in Mid-Nineteenth Century New South Wales (St Lucia, Queensland, 1983).

Sweeney, Christopher
Transported in Place of Death. Convicts in Australia (Melbourne 1981).

Tardif, Phillip
Notorious Strumpets and Dangerous Girls: Convict Women in Van Diemen's Land 1803-1829 (London 1990).

Tench, Watkin
Sydney's First Four Years: A Narrative of the Expedition to Botany Bay and a Complete Account of the Settlement at Port Jackson (Sydney 1962).

Thomas, J. E and
  Stewart, Alex
Imprisonment in Western Australia. Evolution, Theory and Practice (Nedlands, WA,.1978).

Touhill, Blanche M.
William Smith O'Brien and His Irish Revolutionary Companions in Penal Exile (Missouri 1981).

Trustees of the
Public Library of
New South Wales
The Hobart Town Gazette and Southern Reporter. Vol. 1/2 (1816-1817) and vol. 3/4 (1818-1819) (Hobart 1965). *The Sydney Gazette and New South Wales Advertiser*, Vol. 4/5 (1806-1807); Vol. 6/7 (1808-1809) and Vol. 8 (1810). (Sydney 1968-1969).

Ward, Russell
Australia since the coming of Man (Darlinghurst, NSW, 1987).

Webb, Sidney and
  Beatrice
English Prisons under Local Government (London 1963).

Weidenhofer, Maggie
Port Arthur: A Place of Misery (Oxford 1981).

Weidenhofer, Maggie
The Convict Years: Transportation and the Penal System 1788-1868 (Melbourne 1973).

West, John
The History of Tasmania (Sydney 1971, 1st pub. 1852).

Williams, David
John Frost: A Study in Chartism (Cardiff 1939, rept. London and New York 1969).

Wright, Reg
The Forgotten Generation of Norfolk Island and Van Diemen's Land (Sydney 1986).

Wyatt, Irene (ed.)
Transportees from Gloucestershire to Australia 1783-1842 (Gloucester 1988).

Index

(1. Not including the Appendices;
2. No indication given if items are mentioned more than once on a page)